Geography
and the
Urban Environment

GEOGRAPHY AND THE URBAN ENVIRONMENT

Progress in Research and Applications

Editors

D. T. HERBERT

Professor of Geography, University College of Wales, Swansea

and

R. J. JOHNSTON

Professor of Geography, University of Sheffield

Geography
and the
Urban Environment

Progress in Research and Applications

Volume V

Edited by

D. T. HERBERT
Professor of Geography
University College of Wales, Swansea

and

R. J. JOHNSTON
Professor of Geography
University of Sheffield

JOHN WILEY & SONS

Chichester · New York · Brisbane · Toronto · Singapore

Copyright © 1982 by John Wiley & Sons, Ltd.

Library of Congress Catalog Card Number: 78-647093

British Library Cataloguing in Publication Data:

Geography and the urban environment.   Vol. 5
  1. Cities and towns—Periodicals
  910'.091732   GF125
  ISBN 0 471 10225 3

Photoset by Thomson Press (India) Limited, New Delhi
Printed at Vail-Ballou Press Inc., New York

For
David Aled and Nia Wyn Herbert
and
Chris and Lucy Johnston

List of Contributors

G. L. CLARK — Department of City and Regional Planning, Harvard University, Gund Hall, Room 311, Cambridge, Massachusetts, 02138, USA

M. G. COOMBES — Centre for Urban and Regional Development Studies, The University, Newcastle upon Tyne, NE1 7RU, UK

R. CYBRIWSKY — Department of Geography, College of Liberal Arts, Temple University, Philadelphia, Pennsylvania 19122, USA

J. S. DIXON — Centre for Urban and Regional Development Studies, The University, Newcastle upon Tyne, NE1 7RU, UK

J. B. GODDARD — Department of Geography, The University, Newcastle upon Tyne, NE1 7RU, UK

R. T. HARRISON — Northern Ireland Economic Council, Parliament Buildings, Stormont, Belfast BT4 3TT.

R. J. JOHNSTON — Department of Geography, The University, Sheffield, S10 2TN, UK

D. N. LIVINGSTONE — Department of Geography, Queen's University, Belfast, BT7 1NN, Northern Ireland, UK

J. LOWMAN — Department of Geography, The University, Columbia, 2075 Westbrook Mall, Vancouver, BC, Canada V6T 1WS

S. OPENSHAW — Department of Geography, The University, Newcastle upon Tyne, NE1 7RU, UK

R. Palm   *Department of Geography, University of Colorado, Boulder, Colorado 80309, USA*

D. J. Parker   *Faculty of Social Sciences, Middlesex Polytechnic, The Burroughs, London, NW44BT, UK*

E. C. Penning–Rowsell   *Faculty of Social Sciences, Middlesex Polytechnic, Queensway, Enfield, Middlesex EN345F, UK*

D. J. Rossiter   *Academic Computing Services, The Open University, Milton Keynes, MK76AA*

J. E. Seley   *Department of Urban Affairs, Queen's College, 67-30 Kissena Boulevard, Flushing, New York, 11367, USA*

P. J. Taylor   *Department of Geography, The University Newcastle upon Tyne, NE17RU, UK*

G. A. Tobin   *Department of Geography, University of Iowa, Iowa City, Iowa 52240, USA*

J. Western   *Department of Geography, College of Liberal Arts, Temple University, Philadelphia, Pennsylvania, 19122, USA*

J. Wolpert   *School of Architecture and Urban Planning, Princeton University, Princeton, New Jersey 08544, USA*

Contents

Preface

This is the fifth in the series of volumes on *Geography and the Urban Environment*, the first of which appeared in 1978. The purposes of the series as a whole, and of the individual volumes, remain the same; we aim to publish substantial research reports, of a length intermediate between the journal article and the monograph, major reviews of particular topics, and contributions to the lively ideological, philosophical and methodological debates which now characterize the geographical literature. All of this is set in the context of the study of the urban environment, although that theme is interpreted in as catholic a way as possible.

In preparing this fifth volume, we have been able to reflect on its predecessors and their reception. Most reviews have been complimentary to the individual pieces that we have published, indicating the high-quality stream of research and writing that we have been able to tap. Some reviewers have commented that the volumes do not cohere individually. But this has never been our intention. The aim has been to produce an annual series of volumes which cohere as a whole because they illustrate both the diversity and commonality within urban research, while at the same time keeping pace with the changing interests of geographers. Thus although each volume is characterized by two or three major themes, to which most of the contributions are linked, we are always alert to the possibility of publishing a chapter which may stand alone within the particular volume but which contributes substantially to the overall purposes of the series. Thus each volume, like many of the chapters it contains, is intermediate in status between one issue of a journal and a book of essays dedicated to a single theme. In producing such a series, we hope to provide a flexible outlet for authors and a valuable source of material for readers.

In a period of considerable philosophical and ideological debate within geography as a whole, we are pleased to include two contributions on this theme in the present volume. In the first chapter, Richard Harrison and David Livingstone discuss the role of language, and especially of metaphor, in geographical work, arguing that the various perspectives currently used by geographers are based on particular metaphors. Alongside their other recent works on philosophy in geography, this chapter contributes substantially to our understanding of ourselves, how we work and what we assume.

The second chapter, by Gordon Clark, takes up a crucial issue in social science in general at the present time, the role of the researcher in policy studies and in decision-making. In a wide-ranging discussion, which links to several of the other chapters in this and previous volumes, he focuses on a number of important points which have been too readily overlooked in geography's 'relevance revolution'. As economic realities become harsher, and the demands for accountability of academic researchers increase, more geographers are becoming involved in a variety of types of applied research. The points raised by Gordon Clark cannot be avoided if such research is to be both sensible and valuable, in all meanings of those words.

In the heyday of geography's 'quantitative revolution', numerical methods of classification and regionalization were extremely popular among researchers. As descriptive tools, they have now lost their novelty, but in recent years their utility has been capitalized on by a number of workers. In Chapter 3, a group of researchers at the University of Newcastle upon Tyne report on their work aimed not merely at producing yet another functional regionalization of Great Britain but at providing a spatial framework which can be used for sensible data analysis, and for which 1981 census data will be made available. In this we see geographical expertise being put to the test, in work that promises a variety of benefits for future cohorts of researchers.

Remaining with the regionalization theme, Chapter 4 reports on another research study into the division of Britain into areal units, in this case parliamentary constituencies. This is not applied research as in Chapter 3, but rather an evaluation of public policies which have clear spatial components and which result in major political impacts. Ron Johnston and David Rossiter, building on the same research tradition which informed the Newcastle study, show how the interaction of a set of bureaucratic rules with a geographical reality must, of necessity, lead to electoral bias. As the reality changes, so does the interaction and the nature of the bias, but—as they and others point out—a non-partisan electoral cartography is impossible in its results, if not in its aims.

In recent years, there have been several calls for a reintegration of physical and human geography, through work on resource analysis and management. As the two types of geography drift further apart with their increased interest in process rather than pattern, the prospects for such an integration remain remote. Nevertheless, much work is now being done in which either physical geographers focus on the impact of man on environmental processes, including those operating in urban areas, or human geographers seek to apply social scientific analyses to man's use and abuse of his physical environment; some geographers combine both. A major focus of such work has been the environmental hazard, and the central block of chapters in this volume presents a series of studies on that topic. In Chapter 5, Graham Tobin reviews the literature on urban planning in relation to natural hazards, illustrating the nature of the problems facing those wishing to devise a less hazardous urban environment and the difficulties confronting attempts at their solution. His overview is followed by Dennis Parker and Edmund Penning-Rowsell's detailed evaluation of flood mitigation measures in Britain. In Chapter 7, Risa Palm presents an analysis of the efficacy of a California programme designed to make earthquake-prone areas less attractive to home buyers by requiring the vendors and/or agents to disclose the extent of the local earthquake risk; to date, the attempt seems largely to have been in vain. Finally, John Seley and Julian Wolpert cast the net wide again, inquiring into various locational issues relating to man-made as well as natural hazards, and tackling some of the issues of applied social science research raised by Gordon Clark in Chapter 2.

To many people, one significant aspect of the hazardousness of many urban places relates to personal security. Various studies of the geography of crime have shown some parts of cities to be much safer than others. In a critique of such work, John Lowman presents a novel approach to this topic in Chapter 9. Finally, Cybriwsky and Western present an analysis of the urban renewal process in central Philadelphia, focusing on who benefits and illustrating further the contentious role of public policy in the restructuring of urban space.

As in several of the other volumes of this series, therefore, many of the chapters in his book tackle different aspects of a group of related themes. Central to many of them is the nature of the urban environment–both its physical and its manmade aspects—and of human response to it, both individually and through the institutions of the state. Apart from substantive information, the discussions range through the nature of the research process to the applied role of the geographer. Together, they illustrate the continued vitality of urban research.

D. T. HERBERT
R. J. JOHNSTON

Geography and the Urban Environment
Progress in Research and Applications, Volume V
Edited by D. T. Herbert and R. J. Johnston
©1982 John Wiley & Sons Ltd.

Chapter 1

Understanding in Geography: Structuring the Subjective

Richard T. Harrison and David N. Livingstone

> HUGH: To return briefly to that other matter, Lieutenant. I understand your sense of exclusion, of being cut off from a life here; and I trust you will find access to us with my son's help. But remember that words are signals, counters. They are not immortal. And it can happen—to use an image you'll understand—it can happen that a civilisation can be imprisoned in a linguistic contour which no longer matches the landscape of . . . fact.
>
> Brain Friel: *Translations. A Play*

During the last decade, geography has witnessed the re-emergence of a critical, reflective attitude towards explanation and understanding. In contrast to the legacy of a positivist philosophy of science, epitomized in geography by an emphasis on quantitative analysis and model-building as fundamental to the development of spatial science, a desire for greater philosophical articulation has typified the various attempts by human geographers to appropriate for their discipline a suitable philosophy of the explanation of human behaviour. Despite this emerging philosophical awareness, however, human geography has continued to exhibit internal tensions both epistemologically and methodologically. This, at least in part, reflects the reactive nature of these alternatives, inasmuch as their concern has apparently been less with the creation of a consistent, consolidated philosophy of geography than with the refutation and abolition of the positivist orthodoxy. But it may also be a reflection of the inherent incompatibility of the several models of man underlying the philosophical positions eclectically imported into geography (Agnew and Duncan, 1981; Hollis, 1977).

HUMANISTIC INDIVIDUALISM

In broad terms the polarization between individualist and holist perspectives, central to the philosophy of social explanation (O'Neill, 1973; Ryan, 1973), has engendered either an individualistic humanism or a macro-social structuralism. Under the panoply of 'humanism' the various attempts to reinstate man as a knowing subject in encounter with an object constitute a confused mélange of subjectivist geographies more or less conjoined to hermeneutic philosophies of the social sciences, such as existentialism, phenomenology and idealism (Ley and Samuels, 1978; Livingstone and Harrison, 1981c). However, as critics have not been slow to point out, the subjectivist alternatives have been little more than introspective esotericism, lacking a cohesive framework for substantive research (Gregory, 1978a; Hay, 1979): 'Whereas a key feature of the positivist/spatial-science approach has been a great numerical supremacy of practitioners over preachers, the phenomenological movement (like the idealist) has been charac-terized by the converse—much preaching and little practice' (Johnston, 1979, p. 138). Recognizing that humanistic geography presents a fragmented mosaic of perspectives—anthropocentricism, the experience of place, and philosophies of meaning—the issue of human agency and the reinstatement of the geographi-cal subject have been isolated as the unifying theoretical *motifs* which provide a philosophical antithesis to uncritical positivism (Ley, 1980).

The attempt to construct a reconstituted human geography which would reintegrate human creativity within an environmental context and synthesize the realms of meaning and structure—in short a dialectical perspective on man and environment—has taken various forms. The importance of acknowledging conscious, and, through critical introspection, latent presuppositions, both philosophically and ethically, has been underlined in Buttimer's appeal for a value-evaluated human geography (Buttimer, 1974). The search for a new synthesis, a more creative and 'humane' approach to the accumulation and application of geographical understanding (Soja, 1974), has focused, *inter alia*, on the existential sense of place and placelessness (Relph, 1976), belonging and alienation (Olsson, 1981), and the way in which the geography of emotional response is structured experientially (Buttimer and Seamon, 1980; Tuan, 1974; Tuan, 1980), hierophanically (Eliade, 1961; Graber, 1976; Tuan, 1976), and epistemologically (Buttimer, 1978; Buttimer, 1979; Samuels, 1978). The con-sideration and empathetic evaluation of the evocation of the poetics of space (Bachelard, 1969), regional ethos, and images of place in literature (Pocock, 1981; Watson, 1974) have been used to uncover personal attitudes to environ-ment and the way in which the perception of regional identity in popular consciousness is structured (Cosgrove, 1979; Moore and Golledge, 1976; Salter and Lloyd, 1977; Pocock, 1979). For Olsson a more humanistic perspective, necessary for rediscovering human sensitivity, would 'allow us to grasp both the certainty of the external and the ambiguity of the internal' (Olsson, 1978, p. 118). It is, in the last analysis, the problems created by the nature of language as the intersubjective medium for the communication of translated meaning that has been central to Olsson's search for a creative synthesis. Like Wittgenstein, for whom 'the limits of my language mean the limits of my world' (Wittgenstein,

1961, para 5.6), Olsson (1979, 1980) has concluded, in effect, that language is neither subtle nor supple enough to express the personal realm of value and intentionality.

MACRO-SOCIAL STRUCTURALISM

The encounter between geography and structuralism dates, it has been argued, from the debate at the turn of the century between Friedrich Ratzel and Émile Durkheim (Gregory, 1978a, p. 81). While it is undoubtedly the case that structuralism in social anthropology and social theory has drawn upon the pioneer work of Durkheim for its substantive theory and method (Bottomore and Nisbet, 1978, pp. 565–80; Harris, 1968, pp. 464–513), the engagement with Ratzel over the question of the incorporation of *morphologie sociale* into sociology (Buttimer, 1971, pp. 27–40) did not contribute in any significant way to the elaboration of a structuralist human geography.

Despite the current vogue for 'structuralist' approaches to the study of geographical realities, structuralism as an organizing concept is far from monolithic. Fundamentally all structuralist theses maintain that:

all mature experience and knowledge possess a universal, necessary structure, and that this structure is derived, not from the empirical properties of the 'external' world of objects towards which experience is directed and about which knowledge is claimed, but from the manner in which human thinkers impose order on their own 'internal' world of perception or thought (Toulmin, 1972, p. 417).

Notwithstanding this common epistemological denominator, structuralism is less a rigorously consistent and distinctive analytical method than a diffuse tendency (Poster, 1976). Since the structures invoked by various 'structuralists' have acquired increasingly diverse significations (Piaget, 1970), structuralism

should not be claimed to constitute a novel, coherent and comprehensive paradigm for sociological and anthropological theory. Whether viewed as a doctrine or a method . . . 'structuralism' as such does not, on examination, stand for a more distinctive standpoint that a belief in the applicability of rigorous models to social behaviour (Runciman, 1970, p. 58).

For this reason, various nuances of structuralist interpretation in a wide range of disciplines—mathematics, logic, physics, biology, psychology, linguistics, anthropology, sociology, economics, philosophy—have been identified (Boudon, 1971; Piaget, 1970; Robey, 1973). In the social sciences in general, as Giddens (1979, pp. 59–60) has observed, 'the term "structure" appears in two main bodies of literature: that of functionalism, which is often in contemporary versions called "structural-functionalism"; and the tradition of thought that has embraced it most completely, structuralism'.

Structural-functionalism

Dating from Henri de Saint-Simon, Charles Fourier, and August Comte, who were the first modern social theorists explicitly to apply organismic metaphors to the study of social behaviour (Cooter, 1979), there emerged an unbroken tradition of biological-physiological analogies which pervasively dominated the reigning theory of sociology and social anthropology (Young, 1973a). The sub-metaphors of function, growth, harmony, and order, popularized by Herbert Spencer (Bannister, 1979; Fine, 1979; Peel, 1971), heralded the structural-functionalist concentration on the nature of relationships between structure and function (D. C. Phillips, 1970; 1977). Structural-functionalists conjoined structure and function, but gave primacy to function: structure arises only to achieve functions (Carneiro, 1973; Coleman, 1971; Honigmann, 1976, pp. 232–46). Thus, to study the structure of society is like studying the anatomy of an organism and the study of its functions is analogous to studying the physiology of the organism—'it is to show how the structure "works"' (Giddens, 1979, p. 60). As a result, function assumed the key role in social explanation while structure, the pattern of social relations, remained an essentially descriptive concept. Within this tradition, which drew upon the original work of H. Spencer (1910) and Durkheim (1960), there developed a number of distinct, but related emphases. At the time when Radcliffe-Brown (1965) was formalizing his theory of social structuralism, Malinowski (1960) proclaimed his biocultural function-alism, in which, in place of social structure, he began his analysis of society and culture with human nature (Voget, 1975, pp. 480–538). Thus, while the former gave rise to a theory of society, the latter produced a theory of culture (Voget, 1975, pp. 311–16).

The direct involvement of geographers, particularly cultural geographers, with functionalism has been mediated through the cultural theories associated with the American anthropologists Alfred Kroeber, Robert Lowie and Leslie White (Duncan, 1980; Grossman, 1977). Following Durkheim's development of the concept of 'collective consciousness', functionalists were committed to the view that 'human social aggregates involve differentiated units which are interdependent' (Moore, 1979, p. 323). With the twin concepts of differentiation and interdependence, functionalists considered the ways in which the interdependence of units was effected and the contribution which the parts make to the whole. From this arose what Durkheim (1960) termed 'organic solidarity', and, although he did not avidly pursue the metaphor of society as an organism, other functionalists did. The major elements of this holistic perspective were perpetuated by Kroeber and Lowie in the thesis of the autonomy of culture and of the individual's relation to his 'superorganic' milieu (Kroeber, 1915; 1917; Lowie, 1917). For them, culture as a determinant of human behaviour was regarded as an order of distinct reality, a superorganic (a term borrowed from Herbert Spencer) in every way 'explainable only in terms of itself' (Voget, 1960, p. 949). Therefore, for the ethnologist a cultural fact was to be accounted for by 'merging it in a group of cultural facts or by demonstrating some other cultural fact out of which it has developed' (Lowie, 1917, p. 66).

It was this functionalist approach to the study of man and culture, exemplified *par excellence* in the theory of culture as a superorganic entity, which came to dominate cultural geography, particularly through Carl Sauer's association with Kroeber and Lowie at Berkeley during the 1920s and 1930s (Leighly, 1976; Spencer, 1974; 1976; Speth, 1979). While cultural geographers in the Berkeley tradition remained ambivalent about Kroeber's superorganic definition, neither rejecting nor replacing it (Duncan, 1980), Wilbur Zelinsky has been explicit in his use of the theory. For him, as for Sauer who regarded human geography as 'a science that has nothing to do with individuals but only with human institutions, or cultures' (Sauer, 1963, p. 358), cultural geography relies upon a holistic conception of culture, which he views as a largely autonomous and virtually '"super-organic" system that functions and evolves according to its own internal logic and presumed set of laws . . . and does so with a large degree of freedom from individual or community control' (Zelinsky, 1973, pp. 75–6). In developing his theory of culture Zelinsky states (1973, pp. 40–41):

> Obviously, a culture cannot exist without bodies and minds to flesh it out; but culture is also something both of *and beyond* the participating members. Its totality is palpably greater than the sum of its parts, for it is superorganic and supraindividual in nature; an entity with a structure, set of processes, and momentum of its own, though clearly not untouched by historical events and socio-economic conditions. The example of language is relevant, for it is both a major component of, and paradigm for, the totality of culture. Languages have a life of their own, and the forces that change their content and structure are beyond the conscious control of any set of individuals. Furthermore, the basic syntax of language, its axiomatic implications concerning the meaning of meaning, are a decisive factor in the ways we think about and look at the world. It is just as correct to say that a language speaks us as to declare that we speak a language.

To this degree at least, human geography has not been totally detached from the structural-functionalism which, drawing on the Spencerian metaphor of the social organism, dominated American anthropology and sociology in the first quarter of the twentieth century.

Structuralism

Despite this link with anthropological structural-functionalism, geographers, with few exceptions (Gregory, 1978a, pp. 91–105; Johnston, 1979, pp. 162–63), have not developed any strong association with the structuralism originating in Lévi-Strauss's 'systematic attempt to uncover deep universal mental structures as they manifest themselves in kinship and larger social structures, in literature, philosophy and mathematics, and in the unconscious psychological patterns that motivate human behavior' (Kurzweil, 1980, p. 1). Indeed by the 1950s, the 'superorganic' concept of culture had been abandoned by most anthropologists (Geertz, 1970; Keesing, 1974), although 'cultural geographers seem blissfully unaware of the controversy and proceed as if 50 years of substantive anthropological debate had not taken place' (Agnew and Duncan, 1981, p. 53).

By contrast with the functionalism of Anglo–Saxon structuralism, associated with Malinowski and Radcliffe-Brown, structuralism as social theory is essentially of French derivation. As H. Stuart Hughes observes: 'French social thought of the desperate years began with history and ended with anthropology' (quoted in Kurzweil, 1980, p. 1). Following the leadership of Saussure (and later the Prague circle), structuralism developed as an approach to linguistics and, in the form of social theory, as 'the application of linguistic models influenced by structural linguistics to the explication of social and cultural phenomena' (Giddens, 1979, p. 9). Thus Barthes (1964, p. 155), for example, observes that he has been 'engaged in a series of structural analyses, all of which are concerned to define a number of extra-linguistic "languages"'. Since 1955, with the publication of Lévi-Strauss's *Tristes Tropiques* (1955) which paved the way for his *Structural Anthropology* (1963), the first substantial adaptation of Saussurean linguistics to the social sciences (Pettit, 1975), both the theory and methodology of French structuralism, despite the central concern with language, have assumed a variety of manifestations: 'Structuralism is neither a school, a movement, nor a vocabulary, but an activity that reaches beyond philosophy, that consists of a succession of mental operations which attempt to reconstruct an object in order to manifest the rules of its functioning' (Barthes, 1964, p. 213).

Nevertheless, variations on the Saussurian model of language 'which postulates that a linguistic *signifier* has meaning only within a specific system of *significations*' (Kurzweil, 1980, p. 228) have served as the basis for a number of structuralist theories. All of these have extrapolated from rules/relations of grammar/speech to explore social phenomena in terms of the oppositions and transformations of the linguistic model (Pettit, 1975). Language, therefore, has remained at the forefront of structuralist analyses for the reason that 'the centrality of language to culture, and of culture to language, and their presence in all discourse (including scientific discourse) were taken as proof of a specific underlying human universality' (Kurzweil, 1980, p. 228). For the French structuralists, therefore, language is no longer to be regarded as a simple transparent medium of thought, but rather the manifestation of thought itself. Thus, for Barthes, Foucault, Derrida, Kristeva, and Lacan, as for Lévi-Strauss, language is fundamental to understanding:

All of them, it could be said, are obsessed by it. They are obsessed by the institutional nature of language, and by its infinite productivity. It is not something we each bring with us into the world at birth, but an institution into which we are gradually initiated in childhood as the most fundamental element of all in our socialization. Language can thus be described as impersonal, it exceeds us as individuals. Any use of language to communicate with others (or even with ourselves) involves us inevitably in the surrender of a portion at least of our uniqueness, since if our language also were unique no one would be able to understand it (Sturrock, 1979, p. 12).

Given this centrality of language, any 'structuralist' human geography would, we feel, have to focus on the significance of language as the basic medium for both the communication of intersubjective meaning and understanding, and the structuration of the cultural identity of societies. This means that a human geography which relies on structural linguistics only for the insights it provides into the nature of *spatial* structures is unnecessarily restrictive. The study of language *qua* language, therefore, we would suggest, is important for understanding the symbolic expression of communal consciousness, and not just for the elucidation of the ways in which grammatical structures parallel social and spatial structures. 'It is now high time', as Gregory notes (1978a, p. 98), 'that we examined the implications of all this for contemporary geography. There are many avenues which could be taken, since the intersections between anthropology and geography have traditionally been as numerous as they have been important'. However, in many ways it is the failure to perceive that the structures of society and the structures of language are metaphorically rather than formally related that has encouraged the development of marxian critical theory in human geography.

With the central conceptualizations in the language of structuralist marxism revolving around such key terms as 'the logic of capitalism', 'social formations', and 'the capitalist mode of production' (all of which refer to structures explicitly defined as holistic, autonomous, and self-determining entities displaying regularities which cannot be accounted for in terms of individual and collective action), the resulting model of man subordinates human creativity, individuality, and agency to the operation of transcendental social structures as the only truly active forces:

> The structure of the relations of production determines the *places* and *functions* occupied and adopted by the agents of production, who are never anything more than the occupants of these places insofar as they are 'supports' (Träger) of these functions. The true 'subjects' . . . are therefore not these occupants or functionaries, are not, despite all appearances, the 'obviousness' of the 'given' of naive anthropology, 'concrete individuals'—'real men'—but the definition and distribution of these places and functions. The true 'subjects'

are ... the relations of production (and political and ideological social relations) (Althusser, 1969, p. 180).

Such a reductionist approach to the study of man is not, however, necessarily inherent in dialectical versions of structuralism. Indeed, if, as Bartels (1973; see also Smith, 1979) suggests, the 'dialectical paradigm' (Albrow, 1974) is emerging in geography, there must be a central commitment to the first step towards the understanding of men which is 'the bringing to consciousness of the model or models that dominate and penetrate their thought and action' (Berlin, 1962, p. 19). This points to the need for the development of a critical theory which

> penetrates beneath the surface grammar of a 'language-game' to uncover the quasi-natural forces embodied in its depth-grammatical relationships and rules; by spelling them out it wants to break their spell. Its internal *telos* is to enhance the autonomy of individuals and to abolish social domination and repression; it aims at communication free of domination. Such a critical theory, consequently, can become 'practical' in a genuine sense only by initiating processes of self-reflection—a self-reflection which would be the first step on the road toward practical emancipation (Wellmer, 1976, p. 258).

THE CENTRALITY OF LANGUAGE

This brief résumé of the diverse strands of contemporary thought which have contributed to the recent evolution of understanding in geography plainly demonstrates that language has been a central concern in the different philosophical perspectives on meaning, intentionality and understanding. This suggests that language, as the medium for intersubjective communication in both social and scientific communities, should become a focal point in geographers' studies of man in society. By thus focusing on the centrality of language it may be possible for human geographers to transcend the traditional dichotomies (individualism-holism; mind-nature; action-structure; internal-external; freedom-form) inherent in the subjectivist-objectivist opposition as articulated in humanistic and structuralist geographies respectively. This is because, as Mepham (1973, p. 126) notes,

> Not only is it impossible to think an objective world as the source of systems of meaning, it is also impossible to identify this source as subjective. For there is not *first* a subject and a world, and then a language created at their point of contact. Because to *be* a subject is already to live in a world. It is very difficult to free ourselves from the metaphor of language as an instrument which a person can use in order to express feelings or communicate thoughts which have their source elsewhere .... To have a world is to have acquired a culturally

determined perceptual life, a language in which to think, an organization of intersubjective experience.

Perhaps the most basic element in the development of a geographico-linguistic epistemology is the exploration of metaphor as the fundamental human means of acquiring the linguistic competence to express both cognitive and affective understanding (Livingstone and Harrison, 1981a). The reason for this is that the expression and communication of meaning involves the construction of sentences *by* individuals *for* other individuals:

> For us, meaning depends on understanding. A sentence can't mean anything to you unless you understand it. Moreover, meaning is always meaning *to* someone. There is no such thing as a meaning of a sentence in itself, independent of any people . . . . [It is necessary] to base both the theory of meaning and the theory of truth on a theory of understanding. Metaphor . . . plays a central role in such a program. Metaphors are basically devices for understanding . . . . The fact that our conceptual system is inherently metaphorical, the fact that we understand the world, think, and function in metaphorical terms, and the fact that metaphors can not merely be understood but can be meaningful and true as well—these facts all suggest that an adequate account of meaning and truth can only be based on understanding (Lakoff and Johnson, 1980, p. 184).

Metaphor is fundamental in the use of language, cognitive development, and the ways in which conceptions about the nature of reality are forged (Jakobson and Halle, 1956; Ortony, 1979a). In the attempt to come to terms with the world, or some aspect of it, we tend to fasten upon some area of commonsense fact and endeavour to understand other areas in terms of this one (Pepper, 1942). The exposition of the metaphorical underpinings of epistemology has a long history. In the eighteenth century, for instance, Giambattista Vico recognized metaphor as being a critical feature of the growth of language and thought (Bergin and Fisch, 1968; Leatherdale, 1973). Mueller's later argument that metaphor was less the carrying over of a word from one concept to another than the creation of a new concept by means of an old name (Mueller, 1871) was further developed by Cassirer (1946; 1955) who regarded metaphor as the key factor in the expansion of understanding beyond its current limits. The crucial role of metaphor in thought as a whole has been emphasized in a bibliographical review which documents its study and treatment within the western intellectual tradition (Shibles, 1971).

Two fundamental questions need to be addressed: what are metaphors and what are metaphors for? In seeking an answer to the 'what are metaphors?' question, Black (1979) believes that the quest for an infallible and universal criterion of 'metaphorhood' is doomed to failure. 'The recognition that something is a metaphor depends, first, on our knowing what it is for something to be a metaphorical statement, and secondly, on our judgment that a metaphorical interpretation is preferable to a literal one' (Ortony, 1979b, p. 5). Just as Wittgenstein (1968) argued that there are no necessary and sufficient conditions for establishing what constitutes a game, it similarly seems impossible to isolate such conditions for something to qualify as a metaphor—metaphors, like games, seem to be related by family resemblance. The reason for this stems from the contextual nature of metaphorical usage, for metaphors are recognized *as metaphors* by language users in particular contexts; this places the study of metaphor in the domain of pragmatics—the study of speech acts and the contexts in which they occur (Stalnaker, 1972). Thus, while the attempt to produce a satisfactory definition of the nature of metaphor is problematic, some attempt can be made to elucidate the manner in which meaning is both created and communicated by metaphor.

A stimulating approach to understanding the contextual nature of metaphorical expressions has been advanced recently by Searle (1979). Recognizing that a metaphor comprises meaning in excess of, or differing from, what can be deduced from the literal meaning of its sentence vehicle, he provides a theoretical framework drawn from the theory of speech acts (Searle, 1969) in which that excess or difference is given an appropriate rendering. Central to his exposition is the distinction between sentence meaning and utterance meaning (Searle, 1979, p. 93):

> It is essential to emphasise at the very beginning that the problem of metaphor concerns the relations between word and sentence meaning, on the one hand, and speaker's meaning or utterance meaning, on the other. . . . Strictly speaking, whenever we talk about the metaphorical meaning of a word, expression, or sentence, we are talking about what a speaker might utter it to mean, in a way that departs from what the word, expression, or sentence actually means. We are, therefore, talking about possible speaker's intentions. . . . To have a brief way of distinguishing what a speaker means by uttering words, sentences, and expressions, on the one hand, and what the words, sentences, and expressions mean, on the other, I shall call the former *speaker's utterance meaning*, and the latter, *word*, or *sentence meaning*.

Sentence meaning, therefore, comprises the literal, or semantic, meaning of the words used in any expression. The meaning of a metaphor, on the other hand, is always the speaker's utterance meaning—the 'communicative implicature' (Livingstone and Harrison, 1981a, p. 96) or intended meaning of the expression beyond the literal meaning of the words used.

The problem of explicating how metaphors work (that is, how it is possible for speakers to communicate to hearers when speaking metaphorically inasmuch as they do not say what they mean) in this context is best approached diagrammatically (Figure 1.1). This illustrates the relationships between sentence meaning and utterance meaning where the sentence meaning is 'S is P' and the utterance meaning is 'S is R'; that is, where the speaker utters a sentence that means literally that the object S falls under the concept P (for example, 'Sally is a block of ice'), but where the speaker means by his utterance that the object S falls instead under the concept R ('Sally is an extremely unemotional and unresponsive person'). In literal utterance (Figure 1.1a) a speaker says S is P and he means S is P; in other words the concepts P and R are identical for the literal sentence meaning and the intended utterance meaning coincide. In simple metaphorical utterances, the speaker says S is P but intends to communicate S is R (Figure 1.1b); in this instance the meaning associated with concept R is arrived

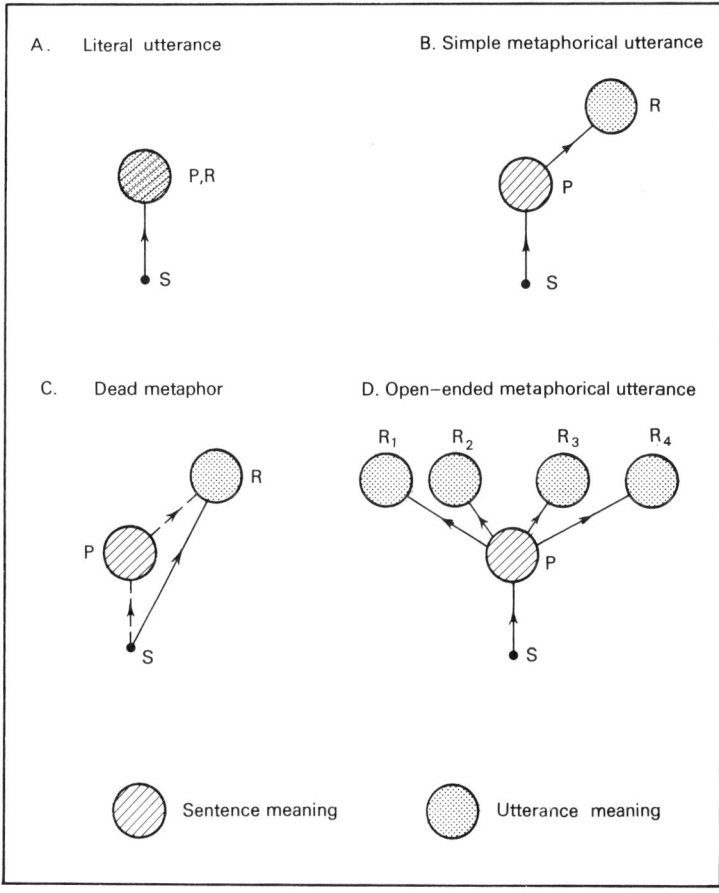

FIGURE 1.1.   The relationship between literal and metaphorical meaning
(after Searle, 1979, p. 122)

at via the literal sentence meaning. In the case of dead metaphor (Figure 1.1c), the original sentence meaning is bypassed and the sentence acquires a new literal meaning identical with the former metaphorical utterance meaning. Finally, in the case of the open-ended metaphorical utterance (Figure 1.1d) a speaker says S is P but intends to communicate an indefinite range of meanings, S is R_1, S is R_2, S is R_3 and so on.

In contrast to simple metaphors, the open-ended metaphor, by its very nature, cannot be paraphrased in a literal expression since it both embodies semantic latencies yet to be fully conceptualized and communicates meaning for which there is no literal equivalent. The expressive power of these metaphors is largely determined by two features: first, the hearer has to figure out what the speaker means and therefore must contribute more to the communication than mere passive uptake; second, to do this, the hearer must go through a separate but related concept (the literal sentence meaning) from the one which is communicated (metaphorical utterance meaning). In general, metaphorical communication occurs when the following, individually necessary and collectively sufficient, principles obtain:

> First, there must be some shared strategies on the basis of which the hearer can recognize that the utterance is not intended literally. The common, but not the only strategy, is based on the fact that the utterance is obviously defective if taken literally.
> Second, there must be some shared principles that associate the P term . . . with a set of possible values of R. . . .
> Third, there must be some shared strategies that enable the speaker and the hearer, given their knowledge of the S term . . . to restrict the range of possible values of R to the actual value of R. The basic principle of this step is that only those possible values of R which determine possible properties of S can be actual values of R (Searle, 1979, p. 120).

The implication of this discussion of the nature of metaphorical expression is that metaphors are only understood in specific social contexts where both the speaker and the hearer share 'the system of associated commonplaces' (Black, 1962, pp. 40–41) embodied in the metaphor's principal and subsidiary concepts. This suggests the closest possible relationship between metaphorical comprehension and the collective consciousness, mythology, or indeed ideology, of any sociocultural group (Livingstone and Harrison, 1980; 1981a). Accordingly, culture, myth, and metaphor are inextricably intertwined:

> That people will understand a metaphor is guaranteed if the metaphor is utilizing cultural, as opposed to private, 'pictures'. The guarantee that such a metaphor will be understood is then, that people within the same culture group have been brought up in roughly similar ways, and become acquainted with

the same sort of thing, and so tend to call to mind the same 'pictures' (McCloskey, 1964, p. 232).

To conclude, our investigation of the mechanisms involved in the communication of metaphorical meaning is, we believe, far from a purely philosophical exercise. Rather, as we shall see, it is at the heart of the nature of scientific understanding in general, and of understanding in geography in particular. In addition to this cognitive role of metaphor, we shall also contend that the formulation of social policy and the structuration of human experience in particular social contexts is equally grounded in metaphor.

UNDERSTANDING IN SCIENCE

Philosophers of science concerned with explicating the mechanisms involved in the construction of scientific models and theories (Black, 1962; Berggren, 1962, 1963; Hesse, 1966; Leatherdale, 1973; Schön, 1963; Turbayne, 1970) have stressed that since they rely on the development of analogies with familiar processes, models can be seen as systemically developed metaphors (Barbour, 1974). As a universal integral constituent of natural language (Lakoff and Johnson, 1980), metaphor is likewise a central element in the constructed language systems of theoretical models. This arises out of the view of scientific inquiry as a creative process 'in which scientists view the world metaphorically, through the language and concepts which filter and structure their perceptions of their subject of study and through the specific metaphors which they implicitly or explicitly choose to develop their framework for analysis' (Morgan, 1980, p. 611).

The metaphorical status of scientific models stems from the fact that in both there is a selective transference of elements from one system of ideas to another in such a way that the subject under investigation is perceived in new ways and new theoretical insights are evoked (Beardsley, 1967; McCloskey, 1964). Thus scientific models share with metaphors the open-endedness which enables the scientist to specify what might otherwise be overlooked and therefore 'to *see new connections*' (Black, 1962, p. 237). The cognitive correspondence between scientific models and metaphors is a reflection of the following five shared characteristics:

(1) *Analogy*: 'metaphor seems to be the key to understanding both the amethodological and creative aspects of scientific discovery and progress . . . in terms of imported analogy and the analogical act' (Leatherdale, 1973, p. 213)
(2) *Open-endedness*: 'It is not an illustration of an idea already explicitly spelled out, but a suggestive invitation to the discovery of further similarities' (Barbour, 1974, p. 14)

(3) *Surplus meaning*: since the theoretical model, like metaphor, is richer (in terms of the associations and implications conveyed) than the phenomenon described, 'it imports concepts and conceptual relations not present in the empirical data alone' (Hesse, 1967, p. 356)

(4) *Systemic concepts*: the subsidiary subject of both open-ended metaphors ('R' in Figure 1.1d) and scientific models is 'regarded as a system rather than an individual thing' (Black, 1979, p. 28). The metaphor-based models of 'the black inner city as frontier outpost' (Ley, 1974) and 'night as frontier' (Melbin, 1978) are not so much about the frontier considered as a thing, but rather about a system of relationships signalled by the presence of the word 'frontier' in both cases (Livingstone and Harrison, 1980)

(5) *Selective transference*: both theoretical models and metaphorical expressions work by '"projecting upon" the primary subject a set of "associated implications", comprised in the implicative complex . . . [or] a set of . . . current opinions shared by members of a certain speech-community' (Black, 1979, pp. 28–29). By both highlighting and hiding relevant elements in the conceptual system, the users of models and metaphors select, emphasize, suppress and organize features of one subject in terms of another.

This approach to the structure of scientific understanding which emphasizes the interpenetration of metaphor and model provides, we believe, a perspective which is both contextual and integrative. 'The metaphorical view,' as Leatherdale (1973, p. 213) observes, 'provides an overall theory of science which is deployable in relation to a large number of problems', such as the relationships among the logic, psychology, and sociology of science, and it does so 'by offering a single unified, synoptic and integrative account of what are often treated as discrete problems'. Conventionally, approaches to the nature of the scientific enterprise have tended to distinguish sharply between the logic of scientific explanation, the psychology of individual insight and discovery, and the sociology of the contextualization of knowledge within scientific communities (Figure 1.2). It is our contention that these three approaches to science (Figure 1.2a) can be individually associated with models (logic), metaphors (psychology), and myths or ideologies (sociology) as their cognitive instruments (Figure 1.2b). The rationale for these associations stems from the kinds of activity or motivation with which both the approaches and the instruments are concerned. The model–logic association is orientated towards the goal of scientific explanation; the metaphor–psychology association leads to a concern with the creation and systematization of original imaginative insight; the myth–sociology association centres on the reconstitution of the social and cognitive contexts of scientific knowledge (Figure 1.2c).

To treat these three sets of associations as necessarily segregated is to overlook the kinds of interpenetration which we have discussed between metaphor and

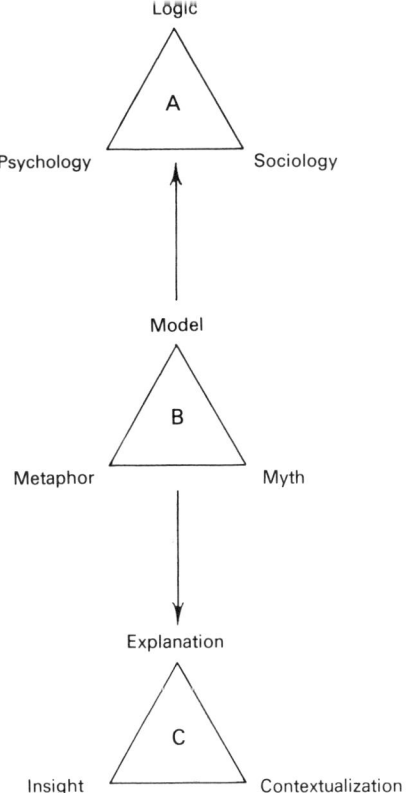

FIGURE 1.2.   The structure of scientific understanding

model development. It also fails to do justice to the increasing recognition that all communication takes place within language communities structured by the possession of shared belief systems, myths, and ideologies. Indeed it is *out of* such communal contexts that analogies with familiar processes arise in the first instance, and it is only *within* such contexts that the necessary cognitive implicatures can be communicated. In short, since the metaphor–myth–model nexus is inseparably interwoven it must follow that the psycho-logy–sociology–logic and the insight–contextualization–explanation triads are similarly interpenetrative. From this we conclude that any attempt to keep the three perspectives separate—reconciliation by segregation—is *de facto* an impossibility. Rather what is needed is the encouragement of pluralistic approaches to the nature of scientific understanding which will be, at the same time, explanatory, insightful, and contextualist. Finally, this metaphor-based perspective on scientific understanding also suggests that it is illegitimate, indeed redundant, to raise the question of assigning primacy to one or other of these avenues of investigation, for the 'fact' of scientific understanding is the eclectic and synthetic outcome of the model-centred logic of explanation, the metaphor-generated psychology of individual insight, and the mythic or ideologically grounded sociology of contextual knowledge.

THE METAPHORS OF GEOGRAPHY

The implication of the previous discussion of the nature of scientific understanding is that metaphor is not only the central link between model as systematically developed metaphor (Black, 1962) and myth as anticipated and expanded metaphor (Lonergan, 1958), but also the dynamic element in the creation, systematization, and communication of insight. Recently indeed, while he does not consider the metaphorical basis of myth (see Turbayne, 1970), Berry (1980) has noted that the specification and exploration of myths is crucial for 'creating future geographies'. Drawing on Fleck's (1979) distinction between 'thought style' (*Denkstil*) at the cognitive level, and 'thought collective' (*Denkkollektiv*) as the social entity through which the thought style is expressed and maintained, Berry (1980, pp. 451–452) states that the 'thought style constrains the ways in which it is possible to perceive reality. One is inducted into a particular thought style through the 'initiation rites' of the thought collective; within it the shape of answers is preformed by the nature of permissible questions'. For Berry this is equivalent to arguing that we are all constrained by our myths. Following Furtado (1975), myths are regarded as lamps which illuminate the perceptions of the social scientist by allowing him to see clearly certain problems while at the same time preventing him from seeing others. This interpretation of myth, of course, closely parallels the selective functioning of metaphor which both *highlights* certain features while *hiding* others. If Berry's programmatic conclusion that 'one of the essentials for a well-adjusted and properly focussed future for our discipline . . . is that we face up to the reality of our myths' (Berry, 1980, p. 452), is to be taken at all seriously then this will, of necessity, involve the exploration of the metaphors underlying the myths and models in the philosophy and research agenda of geography.

That these foundational metaphors are rarely made explicit is not surprising, for as cognitive presuppositions they are the lenses through which the world is viewed rather than the objects of study in their own right (Harrison and Livingstone, 1980). Like Mannheim's peasant boy who could only substitute critical detachment for the taken-for-granted attitude towards his rural milieu by moving to the city and adopting an urban mode of living and thinking (Mannheim, 1936), it is often only possible to see such a presuppositional metaphor as a metaphor by substituting for it another. As Turbayne, in his study of the metaphorically grounded myth of mechanism, has argued:

The metaphysics of mechanism can be dispensed with. The best way to do this is to show that it is only a metaphor; and the best way to show this is to invent a new metaphor. I therefore treat the events in nature *as if* they compose a language, in the belief that the world may be treated just as well, if not better, by making believe that it is a universal language instead of a giant clockwork (Turbayne, 1970, p. 5).

Within contemporary human geography, as we have already indicated, two diffuse and largely antithetical strands of thought—subjectivism and structuralism—have emerged as alternatives to the legacy of a positivistic functionalism. These three orientations comprise the current axes that delimit the conceptual space of geographical praxis which is underlain by a variety of metaphorical presuppositions as to how the real world should be viewed and out of which develop specific models, theories, and disciplinary puzzle-solving activities (Figure 1.3). Some of these metaphors, of course, have longer historical

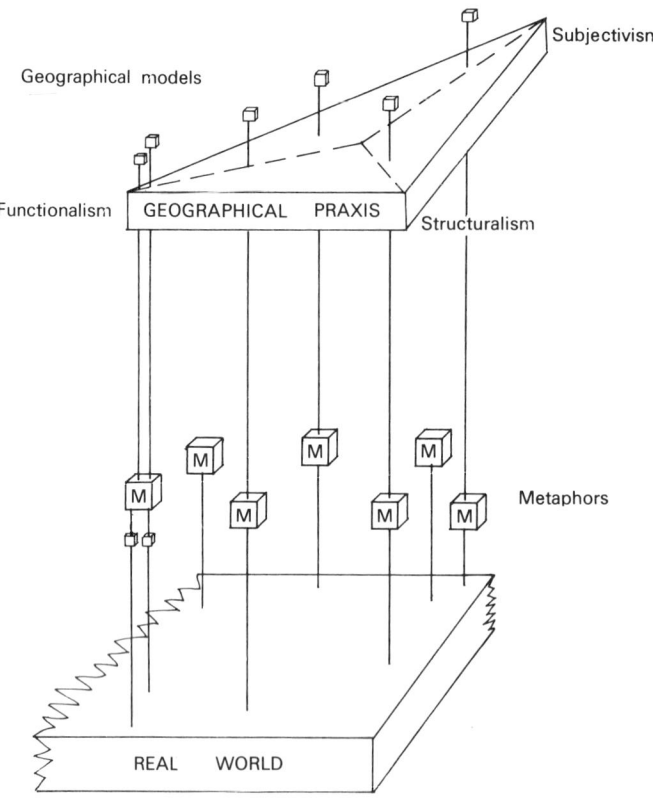

FIGURE 1.3.   Geography as metaphor

traditions than others, and have, accordingly, given rise to a range of more specific sub-metaphors. The ubiquitous presence of metaphors and sub-metaphors in the evolution of geographical understanding suggests that the exploration of geography as metaphor will provide a fruitful perspective for reconstructing the history of geographical thought and practice in such a way that recent demands for a history that is dynamic rather than static (Stoddart, 1981), contextualist rather than internalist (Berdoulay, 1981), may be satisfied (Livingstone, 1979).

Underlying the practice of geography a number of central metaphors. some with longer histories than others, can be identified. The implicit or explicit adoption by geographers of the associations inherent in particular metaphors tends to reflect the basic philosophical orientation of their work—an orientation which delimits the range of questions that may be asked, and constrains the scope of possible answers. In other words, metaphor both legitimizes and is legitimated by the geographer's presuppositional alignment. Some of the more important metaphors of geography can be conceptually located with reference to the functionalism–subjectivism–structuralism axes which provide basic orientations for the pratice of contemporary human geography (Figure 1.4).

Much of what passes for orthodoxy in contemporary geography has been based predominantly on the metaphors of *machine* and *organism*. The *machine*

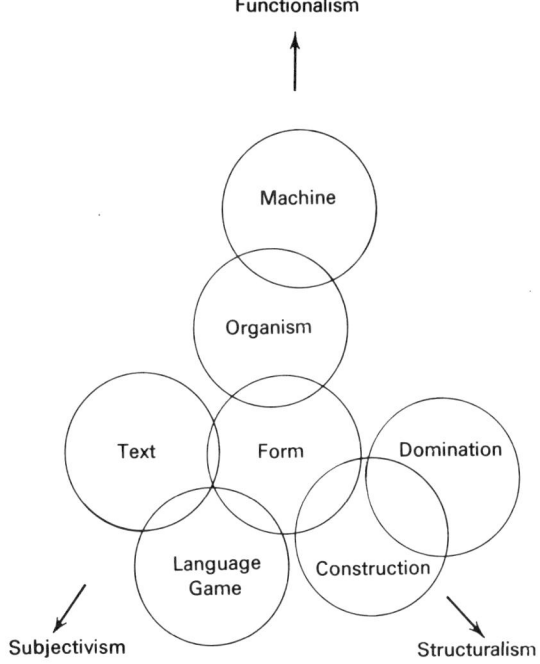

FIGURE 1.4.   Metaphors of geography

metaphor has had a long history, originating with the Greeks and developed, in its modern form, by Descartes and Newton (Pepper, 1942; Turbayne, 1970). Based upon the assumption that phenomena have a concrete real existence and a systemic character orientated to the production of an ordered and regulated state of affairs, mechanistic metaphors have tended to apply such machine characteristics as efficiency, design, purpose, components and control to the study of nature, man, and society. At different times in the history of geographical thought, different aspects of the functionalist metaphor of machine have been emphasized. In the post-Reformation era, for instance, the design element was uppermost in the science practised by advocates of natural and physico-theology for whom the concept of the world as a machine was an image 'connected with that of a maker apart from itself' (Hooykaas, 1972, p. 14; see also Glacken, 1967). In contrast, the *motifs* of control, and consequently prediction, typify the cybernetic environmental systems approach which is perhaps the most conspicuous manifestation of this metaphor in contemporary geography (Bennett and Chorley, 1978, Chapman, 1977). Drawn from the sciences of control engineering, thermodynamics, and communications engineering, this application of 'the ideology of control' (Gregory, 1980) within geography has been characterized as an attempt 'to engage complexity and ... reduce it to understandable proportions in order to control the trajectories describing the courses of individual lives and the larger societies in which they are embedded' (Gould, 1979, p. 136). It is the apparently reductionist nature of this approach, together with its major aim of successfully manipulating systems so that 'mankind achieves world domination in the most complete and efficient fashion' (Kennedy, 1979, p. 553), that have led critics to suggest that it offers a technology rather than a science, *techne* rather than *episteme*.

Despite the diffuse historical configurations of the mechanistic metaphor, a persistent underlying theme seems to be located in the concern with *function*, of how natural and social systems 'work': 'the system concept is essentially functional' (Langton, 1972, p. 131) in that the fundamental aim of systems theory is the analysis and control of 'complex *functioning* wholes' (Chapman, 1977, p. 4). It is at this precise point—the concern with function—that the less reductionist, more holistic, metaphor of *organism* overlaps with the machine metaphor as a vehicle for functionalist analyses. While organismic metaphors have a long history in the western tradition (Lovejoy, 1936) they were revitalized during the eighteenth and nineteenth centuries under the influence of German *Naturphilosophie* and biological evolutionism (Hofstadter, 1944; Jones, 1980; D. C. Phillips, 1977; Young, 1973b). The twin axes of the organic metaphor derive from the concern in biology with the reciprocal relationships between organic form and function (Coleman, 1971):

The term 'organism' has come to be used to refer to any system of mutually connected and dependent parts constituted to share a common life and focuses attention upon the nature of life activity. An organism is typically seen as a combination of elements, differentiated yet integrated, attempting to survive within the context of a wider environment (Morgan, 1980, p. 614).

Within geography there has been a widespread application of analogies drawn from the organic metaphor. The geopolitical conception of the state, Davisian geomorphology, plant ecology and early pedological study, the regional school, and human ecology and urban sociology have all been shown to have drawn inspiration from the organic analogy (Stoddart, 1967). Indeed this metaphor has been so attractive that it has given rise to a number of sub-metaphors, among them the metaphors of growth, cycle, *Gestalten*, adaptation/adoption, and urban frontier, which continue to reappear in much contemporary human geography (Livingstone and Harrison, 1981a). This means that, despite repeated re-pudiations of the organic metaphor on both epistemological and ideological grounds, it continues to exert an influence on the taken-for-granted practice of geography and sporadically resurfaces in new manifestations.

Associated with the metaphor of organism, though less concerned with function, is the metaphor of *form* or structure. While in some ways the concern with forms may be connected up to Kantian philosophy (Livingstone and Harrison, 1981c), it is in the notion of the morphology of landscape, associated with Sauer and the Berkeley school (Sauer, 1963), that the metaphor of form has its most conspicuous manifestation in geographical thought. In his approach to regional geography Sauer believed that there was 'no dualism of landscape . . . since attention is directed to natural and cultural *forms*' (Speth, 1979, p. 17). With his belief in the fictive device that the geographical area is a corporeal 'thing', possessing forms and structure and understood in terms of such organic categories as origin, growth, and function (Speth, 1979), Sauer could say of landscape, that

> Its structure and function are determined by integrant, dependent forms. The landscape is considered, therefore, in a sense as having an organic quality. We may follow Bluntschli [1921] in saying that one has not fully understood the nature of an area until one 'has learned to see it as an organic unit, to comprehend land and life in terms of each other' (Sauer, 1963, pp. 321–322).

A reliance on the metaphor of form, however, cannot be restricted to the Berkeley landscape tradition. The emphasis on the cartographical representation of empirical observations, the concern with morphology, and the stress on spatial pattern and structure, which have typified a number of quantitatively based developments in postwar human geography, perpetuate a formist perspective. In essence Social Area Analysis and Factorial Ecology were methodologies developed to provide 'accounts of the various social and economic mechanisms

which produce a mosaic of districts of different character and of the spatial form which these districts take' (Johnston and Herbert, 1976, p. 5). The identification of underlying socioeconomic processes, it was believed, could be inferred from the specification of the ways in which social, ethnic, and economic residential 'spaces' were integrated (Murdie, 1976). Form, therefore, became the key to explicating process. Indeed in much factorial ecology, formism was so dominant that pattern and process were all but conflated for, according to Berry (1971, p. 215), factorial ecology asks: '"How does the system cohere and pattern?" The answer is sought by trying to identify repetitive sequences of spatial variation present in many observable attributes of areas' (see also Johnston, 1976; Rees, 1972).

The growth of perception studies and cognitive mapping, as important elements in contemporary behavioural geography, is similarly premised on the metaphor of form. The metaphorical status of form lies in the fact that the diffuse, latent, or even subliminal cerebral images held by individuals and groups are regarded as possessing a potential 'form' or 'structure' which may be reconstructed and given material expression in map form. Thus the very concept of 'mental map' is itself a metaphor and its definition and characterization has been expressed in fundamentally metaphorical terms:

> It is preferable . . . to restrict the use of the term [mental map] to the spatial or skeletal framework—the background to the more rounded phenomenon of the image . . . [I]t is logical to assume that the environment as an entity only properly or fully makes sense when the separate parts are mentally structured in some sequential or relational context (Pocock, 1976, p. 493).

Since the mental map represents a 'subjective' space, it has been inferred that it is underlain by norms or laws relating to the nature of consciousness itself (Richards, 1974), the process of perceiving (Lee, 1970; Stea, 1969a), or to social preferences and prejudices (Downs and Stea, 1973, 1977; Gould and White, 1974), which can, in some way, be held to 'explain' the map image. Thus the 'form' of the mental map is seen as related, directly or indirectly, to other structural forms—epistemological, psychological, and sociological—through which multifarious environmental stimuli and diverse everyday experiences are meaningfully constructed. Some indeed, recognizing, implicitly though not explicitly, the metaphorical status of 'mental map', come close to regarding it as an abstraction or, to use Whitehead's (1925) terminology, a 'useful fiction': 'it matters not a whit that we cannot directly observe a "mental map" or even that we cannot know for sure that it is actually "there"; if a subject behaves as if such a map existed, it is sufficient justification for the model' (Stea, 1969b, p. 235).

The closely associated metaphors of *construction* and *domination* have come to characterize the fashionable structuralist perspective on the relations between nature, man, and society in geography. In essence, structuralism:

holds that the identification of the elements of manifest reality must be mediated through a concealed structure. Adoption of this perspective by geographers would involve accepting that the landscape does not have the key to our understanding of it within itself, that these structures 'are not self-evident and inscribed into the nature of things' [Gellner, 1971, p. 165], and that there is an important distinction to be drawn between the self-evident appearance of things . . . and the way they really are (Gregory, 1978b, p. 40).

This distinction between appearance and the essence of things (Glucksmann, 1974), and the belief that concealed structure is both real and knowable, suggests that 'this real-world structure cannot be opposed to the theoretical structure *built* to represent it. . . . [T]he ontological and theoretical structures have to be isomorphic or . . . both structures and theories are *"objects to be constructed"'* (Gregory, 1976, p. 296, emphasis added; see also Vilar, 1973, p. 188).

The fundamental constructional categorization of foundation and edifice, which is an important constituent of everyday conceptual apparatus and language (Lakoff and Johnson, 1980, pp. 97–105), has been metaphorically applied to the structure of society, in the context of the classical marxian distinction between infrastructure as the material base, and superstructure as the political and ideological forms of society (Godelier, 1978; McQuarie, 1978, pp. 20–32; Smart, 1976, pp. 61–64; Williams, 1973). The refinement and application of this constructionist social theory has followed Althusser's conception of over-determination as the relationship between 'determinant instances in the [infra] structure–superstructure complex which constitutes the essence of any social formation' (Althusser, 1969, p. 111). This reconception of the relationship between the (economic) mode of production and the political and ideological levels of society implies that 'although the infrastructure is primary and, as it were, provides the unalterable preconditions of human life and thought, it does no more than this; it supplies the pack of cards, and deals the hands, but the rules of the game and the way the hands are played are left to the players to decide' (Barnes, 1971, p. 109; see also Althusser and Balibar, 1970, pp. 145–157; della Volpe, 1974, pp. 246–254).

Though less developed than the metaphors of machine, organism, and form in geography, the construction metaphor, in its Althusserian expression at least, has been implicitly adopted as an organizing principle in recent philosophical discussion within the discipline. Gregory (1978a, p. 102), for example, believes that only by reference to this Althusserian–marxian structuralism will it be possible 'to construct a conception of spatial structure in terms of . . . the structuration of society'. The validity of the construction metaphor, moreover, has been retained in, for example, Johnston's recent questioning of structuralist geography. His critique, however, stems not from dissatisfaction with structuralism *qua* structuralism but rather from its overemphasis on the macro-scale: 'there is an interest among at least some structuralist in macro-socio-economic processes which have spatial impacts, but a lack of concern with the details of those impacts' (Johnston, 1980a, p. 407). To remedy this Johnston believes that geographical work set within and guided by the structural mould [and reflected in his recent reinterpretation of contemporary urban geography (Johnston, 1980b)], must be firmly grounded in the detailed analysis of the morphology of regional mosaics through the construction and reconstruction of regional social formations, articulations and transformations.

Given the structuralist's concern with the process of structuration as the 'attempt to determine the conditions which govern the continuity and dissolution of structures or types of structure' (Giddens, 1976, p. 120), and the belief that 'the structural properties of social systems are both the medium and the outcome of the practices that constitute those systems' (Giddens, 1979, p. 69), the particular focus on class structure and its legitimation in contemporary capitalist society has generated a further metaphor—that of *domination*. Fundamental to this metaphor is the idea that the structures of society are not neutral but can be seen as oppressive and exploitative—in short, they are seen as instruments of domination. In the application of the metaphor of domination a number of sub-metaphors have emerged: power structures, class struggle, and structural conflict, all of which are regarded as modes of socioeconomic exploitation (Clegg, 1975):

> Power as a particular type of social action is constructed and acted out by individuals as a ruled enactment. Such enactments occur in the context of an economically conditioned structure of domination. . . . The individual is essentially a social being, who, as a bearer of social relations, is ruled and dominated in the last instance by economic power. This economic power is embedded and displayed within the framework of a 'structure of domination' which is articulated through different types of 'rule'. Domination thus concerns, and grants, the prior capacity to be able to 'exercise' power at all (Clegg and Dunkerley, 1980, p. 456).

With a materialist conception of the social world (comprising concrete, ontologically real structures, and characterized by intrinsic tensions and contradictions between opposing elements), the instrument of domination metaphor in radical structuralist geography has led to an exploration of the way in which the power structure within classes, organizations, and regions is linked to power structures within the world political economy. Thus Lipietz, in his recent study of the polarization of space through the unequal development of regions in terms of economic power, incomes, and skills, and the expansion of the tertiary sector, concludes:

> From the moment that these [centre–periphery] relationships are recognised as the spatial dimension of the dynamics of capitalism there is nothing to prevent

an understanding of the industrialisation or even the tertiarisation, of the periphery. However, such industrialisation, or tertiarisation, would be 'deformed', 'misshapen', *dominated* (Lipietz, 1980, pp. 16–17; see also Carney, Hudson, and Lewis, 1980; Perrons, 1981).

In addition to the study of uneven development, the instrument of domination metaphor underlies much of the discussion of contemporary social issues by radical geographers (Peet, 1977) and has generated an extensive literature on the residential pattern of cities and the structure and operation of housing markets (Gray, 1975; Harvey, 1975; Johnston, 1980b). However, despite the wide range of these studies, they are united in adopting a conflict model of society which 'sees sectional interests as being the basis of social life which is, therefore, divisive, involving inducement and coercion as well as generating the structural conflicts . . . [which are] the central element in a social system' (Eyles, 1974, p. 39).

The interpretative metaphors of *language game* and *text* differ from functionalism, on the one hand, by focusing on understanding the nature of social realities through asking questions of meaning and intentionality, and from structuralism, on the other, by emphasizing the intelligibility of human thought and action without recourse to determinant, deep, universal structures. The metaphor of *language game*, first developed by Wittgenstein (1968), presents social activity as a game of words, thoughts, and actions. It suggests that social realities emerge as 'rule-governed symbolic structures as individuals engage their words through the use of specific codes and practices, in order to vest their situations with meaningful form' (Morgan, 1980, p. 616). Adoption of this metaphor involves the belief that these social realities are identified by their use of different kinds of verbal and non-verbal language. This suggests that the 'language game' metaphor applies on the one hand as a metaphor for our understanding of the social world and, on the other, to the treatment of language itself as a game or rule-governed activity. As a result the former has encouraged, in social theory, the development and application of the concept of 'form of life' as the concrete expression of language as the medium of intersubjectivity in definite social practices (Giddens, 1979) and cultural frames or traditions (Gadamer, 1975). While this approach to the study of the meaningful organization of human social life has been developed by interpretative sociologists (see D. L. Phillips, 1977), the adoption of such a perspective has received little more than passing reference in human geography (Harrison and Livingstone, 1979, p. 78). The latter, closely associated, conception of language as a game is premised on Wittgenstein's view that language is not simply communicative and descriptive; it is ontological: 'we cannot think what we cannot think; so that what we cannot think we cannot *say* either' (Wittgenstein, 1961, para 5.61). Olsson (1975, p. 31), adopting this Wittgensteinian perspective, believes that 'by repeatedly focussing on the connections between what I say and the language in which I say it, I hope to arrive at a better understanding not only of reality, thought, and action, but also of the philosophical and methodological problems of action oriented research'. Despite this objective, Olsson's realization that 'facts can not exist outside of conception and my conception reflects the particular language I am using' (Olsson, 1975, p. 9) has led to an increasingly idiosyncratic and individualistic perspective which stems from the limitations of the nature of language itself (Olsson, 1980). It is because scientific language effectively imprisons meaning (Olsson, 1979, p. 302) that he has attempted 'to grasp both the certainty of the external and the ambiguity of the internal, of jibberish and silent communication' (Olsson, 1978, p. 118).

Concern with the interrelations between language, communication and meaning need not, however, necessarily lead to the conclusion that language imprisons meaning. Wittgenstein's later writings suggest that the 'limits of language', the 'that whereof we cannot speak' (Wittgenstein, 1961), lead not to 'a blank void which looms when we have exhausted the logical elucidation of language', but are 'intrinsically involved with the *practices that comprise forms of life*' (Giddens, 1979, p. 34; see also Disco, 1976). The attempt to explicate the way in which meaning is incorporated in the practices—temporal, material, and social—of these nonverbal languages, has suggested that a useful approach to the understanding of social worlds might be found in developing the metaphor of *text* (Ricoeur, 1971; see also Ricoeur, 1973; 1977a). According to this view social activity is regarded as if it were a symbolic document—a text to be interpreted by the use of hermeneutic methods of analysis as a means of unravelling its nature and significance. The central concern of interpretative or hermeneutic perspectives is with understanding the manner in which these texts are authored, read, and translated, 'the way in which the structure of discourse may explore certain key themes and develop particular kinds of imagery' (Morgan, 1980, p. 617).

According to Rose, the practice of text interpretation has come to characterize a growing body of literature in contemporary human geography. For him:

doing human geography consists of interpreting *texts*—an activity much like that of ordinary reading. A text can be considered as any set of signs, symbols, verbal or non-verbal gestures and actions housed in a pattern of linguistic meanings. The texts of human geography . . . comprise not only words, numbers and geometric symbols such as are found in the usual definition of texts as any piece of written communication, but also the whole gamut of expressive signs, whether these signs are found on maps, in the field, in equations, in spoken or written accounts, or as acted out in the events which the geographer is attempting to comprehend. . . . [T]he activity of human geography is the interpretation of such texts: the apprehension of meanings openly expressed by the signs and symbols as well as those meanings which are only implicit in the text taken as a whole (Rose, 1980, p. 124).

In his exposition of geography as text interpretation, Rose has identified Dilthey as a key antecedent of contemporary humanistic geography in view of his emphasis that 'the proper object of understanding in the *Geisteswissenschaften* is the text to be deciphered and understood and that every encounter with a text is likewise an encounter with the transmitting tradition itself' (Rose, 1981, p. 117). As a result, text interpretation, he argues, following Gadamer (1975) and Ricoeur (1977b), must be seen as a text-event involving both the text and the interpreter. Accepting text interpretation as a fundamental way of knowing the geographical world involves the recognition that to understand a text-event the interpreter and the interpretation are continuously bound up with each other (Rose, 1981).

While the metaphor of text interpretation has implicitly underlain much contemporary humanistic geography (Rose, 1981, pp. 120–24), perhaps its most conspicuous manifestation is apparent in the application of the notion of 'reading' as a method of interpretation. Building on the early work of Hoskins (1955) and Jackson (1970), the idea of 'reading the landscape' (Meining, 1979b), for example, has emerged from the belief that 'every landscape is a code, and its study may be undertaken as a deciphering of meaning' (Meinig, 1979a, p. 6). Since the basic principle of this perspective is that all human landscapes have cultural meaning, it follows that the landscape can be read as we might read a book; in a very real sense landscape is unwitting autobiography (Watts, 1975). Nevertheless, in keeping with metaphorical usage as the selective transference of meaning between contexts, Lewis (1979, p. 12) observes that 'reading landscapes is not as easy as reading books . . . [O]rdinary landscape seems messy and disorganized, like a book with pages missing, torn, and smudged; a book whose copy has been edited and re-edited by people with illegible handwriting. Like books, landscapes *can* be read, but unlike books, they were not *meant* to be read.' The problems of interpreting an illegible text are possibly most clearly demonstrated in attempts to read the urban landscape (Clay, 1973). Its unintelligibility and apparent illegibility have both engendered and come to symbolize for many the experience of estrangement and alienation (Paterson, 1976; Strauss, 1961; White and White, 1962), not least because the city 'is not perceived as a coherent system of signs, as an environment communicating to us in a language that we know' (Marcus, 1973, p. 257). However, just as Ruskin argued that it was necessary to read a building and perceive it as a total intellectual and imaginative structure, so also with the city. Attempts to read the city, to decipher its meaning-as-text, operate at two scales. On the one hand cities have been viewed as 'the cultures of their countries made graphic in the landscape' (Watson, 1976, p. 79), as symbols or images 'to which one can orient oneself' (Tuan, 1974, p. 224). Experientially, on the other hand, the cityscape itself can be read as a text which encapsulates the intimate experiences of its inhabitants (Craik, 1968; Lynch, 1960), inviting understanding as an actor, rather than explanation as a spectator (Beck, 1975), and encouraging the adoption of the methodology of participant observation—the practice of reading with eyes, nose, ears and feet (Marcus, 1973).

To conclude, our brief résumé of a variety of perspectives within geography has demonstrated that, implicitly or explicitly, geographers have employed a wide range of metaphors in their attempts to come to terms with nature, man, and society. The centrality of metaphor in the theory and practice of geography must not therefore be underestimated, but rather its value in generating insight and understanding must be actively encouraged. Nevertheless, we must not be uncritical in our use of metaphor. There are drawbacks as well as benefits in metaphorical understanding, perhaps the most important of which arise from the reductionism inherent in mistaking the metaphor for the reality it represents. The use of metaphor, as we have already seen, involves the pretence that something is the case when it is not.

Just as often, however, the pretence has been dropped, either by the pretenders or by their followers. There is a difference between using a metaphor and taking it literally, between using a model and mistaking it for the thing modelled. The one is to make believe that something is the case; the other is to believe that it is. The one is to use a disguise or mask for illustrative or explanatory purposes; the other is to mistake the mask for the face. . . . After the disguise or mask has been worn for a considerable time it tends to blend with the face, and it becomes extremely difficult to 'see through' it . . . . It is not necessarily a confusion to treat items belonging to one sort in the idioms appropriate to another . . . . On the other hand it is a confusion to present the items of one sort in the idioms of another—without awareness . . . . It is to mistake, for example, the theory for the fact, the procedure for the process, the myth for history, the model for the thing, and the metaphor for the face of literal truth (Turbayne, 1970, pp 3–4).

LANGUAGE IN PRACTICE AND PRACTICE IN LANGUAGE

If, as philosophers of science have argued, the formulation of models in science is premised upon that enigmatic (though universal) form of mental activity—metaphorical thinking—and, as we have contended, the theory and practice of geographical discourse is likewise predicated on metaphorical representations of reality, it seems that language as the organ for the creation and transmission of scientific meaning must be a focal point for future research. 'What now seems required is an emphasis on meaning, and on . . . language, as communicator of meaning' (Campbell, 1978, pp. 68–69). However, it would be unnecessarily restrictive to limit the study of language within geography solely to the examination of the cognitive role of metaphor in theory formation. There seem to be at least two further directions in which the awareness and exploration of language and metaphor may provide a fruitful stimulus for human geographical research.

The recognition that language is a fundamental human experience suggests the first such direction: the examination of the ways in which different social groups organize their conceptions of the world and communicate them in linguistic and symbolic form. The metaphors they invent, the meanings they share, the symbols they create, and the myths they believe—which both embody and are embodied in language—coalesce in their particular form of life to provide communal identity and social cohesion: 'it is not the literal past, the "facts" of history, that shape us, but images of the past embodied in language. . . . we must never cease renewing those images; because once we do, we fossilise' (Friel, 1981, p. 66). Of course, this research agenda will encounter many difficulties, not the least of which will be the problems of penetrating the community's core-meanings, even if we do succeed in immersing ourselves, as actors, in the culture of the group. This fundamental impasse is encapsulated in Brain Friel's recent play *Translations*, when George Yolland (an orthographer attached to the toponymic department of the Royal Engineers, engaged in the first Ordnance Survey of Ireland and stationed in a Gaelic-speaking community in County Donegal) observes:

> Even if I did speak Irish I'd always be an outsider here, wouldn't I? I may learn the password but the language of the tribe will always elude me, won't it? The private core will always be . . . hermetic, won't it? (Friel, 1981, p. 40).

Perhaps this core will always be elusive, hermetic. But if we want to understand even the surface meanings of any social group, we must go beyond the exploration of the semiotic study of space (Bailly, 1981; Zeitoun, 1979), environmental symbolism (Rowntree and Conkey, 1980), signs as territorial markers (Boal, 1969; Ley and Cybriwsky, 1974), and the linguistic geography of dialect (Milroy, 1980; Milroy and Milroy, 1978; Trudgill, 1975), to the study of language itself as the intersubjective medium for the creation, communication, and unification of shared meaning (Livingstone and Harrison, 1981b, p. 71). This will permit the identification of the social and spatial arrangement of the spheres in which the significations implied in particular linguistic signifiers are understood—the characteristics of individuals who understand, for example, the implications and meanings encapsulated in particular modes of verbal and non-verbal expression.

Since metaphor is central to the task of accounting for our perspective on the world—how we think about things, make sense of reality, and set the problems we later try to solve—it underlies the ways in which social problems are perceived, formulated, evaluated, solved, and recreated (Harrison and Livingstone, 1980, pp. 27–30). This suggests that social policy can be considered less as a problem-solving enterprise than as a problem-setting one which has 'more to do with the ways in which we frame the purposes to be achieved than with the selection of optimal means for achieving them' (Schön, 1979, p. 255; see also Rein and Schön, 1977). The framing of problems—the genesis of problem-setting and the directions for problem-solving—often depends upon an implict or explicit perception of the 'problem-situation' in metaphorical terms. Dominating the theory and practice of urban housing policy, for example, are metaphors which set out a view of what is wrong and, by implication, what needs fixing. In identifying the nature of these problems, some practitioners and policy analysts have adopted such pathological metaphors as disease, blight, decay, and ageing, while others have relied on preservationist metaphors such as urban village and the slum as natural community:

> Once we are able to see a slum as a blighted area, we know that blight must be removed . . . and the area must be returned to its former state. . . . The metaphor is one of disease and cure. . . . Once we are able to see the slum as a 'natural community' . . . then it is also clear what is wrong and what needs doing. What is wrong is that the natural community, with its homelike stability and its informal network of mutual support, is threatened with destruction—indeed, by the very prophylaxis undertaken in the name of 'urban renewal' (Schön, 1979, p. 265).

From the putative redescription of the slum as a blight or a natural community, it is clear that the metaphors of policy are inherently normative—they involve intrinsic evaluations of both the setting and solving of problems. Accordingly,

> the notion of generative metaphor then becomes an interpretive tool for the critical analysis of social policy. My point here is not that we *ought* to think metaphorically about social policy problems, but that we *do* already think about them in terms of certain pervasive, tacit generative metaphors; and that we ought to become critically aware of these generative metaphors, to increase the rigor and precision of our analysis of social policy problems by examining the analogies and 'disanalogies' between the familiar descriptions— embodied in metaphors . . . and the actual problematic situations that confront us (Schön, 1979, p. 256).

TOWARDS AN EXPERIENTIAL SYNTHESIS

The ubiquity of metaphor in the theory and practice of geography and social policy, as creator and communicator of understanding, is a consequence of its universality in human experience. Since metaphors are invented to give expression and form to otherwise incommunicable insights through the creation of radically new categories of meaning, it follows that the subjective, on the one hand, and the structural, on the other, are neither incompatible nor antipathetic.

This is because metaphor, we believe, forms a bridge between the subjectivist and the structuralist polarities by signifying that understanding is never purely individual but communal (metaphor communicates shared meaning), never purely intellectual but experiential (metaphor arises out of shared experience), never purely theoretical but practical (metaphor is practised in a shared context).

The reason we have focussed so much on metaphor is that it unites reason and imagination. Reason, at the very least, involves categorization, entailment, and inference. Imagination, in one of its many aspects, involves seeing one kind of thing in terms of another kind of thing—what we have called metaphorical thought. Metaphor is thus *imaginative rationality*. Since the categories of our everyday thought are largely metaphorical and our everyday reasoning involves metaphorical entailments and inferences, ordinary rationality is therefore imaginative by its very nature (Lakoff and Johnson, 1980, pp. 192–193).

In adopting the metaphorical perspective there will emerge a synthesis of event and meaning, observation and interpretation, fact and value, objectivity and subjectivity, because, in short, metaphorical understanding structures the subjective.

CODA

And as history proceeds on the heels of art, the wings it takes off on are the wings of metaphor. I would even suggest that language itself is nothing but a giant metaphor, indeed that all meaning is at bottom metaphoric. Without metaphor we could never see the new in the old and never come to appreciate that creation is expression in search of a meaning. Without it we could never produce new worlds from old words and never generate new ideas like magicians pulling rabbits out of their sleeves (Olsson, 1979, pp. 302–303).

When we pass beyond pointing to individual sensible objects, when we begin to think of causes, relations, of mental states or acts, we become incurably metaphorical. We apprehend none of these things except through metaphor. . . . Our only choice is to use the metaphors and thus to think something, though less than we could wish. . . . For me, reason is the natural organ of truth; but imagination is the organ of meaning. Imagination, producing new metaphors or revivifying old, is not the cause of truth, but its condition (Lewis, 1963, pp. 263, 265).

REFERENCES

Agnew, J. A. and Duncan, J. S. (1981). The transfer of ideas into Anglo-American human geography. *Progress in Human Geography*, **5**, 42–57.

Albrow, M. (1974) Dialectical and categorial paradigms of a science of society. *Sociological Review*, **22**, 183–201.

Althusser, L. (1969). *For Marx*, New Left Books, London.

Althusser, L. and Balibar, E. (1970). *Reading Capital*, New Left Books, London.

Bachelard, G. (1969). *The Poetics of Space*, Beacon Press, Boston.

Bailly, A. S. (1981). Behavioural geography in the French-speaking world: developments, approaches and planning experiences. Paper presented at the IBG annual conference, Leicester.

Bannister, R. C. (1979). *Social Darwinism. Science and Myth in Anglo-American Social Thought*, Temple University Press, Philadelphia.

Barbour, I. G. (1974). *Myths, Models, and Paradigms: The Nature of Scientific and Religious Language*, SCM Press, London.

Barnes, J. (1971). *Three Styles in the Study of Kinship*, Tavistock, London.

Bartels, D. (1973). Between theory and metatheory. In R. J. Chorley (Ed.), *Directions in Geography*, Methuen, London, pp. 25–42.

Barthes, R. (1964). *Essai Critiques*, Éditions du Seuil, Paris.

Beardsley, M. C. (1967). Metaphor. In P. Edwards (Ed.), *The Encyclopedia of Philosophy*, *Vol. 5*, Macmillan and the Free Press, New York, pp. 284–289.

Beck, L. W. (1975). *The Actor and the Spectator*, Yale University Press, New Haven.

Bennett, R. J. and Chorley, R. J. (1978). *Environmental Systems: Philosophy, Analysis and Control*, Methuen, London.

Berdoulay, V. (1981). The contextual approach. In D. R. Stoddart (Ed.), *Geography, Ideology and Social Concern*, Basil Blackwell, Oxford, pp. 8-16.

Berggren, D. (1962). The use and abuse of metaphor: I. *Review of Metaphysics*, **16**, 237-258.

Berggren, D. (1963). The use and abuse of metaphor: II. *Review of Metaphysics*, **16**, 450-472.

Bergin, T. B. and Fisch, M. H. (1968). *The New Science of Giambattista Vico*, Cornell University Press, Ithaca.

Berlin, I. (1962). Does political theory still exist? In P. Laslett and W. G. Runciman (Eds.), *Philosophy, Politics and Society*, Blackwell, Oxford, pp. 1-33.

Berry, B. J. L. (Ed.) (1971). Comparative factorial ecology. *Economic Geography*, **47**, 207–368.

Berry, B. J. L. (1980). Creating future geographies. *Annals of the Association of American Geographers*, **70**, 449-458.

Black, M. (1962). *Models and Metaphors*, Cornell University Press, Ithaca.

Black, M. (1979). More about metaphor. In A. Ortony (Ed.), *Metaphor and Thought*, Cambridge University Press, Cambridge, pp. 19–43.

Bluntschli, H. (1921). Die Amazonasniederung als harmonischer Organismus. *Geographische Zeitschrift*, **27**, 49–68.

Boal, F. W. (1969). Territoriality on the Shankill–Falls divide, Belfast. *Irish Geography*, **6**, 30–50.

Bottomore, T., and Nisbet, R. (1978). Structuralism. In T. Bottomore and R. Nisbet (Eds.), *A History of Sociological Analysis*, Heinemann, London. pp. 557-598.

Boudon, R. (1971). *The Uses of Structuralism*, Heinemann, London.

Buttimer, A. (1971). *Society and Milieu in the French Geographic Tradition*, Rand McNally, Chicago.

Buttimer, A. (1974). *Values in Geography. Association of American Geographers Commission on College Geography Resource Paper* 24, Association of American Geographers, Washington, DC.

Buttimer, A. (1978). Charism and context: the challenge of *La Géographie Humaine*. In D.

Ley and M. S. Samuels (Eds.), *Humanistic Geography.Prospects and Problems*, Croom Helm, London, pp. 58–76.

Buttimer, A. (1979). Reason, rationality, and human creativity. *Geografiska Annaler*, **61B**, 43–49.

Buttimer, A., and Seamon, D. (Eds.) (1980). *The Human Experience of Space and Place*, Croom Helm, London.

Campbell, J. A. (1978). Review of R. M. Downs and D. Stea, *Maps in Minds: Reflections on Cognitive Mapping*. *Geography*, **63**, 68–69.

Carneiro, R. L. (1973). Structure, function, and equilibrium in the evolutionism of Herbert Spencer. *Journal of Anthropological Research*, **29**, 77–95.

Carney, J. G., Hudson, R., and Lewis, J. R. (Eds.) (1980). *Regions in Crisis*, Croom Helm, London.

Cassirer, E. (1946). *Language and Myth*, Dover, New York.

Cassirer, E. (1955). *The Philosophy of Symbolic Forms*, Yale University Press, New Haven.

Chapman, G. P. (1977). *Human and Environmental Systems: A Geographer's Appraisal*, Academic Press, London.

Clay, G. (1973). *Close-Up: How to Read the American City*, Praeger, New York.

Clegg, S. (1975). *Power, Rule and Domination: A Critical and Empirical Understanding of Power in Sociological Theory and Everyday Life*. Routledge and Kegan Paul, London.

Clegg, S. and Dunkerley, D. (1980). *Organization, Class and Control*, Routledge and Kegan Paul, London.

Coleman, W. (1971). *Biology in the Nineteenth Century. Problems of Form, Function, and Transformation*, Wiley, New York.

Cooter, R. (1979). The power of the body: the early nineteenth century. In S. Barnes and S. Shapin (Eds.), *Natural Order. Historical Studies of Scientific Culture*, Sage Publications, Beverly Hills, pp. 73–92.

Cosgrove, D. E. (1979). John Ruskin and the geographical imagination. *Geographical Review*, **69**, 43–62.

Craik, K. (1968). The comprehension of the everyday physical environment. *Journal of the American Institute of Planners*, **34**, 29–37.

della Volpe, G. (1974). *Rousseau et Marx et autres essais de critique materialiste*, Maspero, Paris.

Disco, C. (1976). Ludwig Wittgenstein and the end of wild conjectures. *Theory and Society*, **3**, 265–287.

Downs, R. M. and Stea, D. (Eds.) (1973). *Image and Environment*, Edward Arnold, London.

Downs, R. M. and Stea, D. (1977). *Maps in Minds: Reflections on Cognitive Mapping*, Harper and Row, New York.

Duncan, J. S. (1980). The superorganic in American cultural geography. *Annals of the Association of American Geographers*, **70**, 181–198.

Durkheim, E. (1960). *The Division of Labor in Society*, translated by G. Simpson, Free Press, Glencoe. First published in French in 1893.

Eliade, M. (1961). *The Sacred and the Profane*, Harper and Row, New York.

Eyles, J. (1974). Social theory and social geography. *Progress in Geography*, **6**, 27–88.

Fine, W. F. (1979). *Progressive Evolutionism and American Sociology, 1890–1920*, UMI Research Press, Ann Arbor.

Fleck, L. (1979). *The Genesis and Development of a Scientific Fact*, translated by T. J. Trenn and R. K. Merton, University of Chicago, Press, Chicago. First published in German in 1935.

Friel, B. (1981). *Translations. A Play*, Faber and Faber, London.

Furtadó, C. (1975). *El Dessarrollo Economico: Un Mito*, Siglo Veintiuno Editores, Mexico, DF.

Gadamer, H. G. (1975). *Truth and Method*, Sheed and Ward, London.

Geertz, C. (1970). The impact of the concept of culture on the concept of man. In E. A. Hammel and W. S. Simmons (Eds.), *Man Makes Sense*, Little Brown and Co., Boston, pp. 46–65.

Gellner, E. (1971). Our current sense of history. *Archives Européennes de Soiologie*, **12**, 159–179.

Giddens, A. (1976). *New Rules of Sociological Method: A Positive Critique of Interpretative Sociologies*, Hutchinson, London.

Giddens, A. (1979). *Central Problems in Social Theory. Action, Structure, and Contradiction in Social Analysis*, Macmillan, London.

Glacken, C. J. (1967). *Traces on the Rhodian Shore. Nature and Culture in Western Thought from Ancient Times to the End of the Eighteenth Century*, University of California Press, Berkeley and Los Angeles.

Glucksmann, M. (1974). *Structuralist Analysis in Contemporary Social Thought. A Comparison of the Theories of Claude Levi-Strauss and Louis Althusser*. Routledge and Kegan Paul. London.

Godelier, M. (1978). System, structure and contradiction in *Capital*. In D. McQuarie (Ed.), *Marx: Sociology/Social Change/Capitalism*, Quartet Books, London, pp. 77–102.

Gould, P. (1979). Signals in the noise. In S. Gale and G. Olsson (Eds.), *Philosophy in Geography*, D. Reidel Publishing Company, Dordrecht, pp. 121–154.

Gould, P. and White, R. (1974). *Mental Maps*, Penguin Books, Harmondsworth.

Graber, L. H. (1976). *Wilderness as Sacred Space*, Association of American Geographers, Washington DC.

Gray, F. (1975). Non-Explanation in urban geography. *Area*, **7**, 228–235.

Gregory, D. (1976). Rethinking historical geography. *Area*, **8**, 295–299

Gregory, D. (1978a). *Ideology, Science and Human Geography*, Hutchinson, London.

Gregory, D. (1978b). Social change and spatial structures. In T. Carlstein, D. Parkes, and N. Thrift (Eds.), *Timing Space and Spacing Time. Volume 1. Making Sense of Time*, Edward Arnold, London, pp. 38–46.

Gregory, D. (1980). The ideology of control: systems theory and geography. *Tijdschrift voor Economische en Sociale Geografie*, **71**, 327–342.

Grossman, L. (1977). Man–environment relationships in anthropology and geography. *Annals of the Association of American Geographers*, **67**, 126–144.

Harris, M. (1968). *The Rise of Anthropological Theory*, Thomas Y. Crowell, New York.

Harrison, R. T. and Livingstone, D. N. (1979). There and back again—towards a critique of idealist human geography. *Area*, **11**, 75–79.

Harrison, R. T. and Livingstone, D. N. (1980). Philosphy and problems in human geography: a presuppositional approach. *Area*, **12**, 25–31.

Harvey, D. (1975). Class structure in a capitalist society and the theory of residential differentiation. In R. Peel, M. Chisholm and P. Haggett (Eds.) *Processes in Physical and Human Geography: Bristol Essays*, Heinemann, London, pp. 354–369.

Hay, A. M. (1979). Positivism in human geography: response to critics. In D. T. Herbert and R. J. Johnston (Eds.) *Geography and the Urban Environment: Progress in Research and Applications, Vol. 2*, Wiley, Chichester, pp. 1–26.

Hesse, M. B. (1966). *Models and Analogies in Science*, University of Notre Dame Press, Indiana.

Hesse, M. B. (1967). Models and analogy in science. In P. Edwards (Ed.), *The Encyclopedia of Philosophy, Vol. 5*, Macmillan and the Free Press, New York, pp. 354–359.

Hofstadter, R. (1944). *Social Darwinism in American Thought*, University of Pennsylvania Press, Philadelphia.

Hollis, M. (1977). *Models of Man*, Cambridge University Press, Cambridge.

Honigmann, J. J. (1976). *The Development of Anthropological Ideas*, The Dorsey Press, Homewood, Ill.

Hooykaas, R. (1972). *Religion and the Rise of Modern Science*, Scottish Academic Press, Edinburgh.

Hoskins, W. G. (1955). *The Making of the English Landscape*, Hodder and Stoughton, London.

Jakobson, R., and Halle, M. (1956). *Fundamentals of Language*, Mouton, The Hague.

Jackson, J. B. (1970). *Landscapes: Selected Writings* (Ed. E. Zube), Harvard University Press, Cambridge, Mass.

Johnston, R. J. (1976). Residential area characteristics: research methods for identifying urban sub-areas—social area analysis and factorial ecology. In D. T. Herbert and R. J. Johnston (Eds.), *Social Areas in Cities. Volume 1. Spatial Processes and Form*, Wiley, London, pp. 193–235.

Johnston, R. J. (1979). *Geography and Geographers. Anglo-American Human Geography Since 1945*, Edward Arnold, London.

Johnston, R. J. (1980a). On the nature of explanation in human geography. *Transactions of the Institute of British Geographers*, NS **5**, 402–412.

Johnston, R. J. (1980b). *City and Society. An Outline for Urban Geography*, Penguin Books, Harmondsworth.

Johnston, R. J. and Herbert, D. T. (1976). An introduction: spatial processes and form. In D. T. Herbert and R. J. Johnston (Eds.), *Social Areas in Cities. Volume 1. Spatial Processes and Form*, Wiley, London, pp. 5–18.

Jones, G. (1980). *Social Darwinism in English Thought: The Interaction Between Biological and Social Theory*, Harvester Press, Sussex.

Kessing, R. M. (1974). Theories of culture. *Annual Review of Anthropology*, **3**, 73–97.

Kennedy, B. A. (1979). A naughty world. *Transactions of the Institute of British Geographers*, NS, **4**, 550–558.

Kroeber, A. L. (1915). Eighteen professions. *American Anthropologist*, **17**, 283–288.

Kroeber, A. L. (1917). The superorganic. *American Anthropologist*, **19**, 163–213.

Kurzweil, E. (1980). *The Age of Structuralism. Lévi-Strauss to Foucault*, Columbia University Press, New York.

Lakoff, G. and Johnson, M. (1980). *Metaphors We Live By*, University of Chicago Press, Chicago and London.

Langton, J. (1972). Potentialities and problems of applying a systems approach to the study of change in human geography. *Progress in Geography*, **4**, 125–179.

Leatherdale, W. H. (1973). *The Role of Analogy, Model and Metaphor in Science*, North-Holland Publishing Company, Amsterdam.

Lee, T. R. (1970). Perceived distance as a function of direction in the city. *Environment and Behavior*, **2**, 40–51.

Leighly, J. (1976). Carl Ortwin Sauer, 1889–1975. *Annals of the Association of American Geographers*, **66**, 337–348.

Lévi-Strauss, C. (1955). *Tristes Tropiques*, Plon, Paris.

Lévi-Strauss, C. (1963). *Structural Anthropology*, Basic Books, New York.

Lewis, C. S. (1963). Bluspels and flalansferes: a semantic nightmare. In W. Hooper (Ed.), *Selected Literary Essays by C. S. Lewis*, Cambridge University Press, Cambridge, pp. 251–265.

Lewis, P. F. (1979. Axioms for reading the landscape. Some guides to the American scene. In D. W. Meinig (Ed.), *The Interpretation of Ordinary Landscapes. Geographical Essays*, Oxford University Press, New York, pp. 11–32.

Ley, D. (1974). *The Black Inner City as Frontier Outpost*, Association of American Geographers, Washington DC.

Ley, D. (1980). *Geography Without Man: A Humanistic Critique*, University of Oxford, School of Geography Research Paper, No. 24, Oxford.

Ley, D. and Cybriwsky, R. (1974). Urban graffiti as territorial markers. *Annals of the Association of American Geographers*, **64**, 491–505.

Ley, D. and Samuels, M. S. (Eds.), (1978). *Humanistic Geography, Prospects and Problems*, Croom Helm, London.

Lipietz, A. (1980). Inter-regional polarisation and the tertiarisation of society. *Papers of the Regional Science Association*, **44**, 3–17.

Livingstone, D. N. (1979). Some methodological problems in the history of geographical thought. *Tijdschrift voor Economische en Sociale Geografie*, **70**, 226–231.

Livingstone, D. N. and Harrison, R. T. (1980). The frontier: metaphor, myth, and model. *The Professional Geographer*, **32**, 127–132.

Livingstone, D. N. and Harrison, R. T. (1981a). Meaning through metaphor: analogy as epistemology. *Annals of the Association of American Geographers*, **71**, 95–107.

Livingstone, D. N. and Harrison, R. T. (1981b). Hunting the Snark: perspectives on geographical investigation. *Geografiska Annaler*, **63B**, 69–72.

Livingstone, D. N. and Harrison, R. T. (1981c). Immanuel Kant, subjectivism, and human geography: a preliminary investigation. *Transactions of the Institute of British Geographers*, NS, **6**, 359–374.

Lonergan, B. J. F. (1958). *Insight: A Study of Human Understanding*, Darton, Longman and Todd, London.

Lovejoy, A. O. (1936). *The Great Chain of Being. A Study of the History of an Idea*, Harvard University Press, Cambridge, Mass.

Lowie, R. H. (1917). *Culture and Ethnology*, D. C. McMurtrie, New York.

Lynch, K. (1960). *The Image of the City*, Harvard University Press, Cambridge, Mass.

McCloskey, M. A. (1964). Metaphors. *Mind*, **73**, 215 233.

McQuarie, D. (Ed.) (1978). *Marx: Sociology/Social Change/Capitalism*, Quartet Books, London.

Malinowski, B. (1960). *A Scientific Theory of Culture and Other Essays*, Oxford University Press, New York.

Mannheim, K. (1936). *Ideology and Utopia*, Harcourt, Brace and World, New York.

Marcus, S. (1973). Reading the illegible. In H. J. Dyos and M. Wolff (Eds.). *The Victorian City: Images and Realities, Vol. 2*, Routledge and Kegan Paul, London. pp. 257–276.

Meinig, D. W. (1979a). Introduction. In D. W. Meinig (Ed.). *The Interpretation of Ordinary Landscapes. Geographical Essays*, Oxford University Press, New York, pp. 1–7.

Meinig, D. W. (1979b). Reading the landscape. An appreciation of W. G. Hoskins and J. B. Jackson. In D. W. Meinig (Ed.), *The Interpretation of Ordinary Landscapes, Geographical Essays*, Oxford University Press, New York, pp. 195–244.

Melbin, M. (1978). Night as frontier. *American Sociological Review*, **43**, 3–22.

Mepham, J. (1973). The structuralist sciences and philosophy. In D. Robey (Ed.), *Structuralism: An Introduction*, Oxford University Press, Oxford, pp. 104–137.

Milroy J. and Milroy, L. (1978). Belfast: change and variation in an urban vernacular. In P. Trudgill (Ed.), *Sociolinguistic Patterns in British English*, Edward Arnold, London, pp. 19–36.

Milroy, L. (1980). *Language and Social Networks*, Basil Blackwell, Oxford.

Moore, G. P. and Golledge, R. G. (Eds.) (1976). *Environmental Knowing: Theories, Research and Methods*, Dowden, Hutchinson and Ross, Stroudsburg, Pa.

Moore, W. E. (1979). Functionalism. In T. Bottomore and R. Nisbet (Eds.), *A History of Sociological Analysis*, Heinemann, London, pp. 321–361.

Morgan, G. (1980). Paradigms, metaphors, and puzzle solving in organization theory. *Administrative Science Quarterly*, **25**, 605–622.

Mueller, M. (1871). Metaphor. In *Lectures on the Science of Language* 2nd series, Scribners, New York, pp. 351–402.

Murdie, R. A. (1976). Spatial form in the residential mosaic. In D. T. Herbert and R. J. Johnston (Eds.), *Social Areas in Cities. Volume 1. Spatial Processes and Form*, Wiley, London, pp. 237–272.

O'Neill, J. (1973). *Modes of Individualism and Collectivism*, Heinemann, London.

Olsson, G. (1975). *Birds in Egg*, Michigan Geographical Publication No. 15, Department of Geography, University of Michigan, Ann Arbor.

Olsson, G. (1978). Of ambiguity or far cries from a memorializing mamafesta. In D. Ley and M. S. Samuels (Eds.), *Humanistic Geography. Prospects and Problems*, Croom Helm, London, pp. 109–120.

Olsson, G. (1979). Social science and human action or on hitting your head against the ceiling of language. In S. Gale and G. Olsson (Eds.), *Philosophy in Geography*, D. Reidel Publishing Company, Dordrecht, pp. 287–307.

Olsson, G. (1980). *Birds in Egg/Eggs in Bird*, Pion, London.

Olsson, G. (1981). On yearning for home: an epistemological view of ontological transformations. In D. C. D. Pocock (Ed.), *Humanistic Geography and Literature. Essays on the Experience of Place*, Croom Helm, London, pp. 121–129.

Ortony, A. (Ed.) (1979a). *Metaphor and Thought*, Cambridge University Press, Cambridge.

Ortony, A. (1979b). Metaphor: a multidimensional problem. In A. Ortony (Ed.), *Metaphor and Thought*, Cambridge University Press, Cambridge, pp. 1–16.

Paterson, J. (1976). The poet and the metropolis. In J. W. Watson and T. O'Riordan (Eds.), *The American Environment: Perceptions and Policies*, Wiley, London, pp. 93–108.

Peel, J. D. Y. (1971). *Herbert Spencer. The Evolution of a Sociologist*, Heinemann, London.

Peet, R. (Ed.) (1977). *Radical Geography: Alternative Viewpoints on Contemporary Social Issues*, Maaroufa Press, Chicago.

Pepper, S. C. (1942). *World Hypotheses*, University of California Press, Berkeley.

Perrons, D. C. (1981). The role of Ireland in the new international division of labour: a proposed framework for regional analysis. *Regional Studies*, **15**, 81–100.

Pettit, P. (1975). *The Concept of Structuralism: A Critical Analysis*, Gill and Macmillan, Dublin.

Phillips, D. C. (1970). Organicism in the late nineteenth and early twentieth centuries. *Journal of the History of Ideas*, **31**, 413–432.

Phillips, D. C. (1977). *Holistic Thought in Social Science*, Macmillan, London.

Phillips, D. L. (1977). *Wittgenstein and Scientific Knowledge: A Sociological Perspective*, Rowman and Littlefield, Totowa, NJ.

Piaget, J. (1970). *Structuralism*, Basic Books, New York.

Pocock, D. C. D. (1976). Some characteristics of mental maps: an empirical study. *Transactions of the Institute of British Geographers*, NS, **1**, 493–512.

Pocock, D. C. D. (1979). The novelist's image of the North. *Transactions of the Institute of British Geographers*, NS **4**, 62–76.

Pocock, D. C. D. (Ed.) (1981). *Humanistic Geography and Literature. Essays on the Experience of Place*, Croom Helm, London.

Poster, M. (1976). *Existential Marxism in post-War France: From Sartre to Althusser*, Princeton University Press, Princeton.

Radcliffe-Brown, A. R. (1965). *Structure and Function in Primitive Society*, The Free Press, New York.

Rooc, P. H (1972), Problems of classifying sub-areas within cities. In B. J. L. Berry (Ed.), *City Classification Handbook*, Wiley, New York, pp. 265–330.

Rein, M. and Schön, D. (1977). Problem-setting in policy research. In C. H. Weiss (Ed.), *Using Social Research in Public Policy Making*, D. C. Heath, Lexington, Mass.

Relph, E. (1976). *Place and Placelessness*, Pion, London.

Richards, P. (1974). Kant's geography and mental maps. *Transactions of the Institute of British Geographers*, **61**, 1–16.

Ricoeur, P. (1971). The model of the text: meaningful action considered as a text. *Social Research*, **38**, 529–562.

Ricoeur, P. (1973). Creativity in language: word, polysemy, metaphor. *Philosophy Today*, **17**, 97–111.

Ricoeur, P. (1977a). *The Rule of Metaphor*, University of Toronto Press, Toronto.

Ricoeur, P. (1977b). *Interpretation Theory: Discourse and the Surplus of Meaning*, Texas Christian University Press, Fort Worth.

Robey, D. (Ed.) (1973). *Structuralism: An Introduction*, Oxford University Press, Oxford.

Rose, C. (1980). Human geography as text interpretation. In A. Buttimer and D. Seamon (Eds.), *The Human Experience of Space and Place*, Croom Helm, London, pp. 123–134.

Rose, C. (1981). Wilhelm Dilthey's philosophy of historical understanding: a neglected heritage of contemporary humanistic geography. In D. R. Stoddart (Ed.), *Geography, Ideology and Social Concern*, Basil Blackwell, Oxford, pp. 99–133.

Rowntree, L. B. and Conkey, M. W. (1980). Symbolism and the cultural landscape. *Annals of the Association of American Geographers*, **70**, 459–474.

Runciman, W. G. (1970). *Sociology in its Place and Other Essays*, Cambridge University Press, Cambridge.

Ryan, A. (Ed.) (1973). *The Philosophy of Social Explanation*, Oxford University Press, Oxford.

Salter, C. L. and Lloyd, W. J. (1977). *Landscape in literature. Association of American Geographers Commission on College Geography Resource Paper 76–3*, Association of American Geographers, Washington, DC.

Samuels, M. S. (1978). Existentialism in human geography. In D. Ley and M. S. Samuels (Eds.), *Humanistic Geography. Prospects and Problems*, Croom Helm, London, pp. 22–40.

Sauer, C. O. (1963). *Land and Life. A Selection from the Writings of Carl Ortwin Sauer*, edited by J. Leighly, University of California Press, Berkeley and Los Angeles.

Schön, D. (1963). *Displacement of Concepts*, Humanities Press, New York.

Schön, D. (1979). Generative metaphor: a perspective on problem-setting in social policy. In A. Ortony (Ed.), *Metaphor and Thought*, Cambridge University Press, Cambridge, pp. 254–283.

Searle, J. R. (1969). *Speech Acts*, Cambridge University Press, Cambridge.

Searle, J. R. (1979). Metaphor. In A. Ortony (Ed.), *Metaphor and Thought*, Cambridge University Press, Cambridge, pp. 92–123.

Shibles, W. A. (1971). *Metaphor: An Annotated Bibliography and History*, Language Press, Whitewater, Wis.

Smart, B. (1976). *Sociology, Phenomenology and Marxian Analysis. A Critical Discussion of The Theory and Practice of a Science of Society*, Routledge and Kegan Paul, London.

Smith, N. (1979). Geography, science and post-positivist modes of explanation. *Progress in Human Geography*, **3**, 356–383.

Soja, E. W. (1974). Preface. In A. Buttimer, *Values in Geography. Association of American Geographers Commission on College Geography Resource Paper* 24, Association of American Geographers, Washington, DC., pp. i–ii.

Spencer, H. (1910). *Principles of Sociology, Vol. 1*, D. Appleton and Co., New York and London.

Spencer, J. E. (1974). The evolution of the discipline of geography in the twentieth century. *Geographical Perspectives*, **33**, 20–36.

Spencer, J. E. (1976). What's in a name?—The Berkeley School. *Historical Geography Newletter*, **5**, 7–11.

Speth, W. W. (1979). Berkeley geography, the formative decade, 1923–1933. Paper presented at conference on 'The Origins of Academic Geography in the United States', Lincoln, Nebraska, April 1979.

Stalnaker, R. C. (1972). Pragmatics. In D. Davidson and G. Harman (Eds.), *Semantics of Natural Language*, D. Reidel Publishing Company, Dordrecht, pp. 380–397.

Stea, D. (1969a). Environmental perception and cognition: towards a model for mental maps. In G. J. Coates and K. M. Moffett (Eds.), *Response to Environment*, North Carolina University Press, Raleigh, NC.

Stea, D. (1969b). The measurement of mental maps: an experimental model for studying conceptual spaces. In K. R. Cox and R. G. Colledge (Eds.), *Behavioral Problems in Geography: A Symposium, Northwestern University Studies in Geography, 17*, Northwestern University, Evanston, Ill. pp. 228–253.

Stoddart, D. R. (1967). Organism and ecosystem as geographical models. In R. J. Chorley and P. Haggett (Eds.), *Models in Geography*, Methuen, London, pp. 511–548.

Stoddart, D. R. (1981). Ideas and interpretation in the history of geography. In D. R. Stoddart (Ed.), *Geography, Ideology and Social Concern*, Basil Blackwell, Oxford, pp. 1–7.

Strauss, A. L. (1961). *Images of the American City*, The Free Press, New York.

Sturrock, J. (Ed.) (1979). *Structuralism and Since. From Lévi-Strauss to Derrida*, Oxford University Press, Oxford.

Toulmin, S. (1972). *Human Understanding, Vol. 1*, Oxford University Press, Oxford.

Trudgill, P. (1975). Linguistic geography and geographical linguistics. *Progress in Geography*, **7**, 227–252.

Tuan, Yi-Fu (1974). *Topophilia. A Study of Environmental Perception, Attitudes, and Values*, Prentice-Hall, Englewood Cliffs, NJ.

Tuan, Yi-Fu (1976). Geopiety: a theme in man's attachment to nature and place. In D. Lowenthal and M. J. Bowden (Eds.) *Geographies of the Mind*, Oxford University Press, New York, pp. 11–39.

Tuan, Yi-Fu (1980). *Landscapes of Fear*, Basil Blackwell, Oxford.

Turbayne, C. M. (1970). *The Myth of Metaphor, 2nd edition*, Yale University Press, New Haven.

Vilar, P. (1973). Histoire marxiste, histoire en construction: essai de dialogue avec Althusser. *Annales ESC*, **28**, 165–198.

Voget, F. W. (1960). Man and culture: an essay in changing anthropological interpretation. *American Anthropologist*, **62**, 943–965.

Voget, F. W. (1975). *A History of Ethnology*, Holt, Rinehart and Winston, New York.

Watson, J. W. (1974). The image of nature in America. In W. R. Mead (Ed.), *The American Environment*, Athlone Press, London, pp. 1–16.

Watson, J. W. (1976). The city and the American way of life. In J. W. Watson and T. O'Riordan (Eds.), *The American Environment: Perceptions and Policies*, Wiley, London, pp. 79–92.

Watts, M. T. (1975). *Reading the Landscape of America*, Macmillan, New York.

Wellmer, A. (1976). Communications and emancipation: reflections on the linguistic turn in critical theory. In J. O'Neil (Ed.), *On Critical Theory*, Heinemann, London, pp. 231–263.

White, M. and White, L. (1962). *The Intellectual Versus the City*, Harvard University Press, Cambridge, Mass.

Whitehead, A. N. (1925). *Science and the Modern World*, Macmillan, New York.

Williams, R. (1973). Base and superstructure in marxist cultural theory. *New Left Review*, **82**, 3–16.

Wittgenstein, L. (1961). *Tractatus Logico-Philosophicus*, translated by D. Pears and B. F. McGuiness, Routledge and Kegan Paul, London.

Wittgenstein, L. (1968). *Philosophical Investigations*, translated by G. E. M. Anscombe, Basil Blackwell, Oxford.

Young, R. M. (1973a). The role of psychology in the nineteenth century evolutionary debate. In M. Henle, J. Jaynes, and J. J. Sullivan (Eds.), *Historical Conceptions of Psychology*, Springer, New York, pp. 180–204.

Young, R. M. (1973b). The historiographic and ideological contexts of the nineteenth century debate on man's place in nature. In M. Teich and R. Young (Eds.), *Changing Perspectives in the History of Science: Essays in Honour of Joseph Needham*, Heinemann, London, pp. 344–438.

Zeitoun, J. (Ed.) (1979). *Sémiotique de l'Espace*, Denoël Gonthier, Paris.

Zelinsky, W. (1973). *The Cultural Geography of the United States*, Prentice-Hall, Englewood Cliffs, NJ.

Geography and the Urban Environment
Progress in Research and Applications, Volume V
Edited by D. T. Herbert and R. J. Johnston
© 1982 John Wiley & Sons Ltd.

Chapter 2

Instrumental Reason and Policy Analysis

Gordon L. Clark

Reason has always existed, but not always in reasonable form. Hence the critic can choose any form of theoretical and practical consciousness and develop the true reality in its 'ought' and in its final goal out of its *own* forms of existing reality. In regard to real life, the *political state* . . . contains the demands of reason in all its modern forms . . . . But everywhere it . . . falls into the contradiction between its ideal destiny and its predispositions.

Karl Marx. September 1843
Translated and edited by Padover
(1979, p. 30)

RELEVANCE AND REASON

Over the past decade geographers have become very interested in questions of policy relevance, policy alternatives, and the design of optimal procedures for policy implementation in the spatial context (Bennett, 1979). Academic leaders of geography have encouraged acceptance, by the discipline as a whole, of applied policy analysis as a legitimate field of scholarly research. Brian Berry's (1972) debate in the early 1970s with David Smith (1973) over the merits of relevance and involvement in policy-making prompted widespread interest in these issues—an interest which has not died over the intervening decade (see also Berry's 1980 presidential address to the Association of American Geographers concerning, amongst other issues, relevance and public policy). Leslie King (1976), in a review of the progress and prospects of positive economic geography, indicated that inquiry should be orientated towards the policy analysis arena and social problem solving in general. Given the successes of the quantitative revolution, the time has come, according to these writers, to apply the discipline's newer techniques to problems of social significance (see Haggett, 1977 for a general overview of these issues; see also Mercer's, 1977 critique). The challenge is certainly there. Not only are policy problems of political significance, they are also typically more difficult, less understood, and less ordered than those problems that academics generally deal with at the theoretical or abstract level.

Thus the application of geography's newer methodologies to the solving of social problems may be both a test of geography's relevance (even usefulness) as well as of its generality (Clark, 1980).

The underlying impetus for academic involvement in policy-making and policy analysis varies widely amongst researchers. Pressure for more relevant research has come from public and private social science research funding agencies as much as from academics themselves. Thus one motivation for involvement in public policy could simply be self-preservation in the face of growing arguments concerning the irrelevance of much academic research and academic ignorance of the really significant social problems of the day (Lynn, 1978). According to Banfield (1977), academics also like to be listened to and acknowledged as experts. Involvement in policy-making may lead to wider recognition, fame and fortune. In many ways academics are not the outside critics of public policy and political debate that they may have been immediately after the Second World War (Howe, 1954). Involvement through policy analysis in political decisions carries with it the charge of co-option and of being the handmaidens of social inequality and oppression (Harvey, 1974).

I suspect, however, and perhaps this is more a hope than a fact, that arguments of self-interest are incomplete explanations of academic involvement in policy research. Many academics are also prompted for altruistic reasons. First, they seek to improve the nature and implementation of public policy in the general interests of society or particular segments of society (like the poor). Academics, as other groups, have the right to promote the acceptance of their own normative views of how society ought to be organized. After all academics are social individuals and have political interests and views. A second reason for involvement has been to understand society through participation in the actions of the public sector. The impact of the state on society is all pervasive. Not only is the state the single biggest employer in many countries but as well its actions, policies, and even non-action in particular fields, affect all individuals and classes (Clark and Dear, 1981). How the state is structured and in whose interests it operates is a useful mirror on society itself. Clearly, the role of government in spatial systems has been neglected in geography and many social sciences. Thus, through greater involvement in and analysis of public policy action, our theoretical understanding of society itself can be greatly improved (Dear, 1979).

Interest in policy analysis is not simply a matter of academics being co-opted or playing out their own ambitions. Motivations are many-sided and more often than not involve legitimate academic and political interests. Thus I cannot subscribe to the fashionable nihilist view of policy science as being yet another example of ruling class ideology. To debate continually the merits of relevance, the analysis of policy outcomes etc. ignores more important debates over the manner and practice of policy science which go unrecognized in the geographical literature. Through this chapter I argue for a greater appreciation of the complexity of substantive policy analysis. It is claimed that the orthodox view of policy science as instrumental rationality (the selection of efficient means for a given end), which incidentally dominates geography, is too narrow and ultimately naive. In order to develop these arguments it is noted in the next section that conventional policy science has sought, under the guise of objective rationality, to impose upon the political process a particular normative vision of reality. This vision is based upon two interrelated assumptions: politics is typically irrational and biased, and, as a consequence, policy decisions are often based upon false and misleading knowledge. Conventional policy science, it is claimed, also ignores the political nature of the state, its internal dynamics and the political agendas of different state units. As a consequence, policy science is often practically irrelevant or, even worse, an increasingly important argument against legitimate political conflict.

My critique of conventional policy science in the third section (p. 48) is based upon a fundamental proposition: it is incorrect to believe that instrumental rationality as the source of objective and unbiased knowledge is in any way a *replacement* for philosophical reason. On the contrary, it is claimed that knowledge and reason are derivative from individual values and experience (Clark, 1981). Rather than being able to discover independent, objectively defined social facts, as conceived in traditional social science, it is argued that social facts and reason are derivative out of individual interpretation: facts are made or constituted through inquiry rather than found in society. This does not mean that facts and/or interpretations are idiosyncratic and random; the individual observer's place in society (what Fish, 1980, termed the interpretive community) is an important determinant of maintaining consistency in social interpretation. Thus in understanding conventional policy analysis we have to understand the organizational structure of the academic/policy science community as well as its philosophical basis.

For a variety of reasons it is shown that the academic community is not independent; there are no objective standards that would enable a neutral choice between competing explanations of social processes and thus policy advice. Reason as an ideal is confounded with the objectives of the institution it seeks to serve—the state—and the ideological predispositions of the academic community. In the fourth section (p. 54), an integrated model of policy analysis is presented in which instrumental reason is shown to be linked with philosophical knowledge. A series of propositions is considered that defines the relationship between academic knowledge and the state. These propositions emphasize the impossibility of reason existing separately from its philosophical base and being simply a commodity available for hire.

POLICY SCIENCE AS RATIONAL PROBLEM-SOLVING

The current model of the role of social science in public policy can be summarized in the phrase 'rational problem-solving' (Wildavsky, 1979), what Tribe (1973)

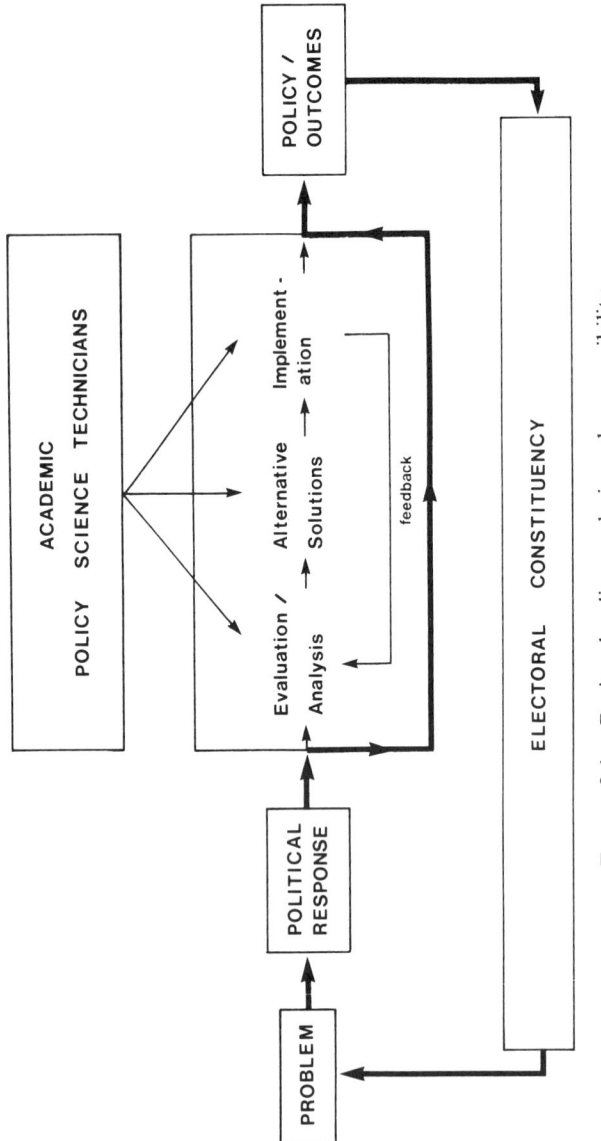

FIGURE 2.1.   Rational policy analysis and responsibility

has termed 'instrumental rationality': the selection of efficacious means to given ends. Although there are many views of the definitive model of policy science (Jenkins, 1978), the orthodox view can be summarized in the following caricature: public policy decisions are often irrational and consequently wrong. Those making policy decisions are overly influenced by political considerations and are often unaware of the implications or unintended consequences of their decisions (Vernon, 1979). Accordingly, social scientists are essential to the policy-making process for the following reasons: social scientists provide independent and objective information on the nature of the policy problem and the implications of following alternative policy options; social science methodology is logical and rational, thus superior to untrained intuitive decision-making; and social science enables rational choices as to the best policies or solutions to the identified problems (Stokey and Zeckhauser, 1978). Figure 2.1 illustrates the separation of academics from direct involvement in the political process and their importance in the substantive issues of evaluation and problem-solving. Academic scientists, according to the rational model, accept the status quo as their context and define the most efficient resolution of the identified problem.

In practice, there is a variety of ways in which social science is perceived to bring about rational policy decision-making. Once a significant policy problem is identified (presumably politically), existing social research and results are applied to its solution. Social science knowledge is used either as a means of informing decision-makers as to the appropriateness of alternative policies and/or as an *ex-post* check of the desirability of proposed policy solutions. Thus social science information is assumed to be more objective, rigorous and complete than the information possessed by the typical policy-maker. Figure 2.2 describes in detail the technical nature of the policy scientists' involvement in the policy evaluation process (a subset of Figure 2.1). Emphasis is on the quantified and objectively stated goals and objectives. Alternatives are also quantitatively evaluated and the results 'fed back' into policy definition/analysis. Notice, however, that in practice the policy analyst may also become involved in problem definition and political response as legitimacy for making the correct policy decision shifts from the policy-maker to the adviser. The constraint on this process is that available scholarly research may not be readily identifiable or even applicable to the problem at hand.

Consequently, a second mode of involvement by social science in policy-making may be direct action-orientated research where the policy scientist is hired to analyse the problem and recommend action (Goldberg, 1977). Here previously developed and refined social science techniques are applied to real world problems (defined politically via sponsoring institutions), on the understanding that the social scientist is to remain independent and objective. In both instances, social science performs a number of functions: it provides the missing information without which 'good' decisions cannot be made or contemplated; it

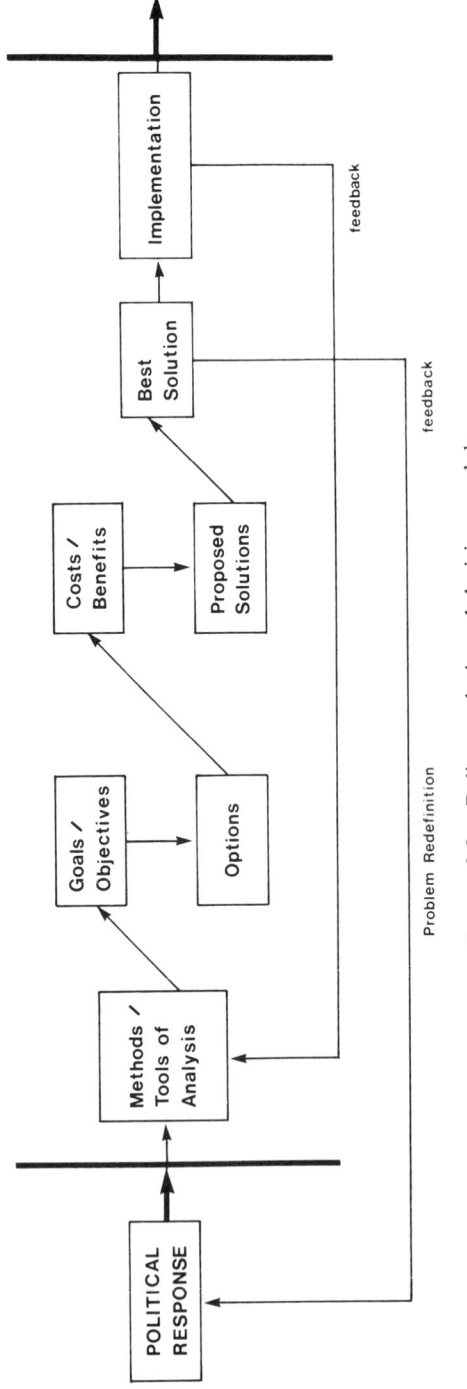

FIGURE 2.2. Policy analysis and decision module

identifies the appropriate means for achieving the desired goals; and it provides the correct information on the best approach to solving the problem (Weiss, 1978). Rational problem-solving is the application of the best of social science theory and practice to significant problems of the day.

Although Figures 2.1 and 2.2 are general and schematic the steps involved in policy evaluation are quite strict and well-defined. For example, Tribe (1973) listed the evaluation procedure used by the National Academy of Engineering for technology planning:

(1) identify and refine the subject to be assessed;
(2) delineate the scope of the assessment and develop a data base;
(3) identify alternative strategies to solve the selected problems;
(4) identify parties affected;
(5) identify the impacts on the affected parties;
(6) evaluate or measure the impacts; and
(7) compare the pros and cons of alternative strategies.

These steps are both focused and systematic, relying upon the nature of the 'problem' at hand as well as the nature and scope of relevant social science methodology. Legitimate policy analysis is presumed to operate *within* the structure of the political processes, serving essentially the institution through which policy outcomes are generated (Tribe, 1972). There is little doubt that the rational model is popular with academics. Numerous governmental agencies in the United States have adopted it as the basis for their own planning and policy evaluation, including, for example, the Dapartment of Housing and Urban Development's (HUD) Office of Policy Research and Development.

Emphasis upon a 'rational' conceptualization of decision-making reinforces the legitimacy of the logical–positivist mode of academic inquiry. Given that universities and research organizations are the sources of such techniques, the academic structure is bolstered by research contracts and rewards to those who expound the rational mode. The rational mode also gives academics power *vis-à-vis* the political process. Academics can both affect and be outside the decision-making system—a valuable asset if the political system is considered to be 'irrational'. Finally, academics are not required to shift methodological gears, but rather apply what is known to yet another problem. In essence, policy problems are subsumed by the hegemony of social science analytical methods. At the extreme, each new policy problem becomes an opportunity for the application of social science analysis. This is not to say the rational model has been universally successful or accepted. There are many examples of failed advice and inadequate analysis using the rational mode (Wilson, 1978). Yet the presumption of guilt remains with the irrational decision-maker; failure on the social science side is presumed to rest with either the individual researcher or the implementation agency not the paradigm of instrumental rationality.

A CRITIQUE OF INSTRUMENTAL RATIONALITY

Clearly, I do not totally accept the assumptions or rationale for the instrumental rationality model. In particular, I would argue that the instrumental rationality model of policy science is misdirected, naive, and a serious threat to the legitimacy of philosophical knowledge. However, I agree with the principle of policy analysis and the involvement of academics in policy-making. What I object to is the instrumental model's implications concerning how the world should be viewed, and the assumptions made by policy-makers and academics alike concerning what are problems, what are solutions, and what the role of social science should be in facilitating choices between competing options.

Rational policy science could as easily be criticized for its dependence upon the logical–positivist model of social science. The conceptualization of a value-free independent observer of society as academic is a central tenet of the positivisit doctrine. Further, the design of social science inquiry in terms of data, hypothesis testing and the search for verifiable truth is a vital element in the practice of positivistic social science. If it could be shown that the logical–positivist methodology was incorrect or irrational itself, then the rational model of policy science would also be devalued (Hollis and Nell, 1975). I would agree with many who have criticized the positivist model, including King (1976) and Rein (1976), for its negation of the role of values and ideology in determining knowledge and the mode of analysis. However, at this time I wish to argue for the rejection of the rational instrumentalist model according to a set of issues which link policy analysis to academic inquiry.

Politics and the policy problem

One of the disturbing aspects of the instrumentalist model is its insistence that politics and politicians are either irrational and/or are not to be trusted with difficult problems. Politics is essentially devalued, held in contempt, and treated with suspicion by policy analysts and mainstream social scientists. Unfortunately the general public probably agrees with policy scientists' assessments of politics. It comes as no surprise, then, that politicians themselves have sought legitimacy by invoking social science support to bolster their public image. Clearly the policy scientist runs some danger of being co-opted by the political system. However, a bigger danger is that of ignoring those legitimate functions of conflict resolution and the representation of alternative views that politics plays by reducing complex social issues to the structure of analytical models.

A basic distinction exists in the policy science literature between social problems and social conflicts. What social scientists might define as social problems, like high levels of unemployment in a particular locality, are, for politicians, social conflicts. An example may help to put this issue in perspective. The mass transit authority of a large north-eastern city and surrounding municipalities in the United States has been attempting to reduce its operating deficit. One solution proposed by policy analysts was to double the price of riding the system in the inner city and institute a limited *fare-for-distance-travelled* schedule for suburban transit riders. While the operating deficit was a very real problem for the politicians, a further issue, in essence the problem as 'social conflict' not acknowledged by the policy experts, was also important: balancing the competing inner city and suburban claims for preference in the fare structure.

Suburban transit riders, through their representatives on the governing board of the mass transit authority, preferred a single uniform fare regardless of the distance travelled, possibly because those riders travel further on average than other riders. Inner city riders, on the other hand, preferred a distance-weighted fare. The policy analysts as consultants did not deal with this issue: values, political interests, equity judgements and the political conflict between interested parties were presumed to be outside the scope of the inquiry. Further, the policy consulting group claimed that their solution was arrived at without reference to the interests of any one group despite the obvious distributional consequences of their recommendations. However, when a decision was reached by the governing board of the transit authority which compromised between the competing political interests involved, that solution was perceived by the policy analysts and their media representatives as being suboptimal and inefficient. It was argued by some commentators that the governing board had in some way given in to special interests. Yet the conflict between different interests was essentially the 'problem' for the political process. The separation of the social problem from its representation in terms of social conflict resulted in the devaluation of the political solution. Unfortunately during the debate between the policy analysts and politicians, the two groups were further polarized through the use by policy analysts of language such as 'objective', 'dispassionate' and the like.

Lack of recognition of the conflict dimension of the social problem by the panel of experts had a number of implications. Clearly, the experts' report and recommendations ignored a vital aspect of the problem but at the same time devalued the initial attempts by the representative board to bring about a solution to the problem outside the parameters set by the experts' report. The experts also ignored fundamental issues of equity and justice although their recommendations had significant, but implicit, equity dimensions: the inner city area was dominated by black and hispanic working-class people who typically cannot afford to use an automobile for journey to work trips. Suburban commuters, on the other hand, were typically white and middle class. The difficulty faced by the governing board was to bring about a resolution between competing classes for 'justice' within a problem context defined by outside experts that omitted the conflict dimension.

Of course it could be argued that policy analysts are not adequate to the task and should not be expected to become involved. Yet within the empirical methodologies there are implicit equity agendas, albeit ignored by the analysts themselves. The issue is how and in whose interests are those methodologies biased? The answer is particular to each case, although, by virtue of the scientific instrumentalist mode of inquiry, it should not be normative. This was the issue faced by the governing board—the resolution of conflict involves implicitly normative knowledge and action. The choice of a normative future based upon a philosophical structure involves weighing different costs and benefits in a manner which may conflict with the technique chosen by the policy analysts. It is extremely difficult to reconcile instrumental knowledge with philosophical knowledge when the assumptions and objectives of each do not agree. The latter is the purpose of the political structure. The danger, however, is that instrumental reason will overtake philosophical reason through the claims of scientific objectivity and methodological efficiency. The political wing is in danger of being dismantled and its very significant contributions ignored.

Theories and action

A central theme of the instrumental model is that policy-makers lack adequate and systematic knowledge of the social and economic processes they wish to affect. The argument is also made that better knowledge of policy alternatives and options would make for more rational and ordered decisions (Coleman, 1980). Social science is presumed to be the source of better knowledge. Two interrelated problems stand out in this regard. First, in reality there is often no single 'best' model or theory of a given process, rather there are competing and often incomplete explanations (Lindblom and Cohen, 1979). Second, once competing explanations are recognized the problem becomes the discrimination between alternatives and choosing the best explanations. The question is: who chooses and according to what criteria?

The first problem is well recognized in the literature and need not detain us for long. Not only are there competing claims of explanation and policy relevance based on differing assumptions and value systems but, more worrying, many models are incomplete and abstract. Thus the full range of causal mechanisms inherent in a given process is often left unspecified and often unknown. Generally, the core dynamics of a given process are specified, if debated over; however, the boundaries of the influences of one process on another are only rarely specified. Yet for the policy-maker, the effects of an action are judged in terms of both intended and unintended consequences. The problems of incompleteness and unintended consequences are crucial to the policy-maker, since in political terms the political constituency is often wider than represented by the issue at hand. However, boundary specifications of the influences of different processes upon one another are not highly valued by the academic profession.

The abstract nature of many theories is also an issue of some importance. Policy-makers deal with concrete issues that typically do not conform to the idealized conceptions of policy scientists. This is not to say that theory is irrelevant, rather the form of the planning problem *vis-à-vis* received wisdom may be such as to make it virtually unique. The question is how many concrete issues are unique and to what extent social science models can be moulded and rearranged to accommodate reality. Informing research and model building through practical application has had a long tradition in social science. As Kuhn (1970) noted, comparison of the expectations derived from theory with reality is a major source of theoretical innovation and reformulation. The danger is that the problem itself may be reinterpreted in terms of analytical methodology such that its original distinctiveness is lost (Habermas, 1971). Perhaps this is inevitable, as suggested in the opening quotation and our initial propositions concerning reason and knowledge. Yet one cannot help but wonder if the rigid nature of many analytical methodologies cures problems through rearrangement and reconceptualization rather than addressing the issues as recognized in the political sphere.

Given the claims of social science for relevance and importance in solving policy-related problems it comes as a surprise to many policy-makers that social science models and theories themselves are typically incomplete. That is, the range and nature of causality in social systems is often only approximated. The 'black-box' syndrome is more prevalent than often formally acknowledged. Consequently the information for making the types of instrumental decisions envisaged by social science policy analysts may simply not be there, or, if available, may be so incomplete as to warrant yet another study before further action. This should not be taken as suggesting that all that is wrong is data availability. Clearly data present a problem, but more fundamental is the poor specification of causality, from which the need for data is defined!

The regularity of incomplete information and the experience of policy-makers in making decisions under uncertainty might prompt us to dismiss these issues as being relatively trivial. However, the policy-maker is still faced with choosing between competing but incomplete models and policy prescriptions. Unfortunately, there is no ready agreement amongst academics about the standards for judging competing explanations of social processes. Popper's (1965) hypothesis-testing method is often invoked, but there are very strong arguments against this method argued by others, such as Feyerabend (1975), Kuhn (1970) and Lakatos (1964). Again the key issue here has been a confusion between empirical knowledge and philosophical knowledge. The rules of selecting between explanations depend upon the values and normative goals of those in the policy-making sphere. The ends determine the means. To assume that empirical rules are alone adequate discriminators is to ignore the ends to which knowledge is being put. Yet it is clear that the instrumental paradigm is very uncomfortable with normative issues—mainly because of the supposed scientific character of academic inquiry. Clearly the policy maker is ill-equipped to adjudicate between competing paradigms. Thus alternative modes of discrimination are often invoked which may have significant exclusionary dimensions.

A crude rule of social science model selection might be to exclude those theories or prescriptions which do not agree in principle with one's own prejudices or values (no marxists need apply): *this might be termed the paradigm choice rule.* A second rule of choice, within a particular paradigm, might be to exclude competing methods on the basis of academic reputation (only the established need apply): *this might be termed the élite rule.* Finally the policy-maker might consult (if she/he has not already) academic leaders for further information (only the famous need apply): *this might be termed the friends and relatives rule.* Clearly these selection rules are a parody of the actual selection process. Yet I suspect that there is enough truth in each for many readers to identify with one or more rules as being representative of their own experience.

Policy analysts and policy-makers have vested interests in using and advancing certain sets of information rather than the full range of alternative explanations as implied in the instrumentalist model (Chomsky, 1971). Selection and sorting of information may not necessarily involve conspiracy to reduce the number of legitimate options. Rather it may be simply an attempt to cut through the confusion and inadequacies of social science information so that order is imposed upon information which is consistent with one's own values and ideology. Note, however, that the potential exists for excluding non-conformist policy options, power threatening (to both policy-makers and academics) solutions, and system-transformation policy alternatives. Consequently it is not surprising that policy-makers complain that few policy options are available in practice, once the sorting process of ideas and alternatives have been completed (Lynn, 1978). But this lack of wide alternatives is derivative of prior decisions taken to exclude those solutions inconsistent with prevailing ideology. Those academics selected, their implicit values, the definition of the 'problem' at hand, and the existing power relations between those in power and those being planned for, all contribute to an homogenizing in the process of information selection.

My argument concerning information and the status of social science in the instrumental model of policy science is clearly cautionary. On the one hand instrumental reason claims a certain objectivity and empirical relevance—presumably greater than the philosophical reason that may dominate the political process in accordance with its normative intent. Yet I am also claiming that within instrumental reason there is also choice concerning the appropriate methods of planning and control. Choice is however constrained by the values and perceptions of those giving advice and those seeking advice. To pretend that such choices are objective is to be naive and scurrilous. As was noted above, the practice of choice can be exclusionary in any number of dimensions, including paradigm rules and élite rules. It is inevitable that choice must be a function of the ends to which knowledge is to be put, yet is not that a normative or philosophical issue?

One final word is needed on the issue of whether or not the assumption that policy makers do not have adequate information is actually useful. The issue may be more the type of knowledge required rather than the volume. Some policy researchers have argued that craft or experience-related knowledge is more significant than content or concept-related knowledge in making good policy decisions (Wildavsky, 1979). Here the argument is that social science research does not equip policy-makers to make decisions. Rather it may only increase the content of policy options. While it is obviously useful to have more information, if the means and processes of making decisions are poorly designed then no amount of extra knowledge will promote better policy. However, it is difficult to decide the relative importance of this issue because few academics themselves have been involved in the policy decision-making process and the problems of dealing with political and institutional structures outside the isolated university setting.

Institutions and academics

If it was concluded above that academics do not understand the functions of politics and prefer to ignore the existence of social conflict in analysing social problems, understanding how institutions behave is even more foreign to the average policy scientist. Bureaucracies, according to the instrumental model, are simply institutional mechanisms for implementing good policy in the interests of society at large (Weiss, 1978). However there is little systematic understanding from policy analysts of the process of how institutions function, despite a great deal of research and analysis (see Wilson, 1977). Typically, as with politics, the view is a stereotype: if actions do not eventuate as anticipated by policy scientists, or if actions do not reflect 'best' policy as defined by the policy research establishment, it is because the implementing institution is perverse or corrupt. Academics from both sides of the political spectrum often share this perception. Conservatives tend to believe that institutions are too big; radicals tend to believe that institutions are controlled in some manner by the ruling class. Both beliefs may have some element of truth; however they remain simplistic explanations. Perhaps these perceptions arise from the very nature and practice of social science. Neither conservative nor radical theories of society have well-articulated theories of the role, nature and behaviour of social structures like the state in organizing outcomes. Conservatives deal principally with individuals, radicals with classes. Institutions are either ignored or seen in purely derivative terms. For example, marxist theories of the state typically derive the state from the existence of irreconcilable class antagonisms (Clark and Dear, 1981). That the state could be autonomous, even controlling its own destiny, is not contemplated. Reason itself may be a different commodity for the state because its interests are basically different from those of individuals and classes which are presumably the clients.

An example may illustrate this issue more clearly. The transit authority mentioned earlier is actually structured according to a number of levels: a board of overseers, whose members are appointed by local towns and cities; a planning staff responsible to the executive director; maintenance staff who are responsible to the rolling stock manager; an operations staff who are responsible to the operations manager; and local station staff who are responsible to the personnel director. Although the lines of authority in the organization are clear-cut, their actual political constituencies do not often overlap. For example, station staff are vulnerable to local sentiment concerning how well the local station is organized while the planning staff typically deal with the governor's office and view the political board as competition.

In deciding what the appropriate transit fare should be, the authority itself was wracked by internal dissant. The overseers' board obviously responded to pressure brought by their own political constituents in their local towns and cities. The planning staff, however, were caught between the political board, their ultimate boss, and the policy experts' advice. The maintenance staff, through their union, argued that a fare-for-distance schedule could decrease ridership, thus lowering staff requirements although the operating deficit would have decreased. In the terms of the opening quotation, the administrative unit of the transit authority reflected the social conflict and discourse existing in the society at large.

This sketch is clearly incomplete, yet the point remains: organizations and their components have differing constituents and interests. Further, although the conflicts of society are reflected in the structures of the decision-making the units of bureaucracy have their own agendas, separate from one another. The policy process must deal with these aspects, not as a complicating detail to an otherwise straightforward problem solution, but as part of the problem itself. The prospect is very real that just as different groups of society have different views as to the nature of any given problem, those views are also likely to be represented within implementation agencies as well. Moreover, interest groups are likely to exist within organizations beyond simply reflecting social views; the power structure of organizations implies that common interests do not automatically develop between different functions. In this manner, instrumental reason and orthodox models of policy science are overly reductionist. Knowledge is thought to be divisible in its definition of ends and means: a theory of action (instrumental reason) separate from a theory of the purposes of action (philosophical knowledge). As long as institutions and political groups have different constituencies and goals, instrumental reason will be subservient to philosophical knowledge. The alternative is to transform the 'problem' itself into the image represented by instrumental reason.

POLICY ANALYSIS AS POLITICAL INTERPRETATION

So far the discussion has been negative—what is wrong with the instrumental model? Yet in criticizing instrumental rationality, readers may have noted implicit arguments about what the field of policy analysis should represent. To re-emphasize a point made earlier, I am not against policy analysis *per se*. In fact I believe it to be a vital aspect of any academic attempt to understand contemporary society as well as of organizing social change. In this section a series of propositions concerning the appropriate function of policy analysis are recorded as hypotheses or initial research statements which could form the basis of an alternative mode of policy inquiry. Clearly these propositions reflect particular values and beliefs. At the same time they reflect a goal of integrating social knowledge with social conflict; a theory of knowledge as a prerequisite for political action (Unger, 1975), and thus of the place of the social scientist in social action.

Proposition 1: Academics must acknowledge their own values and beliefs in presenting policy alternatives and impact assessments

This proposition is quite straightforward and reflects my belief that social scientists have, implicitly or explicitly, sets of norms from which they base their judgements. Notice a fundamental implication: imagine going before a policy hearing to argue the case for increased transit fares and at the same time being forced to make known that you believe that users should bear equally, regardless of wealth, the complete burden of the provision of public goods and services. Values and beliefs (philosophical knowledge) would be matched directly with policy recommendations (instrumental reason).

Figure 2.3 summarizes the place of the policy analyst in the overall process of planning and social conflict. Values, ideology and class structures are seen as impict in political discourse. Following Marx's suggestion, noted in the introduction of this chapter, policy science knowledge is derivative of one's place in society *vis-à-vis* existing social conflict. Ideology, values and structure should not be seen simply as screens to otherwise rational behaviour; rather they are attributes of political conflict and ultimately are conflicting normative views of how the social system ought to be structured. My argument has been that social scientists implicitly conduct policy analysis in this framework. Rather than this being a barrier to consensus as suggested in the instrumental model, it should be recognized as being representative of an inevitable social structure of conflict that should be encouraged rather than eschewed in favour of technical reason.

Proposition 2: Policy analysts must be advocates for particular cases rather than supposedly independent and objective adjudicators of knowledge

This role orientation would provide a means of expressing a wide range of alternative options and an opportunity for cross-examining expert witnesses for various sides. In essence, instrumental reason would still be important in terms

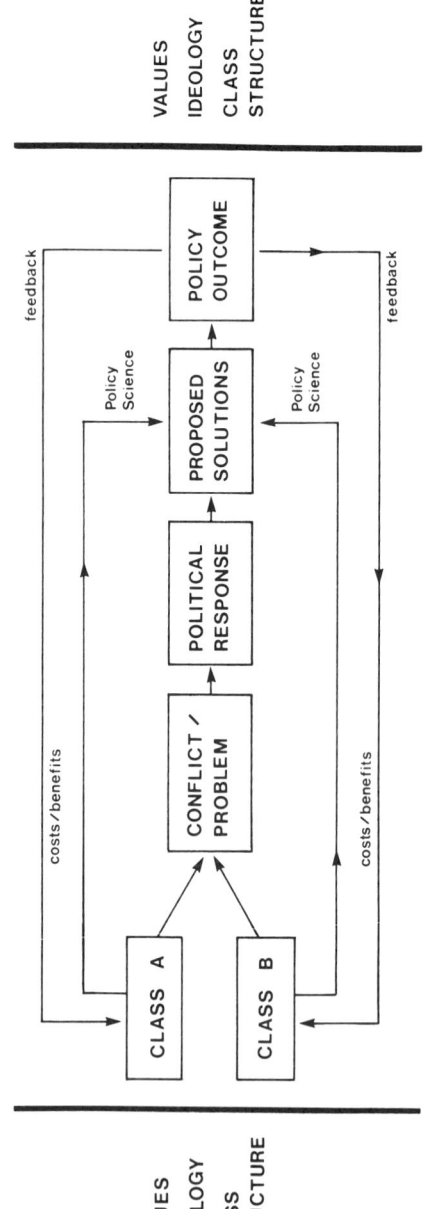

FIGURE 2.3.   Political conflict and policy

of its contribution to actual implementation and planning. However, it would be seen as being derivative out of philosophical knowledge rather than being the only legitimate source of knowledge. The issue here is an explicit recognition of two aspects of policy science: the conflicting nature of much of current academic research, and the inevitable 'taking of sides' that academic research implicitly or explicitly involves. My claim here is that academics should be held accountable for their recommendations and that accounting should be in the political forum where the ends of policy are integrated with its means.

Here I am *not* re-enacting advocacy planning or activist planning of a decade ago. Advocacy planning depended, in part, upon an adjudicating agency for the resolution of competing claims. However, given my earlier argument that social conflict is implicit in the operation of social institutions, no one agency is likely to be neutral. Consequently advocates of policy analysis should be thought of as academics being part of the political process not apart from policy-making and implementation. Further one could claim that advocacy planning reflects the worst aspects of instrumental reason: knowledge as a commodity separate from its philosophical roots; choice between solutions based upon objective criteria; means separate from ends. In Figure 2.4 my argument is summarized as implying that knowledge itself is derivative out of social discourse and social location. Instrumental reason is closely matched to its philosophical roots. Notice as well that the power structure that defines social relations would also define policy scientists' roles: antagonistic when arguing against the status quo; conciliatory when representing the status quo. This leads us to a further proposition.

Proposition 3: Policy science should be critical of the status quo

A fundamental aim of policy analysis should be to avoid co-option and being used to perpetuate existing power relations. Policy scientists as advocates is one solution; as well, academics must be able to step outside their business relationships with government to assert political (normative) judgements about the nature of society and government action. Again this reflects my belief that not only does the public have a right to know the value systems of experts but as well experts themselves should participate, as members of the political structure of society, actively in the political process. The academic as social critic is a traditional role, yet one that is being quickly forgotten. Figure 2.4 briefly describes the internal mechanisms of policy advocacy as represented in Figure 2.3. Notice, in contrast to Figures 2.1 and 2.2, that the 'problem' definition is placed squarely within the conflict structure. Also, it should be acknowledged that the resolution of conflict depends upon the balance of competing interests within the political state and between classes.

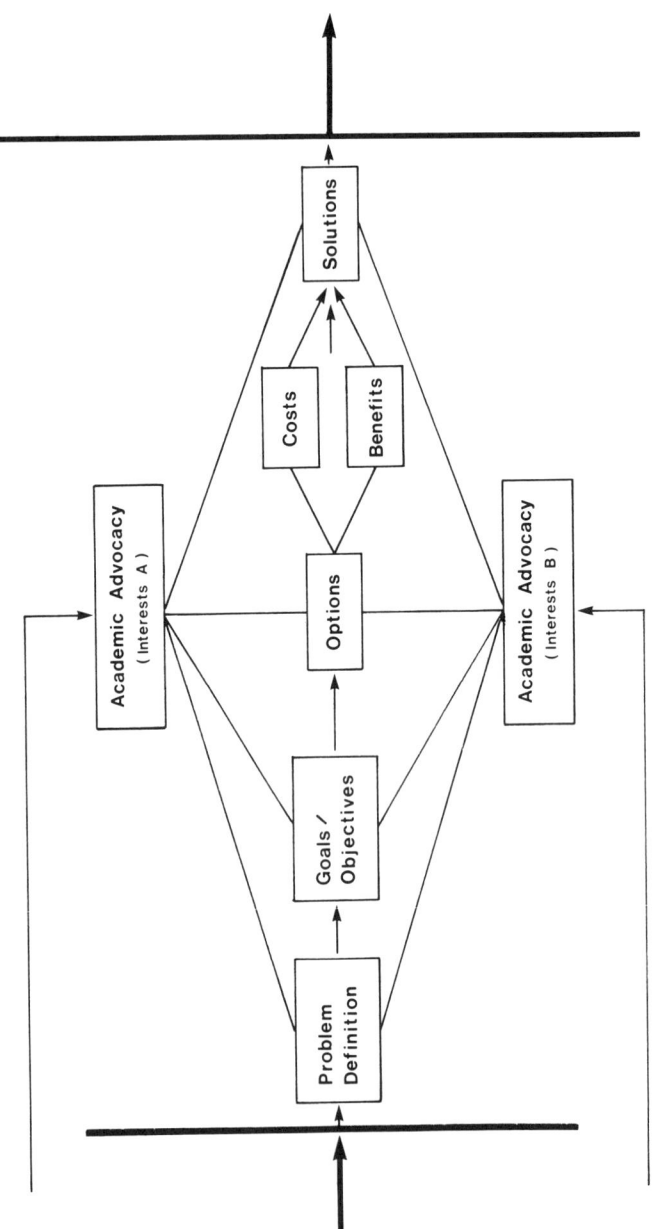

FIGURE 2.4.   Advocacy and policy analysis.

Proposition 4. Sponsoring institutions must encourage advocate briefs and make these briefs accessible to the public

We noted earlier that institutions themselves tend to avoid controversy by using selected expert witnesses to bolster their own dispositions. A requirement for 'advocate briefs' as opposed to 'studies' would open up the system to alternative options as well as broadening the information base of participants in the political system. The choice between competing briefs would still remain and would likely become accentuated. Yet at the same time, the recognition of alternatives and options might make the political process more fluid and encourage a wider debate of the issues. Choices would be brought squarely into the open and be dependent upon the political, as opposed to expert, process. This is a worthy goal that is hardly controversial. Yet there are significant barriers to its implementation; in particular the links between the production of knowledge and the purposes of reason *vis-à-vis* institutional requirements of particular reason according to political agendas. In this proposition I have summarized my fears concerning the devaluation effects that current policy science has in the political process. Knowledge must be made once again part of the political system—not as a substitute for political debate over means and ends.

CONCLUSIONS

Public policy-making deserves a more responsive and political academic science. The instrumental problem-solving model is inadequate and misleading. The art and craft of decision-making is ignored, perhaps even devalued. Politics is unfortunately delegitimized as a sorting mechanism of alternative interests and options. The rational model empowers academics who are themselves often outside the decision-making process. Experts are idolised while disorder and conflict are simplified and trivialized through 'objectivity' and 'reason'. Under these conditions, the policy scientist is a real danger to society. A means must be found to widen the context in which experts function so as to break down the myths of social science.

The four propositions argued for in this paper are an attempt to deal with these problems. In essence, academic policy scientists' values, interests and normative views of the world are recognized in order to bring the system of policy choice into the open. This does not mean that researchers are to be less scholarly or less rigorous in analysis. Simply, researchers should be required to participate in policy decisions as part of the political process not apart from the interests of competing groups. In the terms of the opening quotation, such an interpretive and philosophical policy science would enable the following: a recognition of the ways in which knowledge and facts are constituted through involvement in the political system; a recognition of why reason is a normative aspect of the goals and interests of those contemplating policy and those who design and implement policy; and, consequently, a recognition of both the inevitability of conflict and the contradictions inherent in any attempt to separate instrumental reason from its philosophical roots.

ACKNOWLEDGEMENTS

Thanks to Michael Goldberg of the University of British Columbia for discussion over issues raised in this paper. Michael Dear, Meric Gertler, Ron Johnston, and Jeremy Rudin also provided useful comments on previous drafts of this paper. The author alone is responsible for any errors or omissions.

REFERENCES

Banfield, E. C. (1977). *Policy Science as Metaphysical Madness*, American Enterprise Institute, Washington, DC.
Bennett, R. J. (1979). Space – time models and urban geographical research. In D. T. Herbert and R. J. Johnston (Eds.) *Geography and the Urban Environment Vol. 2*, Wiley, New York, pp. 27–58.
Berry, B. J. L. (1980). Creating future geographies. *Annals of the Association of American Geographers*, **70**, 449–458.
Berry, B. J. L. (1972). More on relevance and policy analysis. *Area*, **4**, 77–80.
Chomsky, N. (1971). *Problems of Knowledge and Freedom: The Russell Lectures*, Vantage Press, New York.
Clark, G. L. (1981). Law, the state and the spatial integration of the United States. *Environment and Planning A*, **13**, 1187–1232.
Clark, G. L. (1980). Urban impact analysis: a new tool for monitoring the geographical effects of federal policies. *Professional Geographer*, **32**, 82–85.
Clark, G. L. and Dear, M. J. (1981). The state in capitalism and the capitalist state. In M. J. Dear and A. J. Scott (Eds.), *Urbanization and Urban Planning in Capitalist Societies*, Methuen, London.
Coleman, J. S. (1980). Policy, research and political theory. *University of Chicago Record*, **19**, 78–80.
Dear, M. J. (1979). Thirteen axioms of a geography of the public sector. In S. Gale and G. Olsson (Eds.), *Geography and Philosophy*, Rotterdam, Reidel, pp. 53–64.
Feyerabend, P. (1975). *Against Method*, Verso Press, London.
Fish, S. (1980). *Is there a Text in this Class?: The Authority of Interpretive Communities*, Harvard University Press, Cambridge.
Goldberg, M. A. (1977). *Plannees and Planners: Toward a Synthetic Planning Process*, Working Paper ‖ 4 Faculty of Commerce and Business Administration, University of British Columbia, Vancouver.
Habermas, J. (1971). *Toward a Rational Society*, Beacon Press, Boston.
Haggett, P. (1977). *Mid-term Futures for Geography, Monash Publications in Geography 16*, Monash University, Clayton.
Harvey, D. (1974). What kind of geography for what kind of public policy? *Transactions of the Institute of British Geographers*, **63**, 18–24.
Howe, I. (1954). This age of conformity. *Partisan Review*, 21, 7–33.
Jenkins, W. I. (1978). *Policy Analysis: A Political and Organizational Perspective*, St Martins Press, New York.

Hollis, M. and Nell, E. (1975). *Rational Economic Man: A Philosophical Critique of Neoclassical Economics*, Cambridge, Cambridge University Press.

King, L. J. (1976). Alternatives to a positive economic geography. *Annals of the Association of American Geographers*, **66**, 293–308.

Kuhn, T. S. (1970). *The Structure of Scientific Revolutions*, Chicago, Chicago University Press.

Lakatos, I. (1964) Proofs and refutations. *British Journal for the Philosophy of Science*, **14**, 1–25.

Lindblom, C. E. and Cohen, D. K. (1979). *Usable Knowledge: Social Science and Problem Solving*, Yale University Press, New Haven.

Lynn, L. E. Jr. (1978). The question of relevance. In L. E. Lynn Jr. (Ed.) *Knowledge and Policy: The Uncertain Connection*, National Academy of Sciences, Washington, DC.

Mercer, D. (1977). *Conflict and Consensus in Human Geography. Monash Publications in Geography 17*, Monash University, Clayton.

Popper, K. (1965). *The Logic of Scientific Discovery*, Chicago, Chicago University Press.

Rein, M. (1976). *Social Science and Public Policy*, Penguin, New York.

Smith, D. M. (1973). Alternative 'relevant' professional roles. *Area*, **5**, 1–4.

Stokey, E. and Zeckhauser, R. (1978). *A Primer for Policy Analysis*, W. W. Norton, New York.

Tribe, L. H. (1972). Policy science: analysis or ideology? *Philosophy and Public Affairs*, **2**, 66–110.

Tribe, L. H. (1973). Technological assessment and the fourth discontinuity: The limits of instrumental rationality. *Southern California Law Review*, **46**, 617–660.

Unger, R. M. (1975). *Knowledge and Politics*, Free Press, New York.

Vernon, R. (1979). Unintended consequences. *Political Theory*, **7**, 57–73.

Weiss, C. H. (1978). Improving the linkage between social research and public policy. In L. E. Lynn Jr. (Ed.) *Knowledge and Policy: The Uncertain Connections*, National Academy of Science, Washington, DC.

Wildavsky, A. (1979). *Speaking Truth to Power: The Art and Craft of Policy Analysis*, Little, Brown and Co., Boston.

Wilson, J. Q., (1978). Social science and public policy: a personal note. In L. E. Lynn Jr. (Ed.) *Knowledge and Policy: The Uncertain Connection*, National Academy of Science. Washington, DC.

Geography and the Urban Environment
Progress in Research and Applications, Volume V
Edited by D. T. Herbert and R. J. Johnston

Chapter 3

Functional Regions for the Population Census of Great Britain

M. G. Coombes, J. S. Dixon, J. B. Goddard, S. Openshaw and P. J. Taylor

The theoretical debate in the urban research literature about the 'nature of the city' and urbanization processes has a long pedigree. More recently discussion has been concerned not only with individual cities but with the set of cities in a nation—the national urban system. However, when it comes to empirical studies either of individual cities or of the urban system researchers have had to make do with official statistics for administrative areas delineated largely on pragmatic or political grounds, definitions which pay scant regard to the geographical principles underlying notions of what constitutes a city. Researchers usually justify such decisions on grounds of practicability—data are simply not available for more appropriate areas or could only be produced by a laborious process of aggregation.

The producers of official statistics can hardly be blamed for providing data for administrative areas. Information is required for central and local government policy-making purposes and governments pay for the collection of the data. However, with the flexibility provided by modern computers and address coding procedures the production of statistics for user-defined areas is not a particularly difficult problem. So perhaps the main reason why urban researchers have not had the data for the areas they want is apathy. Few have been prepared to grapple with the technical problems that arise in translating concepts into criteria that can be operationally applied to real world data or have been prepared to campaign to get the resultant areas adopted by official statistical agencies.

This chapter summarizes an attempt to come to grips with methodological and practical problems of defining a set of functional urban regions for use in the 1981 Population Census of Britain. The first section discusses the conceptual problems that invariably arise in any regionalization exercise. This leads to the suggestion that the 'daily urban system' is the most meaningful unit for the presentation of spatial data. A discussion of how this concept might be applied in Britain in general terms acts as a prelude to a detailed presentation of an operational algorithm developed by the authors in order to identify British 'daily urban systems'. The results of the application of the algorithm to 1971 census data are described in the last section and compared with other official and unofficial regionalizations of Britain. The chapter concludes with a discussion of the future availability of statistics for the recommended areas.

Background to the study

Before proceeding it is appropriate to provide some background to the study. The proper beginning must be in the United States, where official agencies have for a long time regarded the need to define cities consistently in functional terms much more seriously than their counterparts in Britain. Standard Metropolitan Areas were first designed for the 1940 census; the criteria were subsequently revised to identify Standard Metropolitan Statistical Areas (SMSAs) for the 1950 census. Although SMSAs have no legal status they are used for a wide variety of statistical reporting purposes. The application of standard criteria means that different cities can be meaningfully compared; it is therefore not surprising that information for SMSAs can influence the allocation of federal resources to administrative areas contained within them.

Because of the political sensitivity of the SMSAs the definitional criteria have been subject to much scrutiny. The fact that important areas dependent on the SMSAs are excluded led to the recommendation that the boundaries should be extended in order to exhaust the national territory (Berry, 1973). The areas resulting from this recommendation have not displaced the SMSAs for statistical reporting purposes, however. SMSAs are redefined whenever more up-to-date statistics become available, but always using the same criteria.

The first attempt to translate the SMSAs to Britain was made by Hall *et al.* (1973). Using 1961 population and employment data for the pre-1974 Local Authority Areas, one hundred Standard Metropolitan Labour Areas (SMLAs) were defined for England and Wales. The SMLA was composed of an urban core and its commuting hinterland; it had a target population of 70 000, although several areas in fact fell below this threshold. In addition an Outer Metropolitan Ring was defined as those local authority areas from which more commuters travelled to a particular core than to any other core. The addition of the Outer Metropolitan Ring to the SMLA produced the Metropolitan Economic Labour Area (MELA), and these areas included 95 per cent of the total population. The residual areas with no connections to the urban core areas were left unclassified. These definitions were later extended to Scotland and updated using 1971 population and 1966 employment and journey-to-work data, producing 126 areas (Drewett, Goddard, and Spence, 1976).

The present study was partly prompted by a desire to evaluate the SMLA definitions, as these areas had been widely used for research purposes. Because the areas were defined by hand and various pragmatic relaxations of the rules had been made, the present authors found that it was impossible to replicate the definition of SMLAs using a computerized version of the algorithm (Coombes *et al.*, 1979a). Moreover it was apparent that the number of areas produced was very sensitive to changes in the density and/or size criteria used to identify urban cores. This led the authors to a more systematic search for a better organizing framework for functional regions which could be readily translated into a computer algorithm, and by so doing replication by third parties would be made possible.

In addition to considerations of academic rigour there were obvious practical reasons for defining a set of functional urban areas for use with a 1981 census. As a result of local government reorganization in 1974 the majority of statistics for the 1981 census are being published for 460 new districts, compared with the 1765 local authorities that were used in 1971. Those nineteenth-century urban districts, metropolitan and municipal boroughs and rural districts were clearly outmoded, but they did have the advantage that statistics for them could be readily amalgamated into more meaningful units like the SMLAs. Irrespective of their geographical appropriateness, the new districts will clearly provide too coarse a mesh of units for the requirements of many forms of analysis. While statistics are being produced for small areas (wards, grid squares, enumeration districts, postcode sectors) any national level analysis will require expensive computer aggregations of national Small Area Statistics (SAS) to some intermediate level. This will be both expensive and time-consuming and would only be possible a few years after the census data were available.

The change in local government boundaries has also meant that provision of statistics for important *ad hoc* areas, such as the 64 subdivisions of the Economic Planning Regions, has been discontinued. These subdivisions were also composed of aggregations of old local authority areas and included the specially defined conurbations for which statistics had been reported in the 1951, 1961, 1966 and 1971 censuses. In the light of these developments there was clearly a need for a set of areas which could meet a variety of analytical purposes and for which comparable data could be made available for both 1971 and 1981. The remaining sections describe the quest for such areas.

THE PROBLEM

All data analyses involve two basic elements: a set of *objects* upon which a series of *measurements* has been made. Hence any data set may be characterized as a box or matrix, with one axis representing the objects and the other the measurements or variables (Cattell, 1966). In geographical studies this data box is termed the *geographical data matrix* (Berry, 1964a), where the objects are 'places' and the variables are characteristics of those places. For individual-confidentiality reasons, it is just such areal-based data that censuses make available to *all* social researchers. All published census tables may therefore be viewed as particular examples of geographical data matrices.

The modifiable areal unit problem

One important argument that follows from the object-variable characterization of data is that we are able to identify an order of priority between them. It is very clear that in any data-collection exercise, definition of object must precede the measurement procedure—we cannot measure before we have decided what it is we are measuring (Chapman, 1977; Langton, 1972). This very obvious point is of particular relevance to geographical research and other areal studies because the definition of 'areal objects' is by no means a simple matter. By its very nature area is a continuous phenomenon, so its division will be arbitrary to some degree. There are no 'natural' areal units to act as objects in the same way as individuals (animals, plants, persons) may act as 'true' objects in non-areal studies.

This dilemma is commonly referred to as the modifiable areal unit problem. For any set of measures over an areal universe there will be innumerable different ways of combining the measures into sets of areal aggregates. The fundamental problem is that for the same set of original measures, different results may be produced for different areal units. This was pointed out by statisticians in the 1930s (Gehlke and Biehl, 1934; Neprash, 1934) and the implications of their work was summarized succinctly by Yule and Kendall (1950, p. 313): 'we must emphasise the necessity, in this type of work, of not losing sight of the fact that our results depend on our units'. This startling admission has recently been rediscovered by geographers and regional scientists (Clark and Avery, 1976; Openshaw, 1977; Openshaw and Taylor, 1979, Williams, 1976; 1977). The whole point is that areal units must never be accepted as given without any thought for the particular effects they may have on subsequent analysis. Williams (1976, p. 16) puts the problem into its correct perspective:

> No self-respecting statistician would just take any selection of individuals as his sample in a study and give it no further thought. Likewise we would hope that the days are numbered for urban and regional scientists who produce zoning systems, as it were, out of a hat and proceed to use them, blissfully unaware of the effects the grouping might have on any subsequent empirical investigation they carry out

In this chapter we attempt to provide 'further thought' on the definition of areal units for the user of the British census of population.

The areal units used for the 1971 census

The implication of the modifiable areal unit problem for census users is quite straightforward. If areal units are arbitrary in nature then the utility of measurements on them is thrown into doubt, along with the geographical data matrices published in the census volumes.

The population census carefully defines basic objects and measurements on those objects in its data-collection phase (Dewdney, 1981). These basic objects are person, family, household, and dwelling. Measures on these objects are obtained by the questions on the census schedule. Such basic individual-level data have to be modified in the data-reporting phase, owing to fundamental confidentiality constraints. It is at this second phase that the areal basis of census tabulations appears. Hence the areal units available for analysis are *not* the carefully defined basic objects referred to above, but aggregations of these units on an areal basis. Unfortunately these areal aggregations are not defined as 'objects of interest' in the same way as the basic units. Rather they normally appear as 'given', their origins deriving from national and local government administrations. Although such administrative units are important and relevant for many research and non-research needs, they constitute rather arbitrary divisions of the country. Figure 3.1 lists all the areal units for which the 1971 census is reported, at various scales, and illustrates the administrative dominance of the exercise.

The basic census publication is the county volume which uses the local authority areas as the unit at three scales of county, district, and ward/parish. In addition special tabulations are available for other administrative units such as parliamentary constituencies and economic planning regions. These administrative areas comprise all but the smallest two scales of the thirteen levels of aggregation listed in Figure 3.1. In effect, therefore, any analysis of Great Britain that is not directly concerned with local scale variations was only provided with data for administrative areas by the 1971 census, which we have previously identified as relatively arbitrary divisions of the country. In particular, this treatment of the objects of the reported data contrasts with the careful specification of the variables in the development of the question schedule (Benjamin, 1970).

In addition, Figure 3.1 shows that there are three sets of areal units defined solely for census purposes and these deserve a brief comment. The first specially designated areas are the seven *conurbations*. These were defined in 1951 by separating out the largest urban areas in Britain and dividing them up into centres and zones. They are considered as 'a different order of things' (Self, 1961, p. 22) from the rest of Britain, and there was no attempt to define special areas to cover the rest of the country. Hence they have never constituted a comprehensive set of areal objects for studying Britain. Elsewhere in 1951, special small social areas were designated in a limited census-tract programme on the lines of the US census (Filkin and Weir, 1972, pp. 133–135). At the local level this census-tract programme was abruptly halted, when in 1961 the Registrar General made available data for *enumeration districts*. These are the small areas within which the census is administered. They are specially drawn for the census but are only based upon their own administrative needs, that is approximately equal populations to equalize the workload of enumerators and to ease boundary

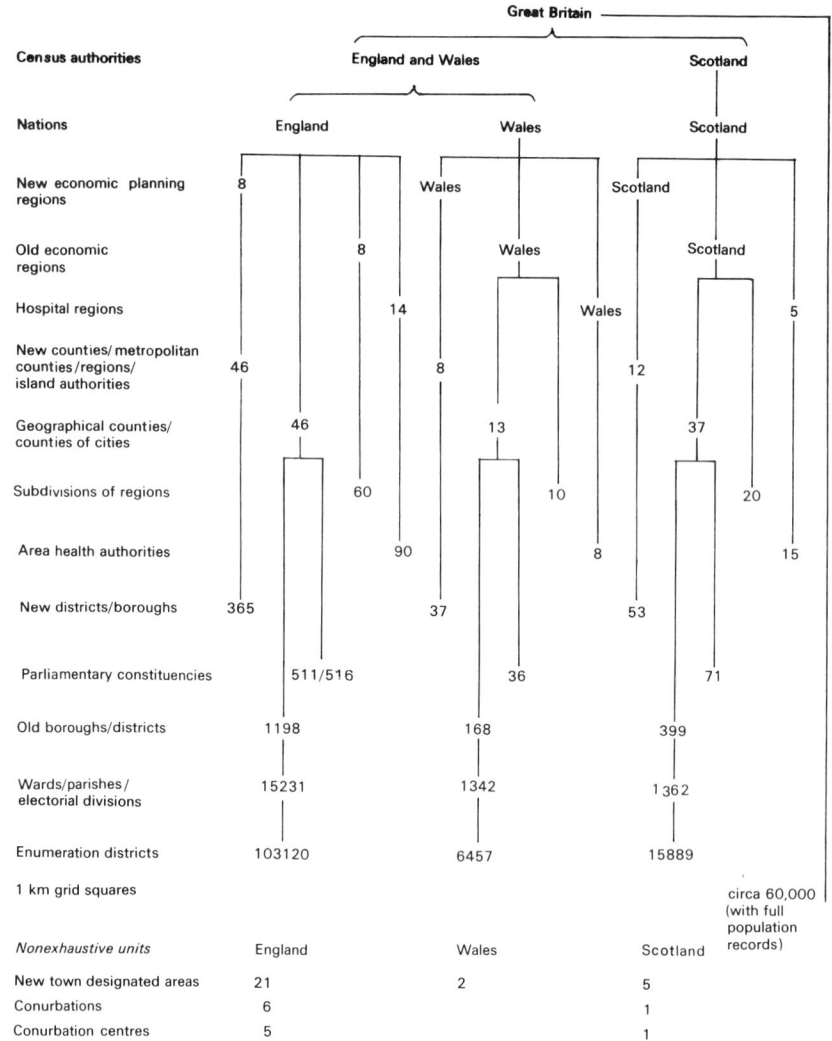

FIGURE 3.1.   Reporting units for the 1971 census.

identification in the field (Benjamin, 1970, p. 135). Hence, although specially drawn for the census, they are as arbitrary as the larger areas derived from existing administrative bodies. In fact their recent popularity in research is due solely to their small size, which enables analysis to come as close as possible to the original individual objects so carefully defined by the census. Finally, from the 1971 census, data have been made available for 1 km *grid squares*. These areal units replace administrative arbitrariness with a new cartographic arbitrariness. The main advantage of a grid system is its immutability, thus it forms a sound base for subsequent intercensus comparability (Benjamin, 1970, p. 153). Of course 'it is clear that neither e.d.'s nor grid squares have any intrinsic sociological relevance' (Filkin and Weir, 1972, p. 133) and hence do not constitute a solution to the problem of arbitrary areal objects in analysis of census data.

Areal aggregates and areal objects

If the areal units, both administrative and specially designated, used by the 1971 census are to be categorized as arbitrary divisions of the country it is incumbent upon us to suggest how we can identify 'non-arbitrary' areal units, which we will work towards in the remainder of this chapter. For this purpose we draw upon the work of Chapman (1977) and, in particular, his distinction between 'areal aggregates' and 'objects of interest', which latter he identifies as 'true entities' for study.

Essentially Chapman argues that objects of interest should have the properties of systems. In primitive terms this means that the 'whole' should be greater than the sum of the parts, or else we are dealing merely with an aggregate. This property of 'wholeness' of an object is reflected in its relative self-containment of activity. Boundaries around an object are characterized as zones of greater impermeability between the object and the outside world. Finally the key characteristic of a true object is the existence of some control mechanism within the object. Hence objects 'respond' to stimuli and therefore can be said to behave. Mere aggregates do not behave. Chapman (1977, p. 22) presents a hierarchy of objects, starting with atoms and molecules (the objects of interest to physical scientists) and continuing through to higher-level objects such as plants, animals, and households (the objects of interest for biological and social scientists). This leaves a difficulty in defining objects above the level of the individual and the household, which is in fact where careful census definitions of objects cease. Chapman (1977, p. 49) is willing to admit that the modern state may constitute an object of interest satisfying his criteria of wholeness and internal control, but is unwilling to recognize any geographical objects that exist between household and state.

THE DAILY URBAN SYSTEM AS SOLUTION

Our task is to design a set of areal units that are not mere 'areal aggregates' but seem to be meaningful entities in their own right. The continuous nature of the areal dimension will make such 'geographical objects' difficult to define, but such an attempt is essential if we are radically to improve the areal basis of census reporting. The only candidate that even vaguely approaches Chapman's criteria for an object at the intermediate scale between household and state is the city region (Chapman, 1977, p. 14).

Daily urban systems

Since 1950 the US census has attempted to go beyond administrative areas in its data presentation to provide information for a set of standard metropolitan areas across the country (Berry and Horton, 1970, p. 251). This initial attempt has been subsequently revised and developed for the 1960 and 1970 censuses, based upon the concept of a 'daily urban system' (Berry, 1967; Berry, Goheen, and Goldstein, 1969; Office of Business Economics, US Department of Commerce, quoted in Berry, 1973). These ideas were originally introduced into the British context by Davis (1959) as part of a worldwide study, and have been subsequently used in several major studies (Drewett, Goddard, and Spence, 1975, 1976; Hall, 1971; Hall et al., 1973). In essence all these definitions of urban regions are based upon employment cores together with their commuter hinterlands. They are daily urban systems (DUSs) in that they describe the pattern of activity around urban areas on a typical working day. Although based upon work trips, Berry (1967) uses the DUS concept to mean the areal zone in which most of the nation's population carry out the vast majority of their daily activities: employment, retail, and social. Hence the concept underlies some recent concern for improving local-government areal structure (for example, Ellman, 1968; Honey, 1977). Furthermore, it has been argued that these urban units constitute a framework within which changes in the national economy should be viewed, both in general terms (Castells, 1977; Pred, 1977) and in the British context (Broadbent, 1977; Goddard, 1974; Keeble, 1977). In this sense urban regions replace the gross development zones and regions which are largely of a non-functional nature.

A very useful way of viewing the DUS concept is as a means for linking the daily activities of the individual with gross trends occurring within the national economy. At the individual level the DUS framework is consistent with the approach to social planning proposed by Hagerstrand under the title 'time geography' (Thrift, 1977). This method of analysis focuses on the individual and specifies the space and time constraints on his day-to-day activities. Given an individual's home base and the need to return there after a day's activity, employment, recreation, shopping, and social opportunities are limited to a region in time and space which Hagerstrand terms the 'daily prism' (Hagerstrand, 1970, p. 13). The maximum extent of a person's prism and hence opportunities will depend on his or her means of transport. Hagerstrand's work defines a set of all possible opportunities for an individual within the personal constraint of home location and transport. This is therefore a theory of what could be and not of what actually does occur in practice (Hagerstrand, 1974). In reality, daily prisms are distorted by the nodality of urban systems both in terms of locationally constrained investment in transport facilities and the long-term land-use trends separating home and workplace. Hence in practice individual prisms will be clustered within the daily urban systems we have described above. The individual household may change residential location within a DUS without any of its members changing employment, and conversely job changes may take place within the DUS without a need for residential mobility. For these reasons Johnson, Salt, and Wood (1974) find Hall *et al.*'s (1973) DUS division of Britain the most suitable units for their study of migration and housing.

Are daily urban systems objects or areal aggregations?

Does a DUS constitute an object of interest that meets Chapman's (1977) severe criteria? Clearly the coining of the term 'system' indicates the confidence of the original researchers in this field that they were indeed dealing with true entities (Berry, 1964b).

Chapman (1977, p. 48) himself concedes that the nodal region is in many ways very close to being an object. In terms of wholeness and organization it consists of different parts (shopping centres, employment zones, and different types of residential area) which make up a functioning whole which is normally relatively self-contained in terms of daily activities. Hence boundaries between DUSs are zones of relative impermeability in terms of actual interactions. These are not, however, the results of controls over those interactions. Chapman points out that the medieval city with its enclosing walls could effectively control its interaction with the outside world, whereas today, although such control on arbitrary access is still exercised with respect to private homes and modern states, this is no longer true of the modern city (Chapman, 1977, p. 51). Hence the DUS's claim to be an object is weakest in relation to the key criterion of control. Therefore a DUS will not respond to stimuli and behave in the way that a true object should.

Nevertheless one should not be quick to dismiss the DUS. It exhibits object-like characteristics without the full control mechanism. Stacey (1969) has confronted a similar problem in equating areally-based community studies with local social systems by admitting that the latter will never normally exist in a pure form but that 'partial' local social systems do in fact exist. Similarly we may assert that a DUS at the very least does form a partial object in the sense that it is far less arbitrary than enumeration districts, grid squares, and administrative areas. If we are going to carry out any analyses at an intermediate scale between individual households and the state, then the DUS concept provides a relatively less arbitrary division than those currently in use.

Problems of application to Great Britain

When we come to apply the concept of a daily urban system to Great Britain several problems arise. In essence this is because the concept is represented in different forms in different parts of the country. Previous applications of the concept to Britain have not adequately coped with the situation. They have emphasized a two-stage process in which first, urban employment centres (frequently called 'cores') are identified, and secondly, commuter hinterlands (or 'rings') are allocated to each core. The first stage involves classifying the base units (local authorities) by size and some measure of metropolitan character (such as employment density). The second stage uses interaction data (journey-to-work flows) to link non-cores to cores. The decision on the thresholds to be used in the criteria of stage one controls the number of DUSs identified, while the level of interaction required in the second stage controls how much of the national territory is incorporated into the DUS regionalization.

The overlap problem

A basic problem of all such regionalization exercises relates to the possibility of overlapping classifications prompted by areas with large commuting flows in different directions. In reality the total DUSs for adjacent cities frequently overlap to some degree and if the cities are relatively close together the overlap in commuting areas may be substantial. A classification for census purposes, however, requires that each class must be discrete so that an area sending commuters to two cities must be allocated to the DUS of only one city. In this way cities in more urbanized regions, for example the North West, have their DUSs spatially restricted by close rivals while in less urbanized regions, for example East Anglia, a city's DUS may expand to the limit of its attraction of the required level of commuting. One particular aspect of this difference in the DUSs defined in contrasting areas of Britain is that the different journey-to-work behaviour of socioeconomic groups is highlighted. The long-distance, mainly white-collar, commuter will normally live and work in the same DUS in the 'rural' areas but may not do so in the more urbanized areas.

The multinodal problem

Related to the overlap problem is the issue of multinodal regions. The DUS approach in practice produces urban systems centred on either a single city or a compact group of urban areas (for example Manchester, Salford and Stretford). In reality this is a simplification of the situation, particularly in the conurbations and similar areas. Hence, whereas a core-and-ring pattern suits East Anglia where large market towns with rural hinterlands are the norm, this framework is less appropriate in older industrial areas characterized by numerous towns amid continuous urban areas. Thus in South Lancashire several 'cores' may be identified, each competing for relatively few non-core units. Instead of such an area being treated as several separate urban regions it is commonly considered to be a composite urban region. This has been conceded in the application of the

DUS concept in the north eastern United States where the census units, SMSAs—Standard Metropolitan Statistical Areas—are combined to produce standard consolidated areas (SCAs) (US Bureau of the Budget, 1967).

The single-tier constraint

Previous British applications of the DUS concept have always produced a single-tier classification. That is to say, the urban hierarchy which underlies the distribution of cities has not been employed as part of the classification. Previous regionalizations have defined DUSs centred on, for instance, London and Swindon with no account taken of the vast difference in nature between these urban regions. A single-tier classification has the basic advantage of simplicity but implies comparability between areal units which most researchers would consider to be unlike. Once again, this is a problem that arises from the differences between the more and less urbanized parts of Britain, posing difficulties for a regionalization that does not take these differences into consideration.

The coverage requirement

Finally, there is the problem of whether the classification should exhaust the national territory. Clearly not all parts of Britain fall into the DUSs around the recognized urban centres and therefore a 'non-metropolitan' residual of small population but large area is typical of previous DUS regionalizations. In the United States Berry (1973) has extended the SMSA definitions to cover that extensive landmass without residual. Hay and Hall (1978) have completed a similar programme not only for Britain but for all of western Europe, recognizing that this moves beyond DUSs, by dividing the peripheral areas into non-urban regions by using non-nodal criteria derived from Smart (1974). This approach therefore employs two distinct classification exercises and so undermines the basic advantage of exhausting the national territory: that by allocating all areas to urban-centred regions a single complete and uniform classification is produced.

To summarise, there are the metropolitan areas where the numerous urban centres are so close together that not only do most 'non-cores' send commuters to several different 'cores', but also these centres of employment themselves house many people working in the principal central city of the region. In contrast, the peripheral areas incorporate districts with only tenuous links with any urban centre, so that the problem in these circumstances is the extension of the regionalization to exhaust all areas, rather than the limitation of rings to prevent overlapping. The critical difference in these types of area is therefore the degree of self-containment of an area with regard to the local provision of jobs for its economically active residents. In the metropolitan areas, even when whole DUSs are considered, there is large-scale inter-area commuting and thus low average self-containment with little or no prior aggregation and these are therefore difficult to bring into the regionalization. Previous DUS regionalizations have failed to include amongst their criteria measures of the proportion of the workers housed in an area who also work within that area—a factor that is considered of overwhelming importance in the definition of the Department of Employment 'travel-to-work' areas (Smart, 1974).

A two-tier solution

There can be no single urban-region framework which will perfectly resolve all the above issues. The aim must be the most realistic mix of concepts which together indicate a classification that will have the general purpose relevance required for the presentation of census data. This requirement of relevance refers not only to the actual statistical criteria but also to their intuitive acceptability. Consequently simplicity of the criteria is necessary, to be balanced against the technical sophistication. In particular we will emphasize the intuitively important criteria of self-containment along with the incorporation of a hierarchical element in our procedure. These two additions are developed to overcome some of the problems inherent in the past applications enumerated above.

   Clearly self-containment and the urban hierarchy are closely related. Logically as we move up the hierarchy to larger urban systems self-containment will increase. Hence any large metropolitan region, based upon London or Manchester or Birmingham, will inevitably be highly self-contained since at that level of the hierarchy most lower-order overlapping urban systems are incorporated into the single larger region. However, at the lower levels of the urban hierarchy towns and cities outside the metropolitan regions will also tend to be self-contained because of their relative geographical isolation. Analysis of the self-containment of DUSs therefore allows a two-tier element to enter into the classification. Three types of DUSs are thereby identified: dominant metropolitan DUSs, subdominant metropolitan DUSs, and free-standing DUSs. This terminology of 'dominance' derives from Bogue (1949), who was also concerned to identify the centres of metropolitan regions. The idea is to recognize the relationships between, say, London and Southend or Liverpool and Southport. In previous classifications these are four separate DUSs despite large absolute commuter flows in each case from the smaller to the larger centre and hinterland. The new flexible approach allows Southport to be recognized as a local subdominant centre within a metropolitan region based upon Liverpool. In contrast free-standing DUSs are based on cities or towns which qualify as separate 'cores' but which neither dominate other DUSs nor are themselves dominated; Scarborough and Carlisle are obvious candidates.

   This solution represents the simplest way of overcoming the problem of the differences between the more urbanized regions and the peripheral areas whose contrasting urban structure will be reflected in the prevalence of free-standing DUSs. Although DUSs remain discrete at each hierarchical level, overlap will be allowed between levels. Hence two types of commuter flow, local and longer-distance, are accommodated in the metropolitan areas—for example, within Southport's DUS and from it to Liverpool. In this way the multinodal character of such areas is also accurately reflected, further emphasizing the inescapable differences in kind between both Southport and Liverpool and Scarborough and Carlisle. Finally, the different journey-to-work patterns of the major socioeconomic groups are reflected in the metropolitan regions where the 'white-collar' workers tend to be employed in the major employment centres but commute from the surrounding areas which are part of satellite DUSs mainly providing local employment for the 'blue-collar' resident workers.

Previous DUS regionalizations made allowance for differentials in work-trip patterns by subdivision of DUSs; this should be considered in conjunction with the remaining problem of extending the application of the DUS concept so as to exhaust the national territory. Extensive use of the data for SMSAs in the USA and the SMLAs in Britain suggests that the practice of defining an 'inner ring' for each urban centre (15 per cent commuting dependence being the common threshold) should be continued. Clearly the need to include the most peripheral areas requires that 'outer ring' criteria be far less restrictive. One possibility is to exhaust the national territory only at the higher tier of freestanding and whole metropolitan regions since this would imply less strict association of these peripheral areas to specific urban centres. This approach would limit the DUSs to the employment centre and its 'inner ring'. Freestanding DUSs and each metropolitan group of DUSs would then be supplemented by 'outer rings' or rural peripheries to form freestanding and metropolitan city regions which would completely cover Britain. The other approach is to follow the established DUS practice by associating outer rings to the individual DUSs before they are considered for grouping into metropolitan regions. This latter approach has the advantage of exhausting the national territory at both upper and lower tiers, and so it is this option which we have chosen.

THE ALGORITHM

The previous discussion specifies the nature of the regionalization we are seeking. This inevitably constrains the available options for developing an algorithm by making the standard statistical classification algorithms inappropriate (see, for example, Brown and Holmes, 1971; Masser and Brown, 1975; Openshaw, 1978; Slater, 1976; Van der Knaap and Sleegers, 1980). This has meant that we have had to develop a special programmable algorithm which codifies the practices of previous researchers who defined urban functional regions, usually manually or with the incomplete use of the computer. The intention is to avoid the dilemma of the standard statistical classification's consistent but arbitrary results and the subjective regionalization's reasonable but non-comparable areas. Adherence to a computerized version of the urban functional region format ensures that our final results will be simple to interpret and meaningful to a wide range of users.

Alongside the goal of interpretability, however, must be added other goals of repeatability and consistency of application. There is no virtue in trying to identify what are considered to be meaningful units if the results are dependent on the occasional relaxation of the rules to avoid anomalous results, activities which have characterized many previous attempts. A regionalization that cannot be replicated by a third party is of little value. Consistency and repeatability have been attained here by developing a computer program without any manual intervention in the process. The algorithm that has been developed consists of nine steps; these are summarized as follows:

TABLE 3.1   Step-by-Step Summary of the Regionalization Algorithm

Step	Summary
0	*Data*: 1971 Census 100% (population) and 10% (employment) files and the journey-to-work matrix for 1930 OPCS/Local Authority areas.
1	*Centres*: All areas are considered by a quotient which compares each area with the national average for retail activity/resident population (which identifies Shop Centres) and for jobs-by-workplace/residents-in-employment (Work Centres); the threshold for Centre status is set at 66% of the national average (all thresholds in the algorithm are set fairly low to allow all plausible candidate areas to go forward, however the large number of criteria that make up the algorithm between them ensure the regions are robust).
2	*Amalgamation*: Any Centre with a journey-to-work outflow to another Centre that exceeds 10% of all its residents-in-employment is joined to that Centre if the flows between the two areas are a substantial proportion of all flows involving those two areas (the exact formula used here is based on that in M. W. Smart 1974).
3	*Consolidation*: Any Centre (or Joint Centre from Step 2) that does not consist of both a Shop and a Work Centre is discarded; for the purposes of data presentation the (Joint) Centre definitions are transformed into approximate built-up Core areas (based on Hall and Hall, 1980) which encompass the principal Shop and Work Centres.
4	*Hinterlands*: Areas outside Cores are assigned as Rings of the Region to whose (joint) Centre they send as commuters over 15% of their residents-in-employment; areas qualifying as Rings of more than one Region are assigned by the formula in Step 2 (in this and all subsequent Steps in the Algorithm contiguity constraints apply).
5	*Exhaust*: All remaining areas are assigned by an INTRAMAX formula (see Dixon and Openshaw 1979) so that the regionalization exhausts the national territory; the parts of Regions assigned in this way are beyond both Core and Ring and termed Outer Areas.
6	*Minimization*: All Regions produced by Steps 1–5 are considered against a measure of both population size and self-containment as a labour market (the different values can, in effect, be balanced against each other in order to meet the single compound threshold); the Region with the lowest value is now disbanded and the constituent areas are then re-assigned by the procedure in Step 5; this continues until all Regions satisfy the Minimization threshold.

(Contd.)

Table 3.1 (Contd.)

Step	Summary
7	*Optimization*: Because the procedure in Steps 5 and 6 is hierarchical it is necessary that the assignments made are tested to ensure that the boundaries produced approximate to 'traffic watersheds' (as far as the original areas allow).
8	*Classification*: Areas assigned by Steps 6 and 7 are assessed by the previous Steps to classify them as Cores, Rings or Outer Areas; any Region with DUS (Core + Ring) under 50,000 population is designated a Rural Area and assigned as such to the Region to which it has the largest outflow (Rural Areas are semi-autonomous labour markets).
9	*Hierarchy*: Regions with large outflow to other Regions are grouped with them into Metropolitan Regions as an upper tier of the regionalization, the other Regions are considered Free-Standing at both tiers (they have no outflow over 7.5% to another Region and form labour markets that are at least 80% self-contained in supply and demand).
10	*Implementation*: The results are replicable due to the automation of the algorithm, but alter when translated onto a different set of areas.

The algorithm step by step

Step 1   Identify urban centres

Since the functional regionalization is to be based on urban centres, defined as a concentration of employment and retail activities, the first stage involves identifying a list of zones[1] that qualify as such centres. To do this two location quotients are defined and a zone has to satisfy at least one in order to qualify as an employment and/or shopping centre.

Let

e_i = employment in zone i,

re_i = retail employment in zone i

rp_i = resident population in zone i

er_i = employed residents in zone i,

a zone qualifies as a retail centre if

$$(re_i/rp_i) \geq 0.66\left(\frac{\Sigma_i re_i}{\Sigma_i rp_i}\right) \tag{1}$$

and as an employment centre if

$$(e_i/er_i) \geq 0.66\left(\frac{\Sigma_i e_i}{\Sigma_i er_i}\right) \tag{2}$$

These criteria were chosen to try and exclude areas which had low levels of self-sufficiency in the provision of jobs, and shops, for their local resident population. This avoids the problems of using absolute size thresholds to select urban cores which simply identify all the heavily populated zones whether they are centres, suburbs or hinterlands. The value of 0.66 was derived after much experimentation and has been selected so as to exclude no significant urban centres. New towns with an underdeveloped retail function were the major problem in 1971.

Step 2 *Amalgamate interdependent centres*

Urban centres that are interdependent need to be in the same functional region. The fact that they may be non-contiguous reflects the nature of the base units that were used and the poor spatial representation they provide of the geography of Britain. The criterion used to identify this interdependence is based on journey-to-work flows. The quotient used here was recommended (but not adopted) by Smart (1974), with the additional restrictions that there must be a minimum 10 per cent outflow and a minimum 1 per cent reverse flow; thus two step 1 centres (i and j) are amalgamated if,

$$T_{ij}^2/(O_i D_j) + T_{ji}^2/(O_j D_i) \geq 0.01 \tag{3}$$

and

$$T_{ij} \geq 0.1 O_i \tag{4}$$

and

$$T_{ji} \geq 0.01 O_j \tag{5}$$

where

T_{ij} is the 1971 census journey-to-work flow from zone i to zone j
(from the OPCS magnetic tapes which, unlike the published volumes used by other studies, show all flows and not just those greater than 50).

O_i is the sum of all flows whose origin is zone i

and

D_j is the sum of all flows whose destination is zone j.

The 0.01 threshold in equation (3) is that recommended by Smart and seems a reasonable value to define interdependent centres, but the application here differs from Smart's in that the quotient is applied only to these large movements whereas Smart applies it to all flows. Furthermore, in our algorithm there is no contiguity restriction during the amalgamation process. This allows binodal regions to occur. It also emphasizes the importance of amalgamating complementary rather than competitive centres, that is centres which share a joint hinterland, rather than adjacent but competitive centres. As rural districts are large enough to include several distinct populated areas, each of which could be amalgamated with a different centre, a chain of centres could be produced linked by those intermediate areas. This is prevented by an additional constraint that rural districts may be linked to only one other centre. Each centre, joint or single, must include at least one employment and one shopping centre; or one area meeting both criteria. The constituent zones of centres failing this requirement are returned to the list of unallocated zones.

Step 3   Adjust definitions of the functional regional centres

It can be argued that perhaps the most useful urban core definition is an approximation to the continuously built-up area. Thus it has been decided to consolidate (joint) centres by adding contiguous areas with definiable urban core characteristics. The analysis of urban areas by Hall, Hall and Morgan (1980) provides the basis for these core definitions. This step is supplementary to the algorithm, and given the nature of the base units used will be fairly crude. In fact this physical definition of cores takes place after the functional regionalization is completed as an additional component for the presentation of census data. It is a manual exercise which does not affect subsequent steps in the computerized algorithm.

Step 4   Identify the hinterlands of the centres

Once the centres have been defined, the next stage is to extend the functional regions by allocating hinterlands. For any unallocated zone i, allocate it as (part of) the ring of centre j, made up of zones k, if

$$\sum_{k \in j} T_{ik} = 0.15\,O_i \tag{8}$$

subject to contiguity restrictions. The commuting flow threshold is set at 0.15 of the unallocated zone's employed residents; this is a standard which is common to nearly all studies of this type and is retained to aid international comparability. Varying this threshold obviously will have an effect on the results but there appears to be no natural cutoff point. Equation (8) is applied by working outwards from each core. If an unallocated zone satisfies the threshold for more than one core then it is assigned to the core with which it has the largest value using the criterion expressed in equation (3). This quotient is as reasonable at this stage as in step 2 because again we are considering sizeable flows; and, as stated in step 3, some of these ring areas have urban core characteristics similar to the centres.

Step 5   Expand the functional regions to exhaust the national territory

The remaining unallocated zones are allocated as outer areas of regions using a contiguity-constrained regionalization procedure based on Openshaw (1974) and Dixon and Openshaw (1979). This assigns any unallocated zone i to region j which is contiguous to i and has the maximum value for the following criterion:

$$T_{ij}/O_i + T_{ij}/D_j + T_{ji}/O_j + T_{ji}/D_i \tag{9}$$

where T_{ij} is the commuting flow from zone i to all the zones currently included in region j.

By this stage in the algorithm the flows between the zones under consideration are relatively small. Consequently any formula similar to that of Smart (1974) will be weighted against these zones joining the larger regions. This is due to the influence of their large values of D_i and D_j in equation (3). The criterion adopted allows the (larger) flows to the larger regions to be influential by separating out the elements of this formula as in equation (9). This formula has been developed from the INTRAMAX procedure of Masser and Brown (1975), but their original criterion was even more unsuitable than that of Smart. It considered the absolute difference between the observed flow and the 'expected' based on O_j and D_j, this being designed for the aggregation of very small zones for transportation studies of, typically, metropolitan areas. As already stated, at this stage we are considering large areas with relatively small flows between them so the absolute difference criterion is using large negative values of 'observed' minus 'expected'. The result is that the smallest region would always be selected as the preferred aggregation for the zone under consideration because it has the lowest 'expected' to be subtracted from the relatively insignificant observed flow. As with many other steps of the algorithm, then, existing 'all-purpose' criteria were found to be inappropriate for many of the different elements needed in a sensible regionalization algorithm. The formula adopted was the product of extensive experimentation upon the data.

Step 6   Impose a minimum size constraint

Due to the uneven distribution of population across the country, any regionalization methodology is liable to produce a large number of regions with only small populations. Consequently a minimum size threshold is introduced. To perform this function the following additional step was devised:

(1) let P_i = the population of the ith region,
     S_i = the ratio of intraregion journey-to-work trips to all trips starting in i, and
     U_i = the ratio of intraregion trips to all trips ending in i, then calculate an index W_i
     $$W_i = \min (P_i/70\,000,1) \times \min (S_i/0.8,1)^2 \times \min (U_i/0.8,1) \qquad (10)$$
     where min (A, B) means the lowest value of A and B;
(2) rank the W_is in ascending order;
(3) if the smallest $W_i < z$ then reallocate all the constituent zones using equation (9), as in step 5: otherwise stop;
(4) update the W_is and return to (2).

The critical value z is set at 0.5263; this was produced by substituting values of 55 000, 0.7 and 0.7 for P_i, S_i and U_i in equation (10), which, like the 'target' values of 70 000, 0.8 in equation (10), are values that have been used in previous studies. The approach here is to set the critical value z at the lowest levels that have been used elsewhere, thus 0.7 and 0.8 represent respectively the minimum and the maximum 'self-containment' values that have been used (Howson, 1979). Similarly, the 70 000 population target was that stated to have been used by Drewett, Goddard, and Spence (1976) though in fact 60 000 was nearer the actual threshold (Coombes *et al.*, 1979b), and whereas Hay and Hall (1978) attempted to adopt 60 000 as their lowest limit, this was not met by all their regions, so that we may take 55 000 to be the minimum regional population for the purpose of equation (10) (Hay and Hall, 1978).

Step 7 Boundary optimization

The functional regionalization is complete but the step 6 procedures are affected by the order in which the assignments are made. One way of resolving this is to employ a boundary/optimizing procedure. This puts all the zones that have been affected by step 6 operations systematically into other regions to optimize equation (9) locally. This is an iterative process similar to the iterative relocation procedure widely used in cluster analysis, except there is a contiguity restriction and a constraint that no change can be made which destroys the internal contiguity of any existing region. After optimization, it is necessary to return to step 6 and repeat steps 6 and 7 until convergence. This process converges after three or four iterations and no further changes are made.

Step 8 Classify the components of the functional regions

The functional regions can now be categorized as either cores, rings, or outer areas: the first two together constitute the daily urban systems. Those zones which have been reallocated or relocated by steps 6 and 7 are recategorized according to the criteria of steps 1 to 5. If the population of any daily urban system is less than 50 000 then it is termed a rural area and that functional region is not subdivided at all. After this, merging of the DUS elements (core and ring) with any outer areas the total rural area population (that is, cases of large groupings of small towns and hinterlands) may exceed 50 000.

Step 9 Classify the functional regions to identify an upper tier

First assign each rural area to the non-rural functional region to which there is the largest commuting flow. Then identify those functional regions which are to be classified as being subdominant in that over 7.5 per cent of all employed residents of that region travel to work in one other particular functional region. These regions are combined as part of a metropolitan city region to create the upper-tier unit in these areas. Elsewhere those functional regions which remain freestanding after this process constitute separate regions at both tiers of the results.

The computer program

This algorithm is operational in the form of a FORTRAN program of approximately 4600 statements. It requires 1500 K of memory and each run takes about 200 seconds of CPU time on an IBM 370/168. Although the next section discusses in some detail the results for a particular regionalization, it should be noted that there is sufficient flexibility in the optional parts of the algorithm to match a variety of user requirements. Thus it is possible to provide both a single recommended functional regionalization and a number of variants to match particular needs.

THE RESULTS

In the preceding sections we have set out the conceptual and methodological criteria for defining a set of functional regions for use in the analysis of the 1981 census of Britain. They have provided a set of objectives against which we can evaluate the results we have produced: each region should be a meaningful geographical individual, part of a set of regions which are consistently defined and constitute a tier in the urban hierarchy, and fitting into a flexible system of areal units which provide a number of options to the user so that there is a reasonable regionalization for most purposes. In the following paragraphs the various levels of the regionalization are described, and illustrated for particular parts of the country. Comparisons are made with some existing sets of areas for which statistics are readily available, notably counties, districts, and the travel-to-work areas of the Department of Employment.

The upper tier

Application of our methodology to 1971 census data has produced 228 functional regions, each one based upon a daily urban system. Just over half of these (115) are located in the less-urbanized parts of Britain and are freestanding functional regions. The remaining 113 functional regions are in areas of longer-distance commuting and more complex urban systems, consequently they can be grouped into metropolitan regions (MR). Each MR is centred on a dominant functional region and contains up to 30 subdominant functional regions. At the upper tier of the regionalization, as a result, Britain is divided into 20 metropolitan regions and 115 freestanding functional regions. This hierarchical structure is summarized in Figure 3.2. The full list of regions, with their population and area, is given in the Appendix, p. 101.

Figure 3.3 shows the 135 upper-tier regions that cover the whole of Britain. Each region has a substantial town or city at its centre with a DUS of upwards of 50 000 people. The metropolitan regions, of course, contain several such DUS-based functional regions (FRs). These upper-tier regions, metropolitan and

Hierarchy of Functional Regions

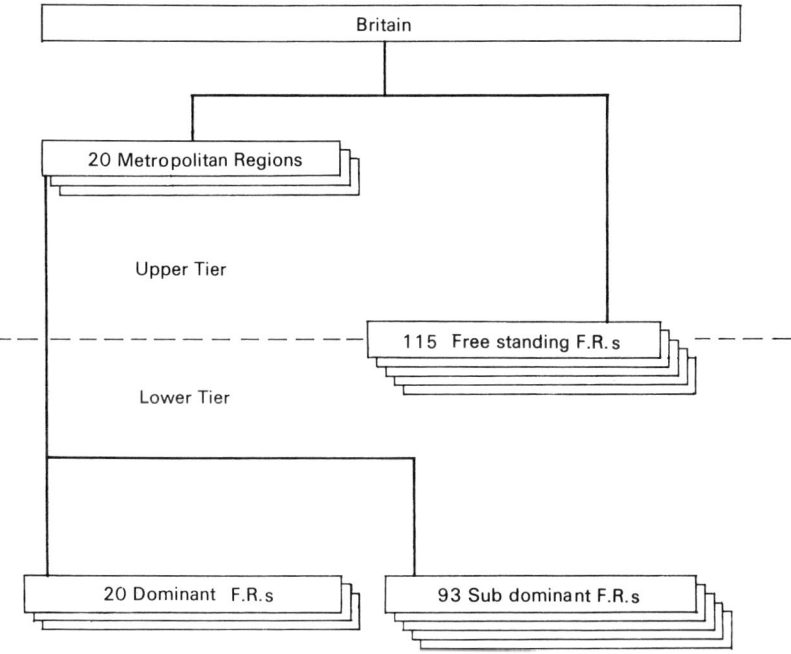

FIGURE 3.2. Hierarchy of functional regions (FRs).

freestanding, together cover the whole of Britain without overlap or exclusion. Areas outside DUSs are allocated according to their principal journey-to-work links so the boundaries tend to follow 'traffic watersheds'. For example, the Glasgow metropolitan region covers the Clyde Valley exactly, and the Shrewsbury freestanding FR extends along road and rail links to include mid-Wales. Each region therefore is a significant element of the British urban system producing a reasonable and meaningful regionalization.

Although the upper tier comprises two contrasting types of region, both the metropolitan and freestanding regions are defined using the same criteria. Each metropolitan region consists of one dominant FR, plus those subdominant FRs having over 7.5 per cent of their employed residents working in either the dominant FR or an adjacent subdominant FR. No freestanding FR is linked in this way (either as dominant or subdominant); the result is that all upper-tier units meet a minimum level of self-containment (or closure) of journey-to-work of 80 per cent on both supply and demand sides of the labour market. Consequently all upper-tier regions share a number of important characteristics: credibility as labour market areas, an effective 1971 population minimum of 50 000 and a substantial urban focus (the DUS). In this way such apparently

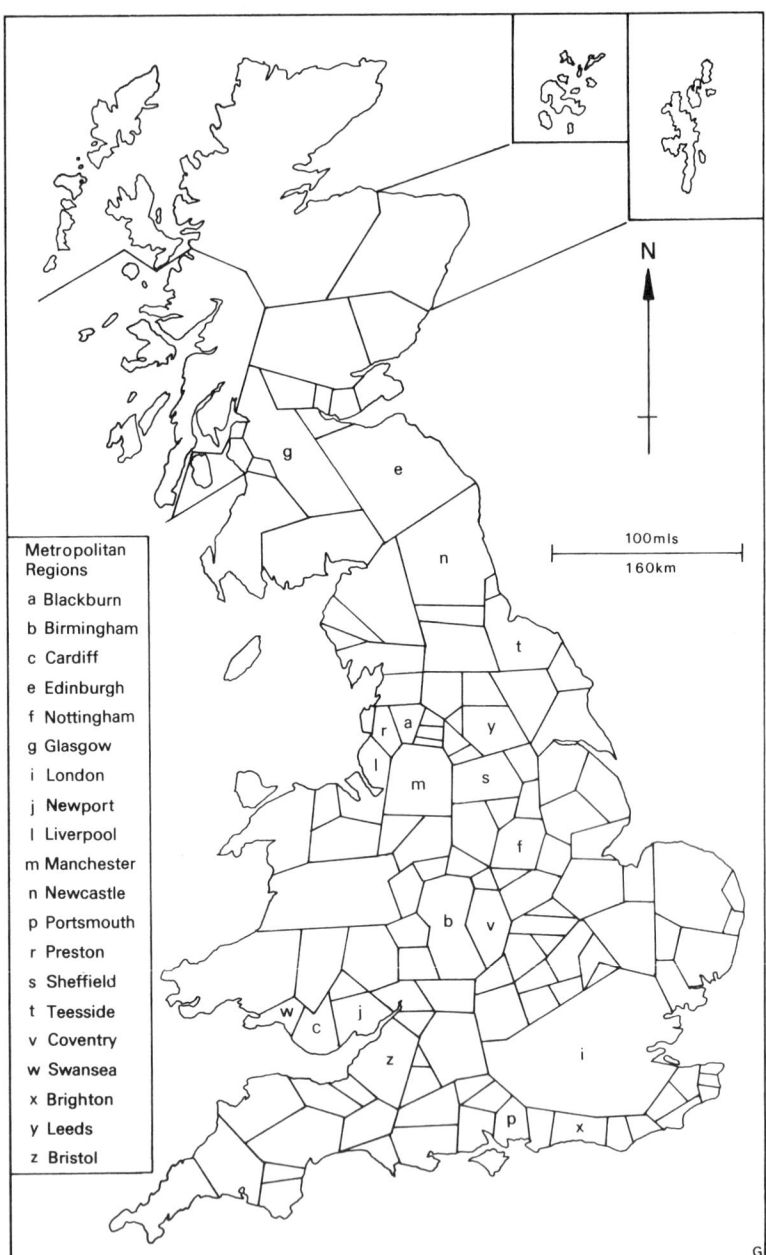

Metropolitan
Regions

a Blackburn
b Birmingham
c Cardiff
e Edinburgh
f Nottingham
g Glasgow
i London
j Newport
l Liverpool
m Manchester
n Newcastle
p Portsmouth
r Preston
s Sheffield
t Teesside
v Coventry
w Swansea
x Brighton
y Leeds
z Bristol

100 mls
160 km

FIGURE 3.3.   Upper-tier regions.

diverse regions as London MR, extending from Newbury to Chelmsford, and Dumfries FR are equally appropriate areal units for analyses.

The regions shown in Figure 3.3 demonstrate that the upper-tier MRs have very large areas and populations owing to the inclusion of subdominant FRs which send commuters to the dominant FRs. There is one MR for each of the conurbations used in the 1951–71 censuses (London, Birmingham, Liverpool, Manchester, Leeds, Newcastle and Glasgow) and for the other large 'regional capitals' such as Cardiff, Bristol, and Edinburgh. The particular criteria used also identify some smaller MRs where there is a clear dominance relationship between two substantial FRs (for example, Blackburn and its subsidiary Accrington). Although there are just 20 MRs in all, East Anglia is the only one of the ten British planning regions not to include a metropolitan FR.

The freestanding FRs are a more heterogeneous group, extending from major provincial cities (such as Southampton and Aberdeen) to extensive thinly populated regions (such as Inverness and Barnstaple) and smaller urban centres, including Scarborough, Stirling and Ebbw Vale. None of these FRs are grouped at the upper tier because they each form a substantial local labour market with its own fairly autonomous urban centre. Consequently it is in this respect that the distribution of upper-tier regions reflects the population distribution of Britain, with the largest number of units in the areas typified by market towns and smaller industrial or resort towns.

South-east England, as shown in Figure 3.4, can be represented by a similar number of either upper-tier regions or counties (for which much data is readily available). It is therefore instructive to compare the relative merits of the two sets of areas as frameworks for spatial analysis. It is clear from the map that the counties form a more regular network of boundaries embracing units of far more equal area (and population). They also have intrinsic importance for some subjects in that they are *de jure* policy areas. The fact that counties do not form meaningful individuals in functional terms has long been recognized (see, for example, Wells, 1903). Subsequent boundary changes have in no way kept pace with developments in population distribution which have ensured that a county such as Surrey has no internal cohesion when separated from London (Ellman, 1968). There is clearly no tier of the urban hierarchy which sets the Greater London area and Buckinghamshire alongside each other as comparable units. Several of the county areas are far from self-contained in labour market terms and so could not be valid units for employment studies.

In fact the counties of South-east England are not only far from adequate alternatives to the upper-tier regions in terms of the criteria we have set for census units, they are scarcely comparable among themselves on any significant criteria. Whereas they are more equal in terms of area and population than the upper-tier regions, the range of size on both these measures is still very large for any study where these are critical factors. Although the boundaries are in many cases now familiar, the time series of data for these particular areas extends no further back

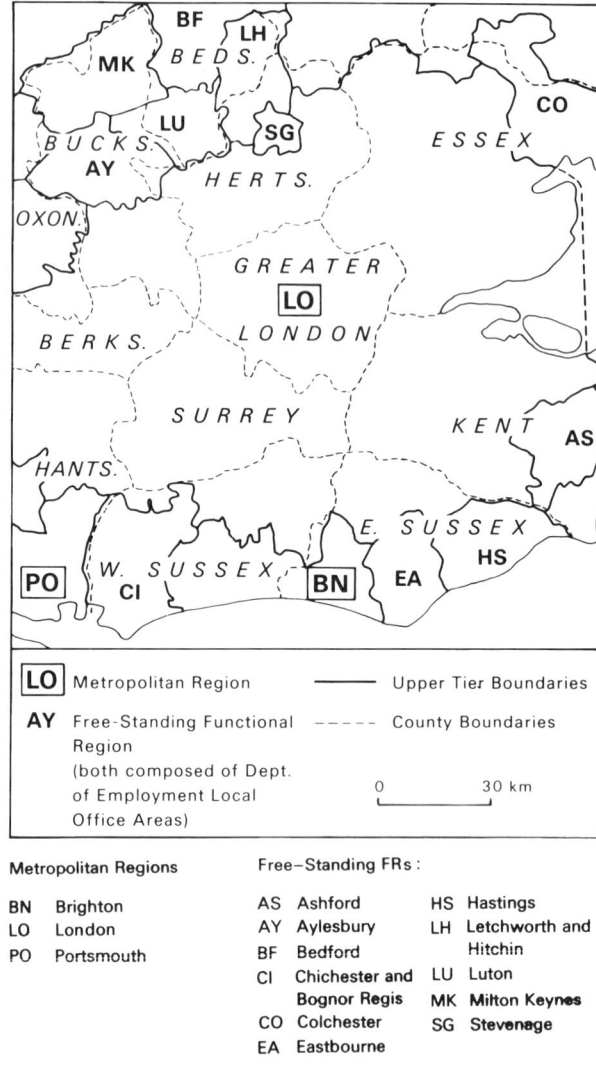

FIGURE 3.4.   South-east England: upper-tier regions and
counties.

than 1971. Thus the historical status of the counties merely acted as a brake on
the boundary changes of 1963 and 1974, ensuring that no criterion was applied
consistently, so the resulting areas are not really comparable. Greater London is
obviously an approach to a formal definition of a built-up area (Rhodes, 1970).
Surrey and Herefordshire could to some extent be considered areas unified by
their physical and, perhaps more plausibly, social characteristics. Kent and

Berkshire could be described as groups of functional areas that are linked by transport corridors but severed from London, of which they are functional extensions. Different again from these two types of area are Essex and the two Sussexes which are not consistent products of physical or functional criteria but perhaps some mixture of the two. Finally, Buckinghamshire appears to have no rationale whatsoever for its grouping of places as distant as Eton and Milton Keynes—except the rigid adherence to the historical boundary.

The post-1974 counties have replaced the Department of Environment's subdivisions of planning regions as 'subregions'. In fact these pre-1974 subregional boundaries (for which data from previous censuses could be produced) provided a fairly reasonable version of the London metropolitan region, although there were no comparable functional boundaries for other MRs or for many smaller city regions or FRs (much of the area in Figure 3.4 was designated 'rest of south-east'). This data series will in any case not be available for the 1981 census. Although in some other parts of Britain the major local authority areas are more reasonable—Scotland is often cited on this point but there are critics of its regions too (see, for example, Dawson, 1979)—the fact is that they are not a consistent set throughout Britain, as shown by South-east England. Even the metropolitan counties fail to conform to functional criteria, in many places being restricted to the built-up areas and excluding their major commuting hinterlands, so resembling the Greater London/Surrey division. Yet elsewhere they extend to include quite separate urban centres; for example Coventry is absorbed into the West Midlands county. In Scotland, Strathclyde regional authority groups with Glasgow the whole of Ayrshire and remote islands such as Mull! Consequently counties can be analysed to emphasize the differences among them (see Craig, 1980), but they cannot be used as analytical tools which will each equally represent the population of a significant area of Britain.

The lower tier

For many purposes, the variation in area and population between the units of the upper tier will be too large. There are also numerous analyses that do not require the additional self-containment conditions that the metropolitan regions meet, so for these purposes the individual functional regions provide additional detail without any critical disadvantages. Where there is no requirement that each area should contain a substantial urban component (a DUS) it is appropriate also to separate out the rural areas. Each rural area is itself a labour market defined on the same criteria as the urban region with which it makes up a functional region. Not all functional regions have rural areas assigned to them, there being 50 rural areas throughout Britain compared to the 228 urban regions or whole functional regions.

Figure 3.5 shows the 278 areas (see the Appendix, P101 for details) which can be considered the lowest tier of coherent labour market definitions available. Separating out the rural areas as well as dividing up the metropolitan regions clearly provides a far smaller range of area sizes. The population size range is smaller also, though less dramatically so because the effective population minimum for rural areas is less than for functional regions. The complete set of functional regions provides a system of areas that recognizes virtually all substantial urban centres in Britain from London to Inverness. The rural areas highlight those districts where urban influence is diffused by dispersed patterns of settlement, employment opportunities, and retail service centres. Many rural areas embrace several smaller competing urban areas which have in common their dependence on the more distant larger centre of their functional region for higher-order services. For example, Yeovil FR includes a rural area embracing Chard, Lyme Regis and Axminster among six small towns in an area just about the size of Anglesey.

The distribution of rural areas around Britain is itself of interest, naturally emphasizing the sparsely settled upland and island parts in the North and West of Britain but also including the thickly populated Fenland districts with their local market towns (such as Spalding and Wisbech). Some larger urban areas are also the centres of rural areas because they belong to types of towns that are surrounded by agricultural areas over which they exert relatively little influence in terms of providing employment opportunities, notably resorts both inland and seaside (such as Malvern and Bridlington) and ports, both fishing and industrial (such as Arbroath and Goole). These form a clear contrast to those relatively small towns which provide substantial employment opportunities for areas populous enough for the core and ring together (the DUS) to pass the 50 000 threshold that confers functional region status (for example, Bridgend and Alloa). The rural area (RA) boundaries in the peripheral areas also provide some valuable insights into subregional groupings (on the modified INTRAMAX criteria explained earlier) such as Skye with the Western Isles, and Caithness with Orkney, while national boundaries are crossed by the rural areas of Berwick and Chepstow which unite the areas on both sides of the Tweed and Wye respectively. Traditional areas that are split include Anglesey (the part by the Menai Bridge joining Bangor instead of Holyhead) and Rutland (no unit being centred within it). Regions where major urban development is close to extensive uplands produce rural areas inside metropolitan regions, for example Hexham RA within Newcastle upon Tyne MR and Lanark RA in Glasgow MR.

The division of metropolitan regions into functional regions at the lower tier serves to emphasize the distinction between satellite towns which are essentially dormitory areas and those with substantial indigenous employment as well. The boundary of the London FR, for example, is pushed back by towns such as Slough and Watford while it encloses equally populous communities like Epsom and Ewell. In Scotland there is a clear distinction amongst the new towns according to whether they were developed principally as overspill housing rather

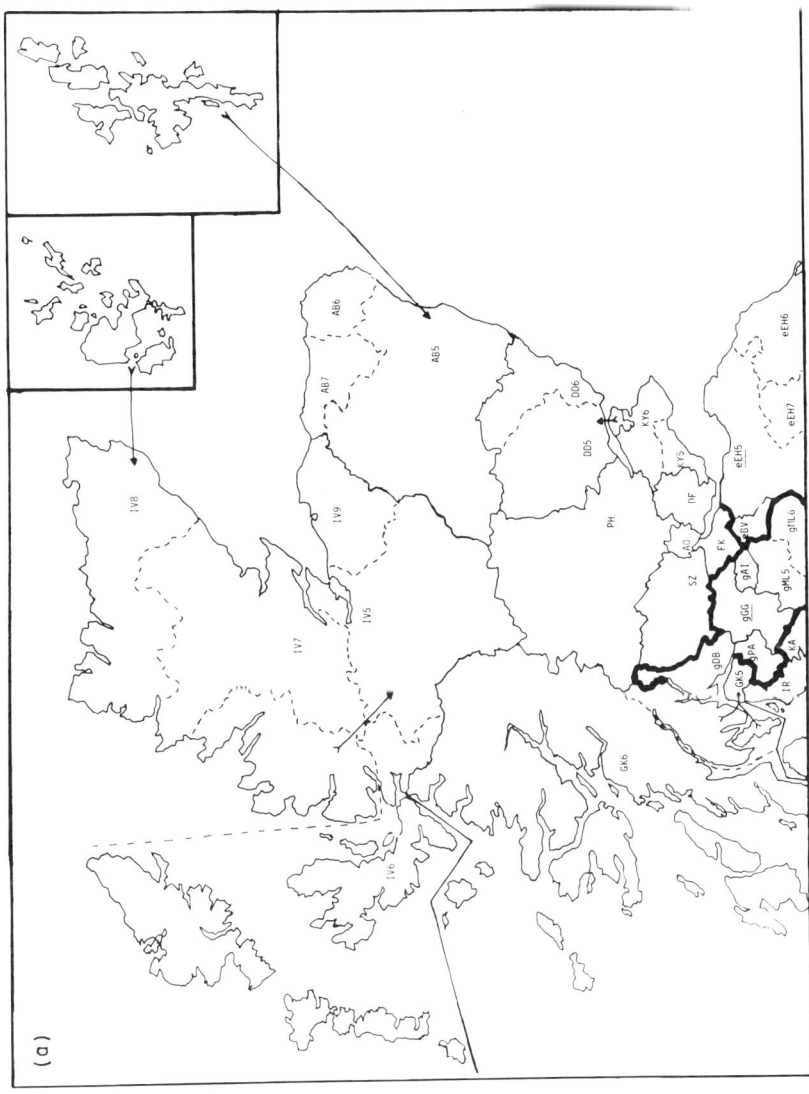

(a)

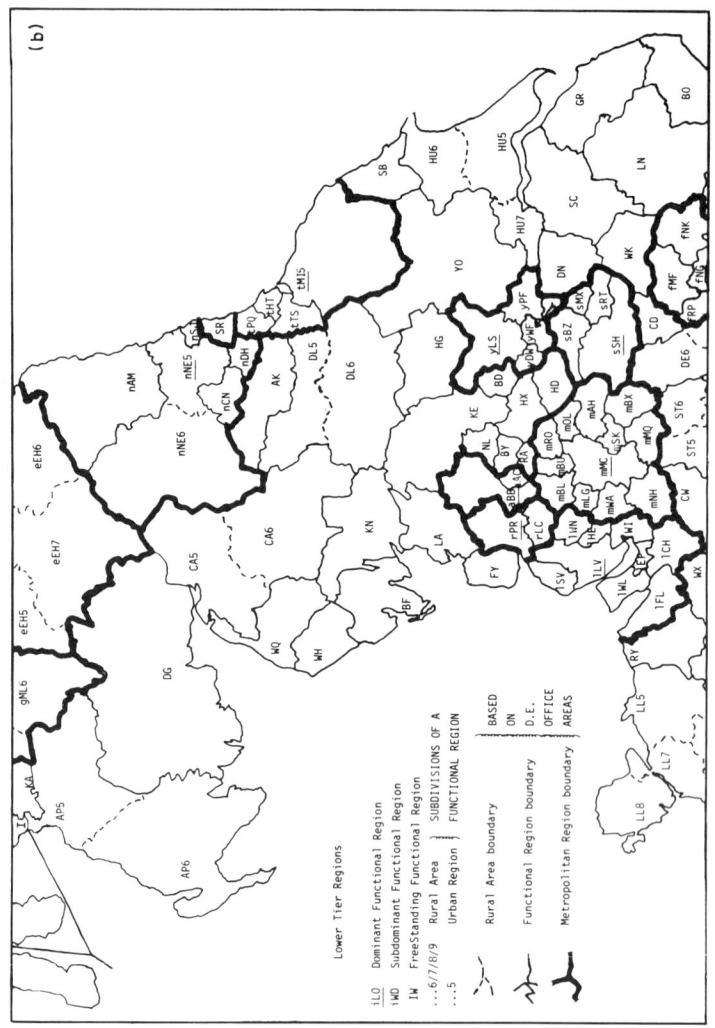

Lower Tier Regions

iLO   Dominant Functional Region
iMO   Subdominant Functional Region
iW   FreeStanding Functional Region
...6/7/8/9   Rural Area } SUBDIVISIONS OF A
                          FUNCTIONAL REGION
...5   Urban Region }

      Rural Area boundary   BASED
                                 ON
      Functional Region boundary D.E.
                                  OFFICE
      Metropolitan Region boundary AREAS

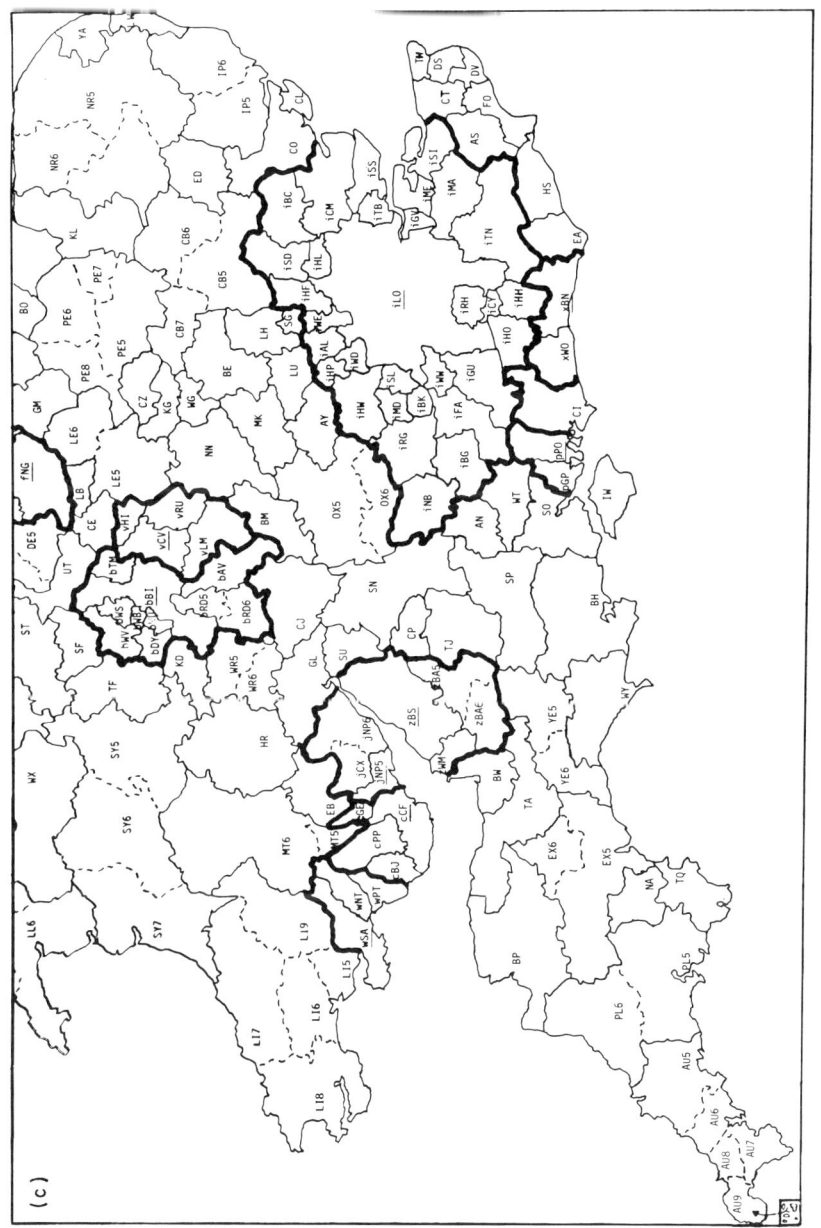

FIGURE 3.5. Lower-tier regions: A. northern Scotland B. southern Scotland and northern England and Wales; C Southern England and Wales

than as more self-contained towns: East Kilbride, Cumbernauld and Livingston all fail to carve out coherent functional regions and become merely parts of Glasgow and Edinburgh rings, whereas Irvine and Glenrothes both become joint centres of FRs with the older urban areas nearby (Ardrossan/Stevenston and Kirkcaldy respectively). Apart from Newtown in mid-Wales (part of an RA), all the new towns in England and Wales are (joint) cores of functional regions except for Skelmersdale (outer area of Wigan FR), Hatfield and Washington (in the rings of Welwyn and Newcastle upon Tyne respectively). A contrasting type of area to the FRs of the new towns are the fairly small FRs clustered around major single employment sources, notably the steel works of Consett and Shotton, though Corby New Town will similarly be a labour market that will attract interest regarding its 1971–81 change in employment levels. As local circumstances vary so much, only data for consistently defined FRs and RAs will make it possible to compare the very diverse urban systems throughout Britain from the large booming oil city of Aberdeen to the small depressed tinmining towns of Cornwall.

Figure 3.6   shows the existing local authority districts in a part of the East Midlands of England contrasted with the lower-tier boundaries of the present regionalization (with RAs shown). In some places district boundaries have united towns with their surrounding countryside (Chisholm, 1975) in the way that was axiomatic to the proposals of the Royal Commissions on Local Government in England (1969) and Scotland (1969). However the inconsistent adherence to this principle (Chisholm, 1976) thwarts many possible comparisons between areas. This is compounded by the excessive respect paid to the historical boundaries; for example Figure 3.6 shows only one county boundary that did not exist prior to 1974 (that of the West Midlands) and only one missing that existed before reorganization (the Leicestershire/Rutland boundary). Moreover, while the pre-1974 local authorities were seemingly far less suitable in scale for urban systems analysis than the current larger areas, they were capable of aggregation to allow more reasonable comparison between units approximating functional regions (for example, Hall 1971). It is therefore important to consider how far existing districts provide a reasonable alternative to functional regions. The 1971 and 1981 census data will be readily available for these areas, but their greatly increased average size means they cannot be aggregated into the same kind of regions as the pre-1974 areas.

From the outset it must be clear that the district boundaries in Figure 3.6 do not constitute a coherent tier of the urban hierarchy. In fact the areas here range from the City of Nottingham to Rutland, areas which cannot possibly be successfully aggregated to form reasonable functional regions. For example, the three districts that surround the City of Derby and include its commuting hinterland also embrace vital parts of other urban systems. Therefore whether South Derbyshire District is allocated to Derby or to Burton-upon-Trent (it includes Swadlincote which is a joint core of the functional region of Burton) the

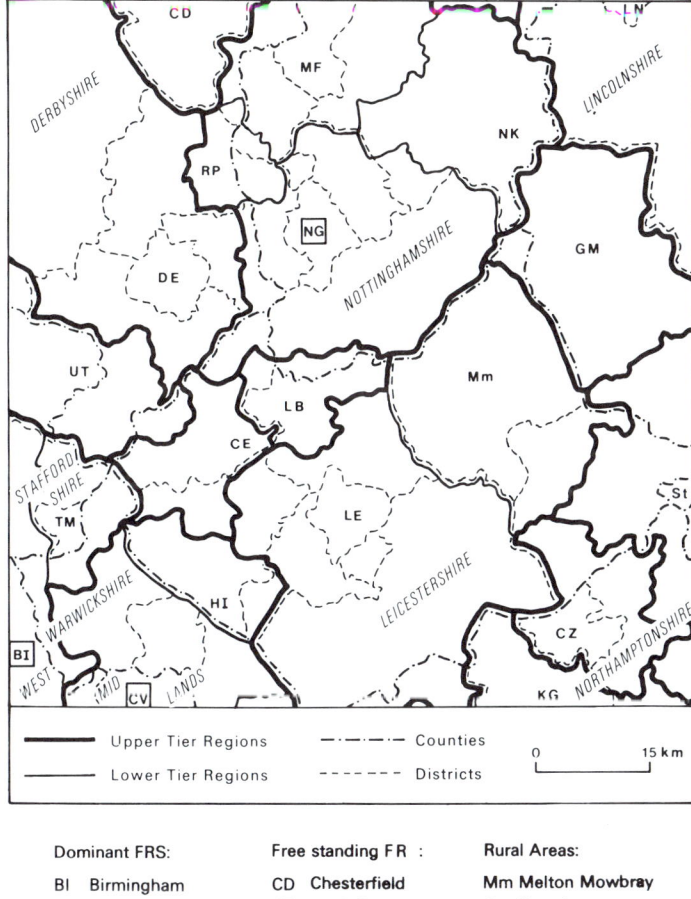

<table>
<tr><td>Dominant FRS:</td><td>Free standing F R :</td><td>Rural Areas:</td></tr>
<tr><td>BI Birmingham</td><td>CD Chesterfield</td><td>Mm Melton Mowbray</td></tr>
<tr><td>CV Coventry</td><td>CE Coalville</td><td>St Stamford</td></tr>
<tr><td>NG Nottingham</td><td>CZ Corby</td><td></td></tr>
<tr><td></td><td>DE Derby</td><td></td></tr>
<tr><td>Subdominant FRS:</td><td>GM Grantham</td><td></td></tr>
<tr><td>HI Hinckley</td><td>KG Kettering</td><td></td></tr>
<tr><td>MF Mansfield</td><td>LB Loughborough</td><td></td></tr>
<tr><td>NK Newark</td><td>LE Leicester</td><td></td></tr>
<tr><td>RP Ripley & Heanor</td><td>LN Lincoln</td><td></td></tr>
<tr><td>TM Tamworth</td><td>UT Burton upon Trent</td><td></td></tr>
</table>

FIGURE 3.6.   Existing local authority districts compared with upper
and lower-tier regions in part of the East Midlands

two urban systems will be non-comparable because the only reasonable
definitions would require a boundary that divides the South Derbyshire district
between them. Another inconsistency can be seen between Tamworth and
Newark, both towns on the periphery of metropolitan regions (Birmingham and
Nottingham respectively). Tamworth district is restricted to the built-up area of

the pre-1972 borough. Newark district extends right across the Nottingham commuting areas and coalmining country, to the very edge of built-up Mansfield. Any comparisons made between these two districts would be bound to be misleading since one area is restricted to the town while the other includes the hinterland (and more).

If we turn to the rural areas we see that not every RA centre is even recognized by the districts despite their larger number and their lower population minimum. The fact that Stamford (an RA centre) is subsumed into South Kesteven District (centred on Grantham) is largely due to the four historical county boundaries which surround Stratford having been considered inviolable. The consequence, of course, is that it is not possible to compare Stamford with neighbouring rural areas such as Melton Mowbray by using data for districts. The converse problem to the non-existence of significant areas can be illustrated by the two tiers of district and county in Nottinghamshire. Ignoring the considerable variations in boundaries, they may superficially appear to be a similar set of areas to the two tiers of Nottingham metropolitan region. However the user of the data for the four functional regions can be assured that each is a meaningful areal unit which stands comparison with each of the other areas at this tier of the regionalization. On the other hand there can be no such confidence about the comparability of such districts as Gedling and Mansfield, since the former is essentially just Nottingham's eastern suburbs whereas the latter is a substantial urban area in its own right. Consequently without the consistent application of objective criteria it is impossible to judge the marginal cases such as Sutton and Kirby-in-Ashfield, which cannot be considered separately to Mansfield, and the Derbyshire towns in the Erewash valley (Long Eaton, Ilkeston, Heanor and Alfreton) which are more closely linked to Nottingham than Derby. In short, the radical differences in the make-up of different districts (Craig, 1977) frustrates meaningful analysis of them.

In sharp contrast to local authorities, the travel-to-work areas (TTWAs) of the Department of Employment are explicitly designed for the presentation of data. Figure 3.7 shows the TTWAs in north-east England and contrasts them with the lower tier of the present regionalization (showing RAs again). The definition of TTWAs derives from Smart (1974), who in turn was attempting to implement the ideas of Goodman (1970). The principal objective is to create regions meeting self-containment thresholds imposed in order to reduce the problem of calculating unemployment percentages from two non-compatible data sources (Howson, 1979). The method of TTWA definition is based on a single criterion applied hierarchically. This criterion has been found to be of limited relevance (Coombes et al., 1980) and any hierarchical application shown to be inherently suboptimal by Openshaw and Gillard (1979). Moreover, any methodology dependent upon a single criterion and threshold greatly increases problems of sensitivity to particular features in the data (Ball, 1980). Despite these important technical issues the objective basis of TTWA definition should still provide a

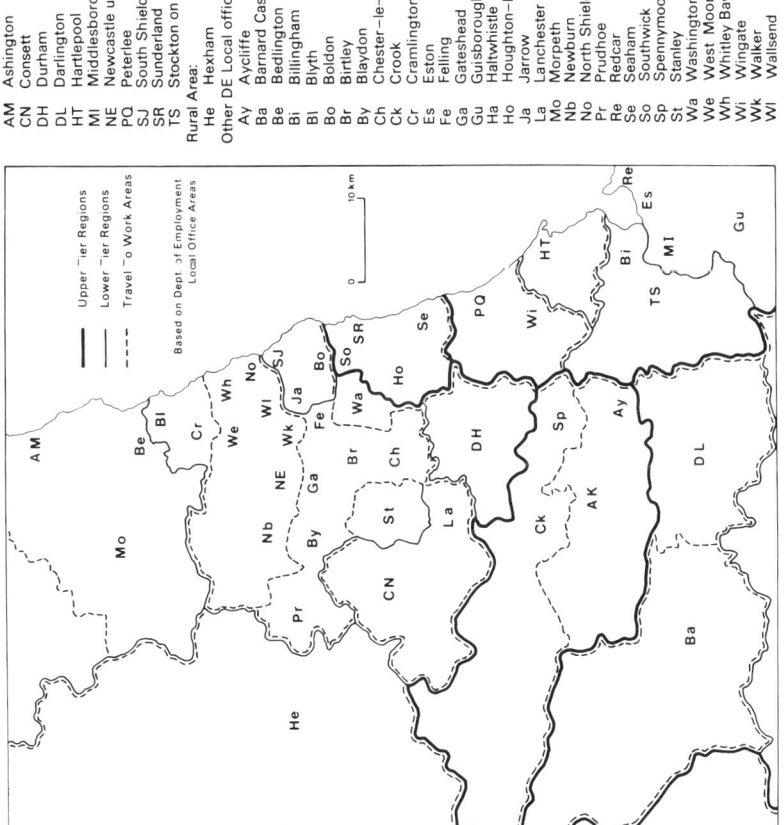

Region Centres:
AK Bishop Auckland
AM Ashington
CN Consett
DH Durham
DL Darlington
HT Hartlepool
MI Middlesborough
NE Newcastle upon Tyne
PQ Peterlee
SJ South Shields
SR Sunderland
TS Stockton on Tees

Rural Area:
He Hexham

Other DE Local offices
Ay Aycliffe
Ba Barnard Castle
Be Bedlington
Bi Billingham
Bl Blyth
Bo Boldon
Br Birtley
By Blaydon
Ch Chester-le-Street
Ck Crook
Cr Cramlington
Es Eston
Fe Felling
Ga Gateshead
Gu Guisborough
Ha Haltwhistle
Ho Houghton-le-Spring
Ja Jarrow
La Lanchester
Mo Morpeth
Nb Newburn
No North Shields
Pr Prudhoe
Re Redcar
Se Seaham
So Southwick
Sp Spennymoor
St Stanley
Wa Washington
We West Moor
Wh Whitley Bay
Wi Wingate
Wk Walker
Wl Wallsend

FIGURE 3.7. North-east England: lower-tier regions and travel to work areas (TTWAs)

Upper Tier Regions
Lower Tier Regions
Travel To Work Areas

Based on Dept of Employment Local Office Areas.

0   10 km

more consistently meaningful set of areas than local authority areas which are the product of far more eclectic considerations.

Unfortunately the output of the TTWA methodology was modified by subjective considerations before the final definitions were constituted in terms of Department of Employment local office (LO) areas. This subsequent step is responsible for serious anomalies that can be identified between existing TTWAs and the product of a computerized replication of the methodology. For example, no grouping based on journey-to-work data is likely to allocate Gateshead and adjacent LO areas to South Shields instead of Newcastle upon Tyne. Less dramatically, the particular criterion used in the TTWA methodology is balanced too strongly against dominant commuting flows so that Cramlington, Washington and Stanley are excluded from Tyneside in favour of Morpeth, Sunderland and Consett respectively. This problem also prevents the TTWAs having a distinct urban perspective; indeed there is no possibility that TTWAs could constitute a consistent tier in the urban hierarchy for there is no explicit minimum size threshold. For example, whereas TTWAs provide an equivalent to the functional region covering the Weardale towns of Crook, Bishop Auckland, Spennymoor and Aycliffe (whose total population exceeds 150 000 and meets the TTWA self-containment threshold of 75/80 per cent) there is a separate TTWA for Barnard Castle's population of less than 30 000. In fact there is an implicit size threshold of a kind because of the distribution of LOs is a major determinant of a large proportion of TTWAs, for example the many very small ones. For example, Hexham RA embraces four potential TTWAs (based on census journey-to-work data, the only available source) but there are only two LOs so the Bellingham district is subsumed by Hexham whilst Haltwhistle (similar in size to Bellingham) not only becomes a TTWA in its own right but it also absorbs the highly self-contained Alston district.

The conclusion here is that TTWAs are not fundamentally superior to Local Authority areas in terms of the criteria set out at the beginning of this section that they should provide a consistent set of meaningful geographical units which portray a tier of the urban hierarchy. The implications of this evaluation are considerable because TTWAs are used for calculating the unemployment levels which determine assisted area status (Townsend, 1980). Consequently the development areas of the Department of Industry are dependent upon TTWA boundaries and inherit their inaccuracies. For example, the absence of a TTWA equivalent to the Bishop Auckland and Aycliffe FR (as mentioned already) results in the South Weardale area being reduced from special development area to intermediate area (*Department of Employment Gazette*, 1979). This is due to the aggregation of Bishop Auckland and Aycliffe with Darlington, a relatively successful medium-size freestanding town. In contrast, the north Weardale towns of Crook and Spennymoor are in Durham TTWA, and as the Durham area is smaller and less successful than Darlington the unemployment percentage for the whole TTWA remains high enough to justify development area status.

Disaggregation of functional regions

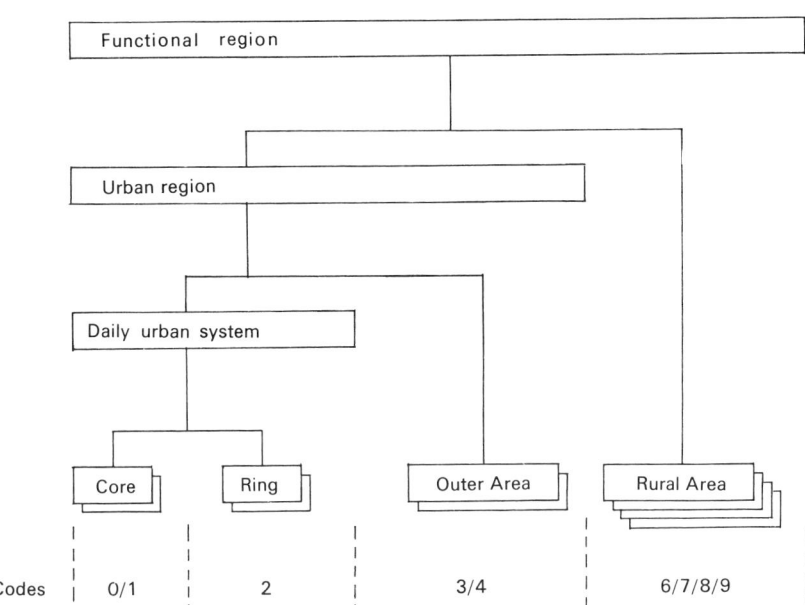

(1) Code number 5 is reserved for the aggregation 'Urban Region' in the system based on DE Local Office Areas
(2) The only component part present in all Functional Regions is a Core (Code 1), additional parts vary between each particular region from none at all (i.e. the Core = the Region) to up to six of the other possible units.

FIGURE 3.8.   Disaggregation of functional regions

This one example illustrates how inconsistency in administrative boundaries can have a potentially critical effect on the level of aid available to the two halves of an arguably homogeneous functional region.

The subdivisions

Figure 3.8 illustrates the system of component parts into which functional regions may be subdivided. These areas will be of particular value for analysis of urbanization within and between functional regions. Separate component areas do not, of course, in themselves constitute meaningful units in the criteria applied to whole functional regions, but they provide an additional facility for studies of, notably, core and ring areas. Once again, other areas for which public statistics are available may in some cases provide similar definitions but of course they do not do so consistently across the country. This can be demonstrated simply by referring back to the discussion of the very different districts for the similar towns Newark and Tamworth, where the lack of an urban perspective in TTWAs compounds their inconsistencies and inability to distinguish between hinterlands and the principal built-up areas they relate to.

In the specification of the functional regions the character of each type of component part could be appreciated from its role in the definitional procedure and its own particular criteria. In addition 'the derivation of each criterion' was given and from this it is evident that the core and ring (which together make up the DUS) follow on from earlier work, notably that which created SMLAs (Drewett, Goddard, and Spence, 1976; Hall et al., 1973). Although the identification of physically built-up cores is very much secondary to our functional region definitions, it may still be of interest to compare our subdivisions with the equivalent SMLA areas which have been used quite widely (see, for example, Champion, 1976; Flowerdew and Salt, 1979; Westaway, 1974).

The first problem in comparing, for example, core definitions of SMLAs and functional regions is that the SMLA cores were the product of a relatively simple criterion. This is illustrated by the fact that the Leeds SMLA core also includes Bradford (Smart, 1979), whereas the possibility of Bradford being part of the core of the Leeds functional region does not arise in our analysis because Bradford is found (on functional criteria) to be separate from Leeds not only at the lower tier but also at the upper as well. The essential conditions for SMLA core status were thresholds of employment total and density, though these were not applied consistently (Coombes et al., 1979b). The SMLA core definitions were also subject to a contiguity constraint, but this too was varied in its application. For example, the three contiguous cores of Guildford, Woking, and Walton and Weybridge were kept separate to produce SMLAs. At the same time, Coventry SMLA core included four towns separated by several miles, a complex version of a joint-centred region for which no definitional rules were specified at all. Our functional criteria indicate that three of these four towns should have individual FRs that are grouped into a metropolitan region (the fourth, Nuneaton, becomes part of the Coventry FR ring). All the other SMLAs with split cores are binodal and in fact they all group towns which are now shown to remain separate even at the upper tier of the CURDS regionalization (with the exception of Milton Keynes New Town).

The FR core definitions are, in part, derived from the analysis of built-up areas by Hall, Hall, and Morgan (1980). This analysis was based on 1971 wards and parishes and had to be adapted not only to fit within the functional region boundaries but also to fit the 1981 wards (and postcode sectors in Scotland) that are the 'building block' areas for the 1981 census FR definitions. The example of Leeds and Bradford is again instructive here; not only does the Hall, Hall, and Morsan (1980) recommended core amalgamate the two cities, it also extends to include large areas that functionally belong with Halifax. The primacy of the functional criteria is rigorously asserted, however, to reject these recommendations which are based only on contiguity of physically urbanized areas (Hall et al., 1979). However within functional region boundaries these same recommendations form the appropriate guidelines for core definitions so that, for example, the London FR core includes all Greater London plus adjoining suburbs—unlike the London SMLA core which excludes eight London boroughs so that is represents no meaningful entity at all. Similar comparisons could be made between the FR and SMLA cores of all the larger urban systems. The major problem remains the inclusion of areas which constitute meaningful lower-tier regions in their own right, rather than the exclusion of suburbs from the cores of the SMLAs.

The division between the SMLAs and all the remaining areas is not dissimilar to that between the DUS and the outer areas (OAs) and RAs, since both are based upon a 15 per cent threshold of commuting outflow to the core/centre. The principal geographical problem with such a criterion is that those areas which possess greater local urban development tend to be nearer this margin than other hinterland areas, which are more straightforward cases of commuting villages and satellite residential developments. The lower-tier FRs recognize the existence of such semiautonomous urban systems as Hertford and Tamworth (as shown above) and designate the cores of subdominant regions in London and Birmingham MRs respectively. In contrast the SMLA definitions consider these to be in the outer rings of 'million city' metropolitan economic labour areas (Kennett and Spence, 1979), a conclusion that suggests these towns are somehow less urbanized than neighbouring Hoddesdon and Lichfield which in reality are only in the (inner) rings because they possess fewer indigenous employment opportunities. To some extend this difficulty remains in our methodology, as with Skelmersdale New Town which becomes an outer area of Wigan because it fails to sustain a separate FR, but the recognition of all major candidates for centre status and the creation of the upper tier greatly ameliorates the problem. Moreover the outer areas of FRs tend to be far more compact than the outer rings of SMLAs and data for non-contiguous areas will be kept separate. Consequently most OAs will be identifiably small proto-FRs (such as Skelmersdale) which are therefore interesting entities in themselves, unlike SMLA outer rings which lumped together diverse places such as Hertford, Bracknell New Town and Bognor Regis in a single data unit.

One of the most dramatic differences between the SMLA and our regionalizations remains the treatment of the more peripheral areas. In the former these remain as unclassified parts of Britain 'beyond' both SMLAs and outer rings, and there are no equivalents of the rural areas. In fact all these residual areas are, if they are considered at all, aggregated into a single data unit which thereby includes 30 or so separate districts. Among these are the cores of ten FRs, ranging from Inverness to St Austell, and from Bury St Edmunds to Llandudno and Colwyn Bay. It is probably unnecessary to make any further comments on a set of areas which classfies Scarborough as non-urban on the same basis as the Isle of Skye. An attempt to improve on SMLAs in this respect in particular was made by Hall and Hay (1978). Here the whole of Britain was allocated to individual urban regions and non-urban regions in what appears to be a direct parallel to our FRs and RAs. Two crucial differences between the two approaches should, however, be emphasized. The non-urban regions are not part of a hierarchical structure so no flexibility is offered to the user who is really interested in a set of areas that cover the whole country but which each possess a substantial urban centre, a common requirement in studies of marketing and service provision. Secondly, whereas RAs are defined by exactly the same procedure as FRs and so can meaningfully compare with them for purposes not requiring each area to have a DUS, the non-urban regions are the product of completely different criteria to the urban regions of the same exercise (Hay and Hall, 1978). This critical disadvantage for the user also serves to explain the nature of the areas that result, varying as they do from 'direct descendants' of SMLAs (which have inherited problems such as the Leeds/Bradford amalgamation and the failure to recognize Tamworth, Hertford and other such important subdominant towns) to dramatically different non-urban regions (two adjacent units in the south-west of England having 1971 populations of 2430 and 211 185).

Summary

The conclusion to be drawn from this evaluation of our results is that the regionalization provides a very flexible set of areas so that census data can be made available for meaningful units for a wide variety of purposes. Unlike local authority areas, for which census data are generally made available, and special purpose areas such as TTWAs and SMLAs, functional regions have been defined consistently and constitute a geographically reasonable description of the urban hierarchy of Britain.

THE AVAILABILITY OF DATA FOR FUNCTIONAL REGIONS

The primary aim of the regionalization that has been described has been to produce a set of areas for which statistics for the 1981 census can readily be made available. In order to meet this objective the functional regions have been defined in terms of 1981 wards in England and Wales and postcode sectors in Scotland. These are the smallest units for which both residence-based population and workplace-based employment statistics will be made available in computer readable form (population data only are provided for enumeration districts). Migration and journey-to-work data are also being coded to this level of aggregation. Although the figures will not be published, users will be able to request any set of census data for the 1981 functional regions from the Office of Population Censuses and Surveys. Alternatively, users could produce their own functional regional tabulation using the functional region codes which will appear on the SAS statistics.

The most obvious disadvantage of the recommended areas is that they are defined using 1971 data. For the purposes of an analysis of change over the intercensal period, areas could be defined on the basis of either the starting or terminal date. Unfortunately it will not be possible to define 'better' 1981 functional regions until small area employment and journey-to-work data become available from the census, and this is unlikely to be before 1984. Clearly a comparison of the results that arise from applying the same definitional criteria to 1971 and 1981 will in itself reveal a great deal about patterns of urban change over the 1970s. In the meantime the availability of the functional region codes on the base units for the 1981 census will permit rapid analysis as each data set becomes available.

The success of the definitions presented here will ultimately be determined by the degree of use made of the areas by researchers and policy-makers. Much emphasis has been laid on the appropriateness of the areas for a wide range of purposes. Practical applications include decision-making on retail and industrial location where it is necessary to calculate the population and labour supply within the hinterlands of particular centres. However the widespread use of the areas for manpower planning purposes will depend upon the availability of employment and unemployment information from the Department of Employment as well as census-based demographic data. In this respect recent suggestions concerning the collection of unemployment statistics indicate that it should be feasible to produce this information for functional regions; as from 1982 it is proposed that all unemployment statistics will be derived not from manual counts at local unemployment offices where the unemployed have in the past been required to register but from the postcode of the place of residence to which employment benefits are addressed. It will be possible to match these postcode areas to functional regions. Workplaces covered by the Census of Employment are similarly being given postcode addresses.

While the details of these developments may appear mundane they provide the basis for integrated accounts of all of the aspects of the local labour market—labour supply and demand and the matching and mismatching process as reflected in the journey-to-work and unemployment. And given the continuing importance of cities as organising foci within the labour market it is appropriate that such accounts should be drawn up for functional regions.

APPENDIX

1971 Population and Areas (Hectares) of Metropolitan Regions, Functional Regions and Rural Areas

The provisional results here are the nearest 1971 equivalents of the 1981 wards (England and Wales) and postcode sectors (Scotland) used for the coding of the 1981 census. The translation of the computerized algorithm's results—whose base units were 1971 local authority areas—into 1981 wards/sectors has necessitated slight adjustments to the boundaries. For example, some of the smallest regions have 'lost' one or two parishes so their 1971 populations for the equivalent 1981 areas have fallen below the 50 000 minimum. There are considerable variations between these sets of results and the 'best fit' to Department of Employment local office areas shown in all the figures (except Figure 3.6). Consequently, the figures below form only an approximate guideline to the populations and areas of the mapped regions; indeed a few rural areas do not appear in both census and local office based systems (due to the peculiarities of the local office areas). The figures are presented in two parts: firstly the metropolitan regions with their associated lower-tier dominant and sub-dominant functional regions (and rural areas, given both as part of their associated functional region and separately in parenthesis); secondly the freestanding functional regions, with rural areas shown separately from the urban region which forms the remainder of that functional region. The first column shows the 1981 census code for each area, as shown in Figure 3.5.

Metropolitan regions (in descending order of population size)

		1971 Population	Hectares
i LONDON MR		12 813 938	1 424 013
iLO	London DFR	8 586 744	335 763
iSS	Southend SFR	305 913	25 471
iRG	Reading SFR	295 896	57 690
iFA	Aldershot and Farnborough SFR	274 948	58 637
iHW	High Wycombe SFR	243 219	54 639
iME	Medway Towns SFR	226 021	19 381
iGU	Guildford SFR	209 171	103 216
iSL	Slough SFR	198 870	20 910
iCM	Chelmsford SFR	188 401	77 358
iWD	Watford SFR	182 860	12 461
iTN	Tunbridge Wells SFR	180 582	76 315
iMA	Maidstone SFR	175 527	57 920
iWW	Woking and Weybridge SFR	165 219	20 427
iTB	Basildon SFR	141 305	17 749
iAL	St Albans SFR	120 957	16 126
iGV	Gravesend SFR	108 590	11 843
iBG	Basingstoke SFR	107 412	67 550
iHP	Hemel Hempstead SFR	107 328	16 050
iSI	Sittingbourne and Milton SFR	100 897	36 914
iHL	Harlow SFR	96 027	15 712
iRH	Reigate and Redhill SFR	89 158	23 824
iMD	Maidenhead SFR	84 127	19 333
iCY	Crawley SFR	76 373	7 538
iWE	Welwyn SFR	75 641	9 491
iHH	Haywards Heath SFR	73 989	27 376
iSD	Bishops Stortford SFR	71 729	64 313
iBC	Braintree and Bocking SFR	68 476	42 253
iHF	Hertford & Ware SFR	65 633	34 599

(Contd.)

Metropolitan regions (in descending order of population size)   (Contd.)

		1971 Population	Hectares
iNB	Newbury SFR	65 163	49 285
iBK	Bracknell SFR	64 596	11 664
iHO	Horsham SFR	63 166	35 205
m MANCHESTER MR		3 066 994	280 129
mMC	Manchester DFR	1 313 276	58 976
mBL	Bolton SFR	262 533	19 369
mSK	Stockport SFR	246 227	12 556
mOL	Oldham SFR	223 970	14 112
mAH	Ashton and Hyde SFR	212 440	21 882
mWA	Warrington SFR	186 486	22 113
mRO	Rochdale SFR	144 172	15 155
mBU	Bury SFR	135 652	10 453
mLG	Leigh SFR	119 010	8 443
mNH	Northwich SFR	102 409	32 523
mMQ	Macclesfield SFR	68 429	30 671
mBX	Buxton SFR	52 390	33 876
b BIRMINGHAM MR		3 015 547	325 439
bBI	Birmingham DFR	1 498 557	103 751
bWV	Wolverhampton SFR	421 932	47 148
bWS	Walsall SFR	279 332	12 758
bDY	Dudley SFR	231 605	19 095
bWU	Smethwick SFR	217 547	5 956
bWB	West Bromwich SFR	136 321	3 887
bRD	Redditch SFR	104 784	57 311
bRD6	(Evesham RA)	(46 403)	(40 261)
bTM	Tamworth SFR	68 882	18 065
bAV	Stratford-on-Avon SFR	54 587	57 468
l LIVERPOOL MR		2 371 539	232 245
lLV	Liverpool DFR	1 111 289	62 412
lWL	Birkenhead and Wallasey SFR	370 497	18 234
lWN	Wigan SFR	218 620	17 364
lHE	St Helens SFR	159 800	12 665
lCH	Chester SFR	113 607	37 200
lWI	Widnes and Runcorn SFR	112 801	14 611
lFL	Shotton SFR	111 724	39 317
lSV	Southport SFR	101 019	17 180
lEP	Ellesmere Port SFR	72 182	13 262
g GLASGOW MR		2 072 485	406 218
gGG	Glasgow DFR	1 376 081	124 427
gML	Motherwell and Hamilton SFR	328 186	188 635
gML6	(Lanark RA)	(41 180)	(132 170)
gPA	Paisley SFR	169 925	28 735
gAI	Coatbridge and Airdrie SFR	119 305	16 717
gDB	Dunbarton SFR	78 988	47 704

(Contd.)

Metropolitan regions (in descending order of population size)   (*Contd.*)

		1971 Population	Hectares
n NEWCASTLE upon TYNE MR		1 425 602	525 718
nNE	Newcastle upon Tyne DFR	989 728	310 205
nNE6	(Hexham RA)	(36 567)	(217 373)
nSJ	South Shields SFR	177 083	6 538
nAM	Ashington SFR	126 096	156 508
nDH	Durham SFR	81 638	18 970
nCN	Consett SFR	51 057	33 677
y LEEDS MR		1 233 994	133 095
yLS	Leeds DFR	762 893	76 325
yWF	Wakefield SFR	199 945	25 158
yDW	Dewsbury SFR	160 277	9 519
yPF	Castleford and Pontefract SFR	110 879	22 093
s SHEFFIELD MR		1 129 005	133 824
sSH	Sheffield DFR	670 569	80 061
sBZ	Barnsley SFR	200 550	31 308
sRT	Rotherham SFR	167 925	15 642
sMX	Mexborough SFR	89 961	6 813
f NOTTINGHAM MR		1 075 513	174 378
f NG	Nottingham DFR	679 225	76 644
f MF	Mansfield SFR	228 515	39 748
f RP	Heanor and Ripley SFR	107 274	13 670
f NK	Newark SFR	60 499	44 316
z BRISTOL MR		1 020 936	237 563
zBS	Bristol DFR	736 461	115 420
zBA	Bath SFR	199 503	92 568
zBA6	(Wells RA)	(51 478)	(51 371)
zWM	Weston-super-Mare SFR	84 972	29 575
e EDINBURGH MR		872 255	706 427
eEH	Edinburgh DFR	806 727	684 631
eEH6	(Berwick upon Tweed RA)	(54 806)	(256 586)
eEH7	(Hawick and Galashiels RA)	(58 541)	(191 831)
eBV	Bathgate SFR	65 528	21 796
c CARDIFF MR		831 973	128 396
cCF	Cardiff DFR	444 997	48 788
cPP	Pontypridd SFR	275 839	41 259
cGE	Gelligaer SFR	75 858	12 379
cBJ	Bridgend SFR	75 299	25 970
t TEESIDE MR		755 340	313 634
tMI	Middlesbrough DFR	403 537	263 287
tMI6	(Northallerton RA)	(41 389)	(73 934)
tTS	Stockton on Tees SFR	177 175	29 667
tHT	Hartlepool SFR	99 450	9 430
tPQ	Peterlee SFR	75 178	11 250

(*Contd.*)

Metropolitan regions (in descending order of population size)   (*Contd.*)

		1971 Population	Hectares
v COVENTRY MR		755 109	147 919
vCV	Coventry DFR	511 542	59 420
vLM	Leamington SFR	108 438	47 082
vRU	Rugby SFR	77 527	26 743
vHI	Hinckley SFR	57 602	14 674
x BRIGHTON MR		542 708	77 482
xBN	Brighton DFR	372 992	50 654
xWO	Worthing SFR	169 716	26 728
p PORTSMOUTH MR		531 882	73 586
pPO	Portsmouth DFR	375 363	63 633
pGP	Gosport and Fareham SFR	156 519	9 953
w SWANSEA MR		431 265	104 867
wSA	Swansea DFR	251 107	53 137
wPT	Port Talbot SFR	111 765	23 335
wNT	Neath SFR	68 393	28 395
j NEWPORT MR		352 248	124 048
jNP	Newport DFR	252 525	90 917
jNP6	(Monmouth RA)	(54 828)	(56 808)
jCX	Cwmbran and Pontypool SFR	99 683	33 131
r PRESTON MR		321 944	71 071
rPR	Preston DFR	220 898	51 955
rLC	Leyland and Chorley SFR	101 046	19 116
a BLACKBURN MR		273 724	70 278
aBB	Blackburn DFR	193 805	64 596
aAC	Accrington SFR	79 919	5 682

Freestanding functional regions (in descending order of urban region population size)

		1971 Population	Hectares
LE5	Leicester UR	539 194	111 375
LE6	Melton Mowbray RA	50 022	57 353
ST5	Stoke-on-Trent UR	530 084	107 897
ST6	Leek RA	35 214	37 773
BH	Bournemouth	441 105	150 127
HU5	Hull UR	432 065	119 426
HU6	Bridlington RA	51 122	76 046
HU7	Goole RA	40 256	43 728
SO	Southampton	416 613	88 143

(*Contd.*)

Freestanding functional regions (in descending order of urban region population size) (*Contd.*)

		1971 Population	Hectares
BD	Bradford	373 943	18 612
NR5	Norwich UR	365 943	229 919
NR6	Dereham RA	47 069	80 604
NR7	Thetford RA	54 026	92 581
OX5	Oxford UR	340 841	164 112
OX6	Didcot RA	59 587	29 514
PL5	Plymouth UR	329 753	148 773
PL6	Launceston RA	40 912	133 866
DE5	Derby UR	323 072	97 570
DE6	Matlock RA	37 217	23 881
AB5	Aberdeen UR	308 424	688 750
AB6	Peterhead RA	37 881	74 404
AB7	Banff and Buckie RA	39 754	91 247
SR	Sunderland	300 002	13 352
LU	Luton	293 613	58 152
FY	Blackpool	282 824	15 225
YO	York	264 264	205 297
DD5	Dundee UR	261 337	216 180
DD6	Arbroath RA	59 721	121 331
DN	Doncaster	248 368	56 922
IP5	Ipswich UR	245 491	130 755
IP6	Woodbridge RA	50 917	74 073
SN	Swindon	239 667	164 971
EX5	Exeter UR	224 821	179 281
EX6	Tiverton RA	36 927	53 334
CB5	Cambridge UR	224 216	126 469
CB6	Newmarket RA	88 709	102 892
CB7	Huntingdon RA	57 008	50 637
GR	Grimsby	212 746	120 666
HD	Huddersfield	209 033	31 474
NN	Northampton	206 373	92 252
LN	Lincoln	196 778	197 674
HX	Halifax	195 189	36 379
CO	Colchester	193 892	85 192
SC	Scunthorpe	177 811	130 702
GL	Gloucester	172 860	85 655
CD	Chesterfield	169 684	31 329
PE5	Peterborough UR	161 441	96 914
PE6	Spalding RA	56 867	72 921
PE7	Wisbech RA	40 271	35 436
PE8	Stamford RA	49 212	75 122
WX	Wrexham	157 140	130 182
CJ	Cheltenham	155 475	95 293
AP5	Ayr and Prestwick UR	153 673	171 389
AP6	Stranraer RA	41 714	239 504
KY5	Kirkcaldy and Glenrothes UR	153 070	46 102
KY6	St Andrews RA	35 556	32 593
AK	Bishop Auckland and Aycliffe	150 679	75 864

(Contd.)

Freestanding functional regions (in descending order of urban region population size)
(*Contd.*)

		1971 Population	Hectares
BE	Bedford	150 083	69 638
TQ	Torquay and Paignton	148 642	69 067
FK	Falkirk and Grangemouth	146 168	30 570
HS	Hastings	143 456	54 031
SY5	Shrewsbury UR	138 805	188 058
SY6	Newtown and Welshpool RA	38 849	170 552
SY7	Aberystwyth RA	43 544	192 129
UT	Burton-upon-Trent	138 248	48 300
LH	Letchworth and Hitchin	137 290	57 225
GK5	Greenock UR	134 894	124 923
GK6	Oban RA	58 805	1 013 257
DL5	Darlington UR	132 803	98 443
DL6	Richmond RA	40 495	124 577
CA5	Carlisle UR	132 679	255 312
CA6	Penrith RA	40 029	200 838
WR5	Worcester UR	131 229	88 687
WR6	Malvern RA	43 753	32 606
LA	Lancaster and Morecambe	130 136	80 627
SP	Salisbury	126 343	138 185
EA	Eastbourne	124 508	42 717
TF	Telford	123 863	78 808
DF	Dunfermline and Rosyth	122 344	61 089
HG	Harrogate	117 606	104 920
TH	Margate and Ramsgate	114 801	10 258
BF	Barrow-in-Furness	113 740	81 343
TJ	Trowbridge	113 107	79 027
CW	Crewe	112 092	48 585
YE5	Yeovil UR	110 305	108 212
YE6	Chard RA	55 818	57 127
CT	Canterbury	110 130	31 057
TA	Taunton	109 695	113 395
IR	Irvine and Ardrossan	109 520	79 172
IW	Isle of Wight	109 512	38 098
KE	Keighley	109 387	105 116
WY	Weymouth	107 525	84 124
CI	Chichester and Bognor Regis	106 795	35 685
WK	Worksop	104 393	104 393
HR	Hereford	103 828	158 631
MK	Milton Keynes	103 460	86 748
EB	Ebbw Vale	100 978	48 479
KL	King's Lynn	99 770	127 807
AU5	St Austell UR	99 111	82 194
AU6	Truro RA	42 030	41 260
AU7	Falmouth RA	58 969	40 104
AU8	Redruth and Camborne RA	45 538	14 219
AU9	Penzance RA	52 061	29 057
KD	Kidderminster	97 290	45 814
DG	Dumfries	97 260	365 526

(Contd.)

Freestanding functional regions (in descending order of urban region population size) (*Contd.*)

		1971 Population	Hectares
PH	Perth	96 495	438 467
BY	Burnley	94 673	10 310
WG	Wellingborough	92 844	24 303
AY	Aylesbury	92 772	45 661
LL5	Llandudno and Colwyn Bay UR	87 632	81 986
LL6	Ffestiniog RA	49 335	167 966
LL7	Bangor and Caernarvon RA	66 401	57 999
LL8	Holyhead RA	47 225	59 030
NL	Nelson and Colne	85 416	16 821
BO	Boston	83 592	90 857
RY	Rhyl and Prestatyn	83 185	87 808
FO	Folkestone	82 016	35 683
KA	Kilmarnock	81 005	37 337
SF	Stafford	79 336	38 247
AS	Ashford	79 083	58 055
LI5	Llanelli UR	76 738	23 348
LI6	Carmarthan RA	40 770	84 132
LI7	Ceredigan RA	39 725	128 876
LI8	Pembroke RA	91 296	126 905
LI9	Annanford RA	41 205	98 763
SG	Stevenage	75 655	44 371
YA	Great Yarmouth	75 575	17 349
NA	Newton Abbot	74 656	44 371
SB	Scarborough	74 409	42 896
BW	Bridgewater	73 521	49 713
WQ	Workington	73 113	69 982
KG	Kettering	72 378	32 922
BP5	Barnstaple UR	70 496	108 616
BP6	Bideford RA	36 100	58 980
LW	Lowestoft	68 592	16 597
BM	Banbury	66 580	50 169
SZ	Stirling	66 492	93 766
LB	Loughborough	65 327	16 064
WT	Winchester	63 806	46 823
SU	Stroud	63 349	32 019
MT5	Merthyr Tydfil UR	63 203	11 163
MT6	Brecon RA	63 077	41 260
WH	Whitehaven	61 569	53 697
CZ	Corby	60 876	28 638
ED	Bury St Edmunds	59 822	61 210
CL	Clacton	59 749	14 374
KN	Kendal	59 038	101 309
CP	Chippenham	58 834	35 817
AN	Andover	56 599	44 686
CE	Coalville	55 186	26 405
IV5	Inverness UR	52 204	289 496
IV6	Hebrides RA	42 543	697 824

(*Contd.*)

Freestanding functional regions (in descending order of urban region population size) (*Contd.*)

		1971 Population	Hectares
IV7	Dingwall and Invergordon RA	39 347	656 422
IV8	Caithness and Orkney RA	37 147	444 945
IV9	Elgin and Nairn RA	43 872	305 688
RA	Rossendale	51 474	9 650
GM	Grantham	50 996	51 962
AO	Alloa	49 872	22 092
DV	Dover	49 594	11 943
DS	Deal	49 444	19 233

NOTE

1. A 'zone' here is a 1971 local authority area (or part thereof) which forms a base unit of this analysis of 1971 census data. This choice is dictated by data availability considerations.

REFERENCES

Ball, R. M. (1980). The use and definition of travel-to-work areas in Great Britain: some problems. *Regional Studies*, **14**, 125–139.

Benjamin, B. (1970). The population census. In *SSRC Review of Current Research 7*. Heinemañ, London.

Berry, B. J. L. (1964a). Approaches to regional analysis: a synthesis. *Annals of the Association of American Geographers*, **54**, 2–11.

Berry, B. J. L. (1964b). Cities as systems within systems of cities. *Proceedings of Regional Science Association*, **13**, 147–163.

Berry, B. J. L. (1967). Functional economic areas and consolidated urban regions of the US. *Final Report of the Social Sciences Research Council Study of Metropolitan Area Classification*, Social Sciences Research Council, New York.

Berry, B. J. L. (1973). *Growth Centres in the American Urban System*, Ballinger, Cambridge, Mass.

Berry, B. J. L, Goheen, P. G. and Goldstein, H. (1969). *Metropolitan Area Definition: A Re-evaluation of Concept and Statistical Practice*, WP, US Bureau of the Census, Washington, DC.

Berry, B. J. L. and Horton, F. E. (1970). *Geographical Perspectives on Urban Systems*, Prentice-Hall, Englewood Cliffs, NJ.

Bogue, D. J. (1949). *The Structure of the Metropolitan Community*, School of Graduate Studies, University of Michigan, Ann Arbor.

Broadbent, T. A. (1977). *Planning and Profit in the Urban Economy*, Methuen, London.

Brown, L. A. and Holmes, J. (1971). The delimitation of functional regions, nodal regions and hierarchies by functional distance approaches. *Journal of Regional Science*, **11**, 57–72.

Castells, M. (1977). *The Urban Question*, Edward Arnold, London.

Cattell, R. B. (1966). The data box: its ordering of total resources in terms of possible relational systems. In R. E. Cattell (Ed.), *Handbook of Multivariate Experimental Psychology*, Rand McNally, Chicago, Ill., pp. 67–128.

Champion, A. G. (1976). Evolving patterns of population distribution in England and Wales. *Transactions of the Institute of British Geographers*, NS (1), 401–420.

Chapman, G. P. (1977). *Human and Environmental Systems: A Geographer's Appraisal*, Academic Press, New York.

Chisholm, M. (1975). The reformation of local government in England. In R. Peel, M. Chisholn and P. Haggett (Eds.), *Processes in Physical and Human Geography*, Heinemann, London.

Chisholm, M. (1976). Academics and government. In J. T. Coppock and W. K. D. Sewell (Eds.), *Spatial Dimensions of Public Policy*, Pergamon Press, Oxford.

Clark, W. A. V. and Avery, K. L. (1976). The effects of data aggregation in statistical analysis. *Geographical Analysis*, **8**, 428–438.

Coombes, M. G., Dixon, J. S., Goddard, J. B., Openshaw, S. and Taylor, P. J. (1978). Towards a more rational consideration of census areal units: daily urban systems in Britain. *Environment and Planning, A*, **10**, 1179–1185.

Coombes, M. G., Dixon, J. S., Goddard, J. B., Openshaw, S., taylor, P. J. (1979a). The standard metropolitan labour area concept revisited. In M. J. Breheny (Ed.), *London Papers in Regional Science 10*, Pion, London, pp. 140–162.

Coombes, M. G., Dixon, J. S., Goddard, J. B., Openshaw, S., Taylor, P. J. (1979b). Daily urban systems in Britain: from theory to practice. *Environment and Planning, A*, **11**, 565–574.

Coombes, M. G., Dixon, J. S., Goddard, J. B., Openshaw, S., Taylor, P. J. (1980). *Functional Regions for the 1981 Census of Britain: A User's Guide to the CURDS Definitions*. DP 30. Centre for Urban and Regional Development Studies, University of Newcastle-upon-Tyne.

Craig, J. (1977). Urban and rural local authorities. *Population Trends*, **8**, 8–10.

Craig, J. (1980). Comparing counties. *Population Trends*, **19**, 22–28.

Davis, K. (Ed.). (1959). *The World's Metropolitan Areas*. University of California Press, Berkeley, Cal.

Dawson, A. H. (1979). Regions and Scotland. In *The Scottish Regions So Far*. Edinburgh University Geographical Society.

Department of Employment Gazette (1979). *Regional Industrial Policy*. HMSO, London, pp. 883–889.

Dewdney, J. C. (1981). *The British Census*. Concepts and Techniques in Modern Geography 26, Geo Abstracts, Norwich.

Dixon, J. S., and Openshaw, S. (1979). *FORTRAN subroutines for the functional regionalisation of large sparse interaction matrices*. DP 24, Centre for Urban and Regional Development Studies, University of Newcastle Upon Tyne.

Drewett, J., Goddard, J. B., and Spence, N. A. (1975). What's Happening to British Cities. *Town and Country Planning*, **43**, 523–530.

Drewett, J., Goddard, J. B. and Spence, N. A. (1976). *British Cities: Urban Population and Employment Trends 1951–1971*. Research Report 10, Department of the Environment, London.

Ellman, P. (1968). The socio-geographic enquiry. In *Research Studies 1*, by the Greater London Group, London School of Economics, London, for the Royal Commission on Local Government in England. HMSO, London, pp. 411–509.

Filkin, C. and Weir, D. (1972). Locality. In E. Gittus (Ed.), *Key Variables in Social Research*, Heinemann, London, pp. 106–129.

Flowerdew, R. and Salt, J. (1979). Migration between labour market areas in Great Britain, 1970–1971. *Regional Studies*, **13**, 211–231.

Gehlke, C. E., and Biehl, K. (1934). Certain effects of grouping upon the size of the correlation coefficient in census tract material. *Journal of the American Statistical Association*, **Supplement 29**, 169–170.

Goddard, J. B. (1974). The national system of cities as a framework for urban and regional policy. In M. Sant (Ed.), *Regional Policy and Planning for Europe*, Saxon House, Teakfield, Farnborough, Hants, pp. 101–127.

Goodman, J. F. B. (1970). The definition and analysis of local labour markets: some empirical methods. *British Journal of Industrial Relations*, **8**, 179–196.

Hagerstrand, T. (1970). What about people in regional science?. *Papers of the Regional Science Association*, **24**, 7–21.

Hagerstrand, T. (1974). The impact of transport on the quality of life. In *Fifth International Symposium on Theory and Practice in Transport Economics*. European Conference of Ministers of Transport, Paris.

Hall, P. (1971). Spatial structure of metropolitan England and Wales. In M. Chisholm and, G. Manners (Eds.), *Spatial Policy Problems of the British Economy*, Cambridge University Press, London, 96–125.

Hall, P., Hall, M. and Morgan, C. (1980). *Definition and Measurement of Urban Areas: an interim Report on Great Britain to the Commission of the European Communities*. Department of Geography, University of Reading.

Hall, P, and Hay, D. (1978). *Growth Centres in the European Urban System*. Department of Geography, University of Reading.

Hill, P., Hay, D., Sammons, R. and Liddell, J. (1979). *Definition and Measurement of Urban Areas: Report to the Commission of the European Communities*. Department of Geography, University of Reading.

Hall, P., Thomas, R., Gracey, H. and Drewett, J. (1973). *The Containment of Urban England*. Allen and Unwin, London.

Hay, D. and Hall, P. (1978). *Urban Regionalisation of Great Britain 1971*. Department of Geography, University of Reading, European Urban Systems WP 1.

Honey, R. (1977). Efficiency with humanity—geographical issues in Scotland's local government reform. *Scottish Geographical Magazine*, **93**, 109–120.

Howson, H. (1979). Travel-to-work areas. *Statistical News*, **46**, 6–10.

Johnson, J. H., Salt, J. and Wood, P. A. (1974). *Housing and the Migration of Labour in England and Wales*. Saxon House, Teakfield, Farnborough, Hants.

Keeble, D. (1977). Spatial policy in Britain, regional or urban. *Area*, **9**, 3–8.

Kennett, S. and Spence, N. A. (1979). British population trends in the 1970s. *Town and Country Planning*, **48**, 7, 221–223.

Langton, J. (1972). Potentialities and problems of adotping a systems approach to the study of change in human geography. *Progress in Human Geography*, **4**, 125–180.

Masser, I. and Brown, P. J. B. (1975). Hierarchical aggregation procedures for interaction data. *Environment and Planning*, A, **7**, 509–523.

Neprash, J. A. (1934). Some problems in the correlation of spatially distributed variables. *Journal of the American Statistical Association*, **Supplement 29**, 167–168.

Openshaw, S. (1974). A regionalisation program for large data sets. *Computer Applications*, **3/4**, 136–160.

Openshaw, S. (1977). A geographical solution to scale and aggregation problems in region-building, partitioning and spatial modelling. *Transactions of the Institute of British Geographers*, **NS 2**, 459–472.

Openshaw, S. (1978). An optimal zoning approach to the study of spatially aggregated data. In I Masser and P. J. B. Brown (Eds.), *Spatial representation and spatial interaction*, Martinus Nijhoff Social Sciences Division, Leiden/Boston, pp. 95–113.

Openshaw, S. and Gillard, A, A. (1979). On the stability of a spatial classification of census enumeration data. In P. W. J. Batey (Ed.), *London Papers in Regional Science 9*, Pion, London, pp. 178–202.

Openshaw, S. and Taylor, P. J. (1979). A million or so correlation coefficients: three experiments on the modifiable areal unit problem. In N. Wrigley (Ed.), *Statistical*

Applications in the Spatial Sciences, Pion, London, pp. 127–144.

Pred, A. (1977). *City Systems in Advanced Economics*, Hutchinson, London.

Rhodes, G. (1970). *The Government of London: The Struggle for Reform*, Weidenfeld and Nicolson, London.

Royal Commission on Local Government in England. (1969). *Report*, HMSO, London. Cmnd 4040.

Royal Commission on Local Government in Scotland. (1969). Report, HMSO, London. Cmnd 4150.

Self, P. (1961). *Cities in Flood*, Faber and Faber, London.

Slater, P. B. (1976). A hierarchical regionalisation of Japanese prefectures using 1972 interprefectual migration flows. *Regional Studies*, **10**, 123–132.

Smart, M. W. (1974). Labour market areas: uses and definition. *Progress in Planning*, **2(4)**, 239–353.

Smart, M. W. (1979). The standard metropolitan labour area concept revisited: comment. In M. J. Breheny (Ed.), *London Papers in regional Science 10*, Pion, London, pp. 160–162.

Stacey, M. (1969). The myth of community studies. *British Journal of Sociology*, 20, 134–147.

Thrift, N. (1977). An introduction to time-geography. concepts and techniques. *Modern Geography* 13, Geo-Abstracts Ltd, Norwich.

Townsend, A. R. (1980). Unemployment and the new government's 'regional' aid. *Area*, **12–1**, 9–18.

US Bureau of the Budget. (1967). *Standard Metropolitan Statistical Areas*, US Government Printing Office, Washington, DC.

Van der Knaap, G. and Sleegers, W. F. (1980). *De structuur van migratiestromen in Nederland: een indeling in Stadsgewesten en Stedelijke systemen*, Deelrapport 1, Economisch Geografisch Instituut, Erasmus Universiteit, Rotterdam.

Wells, H. G. (1903). A paper on administrative areas read before the Fabian Society. In E. G. Wells *Mankind in the Making*, Chapman and Hall, London.

Westaway, J. (1974). Contact potential and the occupational structure of the British urban system 1961–6: an empirical study. *Regional Studies*, **8**, 57–73.

Williams, I. N. (1976). Optimistic theory validation from spatially grouped regression: theoretical aspects. *Transactions of the Martin centre*, **1**, 113–145.

Williams, I. N. (1977). Some implications of the use of spatially grouped data. In R. J. Bennett, N. J. Thrift and R. L. Martin (Eds.), *Dynamic Models for Urban and Regional Systems*, Pion, London, pp. 53–64.

Yule, G. U. and Kendall, M. G. (1950). *Introduction to the Theory of Statistics*. Griffin.

Geography and the Urban Environment
Progress in Research and Applications, Volume V
Edited by D. T. Herbert and R. J. Johnston
© 1982 John Wiley & Sons Ltd.

Chapter 4

Constituency Building, Political Representation and Electoral Bias in Urban England

R. J. Johnston and D. J. Rossiter

The British House of Commons has always been dominated by members elected to represent spatially defined constituencies. Since the 1950 general election, each member has been the sole representative of his constituents, so that the current (1981) membership of 635 means that the United Kingdom is divided into 635 separate electoral units. The process of defining constituencies, and the electoral consequences that follow from it, are the focus of this chapter.

ELECTORAL BIAS AND THE PLURALITY SYSTEM

The electoral system used in Britain and a number of other countries (notably Canada, India, New Zealand, South Africa, and the United States) is termed the plurality system. At an election, the victor in each constituency is the candidate with a plurality (that is, the largest number) of votes. This plurality may be well short of the majority of the votes cast; as Loosemore and Hanby (1971) have shown, the minimum plurality in any contest is

$$MP = (V/N) + 1 \tag{1}$$

where V is the number of votes cast, N is the number of candidates, and MP is the minimum plurality. Thus a constituency with 100 voters contested by four candidates could be won with only 26 votes (two of the others would get 25 votes, and the third 24); with six candidates it could be won with only 18 votes. As a consequence, an elected Parliament need not represent a majority of the voters.

British parliamentary elections (like those in the other countries mentioned above) are contested by political parties. In recent decades two of these parties, and in the last decade three, have nominated candidates for virtually every seat. Thus it is possible to compare the percentage of the votes that a party obtains with the percentage of the parliamentary seats that it wins. To many observers, any difference between these two percentages constitutes electoral bias: a party getting a lower percentage of seats than votes is discriminated against by the electoral system, whereas one getting more seats than votes is unfairly favoured (Gudgin and Taylor, 1979).

Many attempts have been made to account for this bias. Several British commentators have paid considerable attention to an empirical regularity known as the cube-law (Kendall and Stuart, 1950). According to this, in an election contested by two parties only,

$$S_A/S_B = (V_A/V_B)^3 \qquad (2)$$

where S_A is the percentage of the seats won by party A, V_A is the percentage of the votes won by the party A, and S_B and V_B refer to the similar quantities for party B ($S_B = 100 - S_A$ and $V_B = 100 - V_A$). Thus, for example, if party A won 55 per cent of the votes according to this 'law' it would obtain 65 per cent of the seats.

As a generalization of the pattern of British election results, during the present century the cube-law is a reasonable representation, although recent arguments suggest that the power to which (V_A/V_B) should be raised is now closer to 2.5 (Laakso, 1979) and analyses of other elections using the plurality system show considerable deviation from the cubic relationship (Tufte, 1973). What is of interest here is why such electoral bias should result at all.

Electoral systems are open to considerable manipulation by those who wish to influence the results of a poll: the plurality system is probably more open to such manipulation than is any other (Taagepera and Laakso, 1980). There are two major forms of manipulation (Taylor and Johnston, 1979): both rely on the supporters of the contestant parties congregating (although not exclusively so) in separate areas. The first is *malapportionment*. The party manipulating the definition of constituencies arranges it so that in the areas in which it has a majority among the voters there is a relatively large number of small con- stituencies (small refers to the number of voters, not to area), whereas in the areas in which its opponent dominates there is a relatively small number of large constituencies. The other practice is *gerrymandering*, which may involve one of three strategies. The first is so to define constituency boundaries that one's opponent wins a small number of constituencies with very large majorities, whereas one's own party wins a larger number with smaller majorities; thus—using what is known as the *packed gerrymander*—the opposition 'wastes' votes through its larger majorities. The second is to define the constituency boundaries so that one's party wins nearly all of them by about the same ratio of votes as it obtains in the system as a whole; this is the *cracked gerrymander*. Finally, constituencies with unusual shapes can be devised (the *stacked gerrymander*) to group pockets of voters of a certain persuasion into con- stituencies which their party will win. Of the two main types, cracked ger- rymanders are more dangerous to the partisan cartographers than are packed gerrymanders, as a relatively small swing in votes can produce a major change in the allocation of seats.

Gerrymandering can be practised with or without malapportionment: both have long been features of the American political scene where the boundaries for constituencies (including those for the Federal House of Representatives) are drawn by the parties in power in each state. What is more important for the present discussion is that results consistent with those that would be produced by gerrymandering occur in electoral systems where there is no partisan manipulation, because the drawing of constituency boundaries is undertaken by a neutral body. This is the case in Britain. In addition, each of those 'unintentional gerrymanders' is likely to be either 'packed' or 'cracked'; 'stacked' gerrymanders are rare because of the implicit shape constraint (see below).

THE BASES FOR ELECTORAL BIAS IN THE ABSENCE OF PARTISAN MANIPULATION

Electoral bias is created in systems where partisan interests play no part in the definition of constituency boundaries because of the interaction between two elements of the geography of such systems; the distribution of the voters of varying persuasions and the rules for creating the lattice of constituencies.

In Britain, more so than in many other countries (Alford, 1963; Rose, 1974), partisan preferences are closely related to class position; in general, the working class tend to vote Labour and the middle class to vote Conservative (Butler and Stokes, 1974). For a variety of social and economic reasons, these class groups are congregated together (Johnston, 1980), at a variety of spatial scales. At the regional scale, for example, there are greater concentrations of working-class, and thus Labour, voters in the older industrial regions (mainly those to the north of the River Trent), with a corresponding greater concentration of middle-class, Conservative voters in the more prosperous regions of the south-east (Taylor, 1979). Within each urban area, there is an even greater spatial separation of the various classes, creating a mosaic of residential areas which is reflected, *inter alia*, in a mosaic of voting patterns (Herbert and Johnston, 1976).

The superimposition of a lattice of constituencies over such a geography of voters creates a geography of election results. Figure 4.1 illustrates this for three hypothetical situations. In each, the population is divided into two groups, one of which votes exclusively for party A and the other votes exclusively for party B. In the maps of the geography of voting, the cross-hatched areas contain only those who vote for A, the blank areas only those who vote for B, and the shaded areas contain an equal balance of supporters of A and B. The same lattice of 34 constituencies is used in all cases. In the first—Figure 4.1a—there is total segregation of the two groups one from the other, and total spatial congregation. As a result, the frequency distribution of voting for party A in the third column shows that most constituencies either have 100 per cent or 0 per cent for A (which is the equivalent of packed gerrymandering); only a few constituencies—those straddling the boundary of the two areas—have a mixture of voters. In the

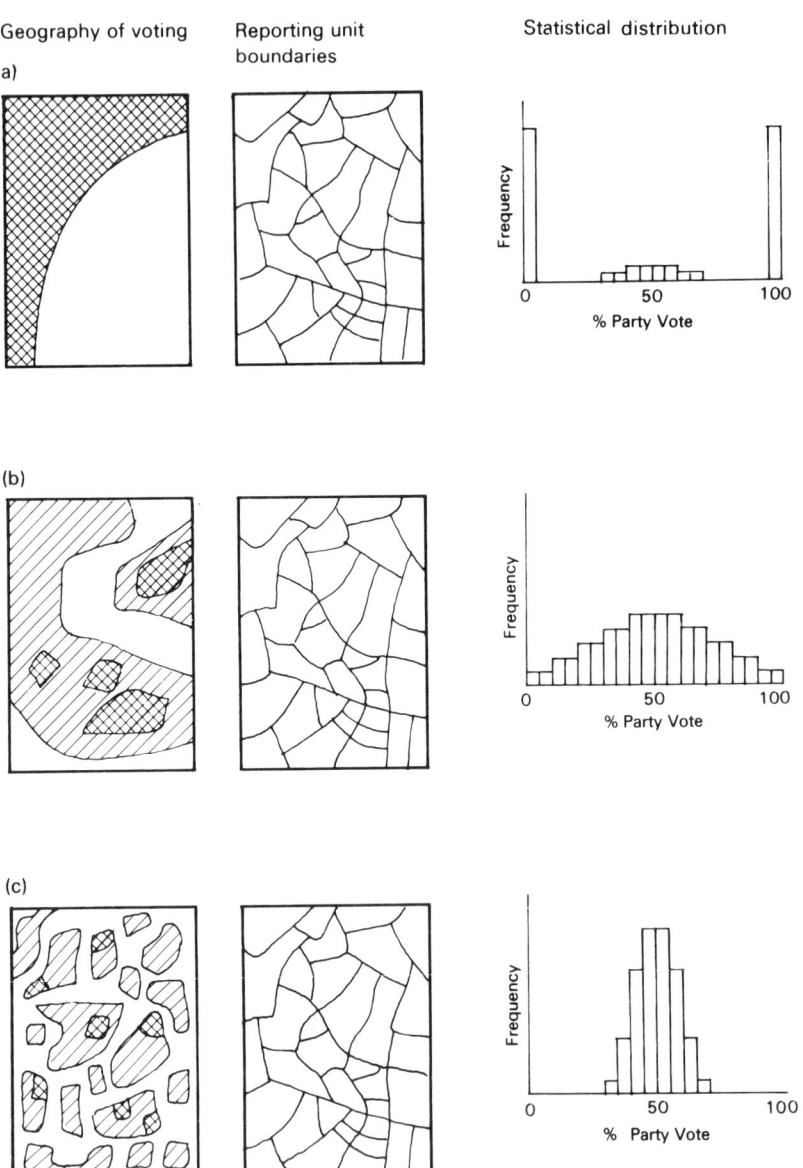

FIGURE 4.1.   Geographies of voting and the distribution of votes by constituencies. (*Source:* Taylor and Johnston, 1979, p. 149)

second case—Figure 4.1b—there are exclusive residential areas for each group, but in addition a mixed zone separating the exclusive areas: the resulting frequency distribution shows a wide spread, with the modal classes showing an almost even division of partisan preferences. Finally, in Figure 4.1c the exclusive areas are as extensive as in Figure 4.1b, but are spatially much more fragmented. Electorally, the result is a much more peaked frequency distribution. (The distributions in Figures 4.1b and c are close to a cracked gerrymander. If the blank areas contained about 5 per cent more of the voters than the cross-hatched areas, then party B would win a much larger percentage of the constituencies than would party A, especially in the case shown in Figure 4.1c.)

Even where there is no partisan manipulation of constituency boundaries, overlaying a lattice of constituencies onto a geography of partisan preferences, as shown in Figure 4.1, is likely to result in electoral bias. The degree of bias will reflect the balance of support between the parties, the spatial patterning of the geography of voting, and the rules for defining the constituency lattice. How this comes about has been investigated by three groups of authors.

The Detroit School Board

In 1969, the State of Michigan reorganized its public education system in an attempt to create greater community control of schools, especially in large cities, thereby hoping to ensure that the provision was suited to local needs. In the City of Detroit, this was to be achieved by creating decentralized school boards. Instead of the one board governing all 21 high-school catchment areas, the latter were to be grouped into not more than eleven and not fewer than seven independent regions, each with between 25 000 and 50 000 pupils.

Within this constraint of number of enrolments, and also with a grouping together of contiguous catchments only, Jenkins and Shepherd (1972) produced a computer algorithm to define the number of possible solutions to the grouping problem. They found 7311 involving six, seven or eight groups: the school board selected a seven-group solution.

Among the 3154 possible seven-group solutions, Jenkins and Shepherd showed the great potential for gerrymandering. It was possible to produce 84 plans in which the white population was in a majority in six, and 24 in which the black population had a majority in five. The modal solution (1662 of the 3154) gave the white population a 4 : 3 majority (the whites formed about 60 per cent of the city's population at the time, although only about 40 per cent of the population of the public school system); the chosen solution, however, produced a white majority in five of the seven regions. In terms of producing integrated school boards, they concluded that: 'Any attempt to promote decentralization as a step toward integration, therefore, could be interpreted by leaders of the black community as deliberate gerrymandering by the existing power structure (Jenkins and Shepherd, 1972, p. 103). Manipulation of the constituency lattice allows such gerrymandering, but it is made relatively easy by the concentration of the blacks in the inner city areas.

Equipopulous gerrymandering

In a series of judgements based on their reading of the Fourteenth Amendment, the US Supreme Court outlawed the practice of malapportionment in the early and mid-1960s. Many believed that this would remove the political element from the districting exercise, and result in 'fair and effective representation' (see Engstrom, 1976). Indeed, what was known as the 'reapportionment revolution' was heralded by some as the basis for introducing districting by computer, with the decision-making being taken over by a neutral machine (see Taylor and Johnston, 1979).

Preventing malapportionment did not end gerrymandering, however. Indeed, it gave it greater impetus, since it was the only remaining method of manipulation available to partisan groups in control of the districting process. Further, the Supreme Court was unwilling to tackle this issue, and so the practice went unchallenged (Engstrom, 1976; Musgrave, 1977).

One aspect of gerrymandering in the United States has been its use (as in the Detroit situation) to minimize the power of the black population. Careful definition of district boundaries can ensure a dilution of black voting power, by ensuring that they form a majority of electors in as few constituencies as possible. The spatial concentration of blacks in most American cities is almost certain to result in some dilution of their voting power since, if they vote in a single *bloc* (Axelrod, 1972; Keech, 1968), they are likely to pile up a large number of wasted votes with substantial majorities in black constituencies, in the manner typical of the packed gerrymander described above. Any intentional gerrymandering would thus dilute the voting power of the black population even more than their spatial concentration would suggest (presumably by splitting the black vote among several constituencies to produce a cracked gerrymander).

To investigate whether such gerrymandering is likely to have been practised in New Orleans, Engstrom and Wildgen (1977) developed a computer algorithm to produce sets of five constituencies for the city council elections. In 1970, the City of New Orleans was approximately 45 per cent black in its population composition and 34.5 per cent black in its electorate: most of the blacks lived in a single ghetto area in central New Orleans (Lewis, 1976).

The five constituencies defined for the City had 52.6, 43.2, 36.8, 23.3 and 22.6 per cent of their electorates who were black. This distribution was compared with that for each of the 165 plans generated by the computer, with the conclusion that the probability of a plan less favourable to the blacks than that selected was 0.7642, which, according to Engstrom and Wildgen (1977, p. 473), is 'a figure that certainly does not support a presumption of gerrymandering. Given the residential dispersion of black voters in New Orleans in a relatively narrow band across the city, a plan that provides a black registration majority is one of five districts does not egregiously dilute the black voting strength'. They did note, however, that it was possible to produce a plan with a black majority exceeding 60 per cent in two districts, and a probability of a less favourable situation than this for blacks was 0.9999: selection of this solution would provide *prima facie* evidence of gerrymandering against *white* voters.

Engstrom and Wildgen's work showed that the distribution of the vote is a crucial element in determining the representation (or potential for representation) of a group. They followed this up in a later study by investigating the seats : votes relationship (percentage of seats won by a party regressed against its percentage of the vote) for hypothetical data sets (Wildgen and Engstrom, 1980). Their voters were evenly distributed across a 10×10 lattice of square cells, which were amalgamated into ten constituencies to form contiguous blocks. For each of 50 simulations, the mean and standard deviation of the percentage of votes won by a party in each of the 100 cells was predetermined, and the relevant cell values were than ramdomly distributed. Addition of the cell values indicated how many of the ten seats the party won.

Figure 4.2 shows the results of their 50 simulations; the r^2 associated with the

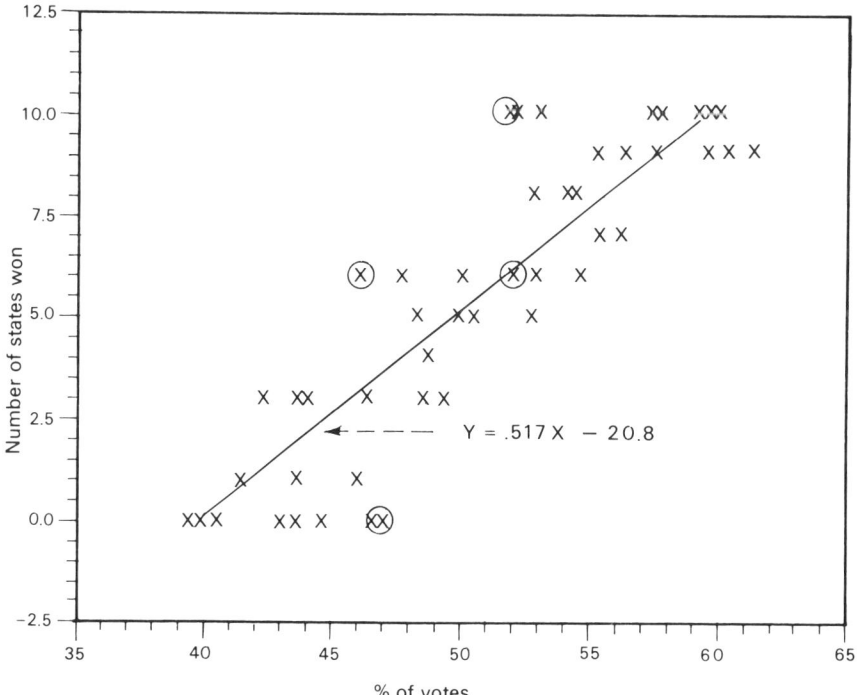

FIGURE 4.2. The relationship between seats and votes in 50 simulated elections. (*Source:* Wildgen and Engstrom, 1980, p. 427)

equation is 0.786, indicating considerable variability in the number of seats won with a given percentage of the votes. A multiple regression, with an R^2 of 0.907, produced the following equation

$$NS_i = -14.96 + 0.34\ PV_i + 0.13\ SDMIN - 0.11\ SDMAJ + 6.33\ GROUP_i$$

$$(3)$$

where

PV_i is percentage of votes won by party i;
$SDMIN$ is standard deviation of vote percentage for the minority party;
$SDMAJ$ is standard deviation of vote percentage for the minority party;
$GROUP_i$ is a dummy variable $= 1$ if party i is the majority party;
and NS_i is the number of seats won by party i.

Thus, as would be expected, a party wins more seats the more votes it gets (PV), especially if it is in the majority ($GROUP$). In addition, a majority party benefits from its votes being relatively evenly distributed across the cells (a negative coefficient for $SDMAJ$) whereas a minority benefits from its votes being spatially concentrated (a positive coefficient for $SDMIN$). This leads to the conclusion that: 'considerable differences in the conversion of votes into seats attributable to residential patterns may be expected under our electoral system independently of gerrymandering (Engstrom and Wildgen, 1977, p. 432)'. Compared to their New Orleans study, however, Wildgen and Engstrom have looked at only one aspect of the residential pattern. The degree of dispersion across cells was investigated, but with no reference to the spatial concentration (that is, the spatial autocorrelation) of cells with similar percentage values.

The British Boundary Commissioners

By far the most detailed examination of this problem of the geographical basis to electoral bias has been undertaken by Taylor and Gudgin. Their work has been concerned with the procedures used by the Parliamentary Boundary Commissions for England (there are parallel Commissions for Scotland, Wales and Northern Ireland). These are entirely neutral in composition but the way in which they operate ensures that there can be no such thing as a 'non-partisan cartography'.

As Taylor and Gudgin's work was the basis for our own, details of their procedures will be outlined later. In general, they built on Jenkins and Shepherd's work, showing how, given a certain geography (a distribution of voters), and a set of spatial building blocks (areas to be amalgamated to form a lattice of constituencies), the equivalent of gerrymandering (without any intent) is almost certain to occur. Indeed '"nonpolitical" approaches will tend to favour the majority party automatically. Hence . . . the Boundary Commissioners in Britain . . . [produce] solutions [which] will usually be similar to those that would result if we allowed [local] councils to gerrymander parliamentary constituencies'

(Taylor and Gudgin, 1976a, p. 55). This conclusion led to their interpretation of the work of the Boundary Commissioners:

> As a non-partisan agency we can expect the Commissioners to choose their solutions independently of the political implications of their decision. However this does not ensure that their solutions are in any sense fair. It simply means that where their solution does favour one party over another this is unintentional (Taylor and Gudgin, 1975, p. 413).

The unintentional biases have a clear geographical element to them, because of the rules prescribed for the Boundary Commission.

> The Labour Party is converted from a moderately urban based party in its support to an extremely urban party in terms of its seats. Conversely the Conservatives are more county based in their seats than in their support—despite their large votes in the cities they win relatively few city seats (Taylor and Gudgin, 1975, p. 414).

Other biases are also introduced, notably against minority parties which have no local nodes of support and are unable to achieve representation via the equivalent of a packed gerrymander.

THE BRITISH BOUNDARY COMMISSIONS REVISITED

All three of the studies discussed in the previous section suggest that electoral bias is not only a potential consequence of manipulation by partisan interests, it is also a likely result of the operation of a set of ostensibly neutral rules when these apply to a geography of voting. Indeed, it would seem that almost any distribution of votes across a territory is likely, when aggregated into contiguous constituencies, to result in one party winning a much larger share of the seats than it does of the votes. This contention is analysed here with reference to the work of the Boundary Commission for England.

Taylor and Gudgin's work

As already indicated, the pioneering work on this topic was undertaken by Taylor and Gudgin (1975, 1976a, 1976b, 1980; Gudgin and Taylor, 1979). Like Engstrom and Wildgen, and basing their procedure on the algorithm developed by Jenkins and Shepherd, they investigated both hypothetical and real situations.

The hypothetical situation referred to an urban area divided into eight districts which had to be amalgamated into two constituencies comprising four districts each. The population of all districts was the same. The percentage of the votes won by the majority party in each was 31, 47, 55, 59, 61, 65, 73 and 89; overall it won 60 per cent of the votes. There were 35 possible ways of producing two constituencies comprising four districts each; the majority party won both in 31 of them, and shared the constituencies 1–1 with the minority party in the other four. For each solution, Taylor and Gudgin (1976a) calculated both the within-constituency variance (in the percentage of votes won by the majority party) and the between-constituency variance. The ratio of the two is the conventional F-ratio of the analysis of variance. The four solutions allocating one seat to the minority party were the four with the highest F-ratios; they showed the greatest degree of between-district variance, and thus the greatest degree of polarization (in other words, a packed gerrymander). The vast majority of the solutions were the equivalent of cracked gerrymanders.

The real situations studied in detail referred to the definition of constituencies for the Newcastle upon Tyne and Sunderland county boroughs. (For the former, Taylor and Gudgin omitted the adjacent Newburn urban district, which was amalgamated with Newcastle by the English Boundary Commission.) Sunderland comprised eighteen wards, which had to be amalgamated into two constituencies. Taylor and Gudgin identified 87 different ways of creating two groups of nine contiguous wards. As with the hypothetical data, the F-distribution was strongly positively skewed. Most of the solutions were the equivalent of cracked gerrymanders, with the Labour Party winning both seats in 73 of the 87, on the basis of an estimated 58.5 per cent of the total vote. Similarly for Newcastle upon Tyne, where 20 wards were to be grouped into four constituencies, Taylor and Gudgin identified a positively skewed distribution of the F-ratio. Labour was estimated to win 58 per cent of the votes, but in 256 of the 337 possible solutions (groupings of five wards into contiguous constituencies) Labour would have won three of the seats, and in 44 others they would have won all four; only 37 of the solutions split the seats evenly between the two parties.

The use of the F-ratio by Taylor and Gudgin makes clear the likelihood of a solution akin to a cracked gerrymander being selected by the Boundary Commission. The skewness of the F-distribution means that the modal category invariably favours the majority party, and a non-partisan neutral body such as the Boundary Commission is more likely to select a solution from the mode than from elsewhere in the distribution; hence their conclusion that 'In . . . Sunderland . . . the result would have been very similar if the Labour Party had been allowed to gerrymander in a true American style' (Gudgin and Taylor, 1979, p. 152). Elsewhere, they point out that the shape of the constituency can be an influence on the degree of electoral bias (Taylor and Gudgin, 1976b). In large urban areas especially, social areas are organized in both sectors and concentric zones (Murdie, 1976). Regarding such organization 'The clearest generalisation which can be made is that sectoral constituencies, stretching from city centre to urban periphery, tend to include a finer range of social areas then non-sectoral ones' (Taylor and Gudgin, 1976b, p. 20). Thus, *ceteris paribus*, electoral bias is likely to be less in urban areas with sectoral constituencies, and they showed this to be the case. Of the six largest county boroughs, Liverpool and Manchester had no sectoral constituencies, and their level of (pro-Labour) electoral bias was more than twice that observed for Birmingham, Sheffield, Leeds or Bristol.

Taylor and Gudgin's work extended

The work reported by Taylor and Gudgin has identified some major elements within the constituency-building procedure in Great Britain that have important consequences for the creation of electoral bias. Their analyses and procedures have formed the basis for the work reported here, which builds on what they did in four ways.

(1) Taylor and Gudgin took no account of variations between wards in their electorates, assuming (as they make clear—Taylor and Gudgin, 1976a, p. 52) that each contained approximately the same number of voters. Thus in their Sunderland example, they assumed that any division of the 18 wards into two groups of nine would meet the electoral quota requirement within which the Boundary Commission must work (for details of that requirement, see below). Wards do vary considerably in their populations, however—especially if their boundaries remain unchanged for a considerable number of years, and in developing their procedure it was desirable to use an algorithm that would produce constituencies of similar population size, rather than constituent number of wards.

(2) In looking at the frequency distribution of solutions with regard to the F-ratio, they assumed that this was the distribution from which the Boundary Commission would make its selection. Many of those solutions might be ignored by the Commission, however, because of the shape of one or more constituencies—a shape that would be suggestive of a stacked gerrymander. That such constituencies were likely to be produced, as part of the distribution, was shown in an application of their procedure to metropolitan Brisbane (Johnston and Hughes, 1978). Thus in studying the set of possible solutions, it seemed desirable to identify the shape of each, and to relate this to the Commissioners' selections.

(3) Taylor and Gudgin were constrained (except in their application of their methodology to districting in the State of Iowa) to using data of unknown reliability to estimate voting in each ward, and thus the result in each constituency in their set of solutions. General election results are not published at the ward level in the United Kingdom (indeed, the count does not take place at this level, the ballot papers being mixed together at a single place prior to counting). Local government elections are conducted at the ward level, but the relatively low turnout, plus the assumption of a close correlation between partisan local preferences and partisan national preferences, introduces some unreliability into using this estimate.

There is no easy solution to this problem. For part of our research, however, we were fortunate in that the general election of May 1979 was held on the same day as local government elections in many places, ensuring a much larger turnout at the latter than is normal. Because of the re-warding activities of the Local Government Boundary Commission for England (see below), the wards used in some places were not those used to define the parliamentary constituencies, and in others parties stood in a ward for the local election but not in the relevant constituency at the general election. Nevertheless, data were available for several large electoral units.

(4) Finally, although Taylor and Gudgin identified the relative frequency of potential solutions consistent with the cracked gerrymander, they did not follow this up by investigating the likely impact of slight changes in the electoral fortunes of parties. Some estimate of the effect of such changes seemed desirable.

The algorithm

Many algorithms have been developed to produce constituencies or similar regions (for instance, Garfinkel and Taylor, 1969). Most were rejected for the present work because they focused on the identification of the optimal solution, within predetermined constraints (see, for example, Sammons 1976, 1978). However, Openshaw (1977) has developed a pseudo-random procedure for producing zoning systems, and this formed the basis for our own algorithm.

Full technical details of the algorithm have been published elsewhere (Rossiter and Johnston, 1981), as has a detailed example of its use in region-building exercises (Johnston and Rosster, 1981a). In brief, it takes a set of wards with known populations, and forms all possible combinations of these into contiguous constituencies within prescribed population limits (a given percentage—plus or minus—of an electoral quota). Thus for the Sheffield county borough, which prior to 1974 comprised 27 wards and six constituencies, it identified 15 937 possible solutions to the constituency-definition problem within the constraint of each constituency being within 12 per cent of the electoral quota. (Some of these solutions are mapped in Johnston and Rossiter, 1980a.)

The evaluation of the shapes of the constituencies in each solution involved the development of a special index. Many such indices have been developed (for a review, see Taylor, 1973) but these invariably apply to individual constituencies only. We required an index of the overall 'shapeliness' of the solution, and not of the shape of individual constituencies. To obtain this, ward boundaries within an urban area being studied were classified into: (a) external—those forming part of the perimeter of the urban area; (b) internal type I—those within the urban area which form part of the boundary of a constituency; and (3) internal type II—those which are neither part of the urban perimeter nor part of the boundary of a constituency. Our index was the length of the type (3) boundaries; the longer these are, the shorter are those in type (2) and thus the less indented (or more shapely) are the constituency boundaries. The index was not standardized, although it easily could have been (type (2) as a percentage of type (2) plus type (3), for example), as our comparisons were being made *within* areas only (for further details, see Johnston and Rossiter, 1981b).

Finally, the algorithm assesses the electoral consequences of each solution by totalling the votes received by each party in each constituency. It also assesses the impact of a 'uniform swing' across all wards (in other words, a defined party either gains or loses a certain percentage of the votes in each), to inquire into the likely 'permanence' of the electoral bias identified.

The algorithm was used to investigate the electoral consequences of the Boundary Commissioners' non-partisan activities. These are constrained by certain rules, and so the remainder of this chapter looks at the rules, their application, and their likely consequences. Three activities of the Boundary Commission for England are studied: the results of its *Second Periodical Report* (1969) in selected urban areas; the results of its definition of European Assembly Constituencies in Greater London (1978); and the results of some of the already published proposals which forms part of its *Third Periodical Report* (due, at the latest, in 1984).

SECOND PERIODICAL REPORT OF THE BOUNDARY COMMISSION FOR ENGLAND

The present method of defining Parliamentary constituencies for the United Kingdom was introduced by the Attlee Labour government in its Representation of the People Act (1949). A more regular redistribution than previously was proposed in order to prevent the development of great differences between constituency populations as a result of population movements, and the original intention was to have a redistribution during the lifetime of each Parliament—that is, once every five years (see Butler, 1963).

The rules by which the Boundary Commissions work are set out in the Second Schedule to the Representation of the People Act (1949), and are reproduced in Table 4.1. They indicate that for the allocation and definition of constituencies, the main building-blocks to be used are the administrative counties and the county boroughs. Under the system of local government existing in England and Wales prior to 1974, county boroughs were entirely independent units forming enclaves within the administrative counties; together the two made up the 'geographical counties'. The county boroughs were, with few exceptions, the largest urban areas (Freeman, 1968); the smaller urban places had the status of either urban district or municipal borough and, with the rural districts, formed the subdivisions of the administrative counties. After the reforms of 1964, the Greater London County was divided into 32 subsidiary metropolitan boroughs each of which, like the county and municipal boroughs and the urban districts, was further subdivided into wards. Using the electoral quota (Rule 7), the

TABLE 4.1   Rules for redistribution of seats

(Second Schedule to the House of Commons (Redistribution of Seats) Act, 1949, as amended)

1.   The number of constituencies in the several parts of the United Kingdom set out in the first column of the following table shall be as stated respectively in the second column of that table:—

Part of the United Kingdom	No. of Constituencies
Great Britain	Not substantially greater or less than 613
Scotland	Not less than 71
Wales	Not less than 35
Northern Ireland	12

2.   Every constituency shall return a single member.

3.   There shall continue to be a constituency which shall include the whole of the City of London and the name of which shall refer to the City of London.

4.   (1)   So far as is practicable having regard to the foregoing rules:—
   (a)   in England and Wales:
      (i)   no county or any part thereof shall be included in a constituency which includes the whole or part of any other county or the whole or part of a county borough or London borough:
      (ii)   no county borough or any part thereof shall be included in a constituency which includes the whole or part of any other county borough or the whole or part of a London borough;
      (iii)   no London borough or any part thereof shall be included in a constituency which includes the whole or part of any other London borough;
      (iv)   no county district shall be included partly in one constituency and partly in another;
   (b)   in Scotland, no burgh other than a county of a city shall be included partly in one constituency and partly in another;
   (c)   in Northern Ireland, no county district shall be included partly in one constituency and partly in another.
   (2)   In paragraph (1) of this rule the following expressions have the following meanings, that is to say:—
      "county" means an administrative county;
      "county borough" has the same meaning as in the Local Government Act, 1933;
      "county district" has, in sub-paragraph (a), the same meaning as in the Local Government Act, 1933, and, in sub-paragraph (c), the same meaning as in the Local Government (Ireland) Act, 1898.

5.   The electorate of any constituency shall be as near the electoral quota as is practicable having regard to the foregoing rules; and a Boundary Commission may depart from the strict application of the last foregoing rule if it appears to them that a departure is desirable to avoid an excessive disparity between the electorate of any constituency and the electoral quota, or between the electorate thereof and that of neighbouring constituencies in the part of the United Kingdom with which they are concerned.

6.   A Boundary Commission may depart from the strict application of the last two foregoing rules if special geographical considerations, including in particular the size, shape and accessibility of a constituency, appear to them to render a departure desirable.

TABLE 4.1 (*Contd.*)

7. In the application of these rules to each of the several parts of the United Kingdom for which there is a Boundary Commission:—
    (a) the expression "electoral quota" means a number obtained by dividing the electorate for that part of the United Kingdom by the number of constituencies in it existing on the enumeration date;
    (b) the expression "electorate" means:—
        (i) in relation to a constituency, the number of persons whose names appear on the register of parliamentary electors in force on the enumeration date under the Representation of the People Acts for the constituency;
        (ii) in relation to the part of the United Kingdom, the aggregate electorate as hereinbefore defined of all the constituencies therein;
    (c) the expression "enumeration date" means, in relation to any report of a Boundary Commission under this Act, the date on which the notice with respect to that report is published in accordance with section two of this act.

Source: Boundary Commission for England (1969, p. 70).

Boundary Commissioners are required to allocate numbers of constituencies to the units and then to subdivide each unit into the relevant number of constituencies, as equal in population as possible (Rule 5). The Commissioners are allowed to override these Rules where they consider it desirable.

The operating procedure—not outlined in the Schedule reproduced in Table 4.1—involves the Commission publishing its proposals for each county and county borough in relevant local newspapers. It then receives comments and criticisms, considers these, conducts a local inquiry if deemed desirable (or required by the Act), and then forwards its final proposals *en bloc* to Parliament. (Each report details how this procedure was carried out.)

The Boundary Commissions are permanent bodies, and they may be called upon by the relevant minister (the Secretary of State at the Home Office) to conduct a review of the constituencies in a particular area at any time. Their main task, however, is to conduct regular reviews of all constituencies (unless the Secretary of State instructs them otherwise). The first general review was conducted in the early 1950s, and although it is the second review which is of particular relevance here, certain aspects of what the Commissioners wrote in 1954 are germane to the present considerations.

The first general review

In its report on the first general review of parliamentary constituencies, the Boundary Commission for England (1954) noted the problems of applying the rules in Table 4.1, given the electoral quota of 57 122 electors. (The Commissions for Scotland and Wales paid much less attention to this issue.) Paragraph 9 of the Commission's report states that

Our aim was to create 506 constituencies each of which would be at or near the electoral quota without cutting across local government boundaries. Where the grouping of the local population permitted of this, the task was simple. The numerous cases where it did not called for special consideration, the choice lying between departing substantially from the quota or disregarding boundaries. In many instances we decided in exercise of the discretion given to us in Rule 6 that we would be justified in recommending the creation or continuance of constituencies with electorates substantially below or in excess of the electoral quota but in no case have we recommended the creation of a constituency with an electorate in 1953 of less than 40 000 or more than 80 000 (p. 2).

The combination of adjacent county boroughs and urban districts into single constituencies was clearly an issue raised with the Commission, on the grounds that such combination might presage local government amalgamation. The Commission replied that

We much doubt whether parliamentary constituency boundaries should be regarded as relevant to the consideration of an application for the alteration of local government areas. . . . The union of boroughs and county districts is not without precedent in parliamentary representation though in general recourse to it becomes necessary only where the electorate contained within boroughs is comparatively small and adjustment is desirable to meet the requirements of Rule 5 (p. 3).

In two cases, this involved overriding rule 4(1)(a)(i): two wards of Reading county borough were detached, one each being allocated to the Newbury and Wokingham constituencies; and three wards in Blackburn county borough were placed in the Darwen constituency.

One aspect of the operation of the Act which the Commission chose to highlight in its report concerned the frequency of redistribution. Another review was needed within seven years, but

It was clear from representations submitted to us that the changes recommended [in the present review], even where they included proposals for additional representation, were not wholly welcome because of the disturbance they would inevitably cause to local political organizations and also because of the feeling of unsettlement they would cause both to the electorate and to their representatives in Parliament . . . we think that consideration should be given to lengthening the minimum and maximum periods between reviews (p. 4).

This advice was taken, and the next review was published in 1969. The import of the advice appears to be reflected in the Commission's decisions, as discussed below: in general, they prefer to tamper with boundaries as little as possible, in order to allow continuity in representation.

The second general review

In its report on the second general review, submitted in 1969 (local reviews for particular constituencies had been implemented in the interim), the Boundary Commission noted that 'The Rules embrace two principles of representative government, equal representation (Rule 5) and territorial representation (Rule 4), which are often difficult to reconcile. The more equality in constituency electorates is sought, the greater the likelihood of disrupting local government units (p. 5).' As pointed out above, when reporting in 1954 the Commission indicated that in meeting Rule 5 they had created difficulties for political parties. In the Redistribution of Seats Act (1958), however, Parliament recognized this and stated in Section 2(2) that:

It shall not be the duty of a Boundary Commission, in discharging their functions . . . to aim at giving full effect in all circumstances to the rules set out in the Second Schedule to the principal Act, but they shall take account, as far as they reasonably can, of the inconveniences attendant on alterations of constituencies other than alterations made for the purposes of rule 4 of those rules, and of any local ties which would be broken by such alterations: and references in that section to giving effect to those rules shall be construed accordingly.

In commenting on the debate on the 1958 Act, the Commission note that there was 'a broad measure of agreement that local ties were of greater importance than strict mathemetical equality' and quote the then Home Secretary that 'The effect of the Bill is to bring in a presumption against making changes unless there is a very strong case for them' (p. 5). Thus continuity became a major element in the review and the Commission proceeded 'with the intention of avoiding, where possible, proposals that would change constituency boundaries for the sake of adjustments in the size of the electorates' (p. 5). (It is of interest to note that the Commission for Wales made similar comments, but the Commission for Scotland did not.)

In discussing their method of working, the Commission point out that in urban areas with more than one seat they adopted the policy of using the existing wards (the electoral units for local government elections) as the basic building blocks. Thus:

For administrative convenience we decided to use ward boundaries for the division of boroughs into constituencies. In some boroughs we were urged to draw constituency boundaries through wards. . . . We took the view, however, that we ought not to depart from existing ward boundaries. Where polling difficulties existed, it was for local authorities to resolve them by ward reviews (p. 5).

Finally, the Commissioners noted that:

We are not required by the Rules to pay regard to future population movement but in the 1954 review the commission took some account of this factor where population change was 'imminent'. The Rules require the use of current electorates.... We cannot, however, escape the fact that the intention of the present law is that a general review shall form the basis of constituency boundaries for at least the next ten years and it would therefore be desirable to make recommendations that would, so far as possible, cushion the effect of gains or losses of electorate so far as they could be foreseen with some degree of certainty . . . we were . . . of the opinion that population trends ought not to be ignored in border-line cases where constituency electorates were close to the upper and lower limits we had decided to apply (p. 7).

Regarding details of procedure, the Commissioners proceeded in the same way at each general review. Rule 1 states that Wales should have not less than 35 constituencies and Scotland not less than 71. Northern Ireland is allocated 12, and the total for Great Britain should be neither substantially greater nor substantially less than 613. Wales has had 36 since 1947, and neither Boundary Commission for that country at the two general reviews proposed a change: Scotland has had 71 over the period. Thus the figure for England should be 'not substantially greater or less than 506' (1969 review, p. 7). There were 511 in the 1954 review and, according to Rule 7(a), this could not be reduced: if they thought it necessary, the Commissioners could have increased the number. In the end, they decided on 516 English constituencies.

The electoral quota was determined by dividing the national electorate of 30 570 683 in 1968 by 511; the result was an 'average' electorate of 59 825. (Although 1968 data were used in the final stages of the second review, most of the work was done on 1965 information.) Using this quota, the Commission then decided the number of seats to be allocated to each geographical county (that is, the administrative counties plus the autonomous county boroughs within their boundaries). These allocations were then distributed within each geographical county with, as far as possible, each county borough (and also each metropolitan borough within the Greater London County) being treated separately from the administrative county. It was this decision to allocate seats by counties in the first instance that led to an increase in the number of seats from 511 to 516.

The procedures for defining constituencies in Great Britain

Inspection of the rules as prescribed by the Representation of the People Act, and their interpretation by the two Boundary Commissions to have completed general reviews prior to 1981, suggests the following set of decision procedures:

(1) The electoral quota is determined.
(2) Constituencies are allocated to geographical counties.
(3) Within counties, constituencies are defined with, as far as possible:
   (a) no violation of county borough and metropolitan borough boundaries;
   (b) All constituencies approximately equal in their electorate, with some
       allowance for likely population changes; and
   (c) As little disruption as possible to existing constituencies.

The relative importance attached to each of these rules has been left to the discretion of the Commissioners, who in many cases were required to define their decisions at local inquiries (70 in all were held during the second general review: an inquiry is mandatory under the 1958 revision of the Representation of the People Act (section 4(2)) if 'objections were lodged by a body of one hundred or more parliamentary electors in the affected constituency or by an interested local authority': 1969 review, p. 3). In addition, as will be detailed below, a further implicit rule appears to have been adopted, relating to constituency shape.

Evaluating the 1969 proposals for England

One of the degrees of freedom remaining with the Boundary Commission (as long as its decisions can be justified and, in the end, are acceptable to Parliament) concerns the degree of variation around the electoral quota—both between counties/county boroughs/metropolitan boroughs and within each of these units. Regarding the latter point, in general smaller towns (all of the evaluation here refers to county boroughs and metropolitan boroughs only) have smaller maximum percentage discrepancies between constituency electorates (Table 4.2). This is presumably because such smaller places in general have smaller wards, allowing greater scope for 'fine-tuning' in the definition of constituencies. Of the 15 cases listed in Table 4.2 as having a maximum percentage discrepancy between constituency electorates exceeding 10.0, in 13 of these this was because the Commission 'honoured' existing boundaries; it preferred to retain the constituencies defined in 1954, despite the relatively large deviations from the electoral quota, rather than impose a totally new set of constituencies with the problems of the break in continuity that this would entail. In only one of the cases studied here (Sheffield) is the maximum percentage discrepancy allowed by the Commission greater than 10.0.

   The case study areas chosen for this evaluation were the four large boroughs in the Yorkshire and Humberside and East Midlands regions in which the 1979 local elections were fought in the same wards as those existing in 1965 (those wards were used by the Boundary Commission to define the constituencies for the second review). The maximum percentage discrepancy from the electoral quota used by the Commission, based on 1965 electorates, in each was:

TABLE 4.2.   Borough size and maximum percentage discrepancy in constituency electorate

Maximum percentage discrepancy in constituency electorate	Constituencies per borough		
	2	3	4+
0–1	4	2	1
2–3	9	1	0
4–5	8	4	1
6–7	3	2	2
8–9	1	7	4
10–11	1	1	1
12–13	1	2	0
14–15	0	2	2
16–17	1	0	0
18–19	0	0	1
20+	0	2	1

Coventry, 9.4; Hull, 5.4; Leicester, 9.4; and Sheffield, 10.9. In the algorithm, the maximum percentages allowed were: Coventry, 10; Hull, 6; Leicester, 10; and Sheffield, 12; the same 1965 ward data used by the Commission were employed to define constituency electorates. The electoral data used were for 1979, and this involved some standardization (notably in Leicester) to allow for variations between party participation in the local and general elections then (for full details, see Johnston and Rossiter, 1979.)

Electoral impact

The total set of results from running the algorithm for each of the four county boroughs is given in Table 4.3. In each case, it will be seen that there is a probable electoral bias towards the majority party, Labour; the modal solution allocates the Labour party a greater percentage of the constituencies than its share of the votes. (The percentages of the total vote won by Labour are not those that it gained in the 1979 general election. These figures have been standardized to accord with that the Labour party would have won in each place if nationally there had been a 50:50 division of the two-party vote between Labour Conservative. The rationale for this is given by the following data on the percentage of the two-party vote won by Labour at each of the last ten general elections:

1950	1951	1955	1959	1964	1966	1970	1974(F)	1974(O)	1979
51	50	48	47	50	53	48	50	52	46

The mean is 49.5. To look at the likely impact of swing, therefore, it was decided to compute Table 4.3 and to centre Table 4.4 (and also Table 4.7, p. 142) on the

TABLE 4.3. The electoral impact of the 1969 review in Coventry, Hull, Leicester and Sheffield

	Coventry	Hull	Leicester	Sheffield
Maximum per cent discrepancy	10	6	10	12
Number of wards	18	21	16	27
Number of constituencies	4	3	3	6
Labour per cent of total vote	57	68	59	65
Number of Solutions	244	100	214	15937
Labour constituency wins				
6	–	–	–	697
5	–	–	–	12327
4	43	–	–	2913
3	193	100	160	0
2	8	0	54	0
1	0	0	0	0
0	0	0	0	0

standardized 50 : 50 split, on the argument that the 1979 result is an extreme case in the modern context.)

The most interesting result in Table 4.2 is that for Hull. In every solution for that county borough the Labour party, with 68 per cent of the standardized two-party vote, won all three constituencies. This reflects the geography of the vote in Hull. The Conservative party had a majority of the two-party vote in only four wards in 1979 (Figure 4.3), three of which were relatively small. They do not form a clear contiguous block, surrounded by wards with only small Labour majorities; indeed, there is only one solution possible which groups all four wards with Conservative majorities into a single constituency (in which Labour wins over 55 per cent of the two-party vote). Thus the social geography of Hull county borough (now defunct) and the Boundary Commission's rules ensure a cracked gerrymander against the Conservative party.

In Coventry, the geography of voting is not as anti-Conservative as in Hull, in part because there are fewer (and hence larger) wards to be amalgamated into more constituencies. The Conservative support is concentrated in the south and west (Figure 4.4), and most of the solutions allocate it one of the four seats based on that core of Tory voters. In the south-east, too, the Labour victories are generally marginal, giving the Conservatives the chance for two seats with a small swing away from Labour. Thus in a town with a more even split between the two main parties than is the case in Hull, the cracked gerrymander-type solution can operate in the favour of either. In Leicester, the Conservative party is disadvantaged because its vote is dispersed around the city's southern and eastern edges (Figure 4.5), so that most of the solutions allocate all three constituencies to Labour. Again, the combination of geography and the rules

TABLE 4.4.   Uniform swing and its electoral impact in the set of solutions

	Percentage swing								
	To Labour					To Conservative			
	4	3	2	1	0	1	2	3	4
Coventry (four constituencies)									
Labour constituencies									
4	189	152	113	75	43	39	29	8	6
3	55	92	131	169	193	195	167	160	142
2	0	0	0	0	8	10	48	76	96
1	0	0	0	0	0	0	0	0	0
0	0	0	0	0	0	0	0	0	0
Hull (three constituencies)									
Labour constituencies									
3	100	100	100	100	100	100	100	100	100
2	0	0	0	0	0	0	0	0	0
1	0	0	0	0	0	0	0	0	0
0	0	0	0	0	0	0	0	0	0
Leicester (three constituencies)									
Labour constituencies									
3	212	208	200	184	160	159	126	96	87
2	2	6	14	30	54	55	88	118	127
1	0	0	0	0	0	0	0	0	0
0	0	0	0	0	0	0	0	0	0
Sheffield (six constituencies)									
Labour constituencies									
6	3 582	2 468	1 586	1 215	697	361	153	92	53
5	12 177	12 807	12 866	12 736	12 327	11 399	10 617	9670	8273
4	178	662	1 485	1 986	2 913	4 177	5 164	6170	7576
3	0	0	0	0	0	0	3	5	35
2	0	0	0	0	0	0	0	0	0
1	0	0	0	0	0	0	0	0	0
0	0	0	0	0	0	0	0	0	0

produces the equivalent of a cracked gerrymander. Only in Sheffield (Figure 4.6). with the Conservative vote spatially concentrated in the western sector, is there sufficient of a 'packed gerrymander-like' distribution virtually to ensure that party one seat (though not more, with over 40 per cent of the vote).

Because the data in Table 4.3 refer to the hypothetical situation of a national 50:50, Conservative: Labour split, it is desirable to look also at the likely impact of uniform swings to and from that position (a 4 per cent swing to Conservative represents the 1979 election result, nationally). This is shown in Table 4.4. Again, the Hull situation stands out; a 4 per cent swing to the Conservative party, giving it well over one-third of all of the votes, will not give it a single seat. Clearly, this is non-partisan cracked gerrymandering. In Coventry and Leicester, too, the pattern is akin to that of a cracked gerrymander, because of the

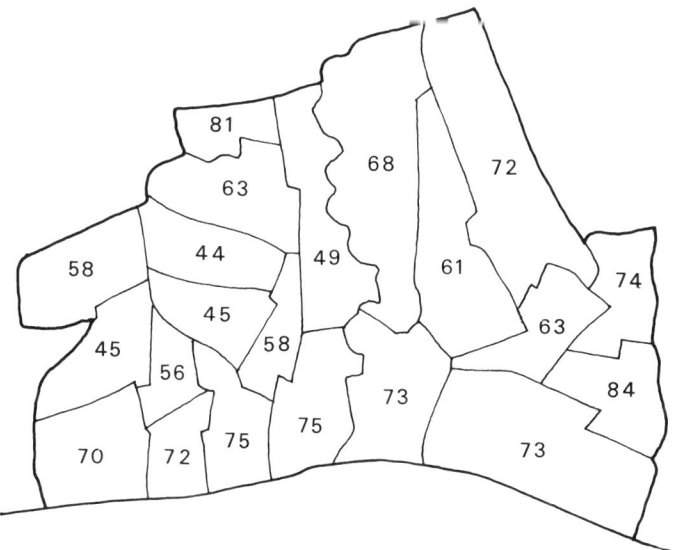

FIGURE 4.3.   Hull: the estimated percentage of votes won by Labour,
by ward, in 1979

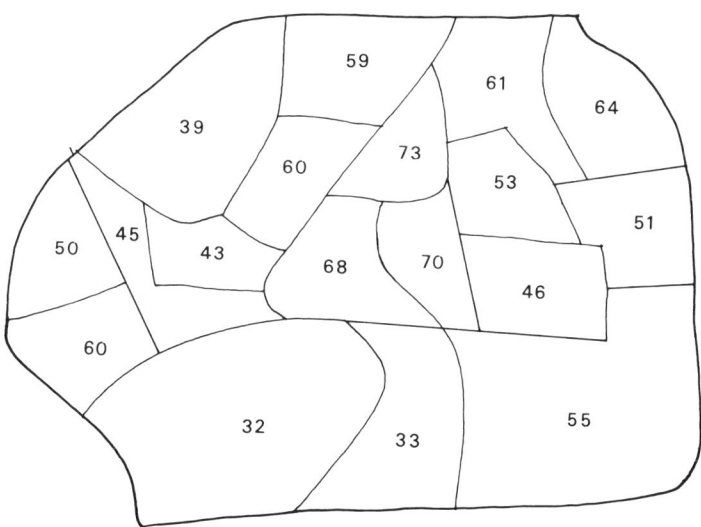

FIGURE 4.4.   Coventry: the estimated percentage of votes won by
Labour, by ward, in 1979

FIGURE 4.5.   Leicester: the estimated percentage of votes won by Labour,
by ward, in 1979

vote distributions shown in Figures 4.4 and 4.5: the greater the percentage of votes won by Labour the greater its chances of winning all of the town's constituencies, but as the Labour vote declines (coming close to a 50:50 split) so there is a strong chance of the Conservative party winning at least one seat (two in Coventry). Only in Sheffield is the situation more akin to a packed gerrymander—largely because of the geography of voting there (Johnston and Rossiter, 1980a). Thus even with 69 per cent of the votes, the Labour party is still most likely to win 5:1 in seats; with 61 per cent, its chances of winning 5:1 or 4:2 are approximately equal.

Taylor and Gudgin's characterization of the operations of the Boundary Commission as akin to a partisan gerrymander favouring the majority party is therefore upheld here. In three of the four cases studied, the gerrymander appears to be of the cracked variety. This reflects the underlying geography of voting, as illustrated in Figure 4.1. Of the four case-study ex-county boroughs, there is pro-Labour bias in every one, because of the gerrymander-like consequences of the Boundary Commission decisions. In three of the cities, the consequence is akin to

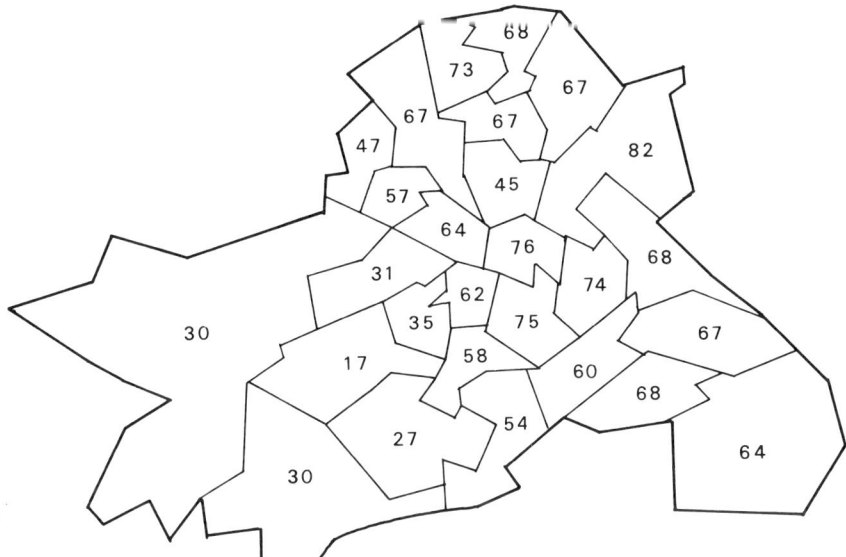

FIGURE 4.6.   Sheffield: the estimated percentage of votes won by Labour, by ward, in 1979

that of an intentional cracked gerrymander; the Conservative vote is too thinly spread to counteract the operation of the rules.

The role of shape

As mentioned above, many of the possible solutions available to the Boundary Commissioners involve combinations of wards into oddly-shaped constituencies (some examples are given in Johnston and Rossiter, 1980a, 1981a). Undoubtedly, these are not favourably considered by the Commissioners and their staffs.

To investigate the potential influence of constituency shapes on the Commissioners' decisions, the shape index outlined above was computed for each of the identified solutions in the four county boroughs. The distributions are shown in Table 4.5. (Because they are unstandardized, Sheffield's are much larger because of its larger number of wards.) Of especial interest here is the relationship between the shape index and the Commission's choice. For each of Coventry, Hull, and Leicester they selected the solution lying within the defined maximum percentage discrepancy with the *largest shape index*. This suggests, as do the data for the eight London boroughs discussed below (see also Johnston and Rossiter, 1981b), that although constituency shape has never been explicitly mentioned as a relevant issue by any of the Commissions it is implicitly very important to them; they aim to produce sets of constituencies which (at least in the terms of the

TABLE 4.5. Distribution of shape indices

Range of indices	Coventry	Hull	Leicester	Sheffield
−300	0	0	0	0
301–400	27	0	19	0
401–500	134	9	119	0
501–600	82	39	71	59
601–700	1	41	4	2121
701–800	0	10	1	7627
801–900	0	1	0	5356
901–1000	0	0	0	763
1001–	0	0	0	11

shape index used here) are compact. (It is of interest to note that in the 1944 Representation of the People Act, the Commissioners were for the first time allowed to depart from the rules 'if special geographical considerations including, in particular, the area, shape and accessibility of a constituency'—Butler, 1963, p. 216—made it desirable. This reference to shape was retained in Rule 6 of the 1949 Act (see Table 4.1, p. 126). Thus although the term shape is never referred to in Commission reports, it is clearly a criterion to which the Commissioners might appeal.) Sheffield provides a partial exception to this: 115 solutions identified by the algorithm had a higher shape index than that selected by the Commissioners (950), although in this case they were dealing with a much larger city with a very great number of potential solutions.

Looking at the relationship between shape and electoral impact, we have investigated only a small group of solutions with the largest indices. (Hull was not considered, of course, since every solution there gave three seats to Labour.) For Coventry, of the top 16 solutions on the shape index, 14 gave Labour a 3:1 victory and there was one each for a 4:0 and 2:2 division. In 12 of the 16, however, a 3 per cent swing to Labour would not bring it all four seats—which is the modal category in Table 4.4; this suggests that the most shapely solutions there are more characteristic of a packed than of a cracked gerrymander. (The 'most shapely' solutions were the log n with the largest shape indices where n = number of solutions identified.) In Leicester, on the other hand, there is greater evidence of a cracked gerrymander in the 15 most shapely solutions. Indeed, in five of those 15, Labour would win only two of the three seats with the given distribution of votes, as it would in six with a 2 per cent swing to Conservative. In six of the other nine, however (including that chosen by the Commission), Labour would continue to hold all three seats even with a 4 per cent swing to Conservative. Clearly the conversion of votes into seats there is very sensitive to the choice of constituency lattice. Finally, in Sheffield the packed gerrymander noted above prevails. Only two of the 122 most shapely solutions give Conservatives two seats at the given percentage of the votes, and only 16 give them two with a 3 per cent swing.

THE DEFINITION OF EUROPEAN ASSEMBLY CONSTITUENCIES (EACs)

Following the United Kingdom's accession to membership of the European Communities in January 1973 and the eventual decision to elect a European Assembly, the various Boundary Commissions were required to create sets of consituencies to be used in the June 1979 elections. (For details of the long process leading to the establishment of the elected Assembly, and the failure of the nine members of the Community to agree on a common electoral system, see Fitzmaurice, 1978.) Under Schedule 2 of the European Assembly Elections Act, passed by the United Kingdom Parliament in 1978, the rules for defining the Euroconstituencies were set out in the following clauses:

9. In Great Britain—
(a) each Assembly constituency shall consist of an area that includes two or more parliamentary constituencies; and
(b) no parliamentary constituency shall be included partly in one Assembly constituency and partly in another.
10. The electorate of any Assembly constituency in Great Britain shall be as near the electoral quota as is reasonably practicable having regard, where appropriate, to special geographical considerations.

England was allocated 66 Euroconstituencies (an average of just under eight parliamentary constituencies each), Scotland eight, and Wales four. (Northern Ireland was allocated three seats, but these were to be contested in a single constituency using the Single Transferable Vote system: Taylor and Johnston, 1979.)

As with the allocation of parliamentary constituencies, the English commission attempted to work at the scale of the administrative counties (those introduced in 1974 under the Local Government Bill of 1971 passed, after amendments, in 1972: Johnston, 1979a). This proved impossible, because of problems of approximating the electoral quota, and the 66 Euroconstituencies were defined within eight areas only one of which, Greater London, was a single administrative county: as the Commission noted, the 92 parliamentary constituencies in the area of Greater London offered an opportunity to recommend EACs [European Assembly Constituencies] of the right size (judged by the electorate) within that administrative area (Boundary Commission for England, 1978, p. 1). Ten constituencies were allocated to Greater London. In reporting on how they conducted the task, the Commissioners state:

We would have liked to have respected the boundaries of all the London Boroughs if that had been possible, but we were of course required to recommend constituencies with electorates which were as near the electoral quota (516 436) as was reasonably practical having regard, where appropriate, to special geographical considerations. We did not regard the observance of London Borough boundaries as a special geographical consideration. Our Rules for the review of parliamentary constituencies provide that as far as practicable no County or London Borough boundary shall be crossed by a parliamentary constituency. No such rule applies to the EAC review. No one borough was large enough to comprise a single EAC . . . and it proved impossible to group whole London Boroughs together throughout the area to form EACs without creating, in some cases, large disparities between their electorates. The electorates of adjoining parliamentary constituencies varied considerably and this together with the divisive effects of the lower reaches of the river largely decided how we should draw the EAC boundaries (p. 18).

The provisional recommendations split 5 of the 32 boroughs between EACs. As a result:

We received a large number of representations about London. Most of them reiterated the view that London Boroughs should not be divided between EACs. . . . All of the representations were considered in detail. While we were anxious to meet the objections to the division of certain boroughs, we found that counter-proposals made to that end resulted in EACs with greater disparities between their electorates than those which we had proposed. However . . . [counter-proposals regarding Enfield and Hackney] had the advantages of reducing the number of divided boroughs to four and improving the equality of representative between the EACs. We decided to adopt that change (pp. 19–20).

Thus Greater London provides a further opportunity to evaluate the Boundary Commission's decisions, this time in a situation where it was operating with two explicit constraints—size and the non-division of boroughs—and, presumably, its implicit criterion of shape. For the analyses, London was divided into two by the Thames (the Commission apparently did this). Only one metropolitan borough straddles the Thames—that furthest up the river, Richmond—and the whole of it was allocated to south London. As the Commissioners did not split any of the boroughs with only two parliamentary constituencies between two EACs, these boroughs were treated as single units. Thus the problems to be tackled were:

(1) Combine the 51 spatial units in north London into six EACs, with a maximum percentage discrepancy in electorate size of 4 per cent (the Commissioners produced a solution with a maximum of 3.5 per cent); and
(2) Combine the 32 spatial units in south London into four EACs, with a maximum percentage discrepancy in electorate size of 4 per cent (the Commissioners produced a solution with a maximum of 2.6 per cent).

The data used were the same as those employed by the Commission.

The results are shown in Table 4.6: 2808 solutions were identified for north London and 521 for south London. In neither case did any solution keep all of the constituent metropolitan boroughs intact. For both, however, it was possible to devise solutions that would split only one borough but none of these (six solutions for north London, five for south London) was among the most shapely; in north London there were more than a thousand solutions with a higher shape index. Thus the Commissioners chose a solution for north London which kept 18 boroughs intact and which had the fourth highest shape index; for south London, they kept ten Boroughs intact in a solution with the second highest shape index. As with their review of parliamentary constituencies, therefore, the criterion of shape appears to have weighed heavily with the Commissioners.

TABLE 4.6. The possible solutions for the London EACs

	North London	South London
Boroughs	20	12
Spatial units	51	32
EACs	6	4

North London

Boroughs kept intact

Shape index	12	13	14	15	16	17	18	19
1401–1500	1	3	6	5	2	0	0	0
1501–1600	0	19	42	52	41	20	15	0
1601–1700	1	27	104	237	296	175	43	3
1701–1800	2	14	68	264	534	276	75	3
1801–	0	1	11	76	152	220	20	0

South London

Boroughs kept intact

Shape index	6	7	8	9	10	11
801–900	1	11	33	10	0	0
901–1000	1	36	140	67	17	2
1001–1100	0	12	79	73	15	3
1101–	0	0	11	8	2	0

TABLE 4.7.   Uniform swing and its electoral impact in the EACs

	To Labour			Percentage swing			To Conservative		
	4	3	2	1	0	1	2	3	4
North London (six EACs)									
Labour EACs									
6	2578	2465	2270	2022	1802	1164	529	161	42
5	230	343	538	786	1006	1611	2062	2197	1311
4	0	0	0	0	0	33	216	444	1269
3	0	0	0	0	0	0	1	6	186
2	0	0	0	0	0	0	0	0	0
1	0	0	0	0	0	0	0	0	0
0	0	0	0	0	0	0	0	0	0
South London (four EACs)									
Labour EACs									
4	238	136	48	9	5	0	0	0	0
3	274	362	339	331	281	202	177	129	110
2	9	23	134	181	235	307	325	350	344
1	0	0	0	0	0	12	19	42	67
0	0	0	0	0	0	0	0	0	0

Estimation of the electoral impact of these solutions should have been relatively straightforward because the 92 parliamentary constituencies were used in the General Election of May 1979. A theoretical analysis could be conducted but, because the turnout—especially of Labour voters—was very much lower in the European election of June 1979 (Johnston, 1979b), this cannot be related to the actual election results. The discussion here is built on the assumption that, if everybody who voted in May had voted again in June, the distribution of votes between the parties would have been identical at the two contests.

The results are given in Table 4.7. In north London, the Labour party won 60 per cent of the votes at the General Election—standardized to a 50:50 share between the two parties (see above, p. 132). With the same turnout at the EEC elections, it was likely to win all six seats. This reflected a probable cracked gerrymander, since a slight swing to Conservative would make a 5:1 split the most probable, with a 4:2 split almost equally probable following a 4 per cent swing; swings to Labour not surprisingly made the probability of it winning all six seats even greater. (One might have anticipated more of a packed gerrymander situation, in that similar seats tend to cluster together, but clearly north London's relatively marginal parliamentary constituencies are widely enough spread to produce the EAC results shown here.) Of the 11 most shapely solutions, seven would have given all six seats to Labour with a 1 per cent swing to Conservative, but all would have given Labour only four with a 4 per cent swing to the opposition.

THIRD PERIODICAL REPORT OF THE BOUNDARY COMMISSION FOR ENGLAND

Following its report in 1969—which, because of political manoeuvrings by the incumbent Labour party (Johnston, 1979a), was not implemented until after the 1970 general election (some minor changes were introduced prior to that election)—the Boundary Commission for England must present its third periodical report by 1984 at the latest. It began its work on this in the late 1970s, after the introduction of a new local government system outside London. Thus its building blocks have been radically altered.

The new local government system

The Local Government Bill of 1971 for England and Wales (amended and passed in 1972) created a new system of local government outside Greater London. Each country was divided into counties, of which six (all in England) were designated metropolitan and the remainder were designated non-metropolitan. Each county was divided into a set of districts; for electoral purposes, under clause 8(b) 'every district shall be divided into wards, each returning a number of councillors which is divisible by three' (Local Government Bill, 1972). The first elections took place in 1973 and the new counties and districts took effect on 1 April 1974.

To oversee the operation of certain aspects of the Bill a Local Government Boundary Commission for each country was established (see Chisholm, 1975; 1976). Section 65 and Schedule 9 of the Bill identified the first major function for the Commission.

As soon as practicable after the first election of councillors for any new district in England, the English Commission shall review the electoral arrangements for that district . . . and . . . shall if they think fit, formulate . . . proposals (Local Government Bill 1972, p. 233).

The Rules to be used are set out in Schedule 11. For counties,

(2) So far as is reasonably practicable—
   (a) the number of local government electors shall be, as nearly as may be, the same in every electoral division;
   (b) every electoral division shall be wholly within a single district; . . .
(3) Regard shall be had to—
   (a) the number and distribution of local government electors of the county and any change in either likely to take place within the period of five years immediately following the consideration;
   (b) The desirability of fixing boundaries which are and will remain easily identifiable; . . .

(d) The boundaries of the wards of the districts in the county.
(Local Government Bill, 1972, p. 237)

For Greater London, excluding the City and the Temples which are considered a
ward of the City of Westminster.

(3) Every other electoral division of Greater London shall lie wholly within a
single London borough.
(4) Every parliamentary constituency wholly within a London borough shall
constitute an electoral division.
(Local Government Bill, 1972, p. 237)

And for districts and London boroughs,

(2) So far as is reasonably practicable the ratio of the number of local
government electors to the number of councillors to be elected shall be, as
nearly as may be, the same in every ward of the district or borough . . . .
(5) Regard shall be had to—
(a) the number and distribution of the local government electors of the
district or borough, and any change in either which is likely to take
place within the period of five years immediately following the
consideration; . . . .
(Local Government Bill, 1972, pp. 238–239)

On completing that task, the Commission was required (under clause 50 of the
Bill) to review all boundaries 'not less than ten or more than fifteen years after 1st
April 1974 and thereafter at intervals of not less than ten or more than fifteen
years' (Local Government Bill, 1972, p. 26). To aid the Commission:

it shall be the duty of the council for each district in England to keep the whole
of their district under review for the purpose of considering whether or not to
make recommendations to the English Commission . . .
(Local Government Bill, 1972, p. 27.)

The general procedures for the Commission to follow were also laid down in
the Local Government Bill; local authorities and others concerned were to be
consulted, and interested persons were to be informed of draft proposals and
given time to make comments on them before final decisions were forwarded to
the Home Secretary for approval. Within this framework the Commission
decided the following timetable (Local Government Boundary Commission for
England, 1973, pp. 4–5):

(1) Notice of intention to review the electoral arrangements in a local authority
will be given, and the local authority will be invited to prepare a draft scheme
in consultation with local interest groups.

(2) The Commission reviews the draft scheme and other local views. It then publishes its own proposals and invites comments.
(3) In most cases, formulation of final proposals will first require a local meeting to resolve differences of opinion: such meetings will be held by Assistant Commissioners.
(4) The Assistant Commissioners' report (where relevant) plus all other materials are considered in the preparation of a final proposal for presentation to the Home Secretary.

The criteria to be used were those set out in Schedule 11 to the Bill, and reproduced above.

Although the Local Government Boundary Commission makes the final decision on the ward system for each district—and hence the electoral arrangement—and its criteria are explicitly non-partisan, nevertheless two partisan elements are introduced. The first is that already presented as the main theme of this chapter: given a geography of partisan preferences and a territorial system of elections, there can be no non-partisan electoral cartography. The second is that by inviting the local authorities to submit draft proposals, in most cases (as most counties and districts were governed by partisan bodies) this was putting a major influence on the districting process into partisan hands. In that the neutral Commission made the final decisions, and that others (many of them minority partisan interest groups) could contest the local authority proposals, the potential for gerrymandering without malapportionment was not as great as in the United States. Nevertheless, it is likely that many of the Commission's final proposals (and they were required to make 377 sets of decisions in at most five years; they were later required to consider the London boroughs as well during this period) contained a significant partisan element.

The nature of the partisan element in the Local Government Boundary Commission's work is of only marginal relevance here. Of greater importance is its role in providing the new building blocks—of approximately equal population size—for the next review to be undertaken by the Parliamentary Boundary Commission. The rules for the latter were not changed, so that their current (1978–84?) review involves definition of a new set of constituencies within the boundaries of the new counties and using the new wards defined by the Local Government Boundary Commission. This final section assesses the likely electoral impact of their decisions in two urban areas—Greater London and Sheffield metropolitan district.

Greater London

According to the Local Government Bill each metropolitan borough is to be considered a separate unit for allocating constituencies. In reviewing population changes there since the previous report, the Boundary Commission for England decided that the Greater London County should lose eight constituencies

TABLE 4.8. Votes and seats in eight metropolitan boroughs, 1979, and possible solutions with electoral impact

| | Borough | | | | | | | |
	Camden	Hackney	Harrow	Haringey	Islington	Lambeth	Wandsworth	Westminster
1979 General Election								
Labour per cent								
Two-party vote	52.5	64.9	53.0	36.1	60.2	53.2	53.5	38.3
Seats								
Labour	2	3	2	0	3	3	3	0
Conservative	1	0	1	3	0	1	1	3
Possible solutions (electoral impact assuming 50:50 national split)								
Wards	26	23	23	21	20	22	22	24
Constituencies	2	2	2	2	2	3	3	2
Maximum per cent discrepancy	2	3	2	5	6	4	9	3
Labour per cent	58	73	61	41	64	57	51	43
Constituencies								
Labour	2	2	2	0	2	2	2	0
Conservative	0	0	0	2	0	1	1	2

according to the national electoral quota (which was based on 1976 population data). The boroughs to lose one seat each are Camden, Hackney, Haringey, Harrow, Islington, Lambeth, Wandsworth, and Westminster. Results there at the 1979 general election are shown in Table 4.8; these show that in every case the winning party got a greater percentage of the seats than of the votes, with especially strong winners' biases in all but Camden and Harrow.

Table 4.8 also shows the modal solution obtained by applying the districting algorithm, using 1979 voting data standardized to a national 50:50 split of the two-party votes. In the six boroughs whose representation has been reduced from three to two seats, the majority party wins both in every case despite its opponent obtaining in one case as much as 43 per cent of the vote. If anything, therefore, the reduction in number of seats appears to have accentuated the degree of electoral bias.

The distribution of results at given levels of uniform swing is indicated in

TABLE 4.9. The electoral impact of uniform swing in eight redistricted metropolitan boroughs

Labour Constituencies		Percentage swing								
		To Labour				0	To Conservative			
		4	3	2	1	0	1	2	3	4
Camden										
Labour	2	878	878	878	878	878	876	872	859	797
	1	0	0	0	0	0	0	0	13	75
Hackney										
Labour	2	284	284	284	284	284	284	284	284	284
Haringey										
Labour	2	334	334	334	334	334	334	323	308	282
Labour	1	0	0	0	0	0	0	11	26	52
Harrow										
Labour	1	120	69	35	17	5	1	0	0	0
	0	340	391	425	443	455	459	460	460	460
Islington										
Labour	2	128	128	128	128	128	128	128	128	128
Lambeth										
Labour	3	85	72	55	54	44	23	9	6	1
	2	12	25	42	43	53	74	88	89	84
	1	0	0	0	0	0	0	0	2	12
Wandsworth										
Labour	3	32	29	19	12	8	0	0	0	0
	2	39	42	52	59	59	47	33	11	5
	1	0	0	0	0	4	24	34	40	41
	0	0	0	0	0	0	0	4	20	25
Westminster										
Labour	1	74	61	52	36	32	21	9	5	2
Labour	0	31	44	53	69	73	84	96	100	103

Table 4.9. In the two most polarized boroughs—Hackney and Islington—Labour win both seats at all vote distributions shown. In the remaining six, however, there is strong evidence of a cracked gerrymander effect in the electoral bias shown in Table 4.8, with considerable variability in the distributions between the different voting levels. (The exceptions to this are Camden and Haringey: see below, however.) Thus in Lambeth, for example, a 4 per cent swing to Labour would give that party all three seats in 85 of the 97 solutions, whereas a 4 per cent swing to Conservative would virtually ensure it two seats, and perhaps bring it three.

As in its other redistricting exercises discussed here, the Boundary Commission produced solutions for these eight boroughs with high shape indices (see also Johnston and Rossiter, 1980b). In rank order position, the shape index for the chosen solution was: Camden, 1st (out of 878); Hackney, 1st (284); Haringey, 10th (334); Harrow, 2nd (460); Islington, 2nd (128); Lambeth 3rd (97); Wandsworth, 6th (71); and Westminster, 6th (105). Inspection of the 'most shapely' solutions shows that the cracked gerrymander is more apparent in these than in the total set. In Camden, for example, only 81 of the 878 solutions would give Conservative one seat with a 4 per cent swing to that party, but this is the case in 19 of the 29 most shapely solutions. (Figure 4.7 shows why this is so. The

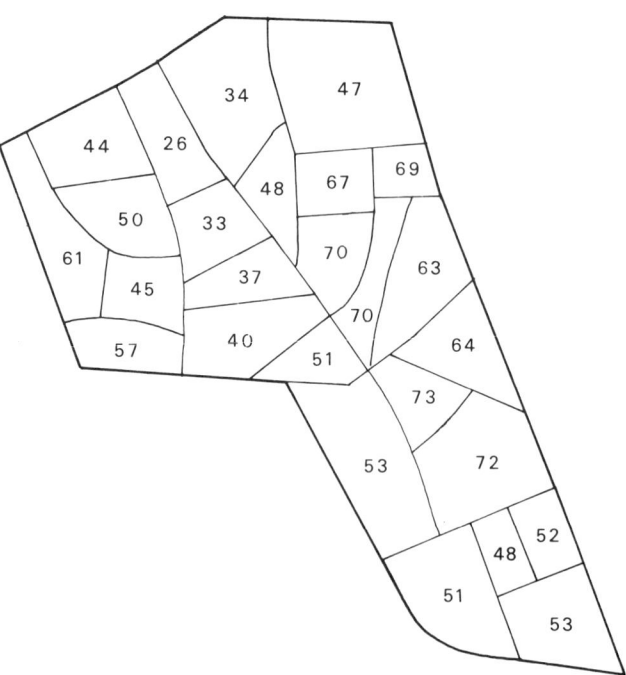

FIGURE 4.7.   Camden: the estimated percentage of votes won by Labour, by ward, in 1979

geography of the borough has a clear packed gerrymander base for all the more shapely solutions, which split it north: south rather than east:west.) Similarly, in Haringey the Conservatives would win one seat with a 4 per cent swing in 13 of the 18 most shapely solutions, but in only 52 of the 334 overall, and in Lambeth, Labour would win only two seats with a swing of 1 per cent or more to it in nine of the ten most shapely solutions, including that chosen by the Commissioners. In Westminster, nine of the ten most shapely solutions—again including the Commissioners' choice—would give Labour one seat at the 50:50 standardized rate, as they would in six cases with a swing of 1 per cent to Conservative. As in most of the other examples discussed here, in situations in which no party gets more than about 60 per cent of the two-party vote, the solutions with high shape indices tend to accentuate a cracked gerrymander.

Sheffield

As a consequence of the addition of uninhabited moorland to the north-west and several formerly independent settlements to the north, the new Sheffield metropolitan district is larger in both area and population than the former Sheffield county borough. Its parliamentary representation was not reduced, therefore, and the Boundary Commission was required to create six constituencies from the 29 wards defined in 1979. Given the relative equality of ward

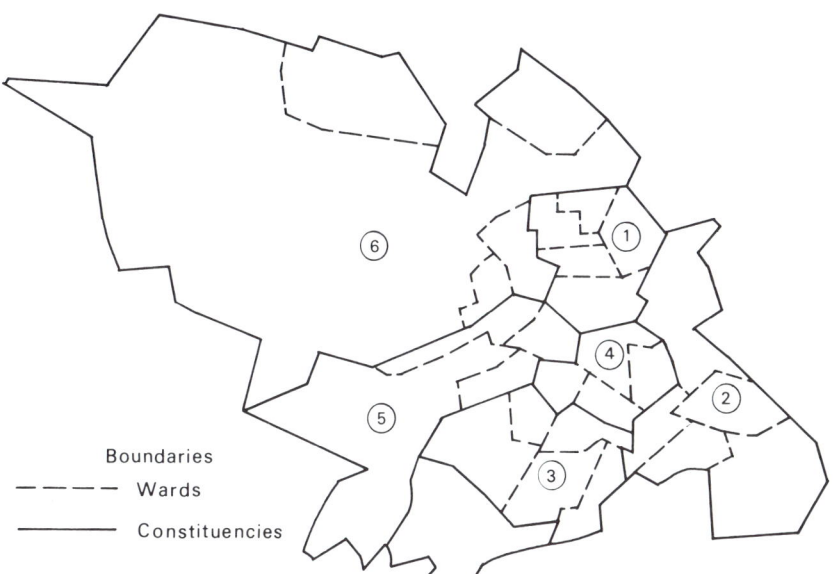

FIGURE 4.8.   Sheffield metropolitan district: the proposed constituencies according to the 1980 proposals of the Parliamentary Boundary Commission for England

populations (in the 1976 data used), this meant five constituencies comprising five wards each and one comprising only four. Their proposal (Figure 4.8) was published in November 1980. Two aspects of it are commented upon here.

The first aspect concerns the use of 1976 ward population data in drawing up a set of constituencies which is likely to be retained almost to the end of the century. The constituency comprising four wards—Park (constituency 4 in Figure 4.8)—already had the smallest population in 1976. By 1980 it had lost over 10 per cent of its electorate, as Table 4.10 shows:

TABLE 4.10   Sheffield constituencies

Constituency	1976 Electorate	1980 Electorate
1. Brightside	67 391	66 492
2. Darnall	75 146	76 220
3. Heeley	75 045	73 412
4. Park	63 590	56 757
5. Hallam	69 961	70 940
6. Hillsborough	69 193	72 818

The maximum deviation from the 1976 mean electorate of 70 054 was 9.2 per cent, and the average was 4.8 per cent. Park constituency contains much of Sheffield's inner city which is experiencing population decline, whereas its neighbour Darnall (2) contains the only area of considerable recent (and likely future) growth. By 1980, changes meant that the maximum deviation from the mean electorate was 18.3 per cent and the average was 7.5 per cent. If current trends continue, then by the time the new constituencies come into effect the maximum deviation could well be close to 25 per cent and when they are replaced in 1999 or thereabouts it could be much larger.

The second aspect worthy of comment is that of constituency shape. The Boundary Commission's proposal includes one constituency—Hallam (5)—which is markedly L-shaped. Using the 1976 population data, our algorithm identified 9949 possible sets of constituencies with a maximum deviation of 12 per cent or less. Of these, the Commissioners' solution ranked only 35th in terms of 'shapeliness'.

The rationale for the Sheffield proposal appears to be as follows. First, the Commission has tried to disrupt existing constituencies as little as possible, within the constraints of the new ward system. (See *The Times*, 2 April 1981, for discussion of its proposals for the West Midlands in which this was not done.) Thus in creating five constituencies within the area of the former Sheffield county borough (the sixth in Figure 4.8 mainly contains the areas added to Sheffield in 1974) the Commission appears to have sought continuity as far as possible, and this is well represented by the similarity between the former and proposed Park constituencies. Secondly, the Local Government Boundary Commission recognized the problem of inner-city population decline and created larger wards in terms of population there; the Parliamentary Boundary Commission does not appear to have realized this and has, at least implicitly, assumed that the wards in Park constituency will remain among the largest in the district. Since the present review is taking a long time, and is using relatively old population data, this means that already the constituencies vary considerably in their electorates and by the time they are used the variations may be very substantial. (The present review should lead to the new constituencies being enacted by 1984. If an early general election is held, however, they might not be used until 1987–8.)

The impact of this proposal is that it will almost certainly reduce Labour's representation in Sheffield from five to four seats. In part, this reflects the changed geography—both the distribution of population and the ward boundaries. Among the 9949 solutions identified using 1976 population data, and with 1980 local election results used to estimate vote distributions, a 4:2 result favouring Labour was almost as likely as 5:1 (Table 4.11A). A small swing to Labour would make 5:1 more likely, whereas a pro-Conservative movement would make 4:2 very likely. A cracked gerrymander for one seat is likely, therefore, whereas in the 1969 review a packed gerrymander, virtually ensuring 5:1, was the typical solution. A similar conclusion is drawn if 1980 population data are used (Table 4.11b), suggesting the importance of the changed geography relative to the Commission's choice of the small constituency as an influence on the character of Sheffield's representation in the 1980s.

TABLE 4.11. The electoral impact of uniform swing in Sheffield metropolitan district

Labour constituencies	To Labour				Percentage swing	To Conservative			
	4	3	2	1	0	1	2	3	4
A—1976 Electorates									
6	2097	1069	433	113	15	1	0	0	0
5	7684	8370	7960	6849	5082	3911	2812	2191	1454
4	168	510	1556	2987	4812	5890	6750	7204	7677
3	0	0	0	0	40	147	387	554	817
2	0	0	0	0	0	0	0	0	1
1	0	0	0	0	0	0	0	0	0
0	0	0	0	0	0	0	0	0	0
B—1980 Electorates									
6	1808	949	395	140	49	6	0	0	0
5	5336	5990	5793	5218	4180	3180	2128	1494	1014
4	51	256	1007	1837	2949	3922	4787	5265	5421
3	0	0	0	0	17	87	280	436	754
2	0	0	0	0	0	0	0	0	6
1	0	0	0	0	0	0	0	0	0
0	0	0	0	0	0	0	0	0	0

TABLE 4.12. Shape and the allocation of seats: Sheffield metropolitan district

Labour constituencies	Shape index < 200	200 224	225 249	250 274	275 299	300 324	325 <
A. 1976 Electorates							
3	0	3	20	15	2	0	0
4	8	243	1302	2248	930	81	0
5	2	220	1065	2264	1303	223	5
6	0	4	6	5	0	0	0
B. 1980 Electorates							
3	0	2	12	3	0	0	0
4	3	122	661	1380	697	85	1
5	2	165	944	1732	1116	215	6
6	0	2	27	17	3	0	0

The discussion in the previous paragraph refers to all of the solutions available to the Commission within a 12 per cent maximum deviation constraint. Cross-classifying seats won against shape, Table 4.12a shows that a 5:1 victory favouring Labour is the likely result in about 70 per cent of the more shapely solutions, including all five of those with the highest indices, produced using 1976 population data. (A similar conclusion is drawn from the solutions using 1980 population data: Table 4.12b.) However, inspection of the likely results among the 'most shapely' solutions with a small swing to Conservative shows that a 4:2 allocation of seats is more likely than 5:1 in three of the five. Again, therefore, it seems that it is the new geography of Sheffield rather than the Commission's selection which has changed the political balance there; one safe Conservative constituency, four safe Labour constituencies, and one relatively marginal constituency is the likely outcome of the population and shape constraints on the Commission's choice.

CONCLUSIONS

Electoral reform is an issue which reappears on the British political agenda every few decades. In the 1970s it was raised by the Liberal party, which won a much smaller percentage of votes than of seats in both of the 1974 general elections. Bias against the Liberals results from the equivalent of a cracked gerrymander; the party has few concentrations of votes and so loses in nearly every seat, whereas a different geography of support could give it a very different level of parliamentary representation.

Less frequently commented on is the bias against one of the two main parties in most of the administrative areas within which Parliamentary constituencies are defined. This is because that bias is not overwhelmingly in favour of one party; in general, Labour benefits in urban areas and Conservative in rural areas. (This relative balance is one reason why neither of the two main parties is in favour of electoral reform, for both would suffer substantially under any system more closely aligned with proportional representation.) The production of that bias has been the subject of the present essay, which has shown how the detail of the geography of voting for the different parties and the spatial building blocks (the wards in urban areas) combine to constrain the delimitation procedure undertaken by the Parliamentary Boundary Commissions. The latter also work within the constraints of a set of rules laid down by Parliament and of their own precedents. The results invariably have the character of a gerrymander, despite the politically neutral status of the Commissions.

Each redistricting exercise undertaken by the Commissions involves a new geography, because of changing partisan preferences and migration patterns. The current (1979) review is also using a new set of building blocks, following the reorganization of local government introduced in 1974 and the new wards defined in the late 1970s. These new constraints may lead to a different pattern of electoral bias. Curtice and Steed's (1981) analysis of postwar election results suggests (to us) a clear break in the general trends when the new constituencies were introduced in 1974. A further break may occur when the next set of constituencies is first used. As county boroughs have been abolished, the likelihood is that—outside Greater London and the six metropolitan counties—this redistribution of seats will favour the Conservative party, because of the removal of many separate, Labour-dominated, urban areas. This could make it much more difficult for the Labour party to win a majority of seats in the House of Commons; it could even lead to change of official Labour policy on electoral reform.

ACKNOWLEDGEMENT

Financial support for this research was provided by the Social Science Research Council under grant HR 5939/2: this support is gratefully acknowledged. Figure 4.2 is reproduced for *Legislative Studies Quarterly*, © Comparative Legislative Research Center at the University of Iowa.

REFERENCES

Alford, R. R. (1963). *Party and Society*, Rand McNally, Chicago.
Axelrod, R. (1972). Where the votes come from: an analysis of electoral coalitions, 1952–1968. *American Political Science Review*, **66**, 11–20.
Boundary Commission for England (1954). *First Periodical Report*, HMSO, London, Cmnd. 9311.
Boundary Commission for England (1969). *Second Periodical Report*, HMSO, London, Cmnd. 4084.
Boundary Commission for England (1978). *Report: European Assembly Constituencies*, HMSO, London, Cmnd. 7348.
Boundary Commission for Scotland (1954). *First Periodical Report*, HMSO, London, Cmnd. 9312.

Boundary Commission for Scotland (1969). *Second Periodical Report*, HMSO, London, Cmnd. 4085.
Boundary Commission for Scotland (1978). *Report: European Assembly Constituencies*, HMSO, London, Cmnd. 7336.
Boundary Commission for Wales (1954). *First Periodical Report*, HMSO, London, Cmnd. 9313.
Boundary Commission for Wales (1969). *Second Periodical Report*, HMSO, London, Cmnd. 4086.
Boundary Conmission for Wales (1978). *Report: European Assembly Constituencies*, HMSO, London, Cmnd. 7362.
Butler, D. E. (1963). *The British Electoral System since 1918*, Clarendon Press, Oxford.
Butler, D. E. and Stokes, D. (1974). *Political Change in Britain*, (2nd edition), Macmillan, London.
Chisholm, M. (1975). The reformation of local government in England. In R. F. Peel, P. Haggett and M. Chisholm (Eds.), *Processes in Physical and Human Geography: Bristol Essays*, Heinemann, London, pp. 305–318.
Chisholm, M. (1976). Academics and government. In J. T. Coppock and W. R. D. Sewell (Eds.), *Spatial Dimensions of Public Policy*, Pergamon Press, Oxford, pp. 67–85.
Curtice, J. and Steed, M. (1981). Electoral choice and the production of government: the changing operation of the UK electoral system since 1955. Paper presented to the Political Studies Association.
Engstrom, R. L. (1976). The Supreme Court and equipopulous gerrymandering. *Arizona State Law Journal*, **2**, 277–319.
Engstrom, R. L. and Wildgen, J. K. (1977). Pruning thorns from the thicket: an empirical test of the existence of racial gerrymandering. *Legislative Studies Quarterly*, **4**, 465–479.
Fitzmaurice, J. (1978). *The European Parliament*, Saxon House, Teakfield, Farnborough, Hants.
Freeman, T. W. (1968). *Geography and Regional Administration*, Hutchinson, London.
Garfinkel, R. S. and Taylor, H. (1969). Optimum political districting by implicit enumeration technique. *Management Science*, **16**, 495–512.
Gudgin, G. and Taylor, P. J. (1979). *Seats, Votes and the Spatial Organization of Elections*, Pion Ltd., London.
Herbert, D. T. and Johnston, R. J. (Eds.) (1976). *Social Areas in Cities*, John Wiley, London.
Jenkins, M. A. and Shepherd, J. W. (1972). Decentralizing high school administration in Detroit: an evaluation of alternative strategies of political control. *Economic Geography*, **48**, 95–106.
Johnston, R. J. (1979a). *Political, Electoral and Spatial Systems*, Oxford University Press, Oxford.
Johnston, R. J. (1979b). Tory voters went to European polls. *Geographical Magazine*, **51**, 785.
Johnston, R. J. (1980). *City and Society*, Penguin Books, London.
Johnston, R. J. and Hughes, C. A. (1978). Constituency delimitation and the unintentional gerrymander in Brisbane. *Australian Geographical Studies*, **16**, 99–110.
Johnston, R. J. and Rossiter, D. J. (1979). *Regionalisation and the Geography of Constituency Boundaries*. Report on Grant HR 5939/2 to the Social Science Research Council.
Johnston, R. J. and Rossiter, D. J. (1980a). Geography is the clue to election victories. *Geographical Magazine*, **52**, 848–849.
Johnston, R. J. and Rossiter, D. J. (1980b). The current redistribution of Parliamentary seats: eight Greater London boroughs. *Area*, **12**, 223–228.

Johnston, R. J. and Rossiter, D. J. (1981a). An approach to the delimitation of planning regions. *Applied Geography*, 1, 55–70.

Johnston, R. J. and Rossiter, D. J. (1981b). Shape and the definition of Parliamentary constituencies. *Urban Studies*, 18, 219–223.

Keech, W. R. (1968). *The Impact of Negro Voting*, Rand McNally, Chicago.

Kendall, M. G. and Stuart, A. (1950). The law of the cubic proportion in election results. *British Journal of Sociology*, 1, 183–196.

Laakso, M. (1979). Should a two-and-a-half law replace the cube law in British elections? *British Journal of Political Science*, 9, 355–362.

Lewis, P. F. (1976). *New Orleans*, Ballinger, Cambridge, Mass.

Local Government Boundary Commission for England (1973). *Report No. 6*, HMSO, London.

Loosemore, J. and Hanby, V. J. (1971). The theoretical limits of maximum distortion: some analytic expressions for electoral systems. *British Journal of Political Science*, 1, 467–477.

Musgrave, P. (1977). *The General Theory of Gerrymandering*, Sage Publications, Beverly Hills, Cal.

Murdie, R. A. (1976). Spatial form in the residential mosaic. In D. T. Herbert and R. J. Johnston (Eds.), *Social Areas in Cities, Vol. 1*, John Wiley, London, pp. 237–272.

Openshaw, S. (1977). An optimal zoning approach to the study of spatially aggregated data. In I. Masser and P. J. B. Brown (Eds.), *Spatial Representation and Spatial Interaction*, Martinus Nijhoff, Leiden/Boston, pp. 96–113.

Rose, R. (Ed.) (1974). *Electoral Behavior*, Free Press, New York.

Rossiter, D. J. and Johnston, R. J. (1981). Program GROUP: the identification of all possible solutions to a constituency delimitation problem. *Environment and Planning A*, 13, 231–238.

Sammons, R. (1976). *Zoning Systems for Spatial Models*, Geographical Paper 52, Department of Geography, University of Reading.

Sammons, R. (1978). A simplistic approach to the redistricting problem. In I. Masser and P. J. B. Brown (Eds.), *Spatial Representation and Spatial Interaction*, Martinus Nijhof, Leiden/Boston, pp. 71–94.

Taagepera, R. and Laakso, M. (1980). Proportionality profiles of West European electoral systems. *European Journal of Political Research*, 8, 423–446.

Taylor, P. J. (1973). A new shape measure for evaluating electoral district patterns. *American Political Science Review*, 67, 947–950.

Taylor, P. J. (1979). The changing geography of representation in Britain, *Area*, 11, 289–294.

Taylor, P. J. and Gudgin, G. (1975). A fresh look at the Parliamentary Boundary Commissions. *Parliamentary Affairs*, 28, 405–415.

Taylor, P. J. and Gudgin, G. (1976a). The statistical basis of decision-making in electoral districting. *Environment and Planning A*, 8, 43–58.

Taylor, P. J. and Gudgin, G. (1976b). The myth of non-partisan cartography, *Urban Studies*, 13, 13–25.

Taylor, P. J. and Gudgin, G. (1980). The decomposition of electoral bias in a plurality election. *British Journal of Political Science*, 10, 515–521.

Taylor, P. J. and Johnston, R. J. (1979). *Geography of Elections*, Penguin Books, London.

Tufte, E. R. (1973). The relationship between seats and votes in two-party systems. *American Political Science Review*, 67, 540–554.

Wildgen, J. K. and Engstrom, R. L. (1980). Spatial distribution of partisan support and the seats/votes relationship. *Legislative Studies Quarterly*, 5, 423–435.

Geography and the Urban Environment
Progress in Research and its Applications, Volume V
Edited by D. T. Herbert and R. J. Johnston
©1982 John Wiley & Sons Ltd.

Chapter 5

Natural Hazards and Urban Planning

Graham A. Tobin

Recent studies of the global extent of natural hazards have indicated that both economic losses and the number of deaths have risen in spite of huge investments in measures to mitigate such events (Dworkin, 1974). Various suggestions have been offered to explain this apparent anomaly. Chambers (1975) put some of the responsibility on poor decision-making criteria at the outset, while others have criticized either the traditional dependence upon engineering 'solutions' (Kazmann, 1972; O'Riordan, 1971; White, 1973) or the limited attention devoted to non-structural measures (Ericksen, 1967). Increased losses have also been attributed to poor individual behaviour and a negative attitude to hazards at the local level (see, for example, Harding and Parker, 1974; James, Laurent, and Hill 1971; Smith and Tobin, 1979). Although all these explanations undoubtedly account for the substantial losses and numerous deaths accruing from hazardous events, the fundamental cause of such problems has been man's encroachment into hazard-prone areas. This situation is aggravated further by increased urbanization, which has put high concentrations of people at risk. A basic failure to plan the development of urban communities in response to natural hazards has produced the present situation where many towns and cities face catastrophic problems in the future.

This chapter is divided into four main parts. A brief examination of human dimensions of natural hazards is followed by a general review of land-use planning principles and the many constraints on the planning process. The third part looks at some of those measures used in urban planning, from mandatory legislation to fiscal inducements and direct public action. The final section takes an overview of the planning process and makes suggestions for further requirements in the form of comprehensive planning models to reduce hazard losses. This chapter does not review the detailed physical processes of each natural hazard, although mention is made of such phenomena where planning decisions are contingent upon them. An analysis of the traditional technological adjustments and non-structural measures is not within the brief of this work, although their importance to comprehensive planning is stressed.

HUMAN DIMENSIONS OF NATURAL HAZARDS

Natural hazards constitute a complex interaction between more extreme elements of the physical environment and activities within the human-use system (Baker, 1976). Certainly, they are natural events in terms of the physical processes involved, but become hazardous only when they conflict with the goals of society. The extent of social disruption varies according to both the intensity of the physical event generated and the level of human activity located in the hazardous area. The potential for disaster, therefore, is particularly high in densely populated industrial centres, where the level of investment is considerable. In addition, the type of structure and development pattern, as well as mitigation measures, will have some bearing upon the impact of such events.

Hazard losses

In an examination of natural hazards at the global scale, direct losses would appear to account for approximately US $25 billion per annum with a further US $15 billion spent on hazard prevention and mitigation (Burton, Kates, and White, 1978). Furthermore, during the average year 250 000 people will die from such events. While these figures indicate the significance of natural hazards around the world, a further disturbing feature is the spatial distribution of such events; 95 per cent of disaster-related deaths occur in poorer nations, which, in

TABLE 5.1.   Disasters to which UNDRO responded, 1979 (adapted from UNDRO, 1980)

Month	Country	Event	Month	Country	Event
January	Bolivia	floods	June	Jamaica	floods
	Mozambique	hurricane	July	Indonesia	tsunami
	Senegal	floods		Nepal	floods
February	Indonesia	floods	August	Ethiopia	floods
	Indonesia	landslides	September	Dominica	hurricane
	Indonesia	volcanic eruption		Dominican Republic	hurricane
	Solomon Islands	hurricane	October	Colombia	floods
March	Fiji	hurricane		Egypt	floods
	Paraguay	floods	November	Colombia	earthquake
	Tunisia	floods		Honduras	floods
April	St Vincent	volcanic eruption		Iran	earthquake
				Yugoslavia	floods
	Yugoslavia	earthquake		Colombia	earthquake
May	Argentina	floods	December	Mauritius	hurricane
	Indonesia	earthquake		Nicaragua	floods
	Malawi	floods			

terms of world population, constitute only 66 per cent of the total. Economic loss, on the other hand, is commensurate with income levels, since 75 per cent accrues in the wealthier nations. However, the relative loss to the community is undoubtedly more severe and of greater significance to the developing nations. Recent trends of hazards do not indicate any substantial improvement, especially for the poorer countries where both deaths and economic losses are increasing (Dworkin, 1974). Given that extreme natural events have probably not increased in frequency or intensity, these trends must be a consequence of a change in the human-use system. Although natural hazards occur regularly on a wide scale around the world, many go unnoticed unless the news media bring the event to the public attention for a few days. The United Nations Disaster Relief Office (UNDRO) attempts to coordinate relief operations in some disaster-prone areas, but this by no means accounts for all hazards. Table 5.1 illustrates UNDRO's response to events in just one year—1979. More detailed figures of hazard losses may be found in the various texts cited above.

Population trends

Indicative of these rising losses has been the corresponding growth in population. The present world population of 4.25 billion is estimated to reach 6.5 billion by the turn of the century, a total increase of about 4 billion during the 20th century (World Bank, 1980). This trend has contributed to the hazard by exposing more people to the danger and has brought more economic investment into direct conflict with the extremes of nature. The situation is further aggravated for the

TABLE 5.2. Population and urbanization of selected nations (adapted from World Bank, 1980)

Country		Popula-tion (million)	Growth average annual per cent 1970–78	Pro-jected popula-tion 2000	Urban per cent 1978	Growth average annual per cent 1970–78
Low-income	Bangladesh	84.7	2.7	143	11	6.6
	Mali	6.3	2.5	11	20	5.5
	India	643.9	2.0	974	22	3.3
Middle-income	Ghana	11.0	3.0	21	36	5.2
	Honduras	3.4	3.3	7	36	5.5
	Peru	16.8	2.7	29	67	4.4
	Turkey	43.1	2.5	65	47	4.6
Industrial	United Kingdom	55.8	0.1	58	91	0.3
	Japan	114.9	1.2	131	78	2.0
	United States	221.9	0.8	252	73	1.2
Centrally	China	952.2	1.6	1251	25	3.1
planned	USSR	261.0	0.9	310	65	2.2

poorer nations, which at present have exceptionally high population growth rates, and therefore will have additional problems in the future (Table 5.2).

The spatial distribution of the population is important since it is from this that an indication of the potential hazard can be obtained. Both the density of population and the intensity of land-use are prime determinants of hazard losses and neither should be overlooked. Urbanization, a prevalent trend throughout this century, has clearly exacerbated some hazard problems by concentrating large numbers of people and economic investment into relatively confined, hazard-prone areas. Many small communities have expanded rapidly into modern industrial complexes with little or no regard for possible constraints of the physical environment. As a result, many cities now face recurring natural hazards from this hasty and ill-conceived development. Despite these lessons, uncontrolled urban expansion is still continuing in many countries, especially in some of the poorer nations where urban populations are rising at twice the rate of the general population (Table 5.2). For example, Colombo (in Sri Lanka) has expanded down into the surrounding lowlands and now suffers from flooding, while Kingston (Jamaica) and Mexico City have both spread onto unstable alluvial material which will lead to large losses from future earthquakes. Without the necessary controls on urbanization, these nations can expect catastrophic losses in many cities in the future.

Hazard problems have been increased further and planning made more complex by the growth of squatter settlements in and around major cities. The populations of these communities may be growing at twice the rate of most urban areas (Torry, 1980). These squatter settlements characteristically occupy some of the most hazardous areas within the city, and the poorly constructed dwellings invariably offer little protection from even minimal geophysical events. For example, the steep unstable hillsides in Lima, Rio de Janeiro and Hong Kong have been settled by squatters, as have the flood-prone marshes and lowlands around Santiago, Karachi and Davao (Philippines), along with the ravines and verges in Caracas, Mexico City, Algiers, Delhi and Manila (Turner, 1969).

These high urban growth rates have not only seen an increase in the physical extent of the community, but have also brought about greater urban densities of population. Densities in some cities of developing nations have risen to 60 000 persons per km^2 although average densities may be around 10 000 persons per km^2. In squatter communities, urban densities as high as 100 000 and 149 000 persons per km^2 have been found in Morocco and India respectively (UNDRO, 1977b). A combination of these densities with high physical risk make these communities particularly susceptible to major disasters. Torry (1980), for instance, has pointed out that in some Turkish cities, many of which are subject to periodic earthquakes, there are very high population densities, with up to 60 per cent of the inhabitants living in the squatter quarters. The relationship of the hazard problem in conjunction with population trends as it pertains to developing nations has been described by UNDRO (1977b, p. 1): "The major regions of the world exposed to violent natural phenomena (especially earthquakes, Tsunamis and tropical cyclones) stretch across the tropical and subtropical portions of Africa, Asia and Latin America. These coincide with areas of rapid population growth and urbanisation and are extremely disaster prone."

The location of dense populations in hazardous areas is not the prerogative of the third world, for many cities in wealthy nations are also hazardously situated and will suffer in the future. For instance, the probability that San Francisco will be devastated by a large-magnitude earthquake is extremely high; the cities of London and Rotterdam are both subject to extensive flooding given certain atmospheric conditions over the North Sea; and Tokyo can expect further earthquakes similar to the one which destroyed the city in 1923, as can many of the towns surrounding the Adriatic Sea. Hurricanes threaten communities such as Miami, New Orleans, Houston and Havana, while damage from volcanic activity will disrupt settlements in Iceland, Italy, the United States, South America and Japan. Obviously, these represent only a few of the towns and cities around the world which occupy hazardous locations. There are of course many other hazards, such as tornadoes, droughts, floods, severe storms and snowfall which add to the risk, and it can be said that virtually all cities are subject to some form of natural disaster.

Hazard impact

The impact of natural hazards will vary depending on the extent of social and economic disruption. Many hazards have had an impact at the global level. For example, the tropical cyclone which devastated Bangladesh in 1970, killing over 200 000 persons, and the Sahel drought in the early 1970s both evoked media attention around the world. However, there are numerous smaller events occurring regularly which are less newsworthy, but which nevertheless produce severe economic consequences at the local, regional or national level. In poor nations, such events may threaten the very existence of the state. Frequent disasters hinder the socioeconomic development of the nation and even individual events can exert losses in excess of 3 per cent of the nation's GNP. It has been estimated that to offset such losses a GNP growth rate of 6 per cent would be required merely to maintain the rising population at current standards. Such growth levels are rarely achieved in developing nations. For instance, the Economic Commission for Latin America estimated that natural disasters in five countries of the Central American Common Market reduced average annual growth rates by 2.3 per cent between 1960 and 1974. This compared with 1.7 per cent for the United States (UNDRO, 1979).

In conclusion, hazards exist because man has built in areas exposed to extremes of nature. The potential for disaster remains high in many communities—a direct consequence in many instances of disorderly urban development bringing dense populations into conflict with the natural environment.

LAND-USE PLANNING—GENERAL PRINCIPLES

In view of the problems presented above, there has been a movement in recent years towards land-use planning as a means of minimizing future hazard losses. The failure of traditional hazard mitigation measures, particularly structural engineering schemes, to reduce such losses has added support to this. Most proposals now advocate that more attention be devoted to the human-use system rather than concentrating on controlling physical processes. Urban planning, therefore, should balance the goals and demands of society against the constraints of nature to achieve a more satisfactory human environment. To achieve this, Baker (1976) advocated that activities with a high loss potential should be discouraged from hazardous areas and uses limited to those which can withstand periodic extremes of nature. The city and the physical environment should be analysed as a single unit so that all relevant factors might be considered. Detwyler and Marcus (1972) proposed that a systems approach to planning, viewing the city as an integrated system of man and environment, would best achieve this objective. Such an approach would at least encourage further consideration of environmental parameters which have generally been ignored in the urban-planning process.

Planning—basic principles

Planning for hazard mitigation involves certain basic principles, all of which should be evaluated before any final plan is adopted. Burton, Kates and White (1978) proposed three areas of consideration.

(1) Hazards always result from interaction of physical and human systems, and to treat them as purely climatic, geological, political, social or economic is to risk omission of components that must be taken into account if sound solutions are to be found.
(2) The use of resources in hazardous areas leads to both social benefits and social costs, and thus it would seem pertinent to examine the trade-off between the two.
(3) In only extremely rare circumstances is there solely one adjustment that merits adoption. Usually there are various alternative schemes which may prove equally effective.

While these three basic principles offer no real advance in our understanding of hazards, they have frequently been overlooked for planning purposes. There has been little recognition of the fact that planners have created many hazardous situations by an inadequate consideration of the physical environment. Socioeconomic factors have also been ignored while decisions have been based on a poor evaluation of the costs and benefits of a limited range of schemes. Even where town plans have existed there has been a failure to apply such basic principles, and hence urban development is still continuing to create hazard problems. Certain criteria, therefore, would seem important to the planning process.

Physical criteria

One of the most significant omissions from any development proposals in the past has been a detailed assessment of the physical environment, an omission which could be viewed as the fundamental cause of current urban hazard problems. Several authors have stressed the need for such physical evaluations, but generally these have been ignored (Legget, 1973; Utgard, McKenzie, and Foley, 1978; Wolman, 1971). Physical criteria have not been fully appreciated in the past, so that towns and cities are full of structures which suffer repeated damage because of their hazardous locations. Urbanization has even aggravated the physical risk of some events. Nakano (1974) described the effect of new town construction on steep slopes in Japan which has added to the landslide potential.

A physical evaluation, however, does not guarantee success in planning. A simple analysis of such basic requirements as water resources was carried out in the Sahel region before nomadic and semi-nomadic pastoralists were encouraged to adopt permanent settlements. However, the whole ecological system was incapable of supporting such lifestyles, and this contributed to the drought hazard which culminated in thousands of deaths (Halderman, 1972). On other occasions, physical studies have been ignored. The town of Anchorage (Alaska) expanded onto clays which were known to liquefy in the event of any seismic activity—a USGS report in 1959 described the problem most clearly. This information was omitted from any planning considerations and apparently deemed unimportant; the fallacy of such blatant disregard of the physical environment was demonstrated in 1964 when an earthquake struck the area.

Socioeconomic criteria

The attraction of particular sites for development has frequently been determined by social and economic factors. All too often decisions have been based on little more than the perceived advantages and disadvantages of such a location in a crude benefit-cost study. The evaluation of physical criteria has seldom warranted detailed considerations, and hazard risks have rarely been appraised accurately. Any awareness of the hazard has invariably been nullified by a complete faith in alleviation schemes to eliminate the risk. Nevertheless, there are many advantages to certain hazardous locations, from the fertile floodplain of the lower Ganges and coastal lowlands of Bangladesh to the aesthetic qualities of mountainous retreats. For example, a large number of settlements derive a variety of benefits from locations adjacent to active volcanoes in Italy, Iceland, Hawaii and many others. Periodically towns in these areas will suffer extensive damage, but the surviving inhabitants will invariably return to the same location. Such destruction has occurred regularly to Indonesian communities around Marapi Volcano with several thousand killed on occasions, but still the survivors return (UNDRO, 1977a). Urban planning, therefore, should recognize these socioeconomic factors. A particular site may well offer sound economic advantages, and there may be a strong social desire to relocate in the same area even after a catastrophic event. The rebuilding of San Francisco much the same as it was prior to the earthquake of 1906 illustrates this point. Planning must balance these demands and try to minimize the impact of future events.

Despite rising hazard losses, urban development is also creating new hazardous areas. Mitchell (1975) has examined the trend in the United States towards coastal locations, which has added not only to potential hurricane losses, but also to coastal erosion problems. It seems the south and south-west have become the areas to which large numbers are moving, many to retire. Ives and Krebs (1978) described another hazard which has been aggravated by recent urban development. Many mountain communities, such as Vail in Colorado, have experienced rapid urban expansion as a consequence of heightened interest in winter sports. This has increased the potential damage and deaths from snow avalanches, because much of this development has been carried out by persons with only limited knowledge of mountain conditions.

Political criteria

While the omission of physical studies from the decision-making process may be the fundamental cause of many hazard problems and socioeconomic factors the spur to such hazardous development, political factors have at times played a significant role. Governments, for instance, have traditionally implemented large-scale engineering schemes to control hazards, with the full support of local populations. These offer protection against hazardous events only to certain design standards, but they invariably instil a feeling of complete safety in the local community. This false sense of security frequently generates further development in the hazardous areas—the so-called levee effect—which can lead to even greater losses than before, when an event exceeds the protection level of the alleviation measure. Other communities which have been exposed to hazards have come to expect some form of relief in the form of a structural alleviation scheme, or, failing this, financial support from a national/regional emergency fund. As a result, many settlements have not worried unduly about the adverse effects of the physical environment. While such alleviation measures should not be disregarded completely, it is suggested that they be incorporated only as part of a fully comprehensive urban plan. Planning as a first priority should attempt to discourage hazardous development and only where absolutely necessary offer structural protection.

Planning goals

The ultimate goal in land-use planning for hazard-reduction is to steer unnecessary development away from those areas subject to severe natural phenomena. In this way, planning is a key factor in the orderly and safe development of urban centres. However, the alleviation of hazard losses is not the sole consideration in urban planning. Planning must translate many social and economic goals into physical patterns of land-use, but should also maintain an appropriate quality of the environment. It is the responsibility of the planner to balance these often conflicting interests and to make a composite plan based on all the basic principles outlined above.

The specific objectives of urban planning in response to natural hazards are fairly straightforward. The initial goal is usually to reduce losses, both in numbers killed and injured and financial damage, so that the society may function more smoothly. White and Haas (1975) have defined such goals as:

(1) reduction in net losses to property;
(2) reduction in the number of casualties;
(3) avoidance of social disruption;
(4) protection and enhancement of the natural environment; and
(5) more equitable distribution of costs and benefits.

Such goals would seem reasonable in any hazard-planning. Ciborowski (1978) examined urban planning in response to the earthquake hazard and put forward similar goals. He stressed the need for planners to incorporate all possible measures into the planning structure to make cities earthquake resistant and safe for human life. He also recognized that these measures, beginning with site selection and regulated land-use patterns, may be in direct conflict with other interests and that certain trade-offs would be necessary.

In practice, these planning goals may be somewhat restricted by the level of development which has already occurred, but for those centres currently experiencing rapid urbanization, careful preplanning offers an ideal opportunity to minimize future problems. Planning may curtail different land-uses particularly vulnerable to local hazards or may enforce legal requirements on the design standards of structures. In more established centres, however, there is less potential for such comprehensive planning, and longer-term projects may be required which establish a policy of gradual change and urban renewal. Certainly much of the present movement into hazardous areas is unwarranted and should be curtailed both in new and older communities. Much of the recent floodplain encroachment in the United States, for instance, derives no economic benefit from such locations (White and Haas, 1975). Planners, therefore, should recognize such trends and encourage more effective locational decisions and rational use of land.

PLANNING CONSTRAINTS

Physical constraints and environmental risk factors

Considerable urban expansion into hazardous areas has occurred because only limited attention has been devoted to environmental factors. One of the initial steps for hazard planning, therefore, should be to heighten awareness of potentially hazardous situations by carefully examining the physical constraints of the environment. Without such basic recognition, there will be little acceptance of urban planning for hazards. Various authors have stressed the need for detailed physical studies as the fundamental key to hazard-loss reduction in urban planning (see for example Andrews, 1978; Bolt et al., 1977; Legget, 1973; Utgard, McKenzie, and Foley, 1978; Vitek and Marsh, 1978).

Detailed natural hazard studies should be made to determine which hazards may occur in a particular area, the spatial extent of such events and the physical characteristics of any hazards, including intensity, duration, speed of onset, etc. Many of these criteria are already available, although they may not be site-specific, and should form the basis of all urban planning programmes. Policies should be contingent upon detailed analyses of the physical environment, because they can influence the efficacy of different schemes. These are the tools for resource planning and management as described by Ringler and Kennaugh (1974). For instance, a zoning programme (see below) may be ideal in certain situations such as flooding, but less satisfactory for a meteorological hazard like tornadoes. The relative patterns and intensities of different hazards, therefore, should help determine the appropriate planning strategy.

The detailed physical effects of hazards are also important considerations in planning. For instance, flash flooding can cause quite intense localized problems which can result in severe structural damage, whereas more extensive down-stream flooding will present problems of longer-term duration and possibly more sedimentation. Any planning programme incorporating structural design will need to assess the intensity and other characteristics of the hazards. Particular problems are found with seismic activity. Ground surface displace-ment along fault lines may occur on occasions; more frequently, however, ground motion and shaking, slope instability problems, and liquefaction of soil materials will occur. These different effects can have a profound influence on earthquake safety in urban areas. For example, several large buildings in Japan and Alaska have collapsed due to the liquefaction of underlying clays. Very detailed local studies, therefore, are required to identify all these potential problems. Furthermore, any planning programme should not be devoted to one hazard, but should also recognize the delicate link between different events. Earthquakes, for instance, can lead to avalanches and slope failures as well as fires and floods. Ciborowski (1978) encouraged consideration of the 'chain of events' in hazard studies, noting that both Tokyo and San Francisco experienced extensive fires following catastrophic earthquakes.

Further information should be collected on the probable frequency of hazardous events. These data could then be used with other physical criteria to determine the relative risk potential of an area. Hazard frequency can be assessed from previous occurrences from which the expected 'return period' may be calculated for specific size events. In terms of flooding, a certain size event (or larger) may be assessed as having a return period or recurrence interval, say of once every 50 years. This means that such an event can be expected an average of once in this time-period, or, expressed another way, has a probability of occurrence in any given year of 0.02. Other hazard frequencies can be calculated in a similar fashion, which can aid planning because damage can be assessed from expected frequencies of different size events. In areas where there are insufficient records for such calculations to be made with any degree of accuracy a more probabilistic approach may be adopted. However, there are other methods of extending records and Allen (1976) has used geological information to improve earthquake records in California, Japan, Turkey and the Philippines.

Mapping programmes

The basic information obtained from the assessment of natural hazards should be used to prepare maps of potential risk areas. These maps are essential for land-use planning in hazard mitigation. They should indicate not only the spatial extent of different hazards, but also the probable intensity and frequency of the events. Only after this detailed research should decisions be made as to appropriate land-uses and investment levels, since from these a full picture of risk involved can be seen. An additional advantage is that such maps can alert the unwary to the possibility of hazard problems as well as indicate which properties are already at risk.

White (1970) advocated more extensive use of such mapping techniques, which in hazard-planning would seem particularly sound advice. However, there has been a fairly long record of such mapping for some hazards, although for the most part they have been neglected by planning authorities. In 1919, for example, the Volcanological Survey of the Netherland Indies prescribed 'areas of danger' around several active volcanoes. This work has recently been continued by the Geological Survey of Indonesia. In fact the volcano hazard has received substantial attention and hazard maps can be found for Kamchatka (USSR), Auckland (New Zealand), Mayon (Philippines), Hawaii, and north-west

United States (Bolt *et al.*, 1977; UNDRO, 1977a). However, most of these maps are of too small a scale to be of practical value for detailed urban planning. For many hazards, more detailed local features are necessary if the planning programme is to be effective. The seismic hazard in particular requires specific information if the various associated problems are to be redressed. Planning strategies must reflect these local factors and hence detailed large-scale maps are essential (Rockaway, 1975; UNDRO, 1978a).

There are now quite a large number of examples of detailed hazard mapping. In the United States, both Colorado and California have adopted legislation to enforce mapping programmes. Colorado became the first state to require each county to map all areas subject to natural hazards and to use these maps as the basis for controlling subsequent development (Ives and Krebs, 1978). This constitutes one of the most forward-looking hazard programmes in the United States. The identification of natural hazards in Colorado by mapping has been discussed by Miller (1977), while Utterback (1977) and Gallant and Robinson (1977) have examined hazard mapping in particular counties. Various authors have looked at specific hazard problems in Colorado. For example, Soule (1977) examined slope stability problems which have been aggravated by poor land-use and was confident that knowledge of slope failure and other geological hazards early in the site-planning process had saved money far in excess of the cost of detailed investigations. In another study, Mears (1977) described the benefits of mapping snow avalanche tracks.

Similarly detailed maps have been prepared for particular sites in California. Waananen and Spangle (1977) used mapping techniques in a study of flood problems, while Nilsen *et al.* (1979) utilized similar procedures in an assessment of slope stability and earthquake hazards. Elsewhere, there are only a few specific case studies. For instance, mapping of the avalanche hazard takes place in Norway and Switzerland (Ramsli, 1974; UNDRO, 1978b).

Hazard mapping is an invaluable tool for urban planning if natural hazards are to be at all considered. However, the effectiveness of any planning programme is dependent upon the accuracy of the map and the skills of the planner to interpret the hazard information. Obviously, accuracy will depend to a large extent upon the quality of the original survey. For instance, how accurate is the delimitation of particular hazards, such as the 50-year flood event? Several authors have examined this issue and found certain problems (Bue, 1967; Burkham, 1978). James *et al.* (1980) looked at the delineation of the 100-year flood in an arid area and found significant areas of concern. Burgess (1979) compared the accuracy of different methods of floodplain mapping and also suggested that errors are indigenous to most techniques. Thus, while the mapping of hazards in terms of their extent and frequency may be based on sound scientific principles, there are some problems in their application.

From this information, the planner must carry out detailed risk assessment studies. The planner, or community, must decide what is an acceptable level of risk and plan accordingly. However, such decisions involve a value judgement. Should, for example, planning criteria be based on the 50-year flood event, or does this constitute either too great or too small a risk? The planner, therefore, must face these decisions and ultimately decide what are the most practical and reasonable uses for each area so that hazard losses may be minimized and the goals of society maximized. Although these maps provide detailed information on the physical aspects of the hazards, clearly data are also needed on the human-use system.

Other planning constraints

The implementation of carefully designed programmes to mitigate hazard losses would appear to be both socially and economically favourable to any urban centre. However, as indicated above, few communities have adopted such positive strategies for hazard reduction. There are many constraints on urban planning which drastically influence the effectiveness of such measures. These may range from political awareness and commitment at the local or national level to legislative and fiscal restrictions. For instance, should planning programmes be administered at the national level to encourage local authorities to adopt a positive attitude to urban land-use, or should the regional and local administrations accept such responsibility? Within the poorer nations, the tremendous losses suffered would suggest that some form of national directive is required, especially since a substantial part of GNP may be going towards hazard relief. In addition, hazards invariably constitute extensive problems which transcend administrative boundaries, and therefore generate more than local interest.

In some instances, local or regional responsibility for hazard relief has failed to reduce losses. In the United States, for example, such land-use planning can only be applied by the state or local community, but this has failed to prevent rising losses. As a result, a closer liaison has developed between national and local government. The federal government has adopted a firmer line for assistance, by insisting that local communities implement local zoning ordinances as a prerequisite to participation in the national flood insurance scheme. In the United Kingdom, similar encouragement has been given to local authorities by the central government. Government circulars have, often with little success, tried to encourage cooperation between local authorities and various water organizations to control floodplain development (Smith and Tobin, 1979). Other studies suggest that locally oriented projects are more effective, not least because they are more site-specific in outlook. The National Science Foundation (1980) *Report* cited several cases of floodplain planning which had been highly successful through sustained effort at the local level. The report makes this one of its final recommendations from the study.

It is probably true that effective planning for hazard mitigation can only be achieved through a combination of national directives and detailed local studies. In a decentralized system the influence of the central body will be limited and hence some cooperation between different administrative levels is necessary if a consistent hazard policy is to be pursued. Alternatively, in a centralized administration, general planning policies may be well defined, but the important local circumstances could be overlooked. While there is not one 'solution' for all hazards, a national commitment would appear to be necessary, but no scheme/plan should be implemented without a detailed survey of local requirements.

The commitment and attitude of local authorities can also be major determinants of the effectiveness of urban-planning programme. On occasions plans have changed due to external pressures. Spangle *et al.* (1980) quoted the case of Xenia (Ohio) which tried to implement local zoning ordinances following severe tornado damage in 1974, but were pressured by certain commercial interests to waive these plans. In Managua, however, following the major earthquake of 1972, a programme to reduce the hazard risk by deconcentrating the downtown area has been adopted. This will probably have long-term benefits but at present is causing hardship to low-income families. The scheme was proposed by a Mexican team which gave inadequate consideration to the immediate demands of the local community.

Local attitude and support can also influence land-use planning programmes. For example, floodplain zoning ordinances were defeated in Davenport (Iowa) and Rock River (Illinois) because local inhabitants failed to support the proposed schemes (Johnson, 1969; Moline, 1974). Similarly, Nelson (1980) implied that local apathy combined with only limited funds brought earthquake disaster planning in California to a virtual halt. In many communities there is a firm belief in 'individual freedom', to the extent that people should be allowed to locate where they choose. In conjunction with this, there is often the attitude that those who occupy hazardous areas should be responsible for their own actions. This is not satisfactory, for unplanned development can directly affect many others in the community by aggravating the hazard. For instance, urbanization of floodplains is known to increase the incidence of flooding (Hollis, 1974; National Science Foundation, 1980). Also, rescue missions, relief and re-habilitation aid as well as general repairs to roads and service facilities are usually borne by the community at large. Butler and Doessel (1980) illustrated this with a study of floods in Brisbane (Australia). It was found that over 22 per cent of flood damage was indirectly supported by the national government. This was particularly true of the appeal fund which collected considerable money primarily because donations in excess of Australian $2 were made tax deductible. On a larger scale, Bowden and Kates (1974) indicated that the coming San Francisco earthquake will affect the whole of the United States through taxation and donations. A *laissez-faire* attitude towards urban development, therefore, is not really conducive to hazard mitigation.

Other constraints on public planning policies include questions on the legality and financial feasibility of such operations. Many nations maintain a firm belief in individual property rights which can seriously impair the effectiveness of land-use planning programmes. The power of the state or local authority to acquire property or regulate land-use may be severely limited. In Costa Rica, for example, the constitution states 'Property is inviolable; no one may be deprived of what is his except for legally proven public interest after compensation in accordance with the law'. This constitutional right is common to many other countries, including Paraguay, Kuwait, Philippines, Turkey or Peru (UNDRO, 1980). Thus even elementary zoning legislation, which restricts land-uses, may be challenged unless it can be proven that general public welfare will be enhanced by the proposal. More active control, such as the public acquisition of land, may be even more severely curtailed. However, in view of the impact hazardous development can have on others, there are strong arguments to support such legislation. Bruun (1972) after examining coastal erosion problems in Denmark, suggested that hazard-planning should be implemented based on similar criteria as those of water supply or public access. In other words, where development on the coastline was likely to be detrimental to others it should be prevented. In the United States, Liebman (1973) maintained that there was no clear-cut division between confiscation of property and valid acquisition of land by the state. Planning, he believed, should guide rather than regulate to achieve those goals of public health, safety and welfare. However, the 'free' system has failed to regulate hazardous development and hence more regulation would appear to be necessary. Zimmerman (1979) illustrated this in a study of three communities in New Jersey. He found that there was no significant difference between property values on the floodplain and those not on the floodplain. Flooding, therefore, has not been a deterrent to development in these communities.

Planning for hazards has also been constrained by limited enforcement opportunities. Well-intentioned legislation has failed in the past because funds were not available for the implementation and operation of the plans. The schemes could not be enforced. Nelson (1980) stated that because of limited finances, there have been too few inspectors in California to enforce earthquake safety building codes. The development and grading of slopes, also in California, has increased slope instability problems, because there has been little attention to enforcement of local ordinances (Griggs and Gilchrist, 1977). In certain less wealthy nations, enforcement problems are probably even more serious, for the administrative structure at the local level may be insufficient to meet the requirements of a sophisticated planning policy. In Ethiopia there have been regional administrative problems in implementing urban planning according to Koehn and Koehn (1979), while Beirut has experienced rapid unplanned expansion along with a substantial squatter community because local legislation has not enforced (UNDRO, 1980).

Given these constraints on urban land-use planning, perhaps it is not surprising that few comprehensive schemes have been implemented. In poorer nations, certainly, a question of priorities might arise. Can the nation afford to restrict development, and is the administrative structure capable of supporting and enforcing such a programme? These nations are facing numerous problems, many more pressing than the control for future or potential hazards. However, a long-term strategy would eventually aid rather than hinder economic development given the significance of some hazard losses. Squatter communities merely add to problems of urban land-use control and enforcement. Some way must be found to enhance the livelihood and personal environments of these people. In wealthy nations a failure to overcome these planning constraints and to recognize the true potential of the hazard has enhanced the hazard risk in nearly every urban community. A more intelligent approach is called for in the future. This chapter now examines some of those measures which have been utilized to plan the urban environment in response to natural hazards.

URBAN PLANNING—LEGISLATIVE CONTROLS

Urban planning to mitigate the harmful effects of natural hazards can be achieved through a series of legislative procedures. Invariably this constitutes some form of zoning ordinance, which attempts to separate certain human activities from the immediate vicinity of any hazard. To enhance the effectiveness of such planning, further legislation to control specific location and structural designs has also been introduced.

Zoning

Many natural hazards lend themselves to zoning legislation because the spatial extent of their occurrence is so well-defined. The delimitation of the potential flood hazard can be assessed relatively easily given hydrological records and topographical information. With little effort those areas prone to earthquakes, volcanoes, tsunamis, coastal erosion, avalanches, landslides and hurricanes can be defined quite accurately. There are some hazards, less spatially restricted, particularly the meteorological events of snow, hail, drought and tornadoes, which are not generally conducive to zoning schemes. However, for many hazards, zoning remains an ideal 'solution' to the problem. Zoning ordinances are designed to restrict development in hazardous areas to those uses which will not suffer extensive losses, while high intensity land-use is encouraged in relatively safe areas.

One of the major problems associated with zoning ordinances has been a question of legality, especially in those nations where individual land-ownership rights are held so highly (see above). This issue is well illustrated by the rather slow acceptance of zoning in the United States. Although zoning was first tried there in 1916, it was not until 10 years later that such policies were given the protection of the law following the *Euclid v. Ambler Realty* court case. This case established the legality of zoning on the basis that the ordinances upheld public health, safety and welfare. However, even 30 years later questions were still being raised as to the constitutionality of such measures (Platt, 1976). Zoning for hazards would seem more than justifiable in terms of public requirements, in that the unwary would be protected, the natural system would suffer fewer changes, and money would be saved on rescue and rehabilitation work. Unfortunately, this has not been the case, for most zoning schemes have been implemented for socioeconomic reasons rather than hazard mitigation. This traditional zoning has been criticized for being relatively ineffective (Neutze, 1978), but for hazard-loss reduction there would seem to be greater potential.

Floodplain zoning

Zoning ordinances have probably been used more extensively for flooding than for any other natural hazard. In general, though, authorities have been rather slow to adopt such measures, as the development of floodplain zoning in the United States illustrates. The Euclid court case in the mid 1920s established zoning as a legal measure in planning, but this did not guarantee the acceptance of zoning ordinances. For example, zoning was considered for New Albany, Louisville and Cincinnati in the 1930s, but these proposals amounted to nothing (Anon, 1937). At this time, technological achievements were seen as the solution of most hazard problems and evidence was not hard to come by to support the success of such engineering schemes (Bennett, 1937). However, the danger of a purely structural response to the flood hazard was recognized fairly early by Segoe (1937). In an advanced comment for the time, he described in detail the process now called the 'levee-effect' and how this could be overcome with land-use planning.

In the 1950s various authors recognized the need for floodplain planning. Kollmorgen (1953) advocated the used of settlement control, which in the long run he saw as more beneficial than flood control measures. Murphy (1958) adopted a similarly strong attitude by suggesting that floodplain development should only be permitted when the economic advantages outweighed the disadvantages, and where there was no serious threat to health or life. During this period he noted that only limited zoning existed for the control of flooding, and that only seven states maintained legislation to prevent encroachment into the stream channel itself. Several zoning proposals were again made at this time, such as that for Lewisburg (Anon, 1937), and there was a further call for local government to take greater control of urban development (Meistrell, 1957). However, it was not until the decision by the General Assembly of States to control floodplain land-use with the expressed objective of reducing flood losses that zoning ordinances became more acceptable (Dunham, 1959).

The federal government has tried to encourage a more consistent policy to flooding since the Federal Flood Control Act of 1936. In 1966 a Unified National Program for Managing Flood Losses was established, and the Task Force concluded that traditional structural measures had helped reduce losses, but that additional action directed towards land-use was necessary to promote the appropriate economic development of floodplains. The aims of the project were to make those who occupy floodplains responsible for their own actions. Further federal schemes were used to encourage more careful planning through such agencies as the Department of Housing and Urban Development and the Federal Housing Administration (Larson and Nikkel, 1969).

Federal influence during the 1970s has been more committed to land-use planning as a viable means of flood-loss reduction. Various publications on the regulation of flood hazard areas have demonstrated this (US Water Resources Council, 1971, 1972, 1979). The federal government has tried to enforce such policies by insisting that those communities wishing to remain within the National Flood Insurance Programme adopt some form of zoning scheme Government attitude has hardened on this, with 27 communities suspended from the project (Natural Hazards Observer, 1978). There is some evidence of success, since over half of the states have at least implemented enabling legislation to permit floodplain zoning (National Science Foundation, 1980). Platt (1976) estimated that over 13 000 local communities had adopted the federal insurance plan which calls for such ordinances. However, some of these may be little more than token gestures, similar to that at Jackson (Mississippi).

Floodplain zoning divides a unit of land into specified areas for the purpose of regulating the intensity of land-use. The zoning plan may incorporate a number of districts although for flooding the dual-zone is perhaps most common. Figure 5.1 illustrates these two divisions—the 'floodway' which represents the stream channel and those portions of the adjoining floodplain necessary to provide reasonable passage of flood flows, and the 'flood-fringe' which occupies the zone immediately outside the floodway. The size of the zones is usually based on an analysis of hydrological data, particularly historical flood records, and topographical factors. From this the expected limits of different magnitude floods can be determined. It is normal in the United States to use the 100-year flood event as the limit for zoning programmes, although the design standards of the zoning plan can be varied according to the acceptable level of risk for particular land uses (Figure 5.2).

In the United States, there is now quite a large number of communities which have adopted some form of zoning ordinance, if only to fulfil the basic requirements of the National Flood Insurance Programme (Natural Hazards Observer, 1978). One of the most advanced states in this respect was Iowa which introduced fairly stringent flood zoning laws in several towns in the 1960s (Blair, 1969, Cooper, 1969; Howe, 1969). Other examples can be found across the country, although perhaps the most detailed has been adopted in the San Francisco Bay Area (Waananen and Spangle, 1977).

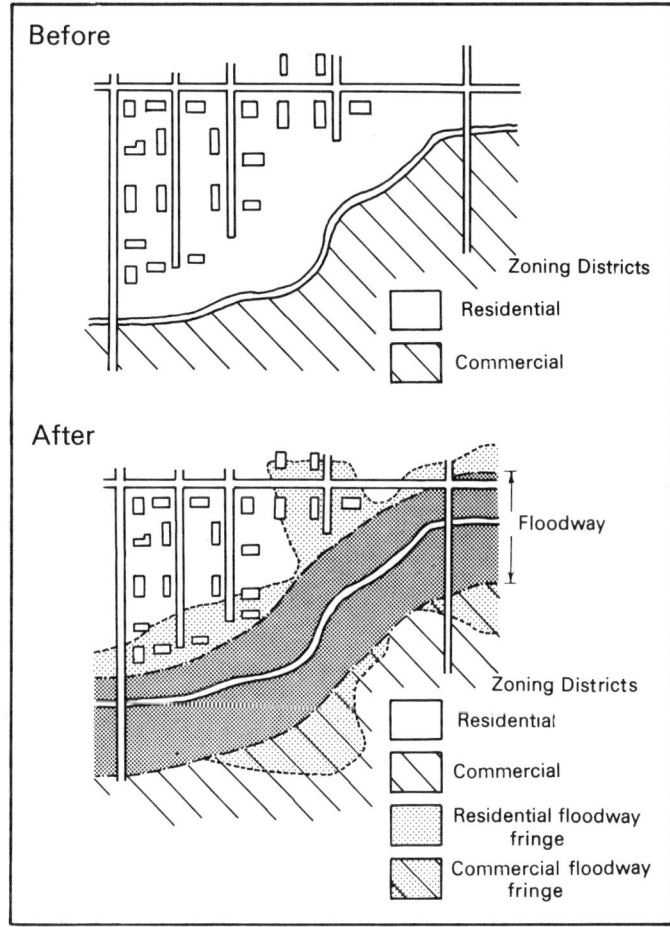

FIGURE 5.1. Typical zoning map before and after addition of flood regulations. (Adapted from US Water Resources Council, 1971, p. 48)

In other countries, examples of detailed zoning and national strategies for floodplain planning are not so common. In the United Kingdom a different system of planning has evolved, although as in the United States this has been relatively ineffective until recently. Until the 20th century little attention was given to flood problems and, particularly during the rapid urban expansion of the industrial revolution, cities continued to spread onto surrounding low-lying lands. Any official response was limited to small-scale structural measures. However, by 1933 attempts were made to control new development with the Medway Letter, which suggested that all new urban development should be

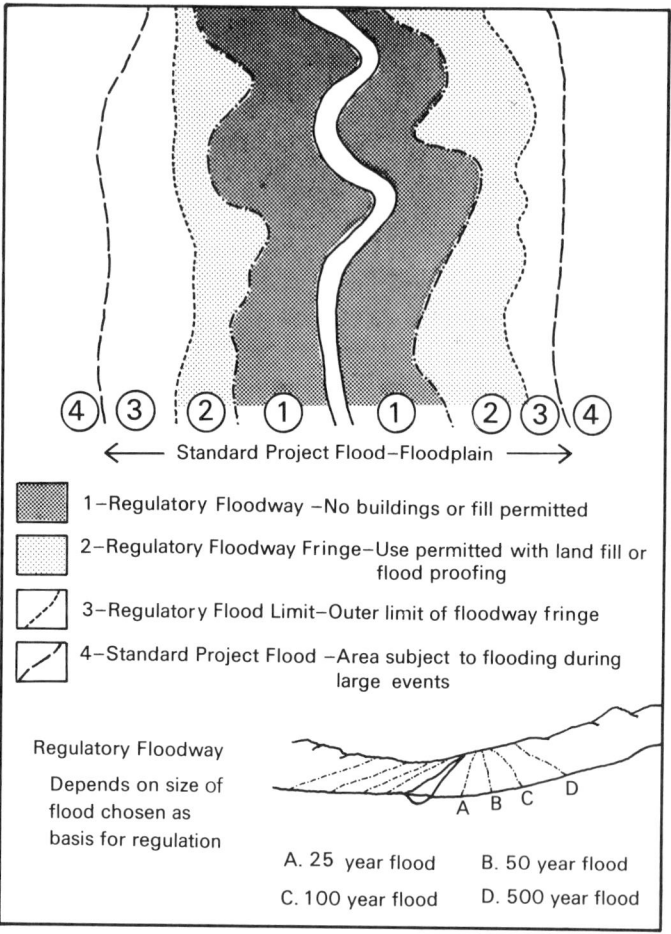

FIGURE 5.2. Floodplain zoning areas, United States (Adapted from
US Water Resources Council, 1971, p. 46)

constructed eight feet above known flood levels. This was usually ignored. With
the passing of the Town and Country Planning Acts, planned urban development became more feasible and government circulars encouraged planning
authorities and local drainage authorities to work more closely together. The
Ministry of Housing and Local Government reiterated these recommendations
in 1962 and 1969, but because of the voluntary nature of such circulars, liaison
between the responsible organizations did not really improve. Penning-
Rowsell and Parker (1974) put much of the blame on poor appreciation of the
hazard by the planners, and as a result very few floodplain zoning programmes
have been introduced in Britain. In Nottingham a zone designated as 'prone to

periodic flooding' has been excluded from further development plans, and various other communities have put localized restrictions on development, as noted by Harding and Parker (1974) in Shrewsbury. However, there is no unified national programme for floodplain management in Britain.

Seismic zoning

In areas of potential earthquakes, any urban planning should be based on a sound evaluation of the physical nature of the event. According to Karnik and Algermissen (1978), this should include not only details on previous seismic activity but also an assessment of the probability of future activity. At the macro-scale such considerations present few difficulties, but at the local level many additional physical parameters must be studied. For instance, surface fault displacement is relatively uncommon, whereas other phenomena associated with seismic activity are more likely to occur, such as groundshaking, slope collapse, landslides and liquefaction of surface materials. Detailed studies of the micro-geological features are essential for effective seismic risk assessment. The areas of potential problems can then be mapped and planned accordingly.

Zoning of seismic areas can be a fairly effective means of mitigating the hazard. Once again, the goal should be to avoid settlement of high-risk areas by dense populations and complex urban structures. Zoning ordinances for seismic risk usually include a series of areas defined by decreasing risk. High-risk zones should include areas of active faults, alluvial soils, unconsolidated landfill and areas where landslides and slope instability are prevalent. Uses of such areas should be extremely low intensity or low risk, such as agricultural, recreational open space or car-parking lots. Clearly very careful consideration of local geomorphological and geological factors is required to delimit precisely such areas. A second zone may constitute a moderate risk environment where low-density usage, such as single-storey dwellings, may be permitted. These uses would be consistent with a zoned area for groundshaking or potentially active faults. Outside of these areas more intensive development should be permitted though not without minimal structural design standards (see below).

Practical zoning programmes have been adopted by quite a few nations to try and reduce future earthquake losses. The Japanese, for example, have developed a sophisticated scheme based on studies of local soil type and how they perform under conditions of seismic stress. Damage was often found to be a function of soil type, so detailed local maps have been produced for this purpose (Petrovski, 1978). A weighting factor is then devoted to different surface materials, such as marshy land (1.5) or alluvium (1.0), whereas tertiary rock warrants only 0.4 (Legget, 1973). Despite such studies, these maps are sometimes ignored and Nichols (1974) quoted the case of a new steel mill built on reclaimed land in Tokyo Bay—an area subject to earthquakes, tsunamis, floods and typhoons. However, because of the simplicity of the Japanese method, other countries have adopted similar zoning criteria, including Turkey, Yugoslavia, Greece and Chile. In the USSR, a slightly different system has evolved based on past experience of damage to low masonry buildings and different soil types (Petrovski, 1978).

The United States has carried out some detailed work in this field incorporating much of the Japanese data. Geological factors, surface deformations, different soil settlement, liquefaction potential and slope stability have all been examined to establish zones of risk. One of the biggest problems, though, has been to assess the degree of acceptable risk based on the expected return periods of different magnitude events. For instance, questions inevitably arise over the potential activity of fault lines. In New Zealand, for urban planning purposes a fault will be considered active if it has moved in the last 20 000 years. For greater risk facilities this may prove too conservative; the US Atomic Energy Commission (now the Nuclear Regulatory Commission), when constructing thermonuclear facilities, considers a fault active if it has moved either once in the last 35 000 years or more than once in 50 000 years (Petrovski, 1978).

Some of the most comprehensive zoning programmes for seismic risk may be found in the United States. Although there is no unified national programme, the federal government has encouraged the adoption of zoning ordinances. Once again in the San Francisco Bay Area of California extensive studies have been undertaken into earthquake problems, and from these, detailed maps of the various risk zones have been drawn up. Blair, Spangle, and Spangle (1979) showed examples of such mapping for geological structure which will affect the speed of seismic wave, potential liquefaction, the relative stability of upland slopes and flood possibilities through failures of bay mud and dikes. From these details an overview of the hazard risk in terms of zones has been produced, which can then be used in conjunction with land capability maps. These systematically evaluate economic, social and political factors of the area and incorporate a human element to the land-use planning programme.

Zoning ordinances have been considered for other natural hazards but few have been implemented. Tropical cyclones, for instance, frequently affect the same areas and hence the spatial extent of both direct and indirect effects can be established with some precision. Unfortunately this involves thousands of square kilometers of land and therefore restrictions on usage would have to be so extensive that they would not be feasible. Immediately adjacent to the coastline, zoning may be a more reasonable proposition, if only to mitigate the effects of tidal surge which often accompanies such storms. In Japan, there has been some planning response to these events; in the town of Nagoya five zones have been designated to counter the hazardous nature of the area. In a high-risk zone little development is permitted, particularly of houses or hotels. In the other zones a series of ordinances control building design, height of ground level, and construction materials (Oya, 1970). These plans are also utilized to combat other hazards, such as tsunamis. Morgan (1979) cited the case of Hilo (Hawaii) which has also introduced zoning laws to control land-use in tsunami-prone areas. In parts of California also threatened by tsunamis some mapping of the risk has been undertaken which may lead to urban planning in the future (Blair, Spangle, and Spangle, 1979).

More effective zoning of coastal areas has been achieved in the management of erosion problems. This is a constant threat to many communities and it would seem reasonable to prevent further development in such hazardous locations. Communities have often discussed this issue, such as Bolinas in California (Rowntree, 1974), but this has not always led to the appropriate action. The US federal government has tried to encourage greater control of these areas with the Federal Coastal Zone Management Act (1972) but its effectiveness is still in question.

In mountainous areas zoning has been proposed to reduce the effects of such hazards as slope instability and snow avalanches. However, once again zoning is contingent upon the initial identification of hazardous areas. Restrictions on urban development in these areas have been fairly common once the local population has been alerted to the problem, even if there has not been comprehensive planning to mitigate such disasters. Switzerland and Norway have treated the issue more seriously than most countries and have restricted further urban development in known avalanche tracks (Ramsli, 1974; Visvader and Burton, 1974). At the local level, there has been some advance in zoning programmes. de Quervain and Jaccard (1980) proposed zoning schemes in the Alps but conceded that major problems would still exist in established communities. In the United States there has been some attention by the federal government, with grants from the Department of Housing and Urban Development and disaster funds being contingent upon detailed physical surveys (Nilsen et al., 1979). Such hazard zoning has been proposed or undertaken in both California and Colorado. Standards on slope steepness and density of construction have been formulated for such communities as Portola and Pacifica (California) to guide planners and developers (Table 5.3). Ives and Kreb (1978) examined the situation in Vail (Colorado) which grew rapidly up to 1973 with little concern for the avalanche hazard. Since then the problem has received more

TABLE 5.3. Slope-density provisions, Pacifica, California
(adapted from Nilsen et al., 1979)

Average slope (per cent)	Per cent of site to remain in natural state
10	32
15	36
20	45
25	57
30	72
35	90
40	100

attention and wise local government has prevented the siting of different properties, including high density condominiums, in known avalanche tracks.

A degree of zoned planning has also been applied to some new desert settlements. Towns in these areas face particular problems from high wind velocities and dust storms, although flooding may also constitute a hazard. The need for careful zoning of properties for protection from such events is of paramount importance (Cones, 1979).

Locational permits

While zoning may constitute the basic aim of land management practices in hazard alleviation, there are a number of legislative tools by which such planning might be enhanced. The control of precise land-uses might be accomplished through a system of location and construction permits. These, issued by the local authority, could be most effective in regulating particular land-uses. In hazard planning this system could be used to inhibit the development of high population densities and excessive investments in areas of significant risk, as well as motivate active investment in 'safe' areas. This form of restriction on hazard zone uses is used fairly frequently by various nations. For instance, urban development on floodplains in the United Kingdom is often prevented in this way. In this case each building application is reviewed on its own merit; a policy which could easily incorporate hazard criteria. This policy does not favour a unified programme, but it does emphasize the importance of local criteria.

A similar concept is the open-space requirement which has now been adopted into many urban development programmes. While these schemes were originally devised for the aesthetic enrichment of the urban environment, there is absolutely no reason why this policy cannot be coordinated with hazard mitigation. Open space policies can prohibit or at least limit intense development from hazardous areas, and provide the additional social benefits associated with green space. Some legal problems have arisen from such procedures because of the apparent selective nature of the legislation, but these have been dismissed by White who maintained that benefits to society far outweigh the costs (see Marx, 1977, p. 241). Open space regulations can fulfil virtually the same role as zoning ordinances in hazard mitigation, and are particularly useful in preserving floodways. In Cedar Rapids (Iowa) parklands and recreational areas have been maintained along the Cedar River (Gardner, 1969). This is typical of a number of communities. Byrne and Ueda (1975) described the benefits of an open-space regulation in Tempe (Arizona) along the Indian Bend Washway. In Dallas (Texas), an open-space greenway was considered as a viable measure to reduce the flood hazard in a fully developed, low-cost housing neighbourhood (Novoa and Halff, 1977). In some areas, open space is considered sufficiently important to the health, safety and welfare of the community that urban plans have incorporated such regulations with little difficulty. For example in Tokyo an urban green space policy has been implemented to minimize the spread of fire. In the 1923 earthquake, many of the 123 000 deaths and much of the considerable damage in the city were the result of fires rather than seismic activity. Similarly, the particular problems of fire in Arctic environments, where water may not be readily available, has inspired some open space requirements in both Alaska and Canada (UNECE, 1980).

Design standards

Having established which land-uses should be allowed in particular hazard zones and the degree or intensity of that use, further control of urban morphology can be maintained through a series of measures that require developers to meet certain minimum standards. In this way additional protection can be afforded those structures which are exposed to some degree of risk. These design criteria may be applied to whole units of land, as with subdivision regulations, or may involve the specific prerequisites for construction standards.

Subdivision

Subdivision regulations are frequently used to define the basic minimum standards for urban development. In the United States, power of enforcement lies with local governments and planning boards, which have been authorized by many state legislatures to adopt design standards. The developer then has to meet these requirements as a precondition to gaining planning permission. Invariably this applies to new development and the subdivision of 'new' land into individual lots. The regulations may prescribe minimum acceptable standards for public facilities and service infrastructure and ensure adequate water supplies and sewage pipelines. Once again, these measures were introduced primarily for contemporary town planning, but there is no reason why hazard regulations should not be included.

In California, a subdivision ordinance has been passed that requires local communities to reject development proposals which do not meet certain conditions. Regulations state that new proposals must be consistent with the general and specific plans for the community. In addition, the site must be physically suitable for the proposed land-use and density of development; the proposed development should not substantially damage the environment and it should not lead to serious public health problems. This legislation has been introduced by the state for a variety of reasons, including the mitigation of hazards. For instance, the regulations clearly state that subdivision ordinances should ensure slope stability factors and prevent extensive interference of natural slopes by grading (Nilsen et al., 1979). Subdivision ordinances are also used in California to control development in earthquake and flood hazard areas (Blair, Spangle, and Spangle, 1979; Waananen and Spangle, 1977).

A carefully administered subdivision regulation programme could bring about more effective management of hazardous areas. New development would be restrained to eliminate piecemeal expansion by coordinating individual and private development and prohibiting subdivision plans for high urban population densities in areas considered at risk. These regulations, however, have not always been adequately applied. Larson and Nikkel (1979) implied that problems had arisen in the past because land had been segmented with little regard to topographic features. Similar arguments were advanced by UNDRO (1977b) which stated that too often subdivision regulations did not guide development appropriately, especially when confronted with unique situations.

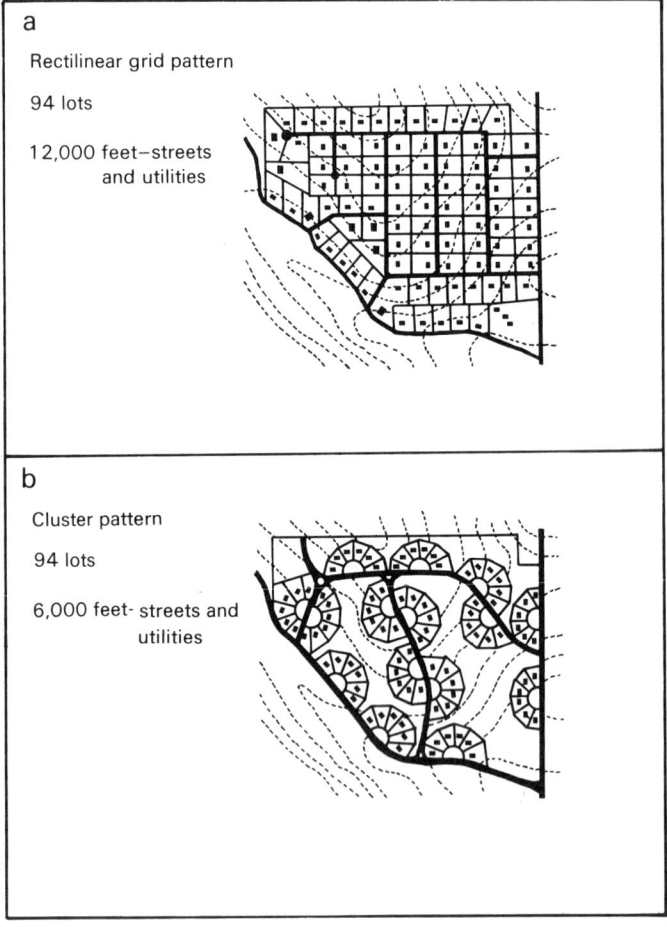

FIGURE 5.3.   Alternative subdivision plans: (a) rectilinear; (b) cluster. (Adapted from California Resources Agency, 1971, p. 53)

Utterback (1977) demonstrated the validity of this in Hahn's Peak Basin (Colorado) where several thousand hectares had been subdivided into numerous small land units. In this case little actual development had occurred because sewage and water capabilities were so limited. Figure 5.3a illustrates a similar case in California where a developer, apparently infatuated with the neat block system, totally disregarded the underlying topography. In this instance, the plan was not pursued because of strict subdivision regulations which exist in the state. Figure 5.3b shows how the scheme was eventually implemented following advice from local officials. In Colorado similar subdivision plans are under way (Shelton, 1977). In this way, the community retains control over spatial and temporal aspects of development, but does not assume responsibility for providing the detailed information required for each proposal. The private developer must provide these data.

Building codes

The effectiveness of zoning and other legislative measures can be enhanced through the use of building codes, which establish minimum design standards for structures in hazardous areas. These codes can delimit not only the design of the structure, but also construction methods and building materials. In combination with a zoning ordinance, appropriate levels of control can be developed so that building codes correlate with defined risk areas. In other words, in designated zones of high risk, more stringent design requirements can be enforced. In addition, such programmes can encourage cities already located in hazard areas to adopt measures of protection. Unlike zoning ordinances, which can be based primarily on physical criteria, the introduction of design standards requires more subtle assessments, on the interaction of buildings and physical events. There is now a wealth of knowledge on the behaviour of buildings in hazardous environments, which should be used as the basis for such regulations. In Japan, for instance, the response of buildings to seismic activity has received considerable attention, and has led to the adoption of improved building codes (Nichols, 1974). In Tokyo, it was found that structures *over* 36 storeys would probably be structurally sound during an earthquake. Evidence from the San Fernando Valley (California) earthquake (1971) attested to these findings since buildings between 20 and 50 storeys performed surprisingly well. Newmark (1970) produced similar findings, and Douglas (1978) suggested that five storeys might in fact prove more hazard-prone in earthquakes. Evidence from different events suggests that some buildings perform consistently well in earthquakes, particularly those constructed of steel and wood frames. These tend to be light and flexible and with careful design can withstand both horizontal and vertical ground movements. On the other hand, masonry and brick constructions have a relatively poor record due to their inflexibility and great weight.

Building codes have been adopted by quite a few countries which suffer from earthquake activity. Such regulations have been viewed for some time as a significant way to alleviate the hazard. For example, in the United States building codes were introduced in the 1933 Field Act. These requirements have been updated fairly regularly as knowledge of building design and construction has improved. Many nations now utilize the 'norms' adopted by the USSR or United States and on occasions Japan, and over 30 nations employ some form of building code for mitigating the effects of seismic activity (UNDRO, 1978a). California in 1971 adopted a Seismic Safety Element Bill which has made it mandatory for all communities in the state to incorporate building codes within general urban plans (Griggs and Gilchrist, 1977). It states that priority should be given to unreinforced masonry structures, buildings constructed prior to the building code jurisdiction and to critical facilities such as emergency buildings, schools and high-occupancy structures.

Building codes have not always been entirely successful, for in California in 1971 several structures failed which were supposedly earthquake-proof, including two hospitals. Another problem has been one of enforcement since many structures have not been altered to conform even with elementary standards. Bolt et al. (1977) estimated that in 1974 there were nearly 200 000 children attending schools which failed to meet even 1933 standards. Sachanski (1978) described further problems associated particularly with recent urbanization and the use of different construction materials. He questioned the resistance of some of the newer synthetic materials to withstand seismic motion. In several countries—Japan, Greece, Turkey as well as the Middle East and Latin America—problems have arisen due to poor design and use of unsatisfactory materials. The Managua earthquake in 1973 showed clearly the benefits of reinforced concrete structures over the local 'adobe' constructions. Nicaragua, Guatemala, and Iran have experienced high death rates because these structures have collapsed (Bolt et al., 1977; Kubo and Katayam, 1978). In recent years, however, various studies have been made of different materials and safe designs for structures from steelframed to prefabricated concrete buildings (Blume, 1970; Degenkolb, 1970; Lin, 1970).

Despite the obvious benefits of safe building design, structural standards have been severely criticized at times as unnecessarily restrictive. This would certainly be the case if building codes were enforced unilaterally across the country or region, but when related to degree of risk the advantages would seem to outweigh the disadvantages. Building codes do raise construction costs, which can exclude low-income families from certain areas, but the protection offered to life would overcome these negative aspects. Clawson and Hall (1973) stated that building codes have been too permissive on occasions, and they recommended that such policies be used more extensively to reduce the impact of natural hazards such as floods, earthquakes and tornadoes.

Building codes introduced specifically for other hazards are not so common. In some areas minimum ground-floor levels have been imposed to restrict flood damage, but widescale application of floodproofing measures has not really been tried. Some communities have enforced floodproofing regulations for property located in the floodway, and certainly the technology exists for such protection (Sheaffer, 1967). A comprehensive building code programme has been implemented in Nagoya (Japan) to control flood losses. In 1959, 5000 people were drowned because of the poor protection offered by their dwellings. In combination with a zoning scheme, therefore, building codes now control minimum ground floor elevations, building types and construction materials in the city (Oya, 1970). Certainly, there is greater potential for the use of floodproofing measures particularly in conjunction with other land management schemes.

Hurricane-proofing of buildings is a less realistic venture. Buildings can be made resistant to quite strong winds but it is more difficult to design structures which withstand the associated sea surge and storm waves. Bretschneider (1972), however, has calculated the associated sea surge and waves of hurricanes upon which design standards might be based. Even minimal standards which strengthen buildings should be enforced to ensure some structural protection to the inhabitants. In Townsville (Australia) standards were introduced to protect against high winds and were subsequently raised following a tropical cyclone in 1971 (Oliver, 1978). Criticism that such regulations make construction costs too expensive are not well founded. For instance, it has been estimated that costs rise by only 6 per cent for protection against winds up to 240 km/h, while the savings based on damage figures would be approximately 60 per cent (UNDRO, 1980). Once again, though, few countries have anything approaching a national programme. Mauritius has made some attempt at this by encouraging the gradual conversion of dwellings from light structures with galvanized iron-sheet roofing to heavy load-bearing structures with concrete roofs.

For other hazards, building codes have been introduced on an *ad hoc* basis. Considerable care is now taken in Arctic environments where the ecological balance can be destroyed so easily. Building codes, therefore, are designed to protect the permafrost conditions which if destroyed could lead to collapsed structures. The classic example of urban planning in Arctic regions is Inuvik in northern Canada, which was a planned new town. The standards employed in this model settlement incorporated detailed studies of the physical characteristics of the area and the latest criteria in construction methodology. Houses were built on stilt foundations above a gravel base while all services (water, heating, sewage) were incorporated into well-insulated utilidors (Price, 1972). Although problems have still arisen, this community represents a genuine attempt to balance the physical environment with societal goals. The USSR has several large cities in sub-Arctic environments which are also exposed to the permafrost hazard, such as Yakutsk and Magadan. However, with careful design prefabricated units rising as high as nine storeys have been safely constructed (UNECE, 1980). Other countries experience similar problems. In Greenland costs for house construction are estimated to be 2.5 to 5.0 times higher than in temperate latitudes;

Sweden has become concerned about the freeze-thaw damage and introduced construction codes to reduce this; and the United States has enforced fairly stringent building codes in these environments to reduce the fire hazard (UNECE, 1980).

Severe winds have led to the adoption of some building codes. In Boulder (Colorado), following the violent windstorms in 1969 and 1972, legislation was introduced to improve roof and fence construction and ensure that mobile homes are securely tied to the ground. In desert environments of the Middle East building codes have been used to reduce wind velocities and assure maximum shade conditions (Cones, 1979). It would seem that most countries have a 'code of practice' toward winds which may be enforced at either national or local level (Sachs, 1978).

Relocation

One of the general aims of these legislative procedures is to separate as far as possible man and his activities from the extremes of nature. Taken to the extreme this would entail the relocation of settlements to hazard-free sites. Clearly, this is not a practical solution for most urban centres, and it is rather simplistic to suggest that all hazard losses would be eliminated in this way. Apart from the socioeconomic factors which would preclude such movements, there may be sound locational benefits in the original site. Given the additional problems of finding a truly hazard-free site, relocation cannot usually be justified on a large scale. Thus land-use management programmes often enforce zoning based on levels of perceived risk.

Despite these problems, some communities have been moved to safer locations. Typical characteristics of such communities include a relatively small size, a well-defined natural hazard, available nearby land and good economic support. Flooding has been the stimulus for several settlement relocations. Two early examples can be found in the United States—Shawneetown (Illinois) and Leavenworth (Indiana) (Anon, 1940). For the most part, however, these were failures because they lacked the full support of the total population (Murphy, 1958). More recently, Big Store Gap (Virginia) was undergoing a voluntary relocation programme which was supported by 80 per cent of the population, and Rapid City (South Dakota) and Prairie du Chien (Wisconsin) were in the process of moving some of the floodplain properties (Natural Hazards Observer. 1976). One of the most significant moves to date has been the relocation of the central business district of Soldiers Grove (Wisconsin). Here the local community has undertaken most of the planning and organization, and should have completed the move by 1982 if monetary problems with the government can be sorted out (Tobin and Peacock, 1981).

There are other examples of relocation. In the Indian state of Gujarat, 300 villages have been relocated to higher ground above the rivers Narmadi and Tupti. A prime consideration in these moves was not to separate the local population from the fertile floodplains. In the more extensive lowlands of Uttar Pradesh about 45 000 villages have either moved or raised ground levels (UNDRO, 1977b). In Alaska, the town of Valdez retreated from the low lying areas which were particularly unstable in earthquakes and also prone to subsidence and tsunamis. In Italy, 9000 residents of Pozzuoli were relocated in 1970 due to volcanic problems (Legget, 1973). In Hawaii, Hilo has been partially relocated following extensive tsunami damage in 1960 which killed 61 and caused US $22 million damage.

URBAN PLANNING—FISCAL INDUCEMENTS

Financial programmes can be instrumental in governing urban land-use. Both positive and negative incentives, through subsidies, loans and differential tax systems, can be formulated to encourage appropriate levels of development in particular areas and discourage unnecessary hazardous investment. Fiscal policies such as these would alter the locational criteria in terms of benefits and costs. Taxation as a basis for urban planning has been advocated for a long time although few fully comprehensive schemes have been tried (Ascher, 1942). However, problems of legality arise from such 'discriminating' schemes. For example, in the United States legislation must be applied 'equally and uniformly' although 19 states do have specific tax incentives to preserve open-space uses (US Army Corps of Engineers, 1976), and Hawaii employs more restrictive codes.

Dangers do exist with such policies. It may seem reasonable to establish a more onerous tax rate for hazardous development, such as floodplain encroachment, if only to make those in the area more responsible financially for their own actions. However, such punitive taxation may merely encourage high-density investment and use of the area, which could lead to even greater hazard-losses. To account for this, other measures should also be used to attract development elsewhere or restrict the subdivision of land units. Another problem is open land in and around cities which is often assessed in the high tax bracket because of the great demand for this land. Waananen and Spangle (1977) suggested that owners may seek to relieve this tax burden by selling the land for further development and thus enhance hazard problems. A lower tax assessment on undeveloped hazard-prone property, therefore, may reduce the economic pressure to sell. Once again, however, further measures may be required to restrict development.

For the most part there has not been widespread use of financial schemes to control urban planning with respect to natural hazards. Certainly bans and subsidies and low mortgage rates have been used to influence urban development, but this has usually been to relieve economic hardship, unemployment, depressed areas or new town development.

URBAN PLANNING—DIRECT PUBLIC ACTION

Direct public action can also be used to enact urban planning programmes. Authorities, at whatever level, may purchase land to control future development which may be costly in the short term, but could lead in the long run to considerable benefits from disaster relief. This may entail buying old established urban lots as they become available or obtaining new land currently undergoing urbanization. To do this government may introduce 'pre-emption right' legislation which gives public agencies first options on the sale of any land. A more extreme measure adopted by some communities is the compulsory purchase order. These measures permit the government to control or even enforce land-use changes and urban development in a variety of geographical locations. For example, Switzerland has adopted widespread pre-emption rights to protect agricultural land from urbanization. In the United Kingdom the compulsory purchase order has been used fairly extensively in urban renewal projects. It would be relatively easy to apply such measures to hazard mitigation.

Having purchased the land the government can then adopt various strategies with which to carry out the urban plan. The government may take prime responsibility for development or alternatively strictly control the designs of subcontracting private developers. As far as initiating development is concerned, this can include anything from small-scale facilities which encourage acceptable private investment to large-scale residential projects or even entirely new settlements. Public action, therefore, may not be entirely negative. Certainly, land may be turned over to less intensive uses such as recreational parks and car-parking facilities, and various communities are considering such action. In the United States, the Federal Emergency Management Agency has introduced a trial scheme to sponsor the acquisition of real properties on the floodplains by local authorities. This programme has been implemented in Arnold (Missouri) and is currently under consideration in Iowa City (Iowa). At the same time, development can be actively encouraged in 'safe' areas—a policy which is also being used in Iowa City (Tobin, 1981).

There are not many examples of nationally designed programmes of direct public acquisition to relieve hazard problems, and even local policies are somewhat restricted. The majority have been introduced for floodplain control to preserve open spaces (UNDRO, 1977b). Harding and Parker (1974) cited the example of Shrewsbury (England) where clearance orders were enforced on the floodplain and the areas subsequently redeveloped for less intensive activities. In Bolinas (California) the public acquisition of land subject to coastal erosion has been one suggestion to alleviate the problem (Rowntree, 1974). In Anchorage (Alaska) new development was encouraged on publicly owned land after an earthquake destroyed much of the old centre in 1964. Saroff and Schoop (1964) stated that development of this relatively safe area was encouraged using a large chainstore to attract further investment.

Another means of public action is through land registration programmes. Since the land market in many countries is so complex, involving public and private activities, it is often difficult for public officials to maintain an accurate inventory of the number, value and types of land transactions. Such records would appear to be essential for effective land control. Registration of land therefore would fulfil this role and would allow officials to introduce other measures, such as zoning ordinances, building codes and financial policies.

CONCLUSIONS—PLANNING ASSESSMENT

An element of risk from natural hazards exists in all settlements, and no measure of planning can reduce this threat to zero. The extended drought in the United Kingdom in 1976 demonstrated that even humid environments can experience severe water shortages, while many other communities around the world have suffered from rare but catastrophic events. Planning for these low-probability events may not be possible because a community is usually faced with many more pressing social problems. However, for the more frequent and identifiable hazard some form of community response is advisable if losses are to be ameliorated. This presents one of the fundamental problems in urban planning programmes: at what level of risk is planning necessary? The level of concern demonstrated by the community for one particular hazard is important for effective hazard planning. Once the need for planning has been established, strategies based on various criteria can then be formulated.

The need for wider planning policies

Several studies cited at the beginning of the chapter have indicated that losses from hazards are still rising in spite of ever-increasing expenditure on alleviation programmes. This apparent anomaly would suggest that something is fundamentally wrong with society's approach to these issues, unless the incidence of extreme geophysical events has also risen. Since this does not appear to be the case, two hypotheses might be tested to account for these trends. Firstly, it has been suggested that mitigation measures have failed to achieve even a modicum of success, and secondly, that urban development has continued in hazardous areas, thus aggravating the problem. In the first case, alleviation schemes have not always had their desired effect, although it should be stated that many adjustments have significantly reduced losses. The implementation of a single-purpose large-scale structural measure may reduce some losses and save lives, but the subsequent effects on community development may present further problems. Such schemes, for example dams and embankments for flooding, have often stimulated further investment in hazardous areas. The scheme instils a false sense of security that the hazard has been eliminated and thus opens the way for further economic development. Once the design capacity of these measures is exceeded, catastrophic losses may result. Single-purpose schemes which attempt to control the natural forces are not sufficient; some form of land-use management would seem necessary for full effectiveness. This aspect has been recognized for some time (Segoe, 1937) but has frequently been overlooked by communities seeking to minimize hazard losses.

Urban development in new areas has also added to rising losses, because frequently construction is undertaken with a complete disregard for the constraints of the physical environment. Even when individuals or communities do consider such exogenous factors, decision-making is too often clouded by limited experience and a failure to appreciate the full costs of particular locations. Before any development decision is finalized, the relative advantages and disadvantages should be evaluated so that all the risks are balanced. Clearly, there are advantages to many locations, such as fertile soils around a volcano or the aesthetic value in some water locations, but these should be carefully weighted against the hazards inherent in such locations. Urban planning for natural hazards, therefore, is necessary to prevent further encroachment into hazardous areas, and to minimize future losses, both financial and life.

Risk assessment

Given that communities normally wish to maximize the use of available land and minimize the detrimental effects of development, it would seem reasonable to expect consideration of potential hazards in any decision-making. However, rational land-use policies are only possible if the decision-maker is aware of possible hazards, and hence a preliminary step in urban planning should entail the identification of potential areas of risk. The basis of urban planning for hazard mitigation rests on detailed studies of the physical environment and the careful application of these findings to the human-use system. The physical criteria can then be used in the preparation of maps which depict areas of relative safety and degrees of risk. These hazard maps can then form the basis of sound urban planning. Details as to the frequency and expected intensity of the event would add to the risk assessment of any area.

A methodology similar to this was proposed by McHarg (1969), who suggested that planning policies could be based on a series of maps, each showing different criteria, so that several factors could be considered at the same time. Arora (1976) described the application of this methodology in environmental planning for Carlisle (Massachusetts). Only fairly recently has attention been given to utilizing this technique in hazard planning. Land capability studies have been made to assess the potential risk of different areas (Laird *et al.*, 1979) while a comprehensive 'vulnerability' map has been constructed for Greater Manila indicating the relative risks from various hazards in different parts of the city (UNDRO, 1979). Perhaps the most comprehensive hazard maps have been drawn for California, which has been subject to exceptionally detailed studies.

This is particularly true for earthquake activity in the San Francisco Bay Area, for which a series of maps depicts areas susceptible to damage from the many processes associated with seismic activity. In addition, a final map attempts to combine all these criteria into one risk map suitable for planning purposes (Blair, Spangle, and Spangle, 1979).

Risk acceptability

The possibility of different hazards occurring in particular areas can be mapped relatively easily and from this a planning policy established. However, since a zero-risk rating is virtually impossible to achieve, any programme will automatically incorporate an element of risk. A decision must be made, therefore, as to the level of risk acceptable to the community.

Two criteria would appear to be of fundamental importance in assessing risk acceptability. Firstly, should an economic value be placed on human life? Any decision, be it for a dam, a levee or a building ordinance, is based on the perceived effectiveness of such a policy, which will include an assessment of the estimated number of lives saved. Nevertheless, an element of risk remains, and hence indirectly an evaluation has been placed on those who will die in the next event. It is quite probable that with stricter zoning regulations or greater financial investment in mitigation measures fewer deaths would have resulted. What value to place on human life therefore presents many further problems, not all of which have been satisfactorily resolved (see Foster, 1980).

The second and perhaps main criterion on which decisions are made is economic. Planning for hazard alleviation has clear benefits in terms of reduced losses, but against this must be balanced the costs of implementing and maintaining any programme. If land is to be left 'open', then costs may include those foregone in not developing the land. This ratio of benefits to costs approach, which has been used for some time, would seem reasonable if decision-makers were seeking to maximize land-uses. However, the full impact of hazards has rarely been considered, if it has even entered into any development policy. Even when individuals accept responsibility for a hazardous location, they rarely pay fully for any losses, as witnessed in an Australian study (Butler and Doessel, 1980). Other evidence of the failure of this approach, whether by design or other external factors (see below), is the continuing rise in hazard losses. If basic economies had been effective, then high-risk areas would be avoided and low-risk ones developed in response to perceived levels of risk. Since communities have continued to expand into hazardous areas, and then call for government assistance, clearly the policy is not working and further controls are necessary.

In terms of hazard planning, there are several other constraints apart from purely economic criteria. Social acceptability of any proposals would seem important to any success, unless the policy is enforced through strict and rigid police powers. For example, zoning has been described as a major factor in the planning process, but its success is contingent upon acceptability of the scheme. To separate man and his activities from the extremes of nature is a sound concept, which in the long run will significantly reduce losses from natural hazards. However, each zoning decision, whether made at the macro or micro level, implies an appraisal of the risk involved, since it is not feasible, nor would it be desirable, to exclude all urban development from hazardous areas. In permitting such development, an element of risk is left. It is up to the planner to evaluate the level of acceptable risk so that the advantages of such a location will exceed the disadvantages.

Political factors may also play a part in urban planning. In some countries the acceptability of different schemes may be in doubt depending on differing constitutional beliefs. Planning programmes, as has been shown, may involve legislation to control zones of development, open space and subdivision requirements or even specific building codes. Alternatively or in conjunction, public officials may opt for financial inducements to coerce developers to establish a more rational pattern of land-use. Finally, governments could take direct action to prohibit unwise development by acquiring the land and strictly controlling investment. While most of these measures can be implemented through national plans or at the local level, they all have the same objective—the rational and safe development of urban areas.

Comprehensive planning

Communities are not usually prepared to leave the future to chance, and many now adopt comprehensive plans to guide future activity. Even Houston (Texas), for a long time the strong proponent of completely free development, has now established some zoning ordinances. Furthermore, urban planning programmes must not be static in nature, but must be continuous and able to encompass a wide range of additional factors. Since physical processes are constantly changing, planning must be vigilant to changing problems, and any policy must be dynamic and sufficiently flexible to deal with new problems. Urban development, for example, can alter the frequency and location of some hazards. Floodplain encroachment can aggravate the flood hazard by blocking the floodway and causing raised water levels. Alternatively, the introduction of a structural alleviation scheme in one part of the drainage basin may have serious repercussions on flooding in another part. In the Netherlands, ten Hoopen and Bakker (1974) described the effect that certain development had on coastal erosion elsewhere. Griggs and Gilchrist (1977) quoted the example of slope failures in California which had been caused by urban development and improper grading. Gupta and Rastogi (1976) described the seismic activity which apparently occurred with the building of Koyna Dam in India; 200 people were killed and over 1500 injured by the subsequent earthquake. They go on to list nearly 20 other cases where seismic activity has been associated with dam and reservoir construction around the world. Urban planning, therefore, must be sufficiently flexible to cope with these changing and unexpected circumstances.

Urban planning should also be comprehensive in design, ideally weighing up all societal goals against the constraints of nature. Comprehensive planning, however, is a fairly recent consideration despite various proposals for such policies in the past. Babroski and Goswami (1979), Sheaffer (1969) and Weathers (1965) looked at or described more comprehensive approaches to flood problems. This is typical of the general trend in flood alleviation away from single-solution engineering schemes to comprehensive management which incorporates a variety of schemes including planning (see for example Dzurik, 1979). Davis (1978) put forward a more substantial methodology for floodplain management which took account of the whole drainage basin rather than focusing on individual communities. Various other comprehensive plans have now been implemented. In Tunisia, a comprehensive programme has emerged as a consequence of dam construction (Eldeen, 1980). In rural Alaska, Stark (1973) advocated careful, comprehensive planning to reduce construction costs. Perhaps more significantly, a genuine comprehensive planning strategy has been proposed for the Arctic environment (UNECE, 1980). The recommendations of this group included an emphasis on detailed local studies to take account of natural hazards, along with the careful design of all structures and facilities. An inventory of settlement hazard sites was proposed and further research encouraged, so that urban development could work with nature rather than against it.

In conclusion, planning for hazards must be comprehensive in nature, but it must also integrate with the other goals of society. Certainly, hazard planning is not the panacea for all society's problems. Nevertheless, hazard assessment should be part of the planning process, even where there are more pressing everyday problems, if only to forestall more serious problems in the future. At present, it would seem that the rapid urbanization of the third world is in many instances creating major future catastrophes which will further add to the poverty level within countries. The spatial inequalities of hazard losses, at least in terms of deaths and proportional wealth, will undoubtedly increase.

Many studies have been made into hazards, and there is considerable information available on urban planning. This chapter has tried to pull the two more closely together, for it seems that planning failures and irrational development have occurred primarily because of neglect rather than lack of information. Various authors have advocated a greater consideration of the physical environment, which is admirable, but this should not go too far the other way and ignore completely the human-use system. A question of priorities also arises, for there are many other problems which society has to face, and this may be particularly true for developing nations currently undergoing rapid urbanization. Nevertheless, planning can reduce hazard losses in the long-term, and there is a moral obligation to encourage the adoption of measures which can reduce human tragedy.

REFERENCES

Allen, C. R. (1976). Geological criteria for evaluating seismicity. In C. Lomnitz and E. Rosenblueth (Eds.), *Seismic Risk and Engineering Decisions*, Elsevier, Amsterdam.

Anon. (1937). River cities zoning against the next flood, *American City*, **52 (May)**, 109.

Anon. (1940). Floods or flood control programs cause four cities to seek new sites. *American City*, **55 (March)**, 107.

Andrews, R. N. L. (1978). Applications of environmental analysis. In W. M. Marsh (Ed.), *Environmental Analysis for Landuse and Site Planning*, McGraw-Hill, New York, pp. 195–210.

Arora, C. R. (1976). Land-use maps for town planners. In P. Laconte (Ed.), *The Environment of Human Settlements*, Pergamon, Oxford, pp. 197–227.

Ascher, C. (1942). *Better Cities*, US National Resources Planning Board, US Government Printing Office, Washington, DC.

Babroski, G. J. and Goswami, S. R. (1979). Urban development and flood control design. *Public Works*, **110**, 78–81.

Baker, E. J. (1976). *Toward an Evaluation of Policy Alternatives Governing Hazard-Zone Land-Uses*, Natural Hazard Research, Working Paper No. 28, Institute of Behavioural Science, University of Colorado, Boulder.

Bennett, C. S. (1937). Does flood protection pay? *American City*, **52 (March)**, 57–59.

Blair, D. J. (1969). Model floodplain regulations for Iowa—a progress report. In M. D. Dougal (Ed.), *Floodplain Management: Iowa's Experience*, Iowa State University Press, Ames, pp. 167–182.

Blair, M. L., Spangle, W. E., and Spangle, W. (1979). *Seismic Safety and Land-Use Planning*, US geological Survey, Report 941–B, Washington, DC.

Blume, J. A. (1970). Design of earthquake-resistant poured-in-place concrete structures. In R. L. Wiegel (Ed.), *Earthquake Engineering*, Prentice-Hall, Englewood Cliffs, NJ, pp. 449–474.

Bolt, B. A. Horn, W. L., Macdonald, G. A., and Scott, R. F. (1977). *Geological Hazards*, Springer-Verlag, New York.

Bowden, M. J. and Kates, R. W. (1974). *The Coming San Francisco Earthquake: After the Disaster*, Natural Hazard Research, Working Paper No. 25, University of Colorado, Boulder.

Bretschneider, C. L. (1972). Revisions to hurricane design wave practices. In Coastal Engineering Research Council, *Thirteenth Coastal Engineering Conference*, ASCE, New York, pp. 167–195.

Bruun, P. (1972). The history and philosophy of coastal protection. In Coastal Engineering Research Council, *Thirteenth Coastal Engineering Conference*, ASCE, New York, pp. 33–74.

Bue, C. D. (1967). *Flood Information for Flood-Plain Planning*, US Department of the Interior, Geological Survey Circular No. 539, Washington, DC.

Burgess, S. J. (1979). Analysis of uncertainty in floodplain mapping, *Water Resources Bulletin*, **15**, 227–243.

Burkham, D. E. (1978). Accuracy of flood mapping. *US Geological Survey, Journal of Research*, **6**, 515–527.

Burton, R. E., Kates, R., and White, G. F. (1978). *Environment as Hazard*, Oxford University Press, New York.

Butler, J. R. G. and Duessel, E. D. P. (1980). Who bears the costs of natural disasters? An Australian case study. *Disasters*, **4**, 187–204.

Byrne, M. G., and Ueda, J. Y. (1975). On rampage through a suburb, *Landscape Architecture*, **65**, 304–311.

California Resources Agency (1971). *Environmental Impact of Urbanisation on the Foothill and Mountainous Lands of California*, Sacramento, Cal.

Chambers, D. N. (1975). Procedures for determining the design flood in engineering works. *Journal of the Institution of Civil Engineers*, **58**, 723–726.

Ciborowski, A. (1978). Some aspects of physical development planning for human settlements in earthquake-prone regions. In UNESCO, *The Assessment and Mitigation of Earthquake Risk*, Paris, pp. 274–284.

Clawson, M. and Hall, P. (1973). *Planning and Urban Growth: An Anglo-American Comparison*, Resources for the Future, Johns Hopkins University Press, Baltimore.

Cones, M. (1979). Planning settlements for upland arid regions: an overview of environmental and building considerations. In D. Soen (Ed.), *New Trends in Urban Planning. Studies in Housing, Urban Design, and Planning*. Pergamon, New York, pp. 283–288.

Cooper, J. F. (1969). The Iowa floodplain management program. In M. D. Dougal (Ed.), *Floodplain Management: Iowa's Experience*, Iowa State University Press, Ames, pp. 219–232.

Davis, D. W. (1978). Comprehensive floodplain studies using spatial data management techniques, *Water Resources Bulletin*, **14**, 587–604.

Degenkolb, H. J. (1970). Design of earthquake-resistant structures: steel frame structures. In R. L. Wiegel (Ed.), *Earthquake Engineering*, Prentice-Hall, Englewood Cliffs, NJ, pp. 427–447.

Detwyler, T. R. and Marcus, M. G. (1972). *Urbanization and the Environment: The physical Geography of the City*, Duxbury, North Scituate.

Dougal, M. D. (1969). Techniques for developing a comprehensive program for flood plain management. In M. D. Dougal (Ed.), *Floodplain Management: Iowa's Experience*, Iowa State University Press, Ames, pp. 53–78.

Douglas, J. H. (1978). Waiting for the Great Tokai Quake. *Science News*, **113**, 282–286.

Dunham, A. (1959). Flood control via the police power. *University of Pennsylvania Law Review*, **107**, 1098–1132.

Dworkin, J. (1974). *Global Trends in Natural Disasters, 1947–1973*. Natural Hazard Research, Working Paper No. 26, Institute of Behavioural Science, University of Colorado, Boulder.

Dzurik, A. A. (1979). Floodplain management: Some observations on the Corps of Engineers attitudes and approaches. *Water Resources Bulletin*, **15**, 420–425.

Eldeen, M. T. (1980). Pre-disaster physical planning: integration of disaster risk analysis into physical planning—a case study in Tunisia. *Disasters*, **4**, 211–222.

Ericksen, N. J. (1967). Changing landuse as an alternative measure for reducing flood losses. *New Zealand Geographical Society: Record*, **44**, 12–13.

Foster, P. D. (1980). *Disaster Planning*, Springer-Verlag, New York.

Gallant, W. A., and Robinson, C. S. (1977). Geologic hazards and land-use study—Eagle County, Colorado. In D. C. Shelton (Ed.), *Proceedings of the Governor's Third Conference on Environmental Geology*, Colorado Geological Survey, Denver, pp. 97–102.

Gardner, D. K. (1969). The role of open spaces in floodplain management. In M. D. Dougal (Ed.), *Floodplain Management: Iowa's Experience*, Iowa State University Press, Ames, pp. 137–146.

Griggs, G. B. and Gilchrist, J. A. (1977). *The Earth and Land Use Planning*, Duxbury, North Scituate.

Gupta, H. K. and Rastogi, B. K. (1976). *Dams and Earthquakes*, Elsevier, Amsterdam.

Halderman, J. M. (1972). *An Analysis of Continued Semi-Nomadism on the Kaputiei Maasai Group Ranches: Sociological and Ecological Factors*, Working Paper No. 28, University of Nairobi.

Harding, D. M. and Parker, D. J. (1974). Flood hazard at Shrewsbury, United Kingdom. In G. F. White (Ed.), *Natural Hazards: Local, National, Global*, Oxford University Press, New York, pp. 43–52.

Hollis, G. E. (1974). The effect of urbanisation on floods in Canon's Brook Harlow, Essex. In K. J. Gregory, and D. E. Walling (Eds.), *Fluvial Processes in Instrumented Watersheds*, Institute of British Geographers, Special Publication No. 6

Howe, J. W. (1969). An introductory philosophy of floodplain management. In M. D. Dougal (Ed.), *Floodplain Management: Iowa's Experience*, Iowa State University Press, Ames, pp. 3–10.

Ives, J. D., and Krebs, P. V. (1978). Natural hazards research and land use planning responses in mountainous terrain: the town of Vail, Colorado, *Arctic and Alpine Research*, **10**, 213–222.

James, L. D., Laurent, E. A., and Hill, D. W. (1971). *The Floodplain as a Residential Choice*, Georgia Institute of Technology, Atlanta.

James, L. D., Larson, D. T., Hoggan, D. H., and Glover, T. F. (1980). Floodplain management needs peculiar to arid climates. *Water Resources Bulletin*, **16**, 1020–1029.

Johnson, E. O. (1969). Co-ordination of urban planning and flood plain development. In M. D. Dougal (Ed.), *Floodplain Management: Iowa's Experience*, Iowa State University Press, Ames, pp. 103–112.

Karnik, V. and Algermissen, S. T. (1978). Seismic zoning. In UNESCO, *The Assessment and Mitigation of Earthquake Risk*, Paris, pp. 11–47.

Kazmann, R. G. (1972). *Modern Hydrology*, Harper and Row, New York.

Koehn, P., and Koehn, E. F. (1979). Urbanisation and urban development in Ethiopia. In R. A. Obudho and S. El-Shakhs (Eds.), *Development of Urban Systems in Africa*, Praeger, New York, pp. 215–241.

Kollmorgen, W. M. (1953). Settlement control beats flood control. *Economic Geography*, **29**, 208–215.

Kubo, K. and Katayam, T. (1978). Earthquake resistant properties and design of public utilities. In UNESCO, *The Assessment and Mitigation of Earthquake Risk*, Paris, pp. 171–184.

Laird, R. T., Perkins, J. B., Bainbridge, D. A., Baker, J. P., Boyd, R. T., Huntsman, D., Straub, P. E., and Zucker, M. P. (1969). *Quantitative Land Capability Analysis*, US Geological Survey, Report No. 945.

Larson, C. J. and Nikkel, S. R. (1979). *Urban Problems*, Allyn and Bacon, Boston.

Legget, R. F. (1973). *Cities and Geology*, McGraw-hill, New York.

Liebman, E. (1973). Legal problems in regulating flood hazard areas, *Journal of the Hydraulics Division (ASCE)*, **99**, 2113–2123.

Lin, T. Y. (1970). Prestressed and precast concrete structures. In R. L. Wiegel (Ed.), *Earthquake Engineering*, Prentice-Hall, Englewood Cliffs, NJ, pp. 475–494.

Marx, W. (1977). *Acts of God, Acts of Men*, Coward, McGann, and Geohegan, New York.

McHarg, I. (1969). *Design with Nature*, National History Press, New York.

Mears, A. I. (1977). Snow avalanche hazard identification and delineation. In D. C. Shelton (Ed.), *Proceedings of the Governor's Third Conference on Environmental Geology*, Colorado Geological Survey, Denver, pp. 21–26.

Meistrell, F. G. (1957). Protection for communities against flood hazards. *American City*, **72 (April)**, 191–195.

Miller, A. E. (1977). The geologic hazard identification process in Routt County. In D. C. Shelton (Ed.), *Proceedings of the Governor's Third Conference on Environmental Geology*, Colorado Geological Survey, Denver, pp. 89–94.

Mitchell, J. K. (1975). The rush to the shore. *Landscape Architecture*, **65**, 170–177.

Moline, N. T. (1974). Perception research and local planning: Floods on the Rock River, Illinois. In G. F. White (Ed.), *Natural Hazards: Local, National, Global*, Oxford University Press, New York, pp. 52–59.

Morgan, J. (1979). The tsunami hazard in Tohoku and the Hawaiian Islands, *Science Reports of Tohoku University, 7th Series (Geography)*, **29**, 149–159.

Murphy, F. C. (1958). *Regulating Floodplain Development*, Research Paper No. 56, Department of Geography, University of Chicago.

Nakano, T. (1974). Natural hazards: Report from Japan. In G. F. White (Ed.), *Natural Hazards: Local, National, Global*, Oxford University Press, New York, pp. 231–243.

Natural Hazards Observer (1976). *Voluntary Relocation*, **1 (December)**, University of Colorado, Boulder.

Natural Hazards Observer (1978). *Flood Insurance Administration Update*, **7 (June)**, University of Colorado, Boulder.

National Science Foundation (1980). *A Report on Flood Hazard Mitigation*, Washington, DC.

Nelson, K. (1980). Are we ready for the big one? *San Francisco*, **22 (March)**, 34–35.

Neutze, M. (1978). *Australian Urban Policy*, Allen and Unwin, Sydney.

Newmark, N. M. (1970). Current trends in the seismic analysis and design of high-rise structures. In R. L. Wiegel (Ed.), *Earthquake Engineering*, Prentice-Hall, Englewood Cliffs, NJ, pp. 403–414.

Nichols, T. C. (1974). Global summary of human response to natural hazards: earthquakes. In G. F. White (Ed.), *Natural Hazards: Local, National, Global*, Oxford University Press, New York, pp. 274–284.

Nilsen, T. H., Wright, R. H., Vlasic, T. C., Spangle, W. E., and Spangle, W. (1979). *Relative Slope Stability and Land-Use Planning*, US Geological Survey Report No. 944, US Government Printing Office, Washington, DC.

Novoa, J. I. and Halff, A. H. (1977). Management of flooding in a fully developed, low-cost housing neighbourhood. *Water Resources Bulletin*, **13**, 1237–1252.

Oliver, J. (1978). *Natural Hazard Response and Planning in Tropical Queensland*, Natural Hazard Research, Working paper No. 33, University of Colorado, Boulder.

O'Riordan, T. (1971). *Perspectives on Resource Management*, Pion, London.

Oya, M. (1970). Land use control and settlement plans in the flooded area of the city of Nagoya and its vicinity, Japan. *Geoforum*, **4**, 27–35.

Penning-Rowsell, E. C. and Parker, D. J. (1974). Improving floodplain development control. *The Planner*, **60**, 540–543.

Petrovksi, J. T. (1978). Seismic zoning and related problems. In UNESCO, *The Assessment and Mitigation of Earthquake Risk*, Paris, pp. 48–65.

Platt, R. H. (1976). *Land Use Control: Interface of Law and Geography*, Association of American Geographers, Commission on College Geography, Resource paper No. 75–1, Washington, DC.

Price, L. W. (1972). *The Periglacial Environment, Permafrost and Man*, Association of American Geographers, Resource Paper No. 14, Washington, DC.

de Quervain, M, and Jaccard, C. (1980). Les catastrophes dûes aux avalanches et leur prevention. *UNDRO News* **(November)**, Geneva, 4–8.

Ramsli, G. (1974). Avalanche problems in Norway. In G. F. White (Ed.), *Natural Hazards: Local, National, Global*, Oxford University Press, New York, pp. 175–180.

Ringler, T. A. and Kennaugh, J. H. (1974). Flood hazard reports: Tools for planning and

Management. *Journal of Soil and Water Conservation*, **29**, 182–185.

Rockaway, J. D. (1975). Engineering geologic data for land-use planning. *Journal of the Urban Planning and Development Division (ASCE)*, **101**, 117–125.

Rowntree, R. A. (1974). Coastal erosion: The meaning of a natural hazard in the coastal and ecological context. In G. F. White (Ed.), *Natural hazards: Local, National, Global*, Oxford University Press, New York, pp. 70–79.

Sachanski, S. (1978). Buildings: codes, materials, design. In UNESCO, *The Assessment and Mitigation of Earthquake Risk*, Paris, pp. 157–170.

Sachs, P. (1978). *Wind Forces in Engineering*, Pergamon, Oxford.

Saroff, J. R. and Schoop, E. J. (1964). Planning in Anchorage after the earthquake, *Journal of the American Institute of Planners*, **30**, 231–233.

Segoe, L. (1937). Flood control and the cities, *American City*, **52** (**March**), 55–56.

Sheaffer, J. R. (1967). *Introduction to Flood Proofing*, Center for Urban Studies, Chicago.

Sheaffer, J. R. (1969). The interaction of urban redevelopment and floodplain management in Waterloo, Iowa, In M. D. Dougal (Ed.), *Floodplain Management: Iowa's Experience*, Iowa State University Press, Ames, pp. 123–136.

Shelton, D. C. (Ed.) (1977). *Proceedings of the Governor's Third Conference on Environmental Geology*, Colorado Geological Survey, Denver.

Smith, K. and Tobin, G. A. (1979). *Human Adjustment to the Flood Hazard*, Longman, London.

Soule, J. M. (1977). Slope failure as a geological hazard and land-use planning problems in Colorado. In D. C. Shelton (Ed.), *Proceedings of the Governor's Third Conference on Environmental Geology*, Colorado Geological Survey, Denver.

Spangle, W., *et al* (1980). *Land Use Planning After Earthquakes*, William Spangle Associates, Inc., Portola Valley, Cal.

Stark, D. A. (1973). Facilities planning in rural Alaska. *Journal of the Urban Planning and Development Division (ASCE)*, **99**, 247–257.

ten Hoopen, H. G. H. and Bakker, W. T. (1974). Erosion problems of the Dutch island of Goree. In *Fourteenth Coastal Engineering Research Conference*, (*ASCE*), New York, pp. 1213–1231.

Tobin, G. A. and Peacock, T. (1981). *Soldier's Grove: A Divided Community*, Paper presented at the Annual Conference of the Association of American Geographers, Los Angeles.

Tobin, G. A. (1981). Acquisition of flood damaged structures under the Federal Emergency Management Agency. In *Proceedings of the 4th Annual Conference of Applied Geographers*, Tempe, Arizona.

Torry, W. I. (1980). Urban earthquake hazard in developing countries: Squatter settlements and the outlook for Turkey, *Urban Ecology*, **4**, 317–327.

Turner, J. F. C. (1969). Uncontrolled urban settlement: Problems and policies. In G. Breese (Ed.), *The City in Newly Developing Nations*, Prentice-Hall, Englewood cliffs, NJ, pp. 507–534.

UNDRO (1977a). *Disaster Prevention and Mitigation. Volume 1, Volcanological Aspects*, United Nations, New York.

UNDRO (1977b). *Disaster Prevention and Mitigation. Volume 5, Land Use Aspects*, United Nations, New York.

UNDRO (1978a). *Disaster Prevention and Mitigation. Volume 3, Seismological Aspects*, United nations, New York.

UNDRO (1978b). *Disaster Prevention and Mitigation. Volume 4, Meteorological Aspects*, United Nations, New York.

UNDRO (1979). *Disaster Prevention and Mitigation. Volume 7, Economic Aspects*, United Nations, New York.

UNDRO (1980). *Disaster Prevention and Mitigation. Volume 9, Legal Aspects,* United Nations, New York.

UNECE (1980). *Human Settlements in the Arctic,* Pergamon, Oxford.

US Army Corps of Engineers (1976). *A Perspective on Flood Plain Regulations for Flood Plain Management,* Department of the Army, Office of the Chief of Engineers, Washington, DC.

US Water Resources Council (1971). *Regulation of Flood hazard Areas to Reduce Flood Losses, volume 1, parts I-IV,* US Government Printing Office, Washington, DC.

US Water Resources Council (1972). *Regulation of Flood Hazard Areas to Reduce flood Losses, volume 2, parts V-VI,* US Government Printing Office, Washington, DC.

US Water Resources Council (1979). A Unified National Program for Flood Plain Management, US Government Printing Office, Washington, DC.

Utgard, R., McKenzie, G., and Foley, D. (Eds.) (1978). *Geology and the Urban Environment,* Burgess, Minn.

Utterback, J. A. (1977). Geologic hazards and land-use decisions in Routt County, Colorado. In D. C. Shelton (Ed.), *Proceedings of the Governor's Third Conference on Environmental Geology,* Colorado Geological Survey, Denver.

Visvader, H. and Burton, I. (1974). Natural hazards and hazard policy in Canada and the United States. In G. F. White (Ed.), *Natural Hazards: Local, National, Global,* Oxford University Press, New York, pp. 219–231.

Vitek, J. D. and Marsh, W. M. (1978). Landslide hazard mapping for local land use planning. In W. M. Marsh (Ed.), *Environmental Analysis for landuse and Site Planning,* McGraw-Hill, New York, pp. 235–249.

Waananen, A. O. and Spangle, W. E. (1977). *Flood Prone Areas and Land Use Planning,* US Geological Survey, Professional Paper No. 492, Washington DC.

Weathers, J. W. (1965). Comprehensive flood damage prevention, *Journal of the Hydraulics Division (ASCE),* **91,** 17–27.

White, G. F. (1970). Flood loss reduction: The integrated approach. *Journal of Soil and Water Conservation,* **25,** 172–176.

White, G. F. (1973). Natural hazards research. In R. J. Chorley (Ed.), *Directions in Geography,* Methuen, London, pp. 193–216.

White, G. F. and Haas, J. G. (1975). *Assessment of Research on Natural Hazards.* MIT Press Cambridge, Mass.

Wolman, M. G. (1971). Evaluating alternative techniques of floodplain mapping. *Water Resources Research,* 7, 1383–1392.

World Bank (1980). *World Development Report, 1980,* Oxford University Press, New York.

Zimmerman, R. (1979). The effect of floodplain location on property values: Three towns in Northeastern New Jersey. *Water Resources Research,* **15,** 1653–1665.

Geography and the Urban Environment
Progress in Research and Applications, Volume V
Edited by D. T. Herbert and R. J. Johnston
© 1982 John Wiley & Sons Ltd.

Chapter 6

Flood Risk in the Urban Environment

Dennis J. Parker and Edmund C. Penning-Rowsell

Urbanization concentrates population, intensifies land-use and increases economic linkages among groups, thus contributing to wealth generation, but it also increases vulnerability to environmental risk, including flooding. This vulnerability threatens social goals such as prosperity, health and security to an extent that environmental hazard control is important for maintaining the quality of urban living.

Environmental alteration due to urban growth and change generates consequences which are difficult to identify, evaluate and control. In cities the risk of flooding is generally both endemic and dynamic; not only is flooding commonplace but alleviated risks tend to be replaced by freshly apparent or newly created risks. Only some of this flooding is serious but reducing urban flood risk poses a wide spectrum of problems. These include the technical difficulties of identifying potential flooding as well as those of planning and implementing flood alleviation schemes. For wise community investment in this area of public expenditure, the economic, social and environmental consequences of flooding need appraisal but for financial and hydrologic reasons it is nearly always impossible to 'prevent' flooding hazards and eradicate risk. This raises the fundamental questions of the standards of protection which are publicly acceptable and the ways of incorporating public expectations and attitudes into the policy-making process, given the public's tendency to be satisfied only with complete protection.

In theory policies and standards of protection should reflect the marginal utility of expenditure on protection from future floods compared with a similar measure of return from other types of public investment. However, this comparison will vary according to the risk perception of different groups and their ability to pay. Again, the impact of urban flooding tends to be selective, often serving to widen inequalities between rich and poor community groups, particularly where flooding is most frequent. Therefore, flooding most affects those least able to withstand personal disaster, who typically are least able to use political pressure to reduce their vulnerability; this differential incidence of the hazard exacerbates the difficulties of defining acceptable standards. Flood protection can be redistributive, safeguarding the vulnerable at the expense of those already insulated. However, such a goal demands a planning system capable of both efficient reaction to randomly occurring events and of being closely attuned and sympathetic to the needs of those vulnerable to flooding.

Over the last 15 years geographical research into urban environmental risks has grown substantially (Hewitt and Burton, 1971; Kates, 1978; Rooney, 1969; White and Haas, 1975). This growth reflects a heightened awareness of the risks associated with urban concentration and the role of environmental control in maintaining the quality of urban life (Chicken, 1975; Detwyler, 1972; O'Riordan, 1976). This chapter reviews progress in research on flooding in Britain and draws upon empirical evidence from a variety of research applications and policy appraisals. In this research literature the influence of the American hazard response paradigm is evident (Kates, 1971; Natural Hazards Research, 1970; Parker and Penning-Rowsell, 1982), with its emphases on floodplain encroachment, economic evaluation methods and individuals' flood hazard perception. These emphases have some serious limitations in the British context as they have been little concerned with agency policy-making and institutional arrangements (Burton, Kates, and White, 1978; White, 1974). However, the value of hazard response research is fully recognized here and the objective of this chapter is to highlight complementary research orientations which are vital for a correct understanding of British urban flood hazard policy.

CONCEPTUALIZATION

The hazard response paradigm

The hazard response paradigm has been a major vehicle for conceptualizing research directions and accumulating empirical evidence concerning the causes, effects and human adjustment to natural hazards (Mitchell, 1979; White, 1973, 1974). The essentials of the paradigm—initially concerned primarily with human adjustment to floods in the United States (White, 1945)—are contained in three related publications (Burton, Kates, and White, 1968; Kates, 1971; Natural Hazards Research, 1970) and are summarized by Burton, Kates, and White (1978).

The paradigm suggests that natural hazards, including floods, are caused jointly by human initiatives and natural events (Figure 6.1); flood hazards cannot exist without human intervention in the form of occupation of flood-prone areas. This simple conceptualization raises several useful questions. Are flood hazards needlessly created through ill-considered encroachment into flood-prone areas? Why do people choose to remain in flood-risk areas? What public policy concerning hazard control in flood-prone areas is liable to be most satisfactory? Questions also concern the perceived or real utility of hazard-prone

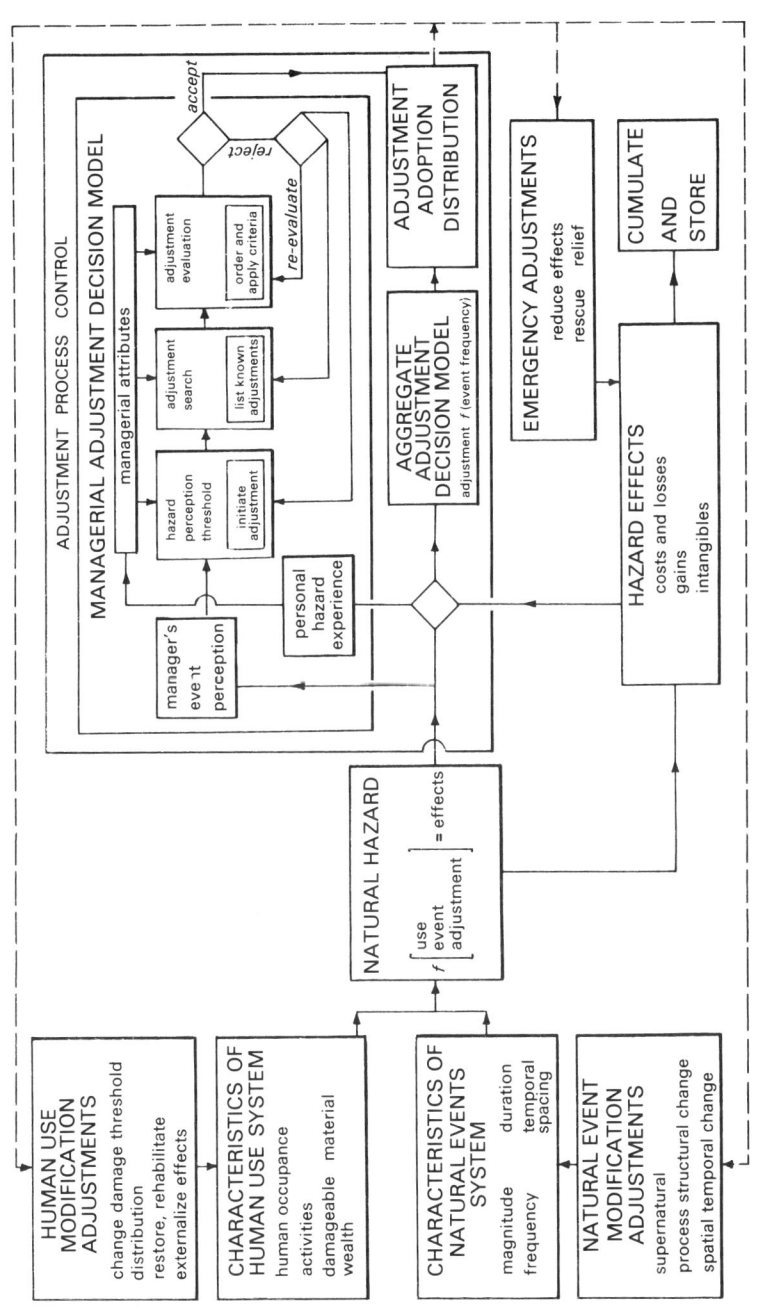

FIGURE 6.1. Kates' (1971) general systems model of human adjustment to natural hazards

areas, relating to the broadly 'ecological' nature of the conceptualization of natural hazard causes, and also the advantages of floodplain use which may counterbalance the disadvantages of flooding. Arising from such questions a major focus of research effort has involved identification and measurement of a wide range of flood effects including property loss, disruption costs and loss of life (Kates, 1965; White, 1964). Only with such an evaluation can the trade-off between potential benefits and costs of using flood-prone areas be determined and the worthwhileness of flood protection be evaluated.

A further major component of the hazard response paradigm is the explanation of hazard adjustment via behavioural parameters (Simon, 1959). The concepts of perception and bounded rationality are introduced to explain why human response to hazards is often not well matched with scientific estimations and historical records of flooding probability (Kates, 1962; Parker and Harding, 1979). Kates' model (1971) postulates a hazard perception threshold for individual floodplain users. This threshold is a function of an individual's hazard experience, personality and time horizon. The model suggests that a search for hazard-reducing adjustments begins only if the perception threshold is reached. An individual's responsibilities and access to information will influence this search and a subsequent listing of adjustments, which is then evaluated according to certain criteria. These criteria and the extent to which they are applied depend upon many variables, including the characteristics of the person and their level of responsibility.

Several sets of hypotheses are suggested by this model. Differences in individuals' hazard perception should be related to differences in the magnitude and frequency of the hazard, to the recency and frequency of personal experience and to other characteristics such as personality. Differences in adjustment adoption between individuals should be related to hazard perception, future hazard expectancy, perceived hazard effects and the perceived range of adjustments and their evaluation. In all cases the focus of attention within the paradigm is on the individual and his propensity to act 'rationally' to 'solve' the flood hazard 'problems'.

The hazard response paradigm also leads to hypotheses concerning the range of alternative adjustments employed in reducing flood hazards (White, 1945). American experience indicates that flood control agencies commonly employ technological or structural measures at the expense of non-structural or social adjustments. The paradigm attributes this to the dominance of these agencies by engineers such that policies reflect their orientations. Individual floodplain users tend also to be narrow in their perception and adoption of adjustments. This is attributed to their lack of knowledge and their limited search for alternatives. These findings led White to investigate the alternative measures which should be used in flood mitigation programmes and their social and economic effect (White, 1974, 1975).

Policy analysis

Policy analysis provides a basis for investigating the decision processes leading to the acceptance or rejection of particular alternatives and has focused almost exclusively upon public agency and government decision-making. Policy research has been developed primarily within political science, public administration and planning (Chadwick, 1971; Dror, 1964; Faludi, 1973; Lindblom, 1959; McLoughlin, 1969).

A basic difference exists between prescriptive and descriptive policy-making models (Mitchell, 1979). The prescriptive or ideal model adopts a linear-deductive approach which initiates decision-making with fundamentals and proceeds through a predetermined 'linear' sequence of steps. This sequence begins with the establishment of planning goals or problem identification and ends with plan implementation and the monitoring of policy effectiveness. Crucial to this process are the exhaustive discussion of goals, the comprehensive review of all possible means to meeting ends, and the systematic evaluation of alternatives. This model prescribes a rational, detached and 'scientific' policy-making process in which decision-makers behave with neutral objectivity.

Most commentators agree that whilst linear-deductive decision-making provides a useful framework for evaluating policy-making, this ideal form is impossible in practice (Dror, 1964). For example, in reality goals are difficult to identify and agree upon; exhaustive goals debate is impracticable and evaluation techniques are deficient. Also planners are inevitably influenced by their values and planning cannot be separated from political processes.

Descriptive policy-making models include 'disjointed incrementalism' (Lindblom, 1959) which characterizes decisions as being made hurriedly in response to crises through a process of 'muddling through'. Goals are not discussed, alternatives are narrowly defined and poorly evaluated and ends are adjusted to suit available means. An intermediate 'mixed scanning' policy-making model has been proposed by Etzioni (1967) to explain why successive incremental policy shifts sometimes give way to more fundamental policy changes. In this model policy-making features a series of incremental decisions but policy-makers are also scanning more radical alternatives which are adopted periodically. This adoption can occur when changes are forced upon individuals or decision-making groups by alterations to their power environment—for example when political power changes hands following elections—such that the previous incrementalism becomes politically unacceptable.

These models can be useful in policy analysis, although the locus of power and decisions cannot always be traced, especially if decision-making is unsystematic. The models pose a series of questions concerning the relationships between stages in decision-making, between resulting plans and some overarching policy framework, and of policy to some overall social goal or goals. The 'political' pressures on decision-makers, and their degree of objectivity, 'rationality' and neutrality may also be questioned. Again, the focus is upon the individual decision-maker as 'expert planner' and the effect of his actions upon policy evolution.

Institutional analysis

Some explanations of environmental policy stress the importance of institutional arrangements (Mitchell, 1979; Sewell, 1978). Urban policy-making, public engineering and planning all take place within an institutional framework which includes the law, administrative rules, organizational structures and financial arrangements (Howe, 1977). Urban flood control policy shortcomings may be related to institutional weaknesses rather than to inadequate planning techniques, insufficient technical ability or public ignorance. In theory the greater the effectiveness of institutional arrangements the more likely it is that policies will be appropriate, although this argument is at least partly tautological in that a key test of effectiveness is clearly the appropriateness of resulting policies!

The law provides 'rules' governing the ownership and use of land and water and prescribes the duties and powers of government, engineering and planning agencies and individuals. These rules are commonly supplemented by established administrative procedures and operating practices. The organizational structure comprises an arrangement of interlocking agencies each having set tasks which relate to overall policy; relationships among agencies are invariably defined both formally and informally. Statute law defines a distribution of power and authority among agencies, usually within a hierarchical structure, and the administrative structure in each agency will determine the level at which decisions are made. Within the organizations there may be key policy-makers who can influence decisions and promote changes in the rules or established procedures if these are acknowledged to be inadequate.

The manner in which responsibilities and powers are divided amongst government departments, other public agencies and individuals may be of particular importance. For practical reasons there has to be such division but its nature is often controversial, reflecting its significance. Excessive fragmentation of responsibility may lead to unclear, ill-defined and contradictory policies, whereas excessive concentration of power may mean decisions are made by those with insufficient detailed knowledge of particular cases and it also removes opportunities for public and local involvement. The public should clearly be represented in the decision-making process concerning public investment but the extent to which this occurs varies and frequently gives rise to protracted debate.

The law and administrative procedures also embrace rules concerning raising and spending revenue. Ultimately planning depends upon finance, the availability of which depends upon government policy and the state of the national economy. If finance is inadequate for tackling particular problems then no amount of attention to other details of policy-making will result in efficient planning.

Less formal components are often included within analyses of institutional arrangements. These include interest groups which seek to influence decisions in their favour and the values of policy-makers, engineers and planners. Ultimately institutional arrangements reflect the traditions, experiences and values of particular societies and are therefore rarely transferable between countries. As societies develop, their needs change and the problems they face alter. Institutional arrangements must keep abreast of these changes and thus require frequent review and periodic alteration (Mitchell, 1971; Porter, 1979).

Institutional analysis can proceed by identifying and applying criteria for evaluating effectiveness of, for example, water-planning institutions (Howe, 1977; Parker and Penning-Rowsell, 1980). Clearly such criteria should seek to evaluate the appropriateness of divisions of power between and within planning agencies, of investments levels, revenue funding arrangements and the adequacy of staffing. The relations between agencies may be a revealing approach to evaluation, as is also the degree of public involvement with decision-making.

However, this process of evaluation is by no means straightforward. Apparently anomalous administrative arrangements may be highly effective; legal limitations may in fact not hinder progress with policy-making if inter-agency cooperation is forthcoming; extensive public involvement may be a charade only developed when established policies are invulnerable rather than genuinely open to change. Institutional analysis, therefore, must recognize the practical and methodological difficulties inherent in this conceptualization of flood control problems.

URBAN FLOODING IN BRITAIN: CAUSES, EXTENT AND EFFECTS

Appraisals of the causes and effects of urban flooding have always been hindered by data deficiencies. During the last decade, however, substantial progress has been made in identifying flooding problems and in assessing their potential impact on urban communities.

Causes of urban flood risk

Flooding has multiple causes and urban areas differ enormously in the combinations of flooding problems they face. Analyses of urban flooding in Britain are frequently oversimplified, focusing predominantly upon classic cases of flood hazard due to extensive urban encroachment (Harding and Parker, 1976; Penning-Rowsell and Parker, 1974a; Perry, 1981; Smith and Tobin, 1979). Where flood hazards are undoubtedly inherited in many settlements from pre-1947 floodplain encroachment, there has been limited recent extensive floodplain development in Britain compared with the United States (Penning-Rowsell, 1981b). The universal land-use regulations which were established in 1947 have limited floodplain encroachment, although this was not their specific purpose. The straightforward transfer from North America to Britain of the floodplain encroachment explanation of flood hazards as developed by White *et al.* (1958) has not therefore been entirely appropriate. The problems inherent in the American 'shadow' over British flood hazard research are explored elsewhere (Parker and Penning-Rowsell, 1983).

Catchment urbanization is a major contributory cause of inland urban flooding in Britain. The aggregate impact of the spread of impervious surfaces and the construction of artificial drainage networks is to increase the speed and magnitude of flooding at a given return period (Hollis, 1979). This process presents severe flooding problems where river channels and flood plains which were formerly sufficient to carry flood flows are no longer adequate because of the effects of upstream urban development. The most common cause of urban flooding is therefore inadequate storm drainage (Penning-Rowsell and Chatterton, 1978).

Several problems associated with urban storm sewer drainage contribute to this flooding. In Britain such drainage is frequently combined with sewage disposal drains and these systems are usually designed to ensure that flood volumes are discharged below ground. In many cities, however, such sewer systems are over 100 years old and are in poor repair following years of neglect and insufficient local authority maintenance. Therefore, in some cases old drainage systems now lack the capacity required to take the large flood volumes resulting from subsequent urbanization.

A second problem is that the replacement of urban storm sewers is far from easy, particularly in inner cities where sewerage systems are oldest and underground congestion is greatest. Sewer replacement is extremely costly. Storm sewerage expenditure in Britain currently totals some £375 million annually and in some areas such as the north-west of England there is a 20-year backlog of maintenance such that sewer collapse and the associated flooding and inconvenience is becoming unfortunately common (North West Water Authority, 1978).

In addition, drainage channels require frequent maintenance and clearance in cities. This is because they rapidly become choked with refuse and rubbish since the public is generally unaware of the flooding implications of this traditional means of waste disposal. Maintenance is both labour-intensive and expensive and is rendered more necessary by vandalism and the public's unwillingness to oversee their own drains.

To take just one example, urbanization of the river Frome catchment upstream of Bristol has contributed to a growing flood problem. This affects the city centre including a new shopping precinct, large commercial districts and an important residential quarter. Up to 3000 properties could be at risk from flooding (Figure 6.2). Other problems exacerbate this risk. Tide levels affect flood

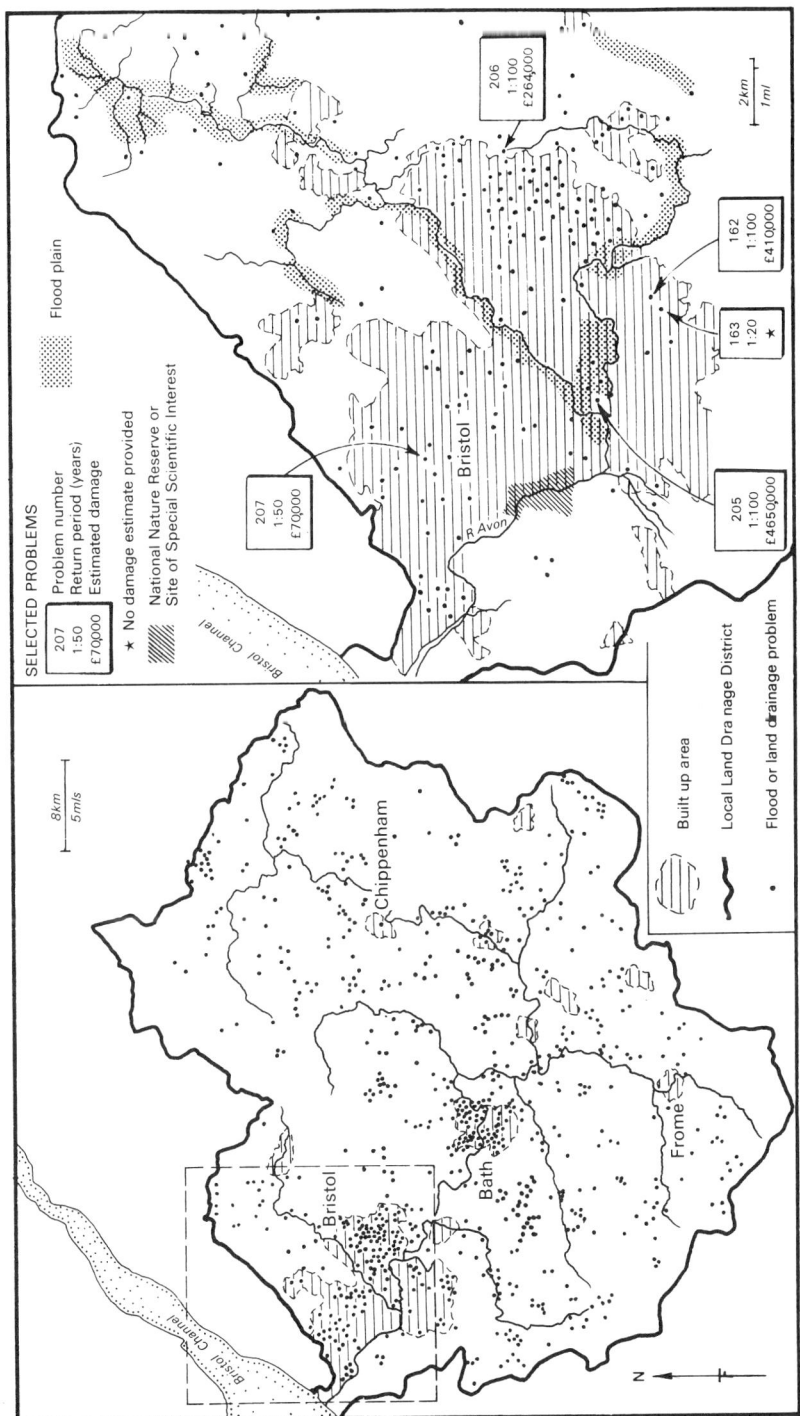

FIGURE 6.2.   The multiplicity of flooding and storm water drainage problems in the Bristol area. (*Source*: Wessex Water Authority)

potential by determining the rate of drainage, yet these levels are difficult to predict for individual flood events. Furthermore, as Bristol developed during previous centuries, the Frome was culverted, so that it now flows almost entirely below ground for several kilometres thus allowing the natural floodplain to become progressively developed. Because of ageing and lack of maintenance the culverts are now silting up, thereby reducing their capacity, just as flood flows due to upstream urbanization are increasing and will be further amplified into the 1990s with the implementation of the city's expansionist structure plan.

Sea flooding is a growing threat to coastal settlements in Britain. Often such settlements have developed behind natural beach defences or behind sea walls, both of which have become less effective over time. The main threat occurs on the east and south coasts of England although localized parts of the west coast are also vulnerable (Perry, 1981; Ward, 1978). Eastern England's fall relative to sea level owing to isostatic readjustment and melting icecaps means that if present trends continue the rise in maximum high tide levels will be 0.76 m over the next century. Because of these shifts in sea levels, and the progressive embankment of the Thames, high tides are 1.22 m higher at London Bridge than 100 years ago, and the chances of flooding due to tides and surges have increased considerably (Horner, 1978). Many towns and ports along the east coast are flood-prone as shown by serious flooding in 1953 and 1978 (Perry, 1981). Sea flooding is also locally a major problem on England's south coast. High tides, storm surges and rare ocean swells, combined with the loss of natural shingle defences, all contribute to this problem which has been recently recognized at Weymouth and the Isle of Portland (Penning-Rowsell and Parker, 1980).

The extent of urban flood risk

A recent major advance in knowledge of flood risk comes from the results of a massive survey programme—known as the Section 24(5) land drainage surveys after the relevant section of the Water Act 1973—which was begun in the mid-1970s and is now almost complete for England and Wales. This survey programme has been overseen by the Ministry of Agriculture, Fisheries and Food and was undertaken by the ten water authorities which have statutory powers concerning the alleviation of urban flooding in their areas (Parker and Penning-Rowsell, 1981a). Not only do these surveys shed light upon the extent of urban flooding potential but they also indicate causes of flooding and the potential benefits of flood alleviation for high priority cases. Preliminary analysis of the survey results suggests that urban flooding in England and Wales is almost ubiquitous and certainly more widespread than is commonly appreciated (see Figure 6.2). This confirms the conclusion from earlier research in the catchments of the Severn, Wye and the south Wales 'valleys' which showed that nearly every urban settlement was flood-prone and that few settlements had full flood protection (Parker, 1976; Parker and Harding, 1978).

For example, the South West Water Authority, with an area covering some 7 per cent of England and Wales, has identified over 450 different locations where urban flooding presents problems (South West Water Authority, 1980). Similarly, over 800 different urban flooding problems have been identified by the Severn Trent Water Authority (1980) in its area comprising 14 per cent of England and Wales (Parker, 1981). The surveys of the remaining eight water authorities suggest a similar relationship between land area and the number of flooding problems so that there could be at least 5000 to 6000 urban flooding problem locations in England and Wales. Much less is known about this type of flooding in Scotland as the regional councils—responsible for Scottish flood protection—have not been obliged to undertake comparable drainage surveys of their areas.

However, crude national statistics concerning urban flooding problems can present a misleading picture of extent and severity. Urban areas with fundamentally different flooding characteristics, as well as those with fringe or minor problems, are all arbitrarily combined. Also a full appraisal cannot be made without accounting either for flooding probability, which naturally varies from place to place, or for the varying degree to which settlements are protected but still have residual flooding problems. Water authority data sources are also very varied in their content and detail. For example, whereas Severn Trent adopted a comprehensive approach by including locations where only a few properties or minor road communications are at risk, the Welsh Water Authority (1979) has identified only principal problems. Nevertheless available data do suggest some basic regularities in the incidence of urban flooding in England and Wales. Burton (1961) noted that British towns and cities are generally less extensively developed on floodplains than in the United States. The Section 24(5) surveys confirm that only a small percentage of flood problems represent the type of major risk common on the large rivers of North America. White (1980), however, indicates that the classic American floodplain flooding picture of major risk may itself be an oversimplification.

By far the most extensive urban flooding potential in Britain occurs in London where over 25 000 houses alone are threatened by a combination of high tides and storm surge conditions in the Thames estuary (Horner, 1979). The Thames tidal barrier is expected to be complete by 1983 affording protection against this threat up to the 1000-year flooding standard. However, this will not 'solve' all of London's flooding problems. The building of the Thames barrier has diverted attention and resources away from the multitude of more minor but still serious flooding in suburban areas. Many of these problems are caused by catchment urbanization which results in an expanded flooded area on land previously flood free and accordingly developed; the problem is dynamic.

Urban flooding effects

The American hazard response paradigm provided an impetus to research into flood damage assessment methods in Britain. Until the early 1970s techniques for

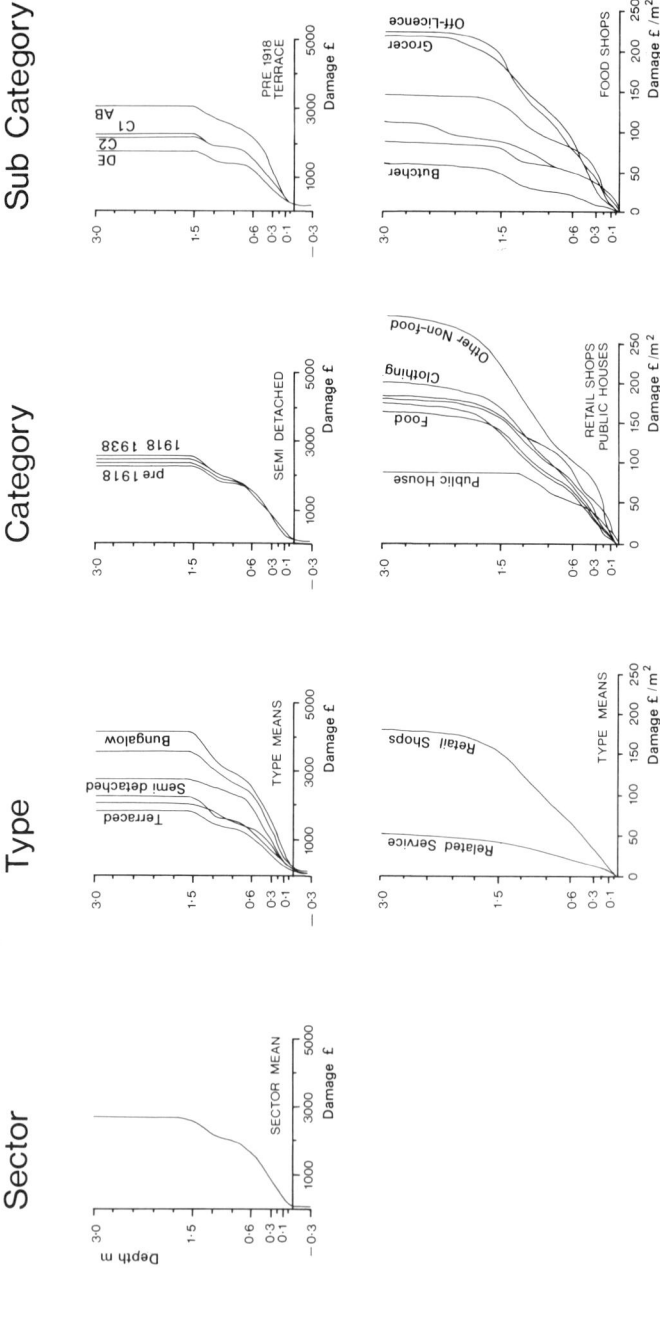

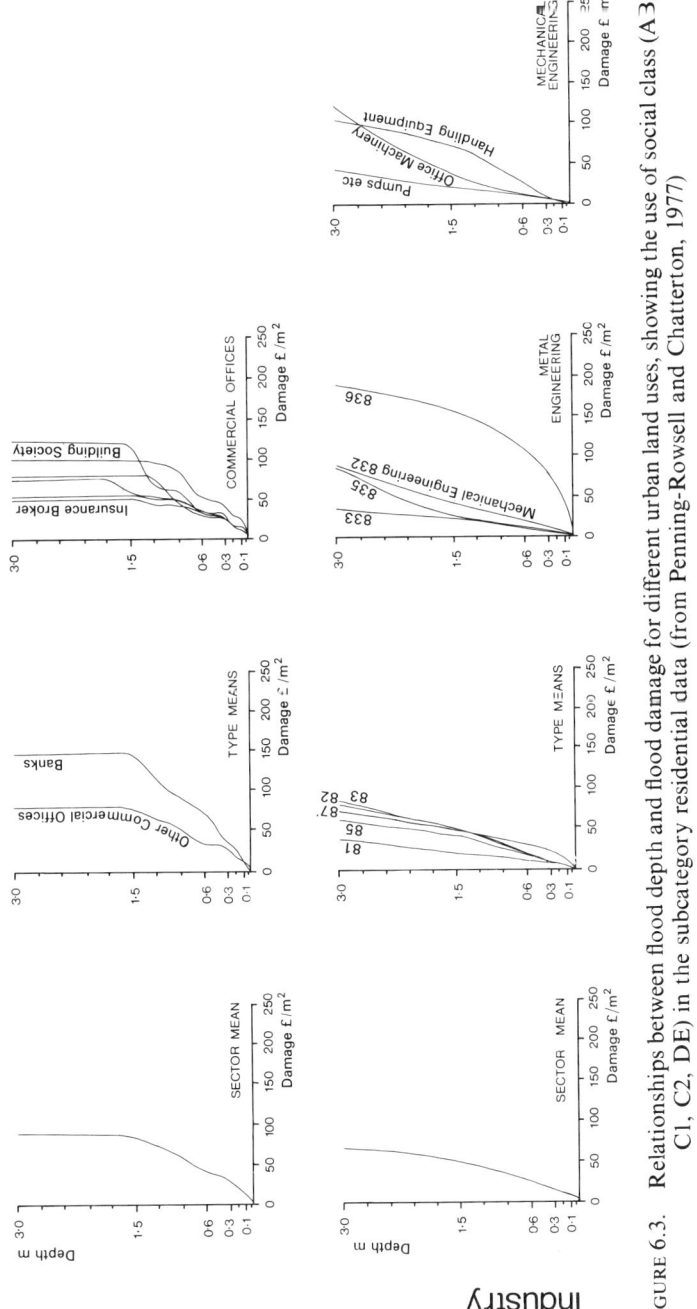

FIGURE 6.3. Relationships between flood depth and flood damage for different urban land uses, showing the use of social class (A3, C1, C2, DE) in the subcategory residential data (from Penning-Rowsell and Chatterton, 1977)

assessing the impact of flooding in Britain and thereby the potential economic benefits of flood alleviation were rudimentary, yet central government demanded cost-benefit appraisals of flood alleviation schemes being proposed for central government grant-aid.

Following the work of White (1964) early British research aimed at quantifying flood damage potential and relating this to property insurance (Porter, 1970, 1971a) and flood frequency (Harding, 1972). Simple depth-damage relationships were established for certain property types and this approach was extended by Parker (1976) who derived standard depth-damage curves for residences following current American practices yet recognizing the important contrasting building types and flood characteristics in Britain (Parker and Penning-Rowsell, 1972). This approach aimed at developing a flood scheme appraisal system similar to that advocated by Kates (1965). A nationally applicable standard flood damage data base has subsequently been created (Figure 6.3) and includes detailed information on the effect of residents' social class on damage susceptibility (Penning-Rowsell and Chatterton, 1977, 1980). Additional data have gauged the relatively small effect of flood warnings on damage reduction (Cole and Penning-Rowsell, 1980; Penning-Rowsell, Chatterton and Parker, 1978) (Tables 6.1 and 6.2) and these data have been linked in an automated method for computing the economic benefits of flood alleviation (Chatterton and Penning-Rowsell, 1978, 1982; Local Government Operational Research Unit, 1973).

Flooding impact is likely to be complex, especially in large urban areas where communication disruption adds considerably to flooding effects. The economic

TABLE 6.1. The relationship between flood warnings and response: individuals' response to warnings (from a survey of nine locations in England and Wales[1])

	Received flood warning		Miscellaneous
	Did not react with damage-reducing actions	Did react with damage-reducing actions	
South-west England locations[2]	36	22	4
Cumbria[3]	1	7	1
Locations in the Midlands of England[4]	11	14	8
Totals	48	43	13
Per cent	46.2	41.3	12.5

[1] For more details see Penning-Rowsell, Chatterton, and Parker (1978) (Table 2).
[2] Weare Gifford; Barnstaple; Bideford; Combe Martin; Braddiford.
[3] Appleby; Keswick.
[4] Attenborough; Newark.

TABLE 6.2. The relationship between flood warnings and response: reasons for respondents' inaction upon receipt of a flood warning' (from a survey of nine locations in England and Wales)

	Number	Per cent
Ill/infirm/old/alone	12	24
Sceptical of flood warning/false warning	25	50
Existing protection assumed adequate	5	10
Others[1]	8	16

[1] For more details see Penning-Rowsell, Chatterton, and Parker (1978) (Table 3).
[2] Includes. 'On standby', 'insured', 'away', 'no time'.

losses due to flooding in such areas include damage to all categories of buildings and their contents and losses to economic activities which are disrupted. While property damage is the most obvious flooding effect, flooded commercial and industrial properties may also suffer substantial loss of trading profits owing to disruption.

It is becoming increasingly recognized that the economic impact of floods can spread well beyond the immediate flood-affected areas. In major River Thames tidal flooding in London the official contingency plans, incorporating road closures, road traffic diversions and the severe curtailment and disruption of public transport services, make it clear that flooding effects would spread at least throughout London and the home counties (Metropolitan Police, undated). In the case of flooding on the Isle of Portland, Dorset, some 48 per cent of total maximum flood damages were indirectly caused by communication disruption which affects employment over 48 km (30 miles) from the scene of flooding (Penning-Rowsell and Parker, 1980).

Further attention is also being directed towards the intangible effects of floods in an attempt to obtain a more comprehensive assessment of their impact. The prediction of loss of life is particularly difficult and controversial yet protection of life is a major objective of urban flood protection and storm sewerage (Penning-Rowsell, 1981b). Recent research indicates strong links between flood experience and adverse health effects (Abrahams et al., 1976; Bennett, 1970; Smith et al., 1980) but the evidence is still too varied for reliable predictions to be made concerning the likely incidence and magnitude of such effects in future flood events.

Causes and effects of sea flooding at Whitstable, Kent

Some of the serious problems concerning Britain's east coast sea defences are exemplified by the flooding risk at Whitstable on the north Kent coast where there is a long history of marine encroachment and sea defence works.

Sea levels have risen by an estimated 4.7 m relative to land levels since Roman times. The risk of flood damage has been exacerbated since then by successive seaward advances of urban development accompanying population and econ-

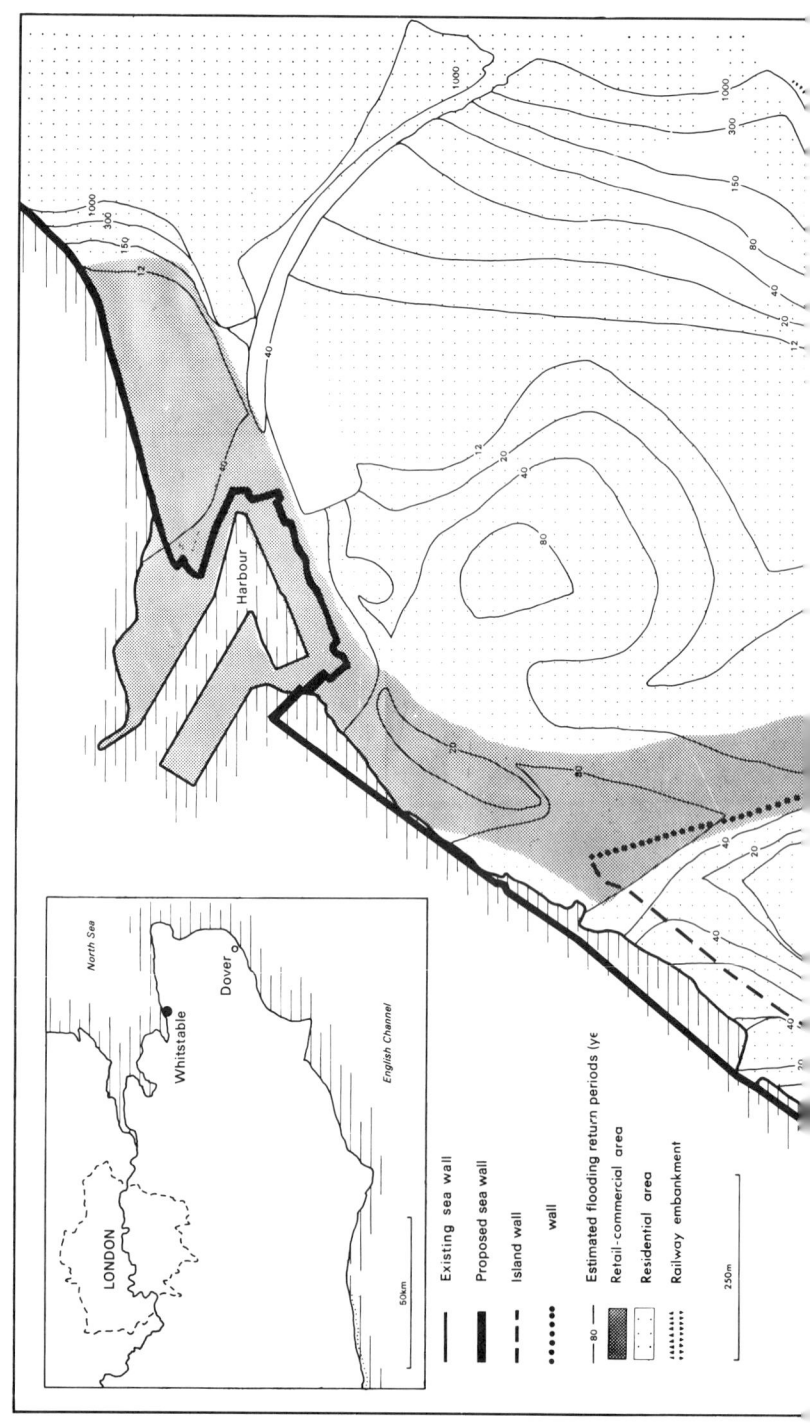

Existing sea wall

Proposed sea wall

Island wall

wall

Estimated flooding return periods (ye

Retail-commercial area

Residential area

Railway embankment

80

250m

Harbour

North Sea

Whitstable

Dover

English Channel

LONDON

50km

FIGURE 6.4. Estimated extent of sea flooding for events of different return periods at Whitstable, Kent. Flood extent boundaries merge together where they meet steep slopes or man-made barriers; numerical values do not always, therefore, follow a sequential pattern

omic growth. Initially, the salt levels in west Whitstable were enclosed during the late 18th and 19th centuries by the 'Island Wall', to promote commercial salt extraction. This encouraged substantial building on the seaward side of the old sea wall known as 'Middle Wall' (Figure 6.4). Subsequently, beach accumulation forward of the new sea defences created a substantial new land feature on which further building developed along the sea front as this became a desirable residential location (Bowler, 1981). During the present century the magnitude of potential flood damage at Whitstable has continued to grow. This has not reflected substantial further encroachment but has arisen with the steady increase in private domestic and commercial investment in both existing and new buildings in the area now estimated to be vulnerable to sea flooding.

Whitstable now has a population of some 16 000 and about 5800 live in the flood-risk area (Figure 6.4). This area includes low-income residential districts, the entire retail-commercial centre of the town and a substantial industrial quarter comprising about 50 businesses. Whitstable has narrowly escaped catastrophic flooding on many occasions, but in 1897 the sea wall was overtopped with flooding in High Street to depths of up to 2.5 m. Serious flooding again occurred in 1953 during the notorious east coast floods. The prediction of sea flooding depths, extents and return periods remains error-prone but serious sea flooding in Whitstable could occur with little warning and to depths of up to 3.5 m in residential districts situated below the height of the existing sea defences.

The existing sea wall, built during the 1950s, is now considered structurally deficient, and catastrophic flooding could occur following wall overtopping or breaching. In either case the flood damage would be substantial, and Table 6.3 gives estimated damages according to different severities of flooding as measured by return periods. The complexity of damage is compounded in this case by extra damage caused by sea water flooding (Penning-Rowsell, 1978) and by structural damage caused by storms accompanying the flood events (Parker and Penning-Rowsell, 1981b). However, estimated indirect losses are not substantial, because the area affected does not include significant road traffic flows, so the geographical extent of flood effects is restricted in this case to the immediately vulnerable area. Nevertheless the intangible flooding effects are expected to be important. Elderly and handicapped residents, many of whom live in the lowest-lying residential districts near to the sea front, are particularly fearful of serious flooding and of their inability to react rapidly to the necessity for evacuation. Loss of life is likely during serious flooding despite a detailed local authority emergency evacuation plan, because of the short warning time available and the extreme depths of flooding.

As the sea rises relative to land levels Whitstable's sea defences promise to remain a continual problem. The latest proposal by the Local District Council is for a new and higher sea wall built with further encroachment onto the existing beach. The proposed wall is designed to protect against flooding up to the 1000-

TABLE 6.3. Flooding at Whitstable, Kent: tangible flood damage with the overtopping of existing sea defences

	Return period estimate (years)							
	6.00	12.00	20.00	40.00	80.00	150.00	300.00	1000.00
A. Direct damage data (Standard flood damage.)								
Damage to residential properties (including damage to motor cars)	63	587 898	1 336 291	3 010 883	5 228 291	7 941 683	9 306 285	10 835 762
Damage to retail and related properties	0	166 509	493 857	607 973	1 942 833	3 707 344	5 098 791	6 735 733
Damage to offices, etc.	0	9 654	25 248	73 130	177 026	330 250	429 718	491 478
Damage to public buildings	0	2 539	8 952	27 875	55 461	109 629	158 959	224 692
Site specific data and supplements to standard data								
Damage to industrial and related premises	0	146 816	194 214	313 595	890 283	1 297 726	1 688 707	2 512 499
Damage to public utilities	0	1 055	10 492	13 806	25 499	35 920	49 114	73 713
Damage to beach huts	0	0	0	6 000	6 000	6 000	6 000	6 000
Structural storm damage	0	0	0	229 325	683 825	683 825	683 825	683 825
B. Indirect damage data								
Loss of retail trading profit	0	0	8 760	31 920	44 400	103 200	112 800	121 440
Loss of trading profits in industrial and related premises	0	14 662	100 625	121 619	336 991	526 598	654 048	793 953
Cost of traffic disruption	0	0	0	0	0	0	0	0
Cost of emergency services	15 000	30 000	45 000	60 000	75 000	75 000	75 000	75 000
Total (£)	15 063	959 133	2 223 439	4 496 126	9 465 609	14 817 185	18 263 248	22 554 000

year return period event, and although similar in standard to the Thames barrier such a high level of protection is unusual in Britain given the costs of such schemes and the likely tangible benefits in terms of flood damage prevented. However, the proposed sea wall will have a design life of only 70 years and after this time further investment will be required to provide protection for the threatened community owing to the finite life of engineering structures and the dynamic relationship between sea and land levels. Nevertheless, public attitudes to the proposal are mixed. The immense cost involved—estimated at £11.8 million (1981 prices)—and the relatively sparse flood experience in Whitstable to date, coupled with the disruption to be caused by the construction works have all engendered opposition. Support, however, comes from those for whom flooding is an inconceivable disaster and from those who see the potential for economic development of the town once the community invests to protect its accumulated capital in the form of domestic property and private businesses. As such these tensions between opposing factions characterize many aspects of the ambivalence in public attitudes to flooding and flood alleviation which have provided much of the stimulus for hazard-response research.

ATTITUDES TOWARDS FLOOD RISKS

Guided mainly by the hazard response paradigm, British geographers have sought to establish a behavioural explanation of flood hazard causality. Attention has thus been consistently directed towards urban encroachment on to flood-prone areas (Hollis, 1976; Penning-Rowsell, 1976; Penning-Rowsell and Parker, 1974b) and towards residents' attitudes, perceptions and actions (Smith and Tobin, 1979; Tobin, 1977). Empirical evidence has contributed to a developing prognosis of urban residential flood risk which suggests that the ability of residents to adjust efficiently to flood risks is limited.

Residents' awareness of flood risk

Since recognition of the flood risk is a basic precondition of risk-reducing actions, lack of awareness amongst residents has received considerable attention. A large proportion of urban residents appear to be completely unaware of the flood risks to which they are vulnerable (Table 6.4). Supporting Kates' (1971) hypotheses and model residents' flood-risk awareness appears almost universally to be related to their experience of floods. Without repeated flooding experience residents do not take risk-reducing actions (Kates, 1962). In research at Appleby and Shrewsbury, Smith and Tobin (1979) and Parker and Harding (1979) found that expectation of flooding and risk recognition were both associated with personal flooding experience. Where flooding expectation was not apparently related to experience this is explained by residents' perceptions—false or otherwise—of the availability of flood protection.

TABLE 6.4. Expectation of flooding amongst urban residents in selected flood-risk locations

Location	Estimated flooding return period	Total number of residents interviewed	Expect future flooding?	Number	Percentage
Shrewsbury UK	10 years	132	yes	35	26.7
(Parker and			no	69	51.9
Harding, 1979)			uncertain	28	21.4
Builth Wells UK	3 years	40[1]	yes	26	65.0
(Parker and Harding			no	7	17.5
1979)			uncertain	7	17.5
Appleby UK	4 years	44	yes	32	73.0
(Smith and Tobin			no	4	9.0
1979)			uncertain	8	18.0
Carlisle UK	11 years	218	yes	148	18.0
(Smith and Tobin			no	39	68.0
1979)			uncertain	31	14.0
Lower Severn Valley UK	25 years	723	yes	522	72.2
(Penning-Rowsell			no	201	27.8
1972, 1976)					
La Follette USA	5 years	31	yes	11	35.5
(Kates, 1962)			no	17	54.8
			undertain	3	9.7

[1] includes interviews at ten commercial premises

The links between flooding experience and risk-reducing actions are clearly demonstrated by Penning-Rowsell (1976), Kates (1962) and Parker and Harding (1979). For example, Penning-Rowsell (1976, p. 150) found for the lower Severn floodplain that only some 15 per cent of those with no flood experience made any damage-reducing adjustments. In contrast, some 69 per cent of those with experience had taken some action. In the same study adjustments were found to be related to the length of time since the last flood was experienced and how optimistic or pessimistic respondents were about the frequency of future flooding. Parker and Harding (1979) provide similar results for Shrewsbury; awareness of flooding is clearly associated with personal experience of flood events. These studies consistently show for residential communities that attitudes to flooding are largely a function of flooding frequency and the degree of residential mobility. Repeated flooding leads to an accumulation of flooding experience and, thereby, to awareness and adjustment. Accordingly those locations in Table 6.4 with frequent flooding have the higher levels of awareness than those with less frequent flooding. However, residential mobility reduces aggregate awareness since residents with flooding experience are almost invariably replaced by those without; experience does not accumulate. High residential mobility in modern urban society is clearly an important factor perpetuating flood hazards as periods of residence are brief compared with the return periods of serious floods which are commonly at least 10 or 20 years. In both Carlisle and Appleby over 40 per cent of residents had lived there for six years or less (Smith and Tobin, 1979). Similar percentages are reported for Shrewsbury and in the lower Severn valley the figure is 35 per cent (Parker and Harding, 1979; Penning-Rowsell, 1976). In each case awareness, and therefore adjustment, is less in the high-mobility urban areas than in the low-mobility rural villages (Penning-Rowsell, 1972).

Low levels of flood awareness, however, cannot be explained completely by limited experience or high mobility. Flooding events are comparatively rare compared with everyday environmental and social 'hazards' such as traffic noise, unreliable public transport, ill-health or vandalism (Harding and Parker, 1974). Whereas the risk of flooding is ever-present it may not be so perceived: relatively infrequent serious events are the only form in which flood risk is perceived. Flooding appears to be of little significance to residents and is thereby largely ignored. Greater concern is directed towards more immediate problems. For example, in the lower Severn valley only some 9 per cent of those citing disadvantages in their location mentioned flooding, whereas 21 per cent mentioned poor provision of bus and other community services. Residents planning a move may not expect—perhaps understandably—to be flooded in the meantime (Burton, Kates, and White, 1978). The overall picture in Britain, as in the United States, is of some public indifference to flooding which is perceived as an infrequent nuisance rather than as a major risk.

Exceptionally, however, the flooding threat may be perceived as sufficiently severe to rank as a daily concern. These attitudes often occur in the stressful period following flooding; flood-risk recognition is commonly associated with the recency of flood experience (Parker, 1976; Penning-Rowsell, 1976). Daily concern over flooding as also related to the severity of recent experience. Residents subjected to deeper and longer durations of flooding are more likely to remain aware of the flood risk. Awareness is also raised when residents, particularly the elderly and infirm, are fearful of flooding and their ability to cope with emergencies (Parker and Penning-Rowsell, 1981b; Smith and Tobin, 1979). A factor clearly complicating flood risk recognition is the probabilistic character of natural events. As well as involving planning for periods of time far longer than those considered in other endeavours, rational response to flooding demands the ability to think in probabilistic terms. The degree to which residents can be expected to think probabilistically must be limited, given that their flooding experience may be either very slight or non-existent, such that inferences must be made from ridiculously small samples of experience (Slovic, Kunreuther, and White, 1974). Kates (1962) found that some residents refused to think of floods as probabilistic events; to do so was beyond their cognitive abilities. Gately (1973) found a similar pattern in Britain, again in the lower Severn valley, where 35 per cent of respondents considered the river would never flood again. However, many interviewees clearly had perceptions of what constitutes a flood and its causes which are somewhat at variance with conventional professional thinking and linked more to a *Genesis* interpretation of events: 'If the water enters the house, that is an act of Nature; if one is driven upstairs or on to the roof, that is an act of God; but if one should have so incurred His displeasure that one is swept away, then *that* is a flood' (Gately, 1973, p. 7).

An almost universal related problem in public comprehension of flood frequency information concerns the return period concept. A '50-year flood' is commonly understood by the public to be the flood which will occur *regularly* every 50 years rather than the flood which will occur *on average* once in 50 years: there is no question of regularity in the concept but there is in the public perception. This tendency towards a determinate ordering of nature by some and a denial of the possibility of recurrence of flooding by others, is commonly encountered in residents' flood risk cognition and profoundly affects their propensity to take risk-reducing actions.

Given the limited opportunity and ability of the public to comprehend flooding occurrences in probabilistic terms, it is perhaps somewhat surprising to find that residents in both Builth Wells and Shrewsbury have a relatively well-informed view of the prospect of further flooding (Parker, 1976). For example, at Shrewsbury 72 per cent of residents subscribed to the sophisticated view that flooding could return in any year rather than to alternative deterministic views. Similar findings are reported from elsewhere in developed societies (Burton, Kates, and White, 1978, p. 99) and these add to the weight of evidence suggesting that perceptions can be highly complex or remarkably sophisticated in some respects and surprisingly crude and over-generalized in others.

Public education and information dissemination concerning flood risks appears to be an obvious means of increasing residents' flood risk awareness and hence provoking individuals to adjust accordingly. Flood hazard reports and maps are made available to residents, developers and local officials in both North America and Australia (Day, *et al.*, 1981; New South Wales Water Resources Commission, undated). However, in Britain, apart from relatively small-scale maps of London's flood risk zone, such information is not generally released, although this may not be so unjustified as might be imagined (Parker and Penning-Rowsell, 1981a). Handmer and Milne (1980) have concluded, for example, that 'the high hopes and ideals often expressed for public information programs based on flood maps seem to be largely without a substantial foundation'. It is becoming clear that efficient flood risk education is far from simple. In Australia the effect of information programmes has fallen well short of expectations partly for perceptual reasons; maps appear to be of limited value in raising flood awareness and in stimulating risk-reducing actions. Such findings, if confirmed elsewhere, suggest that a 'behavioural' approach to flood damage reduction—via increasing awareness—is likely to be less successful as an alternative to structural solutions than many early hazard-response paradigm researchers had hoped.

Residential choice, social class and flood risk locations

The hazard response paradigm predicts that occupation of risk zones persists because such zones are perceived to be in some respect superior. It is clear that many people choose either to locate or remain in flood risk locations because of their perceived advantages. In Shrewsbury only 24 per cent of residents emphasized the disadvantages of their home location; in the lower Severn valley over 30 per cent had apparently considered the flood risk when moving to their flood-prone house; and in Carlisle and Appleby 87 per cent rejected moving house despite the flooding problem. Evidence for factors attracting urban residents to flood-prone areas is somewhat scarce in Britain. However, at Whitstable the perceived amenities at the vulnerable sea-front zone have attracted residents who are able and prepared to renovate old properties and therefore take advantage of low initial purchase prices. Many of these residents are among those now opposed to the higher sea wall, despite this alleviating the risk of catastrophic flooding, because they will lose part of their sea view. For Atlanta in the United States, James (1974) concluded that 'convenience', 'seclusion' and 'attractiveness' were more important to residents than economic considerations such as house price or potential flood damage.

On balance, British and North American evidence from studies based upon the hazard response paradigm favours the conclusion that flood risk recognition and risk-taking action are only marginally explained by socio-economic variables such as educational achievement, social class, occupation, age, sex and tenure (Kates, 1962; Parker, 1976; Smith and Tobin, 1979). However, an alternative interpretation is emerging of the significance of social class in relation to hazard vulnerability (O'Keefe, Westgate, and Wisner, 1976; Torry, 1979). This is linked with the observation, in Britain at least, that unprotected urban floodplains are frequently occupied by low or fixed-income groups, as for example at Shrewsbury. Munro et al. (1980) also found that low land prices were the major attraction to the residents of the Lismore floodplain in Australia where aboriginals and other less-favoured social groups congregate in cheap flood-prone housing.

This evidence suggests that those most vulnerable to flooding comprise those least able to withstand property losses and personal stress. However, there is a gap between empirical evidence from hazard-response paradigm studies and the emerging class interpretations and observations. This gap arises because British investigations have almost without exception focused upon low and middle-income residential areas where income differentials are narrow and have ignored middle-class, amenity-rich locations. The choice of study locations has so far been dictated more by the need to find a severe flooding problem than by the desire to pursue a social-class interpretation but the consequence is limited rigorous analysis of social class effects. This lack of evidence emphasizes the methodological rigidity of the hazard-response paradigm. Surveys were not done in flood-prone areas but in prestigious Maidenhead or Henley. Researchers realised intuitively that here amenity gain from river locations far outweighs the flood risk for those affluent enough to give priority to scenic river views and prospects of regattas over the possibility of flood losses which for others might present personal economic disaster. The paradigm has implicit welfare con- notations, specifically focusing on protecting those less knowledgeable or less able to withstand natural disasters from the follies of their ignorance or the inadequacy of their economic lot.

The new social-class explanation of residential community flooding vulnera- bility has the following features. Unprotected residential communities are characterized by high proportions of low and fixed-income groups, and by high proportions of elderly, infirm and widowed inhabitants. Such residents are attracted to the older housing often found in floodplains. This housing is comparatively inexpensive partly because of repeated flooding which lowers housing quality and increases dry-rot and damp. Low and fixed-income groups may be under-insured and for them flooding is a financial disaster. The elderly, infirm and widowed are least able to act in a flood emergency and are therefore more vulnerable to injury and loss of personal belongings; they are also more likely to suffer ill-health related to stress during and following flooding. Above all these groups are often 'poorly connected', inarticulate and ignorant about their rights and institutional responsibilities; they will be least inclined to organize effective political pressure for flood protection. Examples of such residential communities exist in many British cities including the flood-prone areas of Lincoln and Cardiff, the St Pauls area in Bristol and the low-income parts of Portland, Dorset (Penning-Rowsell and Parker, 1980).

On the other hand, middle-class professional and élite residential communities, perhaps attracted to prestige or amenity riverside locations, can be expected to be articulate, well-insured, 'well-connected', and more able to recover financially from a flood event. Such groups are quick to organize residents' pressure groups and are well able to make political pressure work in their favour so as to obtain flood protection. These groups may also be able to insist on a higher standard of flood protection than others, thus reinforcing the inequities which already exist in urban communities. A further advantage which these groups have is that they are often able to insist on higher standards of amenity improvement associated with flood protection schemes.

The relevance of residents' flood risk attitudes

A pervasive assumption of the hazard-response paradigm is that risk-reducing actions of individuals are critical to effective flood hazard reduction. This may be valid in North America where landowners and residents have been significantly less constrained by planning controls than in Britain. However, in Britain comprehensive land-use regulations embodying development controls date from 1947 and there has been less scope for individuals to create risks by unwise individualistic building development in flood-prone areas and hence less need to react to flood risks (Parker and Penning-Rowsell, 1982).

The most effective response for a British floodplain resident to the flood risk is to contribute towards political pressure for comprehensive flood protection, usually by structural means. For this action, residents' perceptions and knowledge of institutional arrangements for flood protection are most important. A major obstacle to flood risk reduction is therefore not so much individual residents' reluctance to keep sandbags available for a flood emergency, but their inability to comprehend the rights, duties and responsibilities of residents, local authorities and water authorities, and to make the local political processes work in their favour to obtain flood protection.

Nevertheless, residents' attitudes towards floods are becoming more important as more sophisticated flood warning systems are being provided for major cities. In some localities flood warning linked to emergency evacuation procedures is the only feasible means of protection while for protected but intensively developed residential areas flood warnings may be the only defence against catastrophic overtopping of flood defences (Chatterton, Pirt, and Wood, 1979). However, response to warnings is commonly low for a variety of reasons (see Tables 6.1 and 6.2), some of which are imperfectly understood. Research is therefore needed to clarify the best processes of warning dissemination so as to capitalize upon investment in flood forecasting and warning generation.

Flood risk perceptions and attitudes also have considerable relevance in gauging the intangible benefits of flood alleviation schemes and are becoming increasingly important. With further research perhaps measures of stress and fear may emerge from analysis of flood risk perception. The trade off people are prepared to make between flood protection and amenity loss warrants further attention in seeking the most appropriate standards of flood protection in particular circumstances (Parker and Penning-Rowsell, 1981b). Such research represents a shift from academic study of flooding attitudes as part of an overall model of environmental behaviour, towards more utilitarian data gathering on the 'social feasibility' of current flood loss reduction strategies (Smith and Tobin, 1979).

THE INSTITUTIONAL AND PLANNING ENVIRONMENT

The legal and administrative framework

Providing flood protection for urban communities is complicated by the uncertainties inherent in randomly occurring events such as floods and also by the complex institutional arrangements. These arrangements involve a multiplicity of agencies, a complex legal system and a financing arrangement which mixes central government grants and a variety of local contributions. When added to the ambivalent public attitudes concerning the incidence of future floods and the acceptable standards of protection these complications make the planning of flood alleviation somewhat problematic.

Flood alleviation legislation in Britain has a long history dating back to the Commissioners of Sewers established in 1427 and the Bill of Sewers 1521 (Wisdom, 1975). The most important statute enacted in recent times was the Land Drainage Act 1930, which replaced the drainage districts established under the Land Drainage Act 1861 and set up Catchment Boards to oversee both agricultural land drainage and urban flood protection (Cole, 1976). The recent Land Drainage Act 1976 merely consolidates pre-existing legislation while the Water Act 1973, which established the water authorities, had only a minor effect on this part of planning the hydrological cycle.

British land drainage law—governing agricultural drainage and urban flood protection excluding coastal flooding—is based on a number of key principles. First, the responsibility for land drainage lies first and foremost with the riparian owner—the owner of land abutting a watercourse (Wilkins, 1980). Secondly, much of the legislation is merely permissive and confers no duties upon agencies to provide flood protection (Hollis, 1980). Thirdly, land drainage is predominantly a local matter and the law and administrative arrangements allow that decisions about it should be made locally. Finally, the law suggests that those who benefit from land drainage or create a need for it should pay accordingly the cost of its provision (Parker and Penning-Rowsell, 1980).

From the third of these principles—local decision-making—arise the main executive planning agencies in the inland flood protection field. While the organization of other water services moved from local government or river authority control to regional water authority control in 1974, special local provisions for land drainage were incorporated into the Water Act 1973. These arrangements allowed for regional and local land drainage committees—paralleling pre-existing catchment boards and river authority areas—as one of the two statutory committees required of each water authority (Hollis, 1980) (Table 6.5). Furthermore, particularly favourable arrangements guaranteed both special representation of land drainage interests on the water authority boards and the continuation of the central government grant-aid system. This system provides the only central government finance to the otherwise deliberately self-sufficient water authorities (National Water Council, 1978).

These special arrangements were by no means accidental. Richardson, Jordan, and Kimber (1978) describe the concerted lobbying campaign which led to the concessions by the Ministry of Housing and Local Government of these arrangements to protect land drainage interests within the large and powerful

TABLE 6.5. The organizational character of land drainage and flood alleviation in England and Wales (from Hollis, 1980)

| Water authority | Divisional organization with regard to land drainage | Authority members | | Local Land Drainage Committees | No of IDBs | IDB Expenditure 1976–77 £ 000 | Water Authority expenditure on land drainage 1974–75 | |
		Local Authority	Ministerial appointments				Capital £ 000	Revenue £ 000
North-umbrian	2 divs S, WS, LD 1 div WS, LD	10	9	0	1	0	47	420
Welsh	7 divs all-purpose	20	15	7	14	210	795	1545
Yorkshire	1 div LD	13	12	0	50	2120	1537	2045
North West	1 div river management incl LD	14	13	3	11	75	1090	2569
South West	3 divs all purpose	8	7	2	1	3	649	802
Thames	1 div S and river management incl LD 1 div river management incl LD	36	22	2	0	—	3126	3247
Severn Trent	8 divs all purpose	22	21	2	36	1206	2033	2420
Wessex	3 divs all purpose	8	7	3	21	288	1365	1547
Anglian	5 divs river management incl LD	18	17	5	136	6428	4576	6153
Southern	3 divs river management incl LD and WS 1 div all-purpose	10	9	4	19	908	1822	2725

LD: Land Drainage; S: Sewerage; WS: Water Supply; IDBs: Internal Drainage Boards.

water authorities. The 'community network' of mutually supporting interests—principally the farming lobby articulated by the Association of Drainage Authorities and senior civil servants from the Ministry of Agriculture, Fisheries and Food—feared that land drainage concerns would be swamped by the more pressing sewage treatment and water supply duties of the multifunctional water authorities. The 'network' strove to maintain their separate administrative and financing system to ensure the continuation and stability of the special status and resources directed to land drainage since the Land Drainage Act 1930 sought to promote agricultural recovery via state investment in agricultural infrastructure including land drainage (Penning-Rowsell, 1980).

Meanwhile local authorities retain a major role in urban flood protection. Land drainage committees and water authorities are only responsible for 'main rivers' whereas minor watercourses are district council responsibilities (Severn Trent Water Authority, 1977). In London the Greater London Council has complete urban drainage responsibilities in addition to responsibility for the Thames tidal barrier (Horner, 1978), thus adding to the administrative fragmentation; in Scotland the situation is again different though still dominated by agricultural interests (Figure 6.5). At the coast the situation is different again. Much coastal flooding is prevented by coast protection schemes—designed primarily to prevent erosion—which are the responsibility of district councils or water authorities. The councils are responsible in this field to the Department of the Environment, which gives grant-aid, but until the Whitstable sea wall proposal by Canterbury City Council the Department did not require full economic appraisal of the flood protection thus provided.

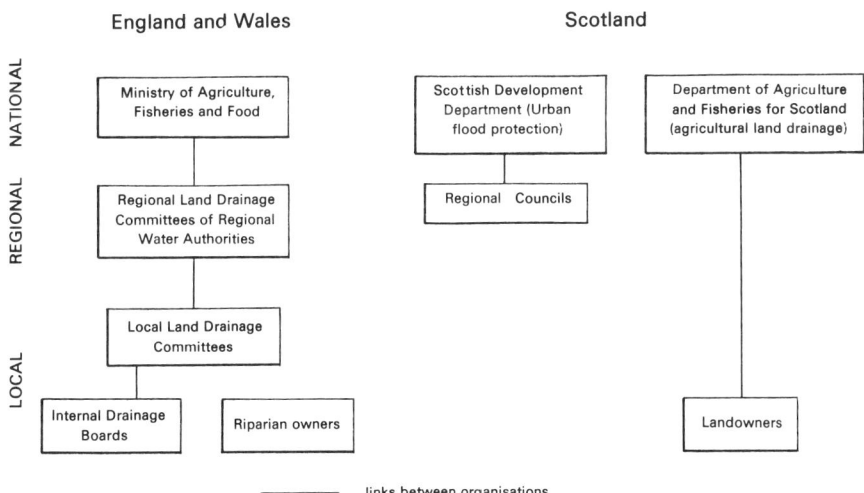

FIGURE 6.5.   Structure of major responsibilities for flood protection and land drainage in Britain (excluding coastal flooding and emergency relief)

In contrast, both agricultural drainage and inland urban flood protection are the responsibility of the Ministry of Agriculture, Fisheries and Food rather than urban drainage being overseen by the Department of the Environment along with other local authority services. Such an arrangement was a further concession to the farming-dominated drainage lobby during the negotiations over the Water Act 1973 (Parker and Penning-Rowsell, 1980; Richardson, Jordan, and Kimber, 1978). In turn, members of the regional and local land drainage committees are either Ministry appointments or county council delegates, the latter because counties pay rate precepts to water authorities for land drainage. This procedure guarantees an inbuilt emphasis in these committees on agricultural drainage rather than urban flood alleviation. Consequently, unless potential beneficiaries of urban flood protection schemes make known their needs there can be a tendency to promote marginally worthwhile agricultural drainage instead of more cost-effective urban programmes.

Applying some institutional criteria

Some of the continuing urban flooding problems are undoubtedly related to institutional shortcomings. Division of responsibility between water authorities and district councils is a continual source of confusion which has caused delay in the execution of flood alleviation plans, especially where inadequate finance has been committed by district councils to this area of their multifarious responsibilities. However, district councils often lack the necessary specialist staff to appraise and implement urban flood control schemes given that their engineering personnel are unlikely to encounter such problems with the frequency with which water authorities are concerned with land drainage problems.

Much of this evidence would suggest that district councils should not have land drainage responsibilities or promote coast protection schemes to prevent sea flooding and that water authorities are better suited to give adequate priority to all urban flood alleviation. However, if all urban flooding problems, however minor, were water authority responsibilities this would remove the local control from the planning process which is the necessary hallmark of this field. Water authorities tend to be large, remote, bureaucratic and insufficiently accountable organizations; excessive time can elapse between flood events and any flood control programme. Water authorities are inherently unsuitable for the control of minor local hazards, and the district councils have a proper role in this area of community welfare. However, greater technical cooperation between councils and water authorities is an essential prerequisite to improved flood alleviation planning (Severn Trent Water Authority, 1977).

A further reason for a continuing—but improved—district council role is that one of the major institutional problems concerns the control of urban development on floodplains. We can see now that this is perhaps not the major problem that researchers working in the hazard response paradigm have considered (Penning-Rowsell, 1976; Penning-Rowsell and Parker, 1974a, 1974b; Smith and Tobin, 1979); the encroachment problem common in the United States has been assumed as of equal significance in Britain but this is an exaggeration (Parker and Penning-Rowsell, 1983). Nevertheless there is a nagging increase in potential flood damages in some areas where local authorities—including district councils—allow factory and residential development in areas liable to flooding. Such problems arise when developers and district councils choose to ignore the flood problems and water authority advice or occasionally where planning permission is given on appeal despite warning against such development by the relevant water authority (Penning-Rowsell, 1981a and b). In general, land-use planning has greatly aided flood plain management in Britain—and such management is probably more advanced as a result than anywhere else in the world—but this nagging problem remains. There is no solution except to give water authorities land-use planning powers in floodplain areas, as occurs in Victoria, Australia, but this would remove the community responsibility for land-use from the locally elected districts to the non-participatory management-orientated water authorities. The only marginal institutional improvement would be for mandatory contributions from developers towards drainage and flood alleviation works and this is currently under consideration for future legislation (National Water Council, 1978). A further improvement in land-use planning in flood risk areas should materialize as more information emerges from water authority surveys of flooding problems, and district councils thereby have a better data base for their floodplain development control decisions (Parker and Penning-Rowsell, 1981a).

By any criterion, the influence of agricultural interests in urban flood alleviation is strong (see Figure 6.5). This might be seen as a disadvantage in removing responsibilities from those urban residents liable to suffer flooding, and also by giving one specific group dominant influence over central government grants for urban infrastructure improvement. However, there also could be advantages in these arrangements. Owing to the strength of the farming lobby the total resources allocated to land drainage have been maintained, even at times of other public expenditure cutbacks, such that the urban community has gained from the maintenance of their flood protection budget. In addition farmers tend to have long memories whereas mobile urban dwellers perhaps would not vote for drainage expenditure unless they had recently been affected by flooding. The land drainage committees and farmers with influence in this area perhaps have the type of collective memory needed to plan flood control schemes which the urban dweller lacks; the latter would rather vote for immediate benefits of a better bus service, which is perceived as of greater priority, than for the longer-term benefits of protection from floods which might not occur for 25 years.

An evaluation of decision-making

The contrast between 'linear-deductive' and 'disjointed incrementalist' decision-making discussed above provides some help in analysing decisions concerning flood protection planning. There is no doubt that some decisions in the past have reflected pure crisis-response following a particularly severe flood, an approach which is often encouraged by ambivalent public attitudes. Local willingness to finance a proportion of flood protection via rates and to agree compulsory purchase arrangements frequently only follows serious flooding. Even then plans must be laid rapidly or public interest in flood protection may wane (Parker and Penning-Rowsell, 1980, p. 225).

Discussion of the socially appropriate standards of flood protection—the goal to be achieved—is sparse. In recent times design standards have risen from the 30–50 year flood event which was the norm in the mid-1950s to encompass designs aimed at the 100 year event or even higher. No good reason exists for these higher standards except that water authority engineers have been chary of designing schemes which will not accommodate the most serious known flood, and this naturally leads to rising standards as records accrue.

Three aspects of flood protection planning hint at the development of more rational decision-making. The first comprises the Section 24(5) surveys currently emerging from the water authorities of flooding problems in their own areas (Parker and Penning-Rowsell, 1981a; Penning-Rowsell and Chatterton, 1976) Here is an attempt to evaluate the range of flooding problems in Britain's urban areas from which to decide both the optimal level of capital expenditure for this type of community welfare investment and also the sequence of schemes to be implemented based on relative cost-effectiveness. This approach to floodplain mapping, as opposed to mere publicity on flood problems which has been the feature of many American and most Australian floodplain maps (Day *et al.*, 1981), will undoubtedly make a real contribution to better flood protection planning.

Nevertheless, some would argue—and Thames' water planners have—that exhaustive analysis of all including the smallest flood problems is not conducive to better planning (Parker and Penning-Rowsell, 1981a). This is because it is not necessarily useful to know at any one time of all possible flood problems when sufficient problems are known for the capital expenditure of the responsible agency, and the problem is in any case continually changing in character and magnitude. Thus, planning based merely on data collection—which at least partly characterizes the Section 24(5) surveys—ignores debate about the standard of service to be given and the necessity for choice between competing uses for scarce capital resources.

Further evidence of improved decision-making comes from the increased public participation in urban flood alleviation. However, water authorities and district councils have only reluctantly accepted demands for public involvement in decision-making and have responded by providing public meetings designed to disseminate information rather than encourage genuine debate. As such this type of public involvement is no different from many 1970s 'participation' exercises where planning agencies presented solutions for agreement rather than choices for decision.

However, public inquiries into flood alleviation schemes are now possible (Hall, 1978; Parker and Penning-Rowsell, 1980; 1981b), and while river engineers in general are increasingly concerned to consult the public when planning capital schemes, the remote and technically based water authorities are not well suited to the needs of public participation. Furthermore such participation does raise serious problems. The public is generally ignorant about institutional powers and responsibilities and commonly believes that water authorities and district councils have a duty to alleviate flooding whereas in fact their powers are merely permissive. Such misunderstandings can create considerable aggravation. This is compounded by delays in planning flood alleviaton, which in part can be traced to ambivalent public attitudes to the desirability of flood protection when there is a trade-off of amenity loss to be balanced against a higher standard of flood protection, as at Whitstable (Parker and Penning-Rowsell, 1981b) and at Pulborough in Sussex (Penning-Rowsell and Chatterton, 1976; 1977). Again, public consultation may simply reflect the power of existing interests in the flood protection field. Little is likely to be threatened by consultation if the power to make decisions remains with the land drainage committees and the Ministry rather than with the public at large or their elected representatives.

The economic evaluation of urban flood alleviation schemes has some of the hallmarks of due consideration being given to a more rational approach to resource allocation by the responsible agencies. This evaluation could perhaps be seen as part of a linear-deductive search for alternative, more cost-effective methods of attaining the goal of adequate urban drainage. This, however, is not quite the truth. In reality water authorities and their land drainage committees—as well as district councils implementing their more substantial river flood protection schemes—are obliged by the Ministry of Agriculture, Fisheries and Food to provide this type of evaluation. If they were not so obliged they would almost certainly not use these techniques which, in any case, are often used at present merely to post-rationalize predetermined designs. However, no grant will be paid by the Ministry without such evaluations and both water authorities and councils find such grants attractive at a time of scarce capital for public investment. In turn, the Ministry has not really adopted this assessment of cost-effectiveness out of a search for the most worthwhile levels of community urban drainage investment but rather because of Treasury pressure. The Treasury, in effect, is trying to ensure that this expenditure—promoted through political pressure by the agricultural lobby—is necessary at all. Indeed, as the pressures on government to curtail public expenditure have grown so the Treasury has insisted on more and more detailed evaluations, particularly on those schemes worth over £1.5 million for which it requires the Ministry to pass on the relevant documentation for final decisions. Thus the pressures to contain public expenditure, rather than the search for better decision-making, has been the real driving force behind this approach to scheme evaluation.

CONCLUSIONS

This chapter has posed significant questions concerning the ability of urban communities to manage environmental risks and flooding in particular. The emerging conclusion is that much American theory in this field is ultimately inapplicable to Britain. We cannot rely upon individuals to help themselves, as is implicitly advocated by the hazard-response paradigm's concern with risk education. Instead we must intervene as a community to forestall future flood damage particularly since flood protection cannot be provided for individuals but only for communities. These therefore need to reach a consensus on the desirability of such investment. In Britain the type of education therefore required would focus less on the nature of flooding problems and more on the institutional mechanisms for urban flood alleviation which in turn might lead to some necessary administrative and planning improvements.

Analysis of the full range of flood hazard research in Britain shows that strong links have developed between research and application. These links have been strongest in the flood damage assessment field where government pressure and research funding has encouraged most effort. This pressure results from the need for water authorities to use consistent and defensible data—but which is not necessarily 'correct'—on which to base the planning of their flood alleviation schemes.

However, much British flood hazard research has concentrated on classic overbank flooding in riverside towns such as Gloucester, Shrewsbury, Lincoln, Carlisle and Nottingham. Little research has tackled either coastal floods or flooding in major urban areas, both of which we now see as having a significantly different flooding character. Coastal flooding is occurring as relative sea and land levels change or existing defences prove inadequate, and is characterized by extensive storm damage and significant threats to public safety. In major urban areas catchment urbanization and storm sewer dereliction are the principal causes of flood risks. These factors once again emphasize the relationship between land-use control and flood hazards, and between such hazards and the basic standards of urban infrastructure.

Nevertheless, the focus of hazard research in small and medium-sized urban communities has tended to ignore the even greater mobility of metropolitan residents and their likely greater ignorance of flooding problems and strategies for risk reduction. In addition to these facets of this policy field a focus on major urban areas would concentrate more on the role of local authorities rather than water authorities and emphasize further the dynamic nature of urban flood risks. Such an analysis would undoubtedly demonstrate that the quality of urban living depends upon many factors amongst which flood alleviation, drainage, and hazard protection are largely forgotten necessities for community welfare.

REFERENCES

Abrahams, M. J., Price, J., Whitlock, F. A., and Williams, G. (1976). The Brisbane floods, January 1974: their impact on health. *Medical Journal of Australia*, **2**, 936–939.

Bennett, G. (1970). Bristol floods 1968: controlled survey of effects on health of local community disaster. *British Medical Journal*, **3**, 454–458.

Bowler, E. (1981). *Coastal Erosion and Sea Defence Work in the Whitstable Area*. A report to Canterbury City Council, Canterbury.

Burton, I. (1961). Some aspects of flood loss reduction in England and Wales. In White, G. F. (Ed.), *Papers on Flood Problems*, Research Paper No. 70, pp. 203–221. Department of Geography, University of Chicago, Chicago.

Burton, I., Kates, R. W., and White, G. F. (1968). *The Human Ecology of Extreme Geophysical Events*, Natural Hazard Research Working Paper No. 1. Department of Geography, University of Toronto, Toronto.

Burton, I., Kates, R. W., and White, G. F. (1978). *The Environment of Hazard*, Oxford University Press, New York.

Chadwick, G. (1971). *A Systems View of Planning*, Pergamon, Oxford.

Chatterton, J. B. and Penning-Rowsell, E. C. (1978). The benefits of urban storm drainage: computer modelling and standardised assessment techniques, *Proceedings of the International Conference on Urban Storm Drainage*, Southampton, pp. 648–665.

Chatterton, J. B. and Penning-Rowsell, E. C. (1982). Computer modelling of flood alleviation benefits. *Journal of the Water Resources Planning and Management Division, American Society of Civil Engineers* (in press).

Chatterton, J. B., Pirt, J., and Wood, T. R. (1979). The benefits of flood forecasting. *Journal of the Institution of Water Engineers and Scientists*, **33(3)**, 237–252.

Chicken, J. C. (1975). *Hazard Control Policy in Britain*, Pergamon Press, Oxford.

Cole, G. (1976). Land drainage in England and Wales. *Journal of the Institution of Water Engineers and Scientists*, **30**, 7, 345–367.

Cole, G. and Penning-Rowsell, E. C. (1980). The place of economic evaluation in determining the scale of flood alleviation works, In *Flood Studies Report—5 Years On*, Institution of Civil Engineers, London.

Day, H. J., Chatterton, J. B., Wood, T. R., Penning-Rowsell, E. C., and Ford, D. (1981). *Comparative Aspects of Floodplain Data Management—Australia, United Kingdom and United States*, Paper presented at American Society of Civil Engineers' Conference, San Francisco, Cal.

Dror, Y. (1964). Muddling through—science or inertia? *Public Administration Review*, **24(3)**.

Detwyler, T. R. (1972). *Urbanisation and the Environment*, Duxbury Press, Belmont, Cal.

Etzioni, A. (1967). Mixed scanning: A 'third' approach to decision making. *Public Administration Review*, **27(5)**, 385–392.

Faludi, A. (1973). *A Reader in Planning Theory*, Pergamon, Oxford.

Gately, J. E. (1973). *The Idea of a Flood*, Middlesex Polytechnic Flood Hazard Research Project, Special Publication No. 1. Middlesex Polytechnic, London.

Hall, C. (1978). Amberley wild brooks. *Vole*, **7**, 14–15.

Handmer, J. W. and Milne, J. (1980). *Flood Maps as Public Information*, Department of Geography, Australian National University, Canberra.

Harding, D. H. (1972). *Floods and Droughts in Wales*, unpublished PhD thesis, University of Wales, Aberystwyth.

Harding, D. M. and Parker, D. J. (1974). Flood hazard at Shrewsbury, UK. In G. F. White (Ed.) *Natural Hazards, Local, National and Global*, Oxford University Press, New York.

Harding, D. M. and Parker, D. J. (1976). Flood hazard reduction: a case study. *Water Services*, **January**, 24–28.

Hewitt, K. and Burton, I. (1971). *The Hazardousness of a Place: A Regional Ecology of Damaging Events*, Research Paper No. 6, Department of Geography, University of Toronto, Toronto.

Hollis, G. E. (1976). River management and urban flooding. In A. Warren and F. B. Goldsmith (Eds.) *Conservation in Practice*, Wiley London.

Hollis, G. E. (Ed.) (1979). *Man's Impact of the Hydrological Cycle in the UK*, Geobooks, Norwich.

Hollis, G. E. (1980). Land drainage and nature conservation: is there a way ahead? *Ecos*, **3(1)**, 3–11.

Horner, R. W. (1978). Thames tidal flood works in the London excluded area. *Journal of the Institute of Public Health Engineers*, **6(1)**, 16–24.

Horner, R. W. (1979). The Thames Barrier Project. *Geographical Journal*, **145(2)**, 242–53.

Howe, C. W. (1977). *The Design and Evolution of Institutional Arrangements for Water Planning and Management*, UN Water Conference, 14–25 March, Mar Del Plata.

James, L. D. (1974). *The Use of Questionnaires in Collecting Information for Urban Flood Control Planning*, Georgia Institute of Technology, Atlanta, Ga.

Kates, R. W. (1962). *Hazard and Choice Perception in Flood Management*, Research Paper No. 78, Department of Geography, University of Chicago, Chicago.

Kates, R. W. (1965). *Industrial Flood Loses: Damage Estimates in the Lehigh Valley*, Research Paper No. 98, Department of Geography, University of Chicago, Chicago.

Kates, R. W. (1971). Natural hazard in human ecological perspective: hypotheses and models. *Economic Geography*, **47**, 438–451.

Kates, R. W. (1978). *Risk Assessment of Environment Hazard*, J. Wiley, New York.

Lindblom, C. E. (1959). The science of 'muddling through'. *Public Administration Review*, **19**, 79–88.

Local Government Operational Research Unit (1973). *The Economics of Flood Alleviation*, Report No. C155, Reading, England.

McLoughlin, J. B. (1969). *Urban and Regional Planning: A Systems View*, Faber, London.

Metropolitan Police (undated). *Thames Tidal Flooding Contingency Plans*, London.

Mitchell, B. (1971). *Water in England and Wales: Supply, Transfer and Management*, Research Paper No. 9, Department of Geography, University of Liverpool Press, Liverpool.

Mitchell, B. (1979). *Geography and Resource Analysis*, Longman, London.

Munro, R. G., Carpenter, R. J., Handmer, J. W., Smith, D. I., and Martin, W. C. (1980). *The Social Attitudes of Lismore Residents to the Flood Problem*, Centre for Resource and Environmental Studies, Australian National University, Canberra.

National Water Council (1978). *Water Industry Review 1978*, London.

Natural Hazards Research (1970). *Suggestions for Comparative Field Observations on Natural Hazards*, Working Paper No. 16, Department of Geography, University of Toronto, Toronto.

New South Wales Water Resources Commission (undated). *The Flood Inundation Mapping Programme.* New South Wales Water Resources Commission, Sydney, Australia.

North West Water Authority (1978). *Underground Dereliction in the North West,* Warrington.

O'Keefe, P., Westgate, K., and Wisner, B. (1976). Taking the naturalness out of natural disaster. *Nature,* **260,** 566–567.

O'Riordan, T. (1976). *Environmentalism,* Pion, London.

Parker, D. J. (1976). *Socio-economic Aspects of Flood Plain Occupance,* unpublished PhD thesis, University of Wales, Swansea.

Parker, D. J. (1981). The value of hazard zone mapping: Water Authority 'Section 24(5) Surveys' in England and Wales. *Disasters,* **5,** 120–124.

Parker, D. J., and Harding, D. M. (1978). Planning for urban floods. *Disasters,* **1,** 47–57.

Parker, D. J. and Harding, D. M. (1979). Natural hazard evaluation, perception and adjustment. *Geography,* **64(4),** 307–316.

Parker, D. J. and Penning-Rowsell, E. C. (1972). *Problems: Methods of Flood Damage Assessment,* Middlesex Polytechnic Flood Hazard Research Project, Progress Report No. 3, Middlesex Polytechnic, London.

Parker, D. J. and Penning-Rowsell, E. C. (1980). *Water Planning in Britain,* George Allen and Unwin, London.

Parker, D. J. and Penning-Rowsell, E. C. (1981a). Specialist hazard mapping: the Water Authorities' land drainage surveys. *Area,* **13, 2,** 97–103.

Parker, D. J. and Penning-Rowsell, E. C. (1981b). *Whitstable Central Area Coast Protection Scheme: Benefit Assessment,* Middlesex Polytechnic Flood Hazard Research Centre, Middlesex Polytechnic, London.

Parker, D. J. and Penning-Rowsell, E. C. (1983). Flood hazard research in Britain. *Progress in Human Geography,* (in press).

Penning-Rowsell, E. C. (1972). *Flood Hazard Research Project,* Progress Report No. 1, Middlesex Polytechnic, London.

Penning-Rowsell, E. C. (1976). The effect of flood damage on land use planning. *Geographica Polonica,* **34,** 139–153.

Penning-Rowsell, E. C. (1978). *The Effect of Salt Contamination on Flood Damage to Residential Properties,* Middlesex Polytechnic Flood Hazard Research Project, Middlesex Polytechnic, London.

Penning-Rowsell, E. C. (1980). Land drainage policy and practice: who speaks for the environment? *Ecos,* **1, 3,** 16–21.

Penning-Rowsell, E. C. (1981a). The simplifications of our radically over-designed urban storm sewer and drainage systems. In *Proceedings of the International Conference: Water Industry 1981,* pp. 149–154, Brighton.

Penning-Rowsell, E. C. (1981b). Non-structural approaches to flood control: flood plain use regulation and flood warning schemes in England and Wales, In *Proceedings of the International Commission on Irrigation and Drainage* (11th Congress), Grenoble, pp. 193–211.

Penning-Rowsell, E. C. and Chatterton, J. B. (1976). Constraints on environmental planning: the example of flood alleviation. *Area,* **8(2),** 133–137.

Penning-Rowsell, E. C. and Chatterton, J. B. (1977). *The Benefits of Flood Alleviation,* Saxon House, Farnborough, Hants.

Penning-Rowsell, E. C. and Chatterton, J. B. (1978). The benefits of urban storm drainage: computer modelling and standardised assessment techniques. In *Proceedings of the International conference on Storm Damage,* pp. 648–665, Southampton.

Penning-Rowsell, E. C. and Chatterton, J. B. (1980). Assessing the benefits of flood alleviation and land drainage schemes. *Proceedings of the Institution of Civil Engineers*, **2, 69**, 295–315.

Penning-Rowsell, E. C. Chatterton, J. B., and Parker, D. J. (1978). *The Effect of Flood Warning on Flood Damage reduction*, Report for Central Water Planning Unit, HMSO, London.

Penning-Rowsell, E. C., and Parker, D. J. (1974a). *The Control of Flood Plain Development: A Preliminary Analysis*, Flood Hazard Research Project No. 4, Middlesex Polytechnic, London.

Penning-Rowsell, E. C. and Parker, D. J. (1974b). Improving flood plain development control. *Journal of the Royal Town Planning Institute*, **60**, 2, 540–544.

Penning-Rowsell, E. C. and Parker, D. J. (1980). *Chesil Sea Defence Scheme: Benefit Assessment*, Middlesex Polytechnic, Flood Hazard Research Centre, Middlesex Polytechnic, London.

Perry, A. (1981). *Environmental Hazards in the British Isles*, George Allen and Unwin, London.

Porter, E. A. (1971a). *The Assessment of Flood Risk for Land-use Planning and Property Insurance*, unpublished PhD thesis, University of Cambridge, Cambridge.

Porter, E. A. (1971b). Assessing flood damage. *British Science News (Spectrum)*, **84**, 2–5.

Porter, E. A. (1979). *Water Management in England and Wales*, Cambridge University Press, Cambridge.

Richardson, J. J., Jordan, A. G., and Kimber, R. H. (1978). Lobbying, administrative reform and policy styles: the case of land drainage, *Political Studies*, **26**, 1, 47–64.

Rooney, J. (1969). The economic and social implications of snow and ice. In R. J. Chorley, (Ed.), *Water, Earth and Man*, pp. 389–401, Methuen, London.

Severn Trent Water Authority (1977). *A Unified Approach to Land Drainage*, Birmingham.

Severn Trent Water Authority (1980). *Land Drainage Survey, Section 24/5, Water Act 1973*, 8 volumes and atlases, Birmingham.

Sewell, W. R. D. (1978). Water resource planning and its future context. *Water Supply and Management*, **1**, 387–397.

Simon, H. A. (1959). Theories of decision-making in economics and behavioural science. *American Economic Review*, **49**, 253–283.

Slovic, P., Kunreuther, H., and White, G. F. (1974). Decision processes, rationality, and adjustment to natural hazards. In G. F. white (Ed.), *Natural Hazards, Local, National, Global*, pp. 187–205, Oxford University Press, New York.

Smith, D. I., Handmer, J. W., and Martin, W. C. (1980). *The Effects of Floods on Health: Admissions for Lismore*, Centre for Resource and Environmental Studies, Australian National University, Canberra.

Smith, K. and Tobin, G. A. (1979). *Human Adjustment to the Flood Hazard*, Longman, London.

South West Water Authority (1980). *Land Drainage Survey, Section 24/5, Water Act 1973*, 1 volume and atlas, Exeter.

Tobin, G. A. (1977). *Some Aspects of the Flood Hazard Assessment and Response with Particular Reference to Cumbria*, unpublished PhD thesis, University of Strathclyde, Glasgow.

Torry, W. I. (1979). Anthropological studies in hazardous environments: past trends and new horizons. *Current Anthropology*, **20(3)**, 517–540.

Ward, R. C. (1978). *Floods: a Geographical Perspective*, Macmillan, London.

Welsh Water Authority (1979). *Water Act 1973, Section 24/5 Land Drainage Survey*, 1 volume, Brecon.

White, G. F. (1945). *Human Adjustment to Floods*, Research Paper No. 29, Department of Geography, University of Chicago, Chicago.

White, G. F. (1964). *Choice of Adjustment to Floods*, Research Paper No. 93, Department of Geography, University of Chicago, Chicago.

White, G. F. (1973). Natural hazard research. In R. J. Chorley (Ed.), *Directions in Geography*, pp. 193–216, Methuen, London.

White, G. F. (1974). *Natural Hazards, Local, National, Global*, Oxford University Press, New York.

White, G. F. (1975). *Flood Hazard in the United States: A Research Assessment*, Institute of Behavioral Science, University of Colorado, Colorado.

White, G. F. (1980). *Overview of the Flood Insurance Program*, Statement to the Senate Committee on Banking, Housing and Urban Affairs, Institute of Behavioral Science, University of Colorado, Colorado.

White, G. F., Calef, W. C., Hudson, J. W., Mayer, H. M., Sheaffer, J. R., and Volk, D. J. (1958). *Changes in Urban Occupance of Flood Plains in the United States*, Research Paper No. 57, Department of Geography, University of Chicago, Chicago.

White, G. F. and Haas, E. J. (1975). *Assessment of Research on Natural Hazards*, MIT Press, Cambridge, Mass.

Wilkins, J. L. (1980). Land drainage legislation and the engineer—a review and discussion paper—Parts I and II. *Chartered Municipal Engineer*, **107**, 123–29, 147–154.

Wisdom, A. S. (1975). *The Law of Rivers and Watercourses*, 3rd. ed., Shaw and Sons, London.

Geography and the Urban Environment
Progress in Research and Applications, Volume V
Edited by D. T. Herbert and R. J. Johnston
© 1982 John Wiley & Sons Ltd.

Chapter 7

Earthquake Hazards Information: The Experience of Mandated Disclosure

Risa Palm

Public concern over earthquake hazards in the United States over the past 20 years has been further heightened by two major disasters in 1964 and 1971. The major centre of earthquake activity is located in the Pacific region, from Alaska to California, although there have been major earthquakes in New Madrid, Missouri (1811–12), Charleston, South Carolina (1886), Massena, New York (1944), and Wilkes-Barre, Pennsylvania (1944). The combined losses from five major earthquakes in California and Alaska in this century totalled 1025 lives and $2 857 500 000 in property damage in 1980 dollars (Table 7.1).

It was estimated that in 1970 approximately 31 million people lived within areas of known distribution of damaging earthquakes corresponding to 8 or above on the Modified Mercalli Intensity Scale of 1931 (US Office of Emergency Preparedness, 1972). Earthquakes of this magnitude have been described as producing general fright, alarm approaching panic, considerable damage to ordinary substantial buildings with some partial collapse, heavy damage to some wooden houses, cracking and breaking of solid stone walls, and twisting and falling of chimneys, columns, monuments, factory stacks and towers (Iacopi, 1971, p. 35). Structural damage and injury may result both from the earthquake directly, and also because of associated disasters such as fires or flooding which may follow the earthquake. Property damage figures thus underestimate the total losses sustained by a population which experiences a major damaging earthquake.

Human responses to major earthquakes provide a further source of increasing costs. During the earthquake, physiological distortions may affect observation of the event: 'It is not uncommon for seismologists to receive long letters describing gaping earth fissures, huge earth waves, and wildly gyrating buildings that seem to touch the ground with each giant swing' (Iacopi, 1971, p. 34). Even more serious are the psychological distortions and fears engendered by an earthquake. Normal body equilibrium may be upset, affecting all of one's senses: 'Small earth waves suddenly loom as large as waves rolling up the beach, and the world seems to turn topsy-turvy before your eyes' (Iacopi, 1971, p. 34). After the earthquake,

TABLE 7.1. Major US earthquakes in this century

Year	Place	Lives lost	Damage ($ million, 1980)
1906	San Francisco	700	168.0
1933	Long Beach, California	115	262.9
1952	Kern County, California	14	152.2
1964	Alaska	131	1181.2
1971	San Fernando, California	65	1093.2
Total		1025	2857.5

Source: Modified from Visvader and Burton (1974), p. 223.

the temporary mental confusion may turn into a fear which may remain with people long after the event is over. This fear is not so much related to the actual damage associated with the earthquake, as the fear of the unknown force of a shaking earth: 'To watch buildings crack and fall, or trees shake, without being able to see the cause behind the effect is a terrifying sensation' (Iacopi, 1971, p. 34).

In California, relatively severe earthquakes are not an infrequent occurrence. The 1971 San Fernando earthquake had a magnitude of 6.6 on the Richter scale, and resulted in over a million dollars worth of damage (in 1980 dollars). This earthquake was particularly damaging because its epicentre was located in a densely populated urban area. The San Francisco earthquake of 1906 was less costly in terms of lives lost and property damaged, although its force at a magnitude of 8.3 on the Richter scale was 80 times greater than that in San Fernando. Should an earthquake of such magnitude recur, losses to life and property would be unimaginable:

> Between 1970 and 2000 we may expect a major earthquake in the San Francisco Bay area of magnitude around 8 Richter and duration of more than a minute. The expected damage to assets would run to 25 billions of dollars at 1970 prices [more than double that figure in 1980 dollars], and loss in life may be in the hundreds or thousands depending on the time of day the quake strikes and the adjustments that are made prior to the disaster and afterwards (Mukerjee, 1971, p. 10).

CALIFORNIA LEGISLATION RELATED TO EARTHQUAKE HAZARDS

The research reported in this chapter is based on legislation adopted by the State of California in the 1970s to attempt to reduce earthquake risks. Before reviewing this law, it is useful to summarize the ways in which the state has been involved in seismic safety regulations.[1]

The first evidence of official state involvement in earthquake hazards was the reprinting of the eighth annual report of the state mineralogist (now called the state geologist) in 1888 on the Owen Valley earthquake of 1872 which damaged the Capitol building in Sacramento. Next, in 1906 following the San Francisco earthquake, the governor appointed a state earthquake investigation commission which published a two-volume report and atlas on the earthquake. In 1933, following the Long Beach earthquake, the state legislature passed the Field Act which required, among other things, that the State Office of Architecture and Construction set up rules and regulations concerning earthquake safety in the design and construction of school buildings. Other building code provisions were passed and strengthened on a state basis (such as the Riley Act and the Uniform Building Code), and also by counties and municipalities. A Joint Committee on Seismic Safety was established in 1969 comprising four Senate members and four Assembly members. This committee, advised by five advisory groups, put together information on structural engineering, geological and seismological factors, dams and soils, city lifelines, land-use planning, disaster preparedness, and government organization and performance. The Joint Committee influenced several earthquake-related measures introduced since its inception and the occurrence of the damaging San Fernando earthquake of 1971. Of those enacted are the following:

1971

Senate Bill 351—Seismic Safety Element: that all general plans consider the following: (a) a land-use element, (b) a circulation element, (c) a housing element, (d) a conservation element, (e) an open-space element, and (f) a seismic safety element consisting of the identification and appraisal of seismic hazards.

Senate Bill 479—Public School Siting: requires a geological investigation of prospective sites for new schools and for additions to existing schools.

1972

Senate Bill 519—Seismic Structural Safety of Hospitals: requires that the State Department of Public Health develop hospital construction standards and regulations to assure adequate resistance to earthquake damage.

Senate Bill 520—Alquist–Priolo Geological Hazard Zones Act: State Mining and Geology Board to prepare policies and criteria for the development of areas encompassing major active fault traces, which are to be mapped by the state geologist.

Senate Bill 896—Dam Safety: requires that owners of dams designated by the Office of Emergency Services prepare inundation maps.

Finally, the committee recommended the establishment of a permanent state seismic safety commission which would 'develop seismic safety goals and programs, help evaluate and integrate the work of state and local agencies concerned with earthquake safety, and see that the programs are carried out effectively and the objectives accomplished' (Joint Committee on Seismic Safety, 1974, p. 11). This body was established in 1975.

MITIGATION OF EARTHQUAKE LOSSES THROUGH THE PROVISION OF INFORMATION

Of the several legislative acts adopted in California, one focused on providing information about the location of fault rupture zones to residents. This is the Alquist–Priolo Special Studies Zone Act. The original legislation was passed in March 1972 and required the state geologist to delineate by the end of 1973 'appropriate wide special studies zones to encompass all potentially and recently active traces of the San Andreas, Calaveras, Hayward, and San Jacinto Faults', as well as other faults which were a 'potential hazard to structures from surface faulting or fault creep'. The zones were to be one-quarter mile (140 m.) in width, or less around the fault trace. In the original legislation, city or county approval would be required for all new real estate development of structures for human occupancy, and 'cities and counties shall not approve the location of such a development or structure within a delineated special studies zone if an undue hazard would be created' (Section 2623, California Public Resources Code). In 1975, several amendments to the act were passed, including one mandating disclosure of the location of the special studies zone to persons considering the purchase of property (developed or undeveloped) within the zone. This amendment stated that 'a person who is acting as an agent for a seller of real property which is located within a delineated special studies zone, or the seller if he is acting without an agent, shall disclose to any prospective purchaser the fact that the property is located within a delineated special studies zone' (Section 2621.9, California Public Resources Code).

The history of this amendment provides certain insights into what its proponents wished to achieve and the compromises they were forced to make. Although there is no full transcript of the public debate in either the State Senate or Assembly, nor of testimony provided in committee hearings, the legislative history of the amendment can be constructed from the voting records in committees as well as from the notes and recollections of some of the principals.

Given the well-recognized strength of the real estate lobby in California, one might have expected that the amendment would have generated controversy in the legislature and a public debate. Instead, the act passed virtually unopposed after only a few phrases were modified in the California Assembly. Part of the reason for the acquiescence of the California Association of Realtors to the amendment was the legislative package of which the disclosure provision was a small part. Along with disclosure, this package contained several changes in the original act favourable to real estate developers and real estate agents, including a change of the name of the zones from 'geological hazard zones' to 'special studies zones', the exemption of new single-family wood-frame dwelllings not part of large developments from geological reports, the exemption of mobile homes and condominium conversions from reports, and the exemption of alterations or additions to existing structures when these alterations were less than 50 per cent of the value of the structure.

Opponents of the amendment such as the California Association of Realtors would have preferred that if disclosure were to be written into the law at all, it would be the responsibility of the seller rather than the agent. However, they compromised on the disclosure language, given the rest of the package (Gillies, 1980). Proponents of the disclosure provison also viewed the final set of amendments as a compromise, in which they had traded the exemption of single-family dwellings for the disclosure provision (Hurst, 1980).

The act itself contained no specific clauses referring to enforcement, although the disclosure amendment is interpreted as referring to a set of 'material facts concerning the transaction that might affect the principal's decision' (*Smith* v. *Zak* (1971) 98 Cal. Rptr. 242, 20 CA 3d 785). As such, enforcement of the disclosure of the special studies zone is within the purview of the California Department of Real Estate which is empowered to revoke real estate licences where evidence of misrepresentation is presented (Section 10176(a), Business and Professions Code, Real Estate Law). In addition, failure to make a disclosure could make the real estate broker liable to a civil suit by the buyer-plaintiff.

After some initial confusion over the question of how real estate agents were to determine if a given parcel was within a special studies zone and how disclosure was to be carried out, a fairly standard procedure was established. This standardization was assisted by the 1977 publication of a manual on special studies zone disclosure and the development of a contract addendum to the deposit receipt which was made available to members of the California Association of Realtors (California Association of Realtors, 1977). Several Boards of Realtors produced coloured maps outlining the location of the special studies zones which they used in their offices or gave to clients.

The state office charged with ensuring the enforcement of the disclosure legislation, the California Department of Real Estate, seemed satisfied that disclosure was taking place (Liberator, 1979). In addition, it was assumed that the legislation was filling a gap in consumer protection by conveying 'complex hydrologic, seismic, and other geologic information . . . to real estate buyers before the sale' (Kockelman, 1980, p. 71). However, there had been little direct measurement of the effects of disclosure on the home-buying public.

THE RELATIONSHIP BETWEEN INFORMATION PROVISION AND BEHAVIOUR CHANGE

Before discussing the results of the empirical study, it is useful to review previous research on the expected impact of new information on behaviour, for mandated provision of information is based on several assumptions of how individuals and small groups use information about their environment in decision-making. These assumptions are derived primarily from work in economics and social psychology/communications on two questions: the response of individuals to uncertainty, and the relationships between the provision of information and changes in attitudes and behaviour. In this section the largely non-intersecting work from these fields is reviewed to provide a set of expectations concerning the response of individuals to special studies zones disclosure by real estate agents.

CHOICES UNDER CONDITIONS OF UNCERTAINTY

Some early research in economics proceeded under the asumption that households attempt to optimize in decision-making. Two conditions are required for optimization: the existence of a set of criteria for decision-making which permits all alternatives to be compared, and behaviour involving the selection of the alternative which is preferred by these criteria to all other alternatives (March and Simon, 1958). Modifications of these conditions allow for the use of 'satisfactory' standards, easing the assumption of the omniscient 'economic man'. In these models, a set of criteria exists that describes the minimum satisfactory condition, and a selection is made if it 'meets or exceeds all of these criteria'. Since it may be assumed *post hoc* that the purchase of a particular residence involved the decision that this alternative met at least the set of 'satisfactory' standards set up by the household, it follows that if a household chooses to locate close to an active earthquake fault (1) they were not aware of this location despite disclosure, or (2) they were aware of the location but for some reason it did not affect their decisions with respect to their set of 'satisfactory criteria'. The second condition would imply that either proximity to an active fault was not one of the criteria used in their home purchase decision or that it was important, but that other factors militated the decision despite the unsatisfactory nature of the decision with respect to this one criterion. It is therefore important to assess the conditions considered in their home purchase decision, whether proximity to an earthquake fault was or would be considered, and if the decision performed satisfactorily on this criterion. One would hypothesize that: if proximity to an earthquake fault is considered of little importance or not considered at all in the home purchase decision, special studies zones disclosure will have little impact on the purchase decision or on subsequent mitigation measures. This hypothesis can be tested by direct questions to home buyers within and beyond the special studies zones to seek differences in attitudes to locations proximate to fault traces, and the impacts of disclosure on their purchase decisions.

The most straightforward application of optimization models is to cases where information, albeit incomplete and possibly poorly used, involves little risk. However, decisions become more complex when under conditions of un- certainty. In general, the response to uncertainty has been described within the framework of expected utility theory, originally advanced by Bernoulli (1738). Under conditions of uncertainty, the decision to take or avoid risk is analysed in the form of a set of utility functions derived from a combination of the sets of possible outcomes and the probabilities that various outcomes will occur.

It is assumed that most behaviour is risk-averse: that is, people would prefer a known but smaller payoff than risk a large loss for a smaller probability of a large payoff. For example, the individual will prefer to accept $50 than to take a chance of winning $100 or $0 in a 50–50 gamble. Such risk-averse behaviour produces a utility function with a concave form (Figure 7.1), and is the basis for expectations concerning the purchase of insurance, in which the individual *will* lose a given amount in a fixed insurance premium against the notion that one *could* lose a much larger amount if one were not insured. In the application of expected utility functions to the case of the decision to purchase a house in an area subject to destruction or damage from infrequent events such as earthquakes, it would be expected that the buyer would behave in a risk-averse fashion; the buyer, upon learning that an area is subject to threat from surface fault rupture, should respond by attempting to avoid the risk or lessen its impact through the purchase of insurance (or a form of self-insurance in which a lower sales price is 'traded' for a willingness to assume the risk of major structural damage).

Several discussions of insurance purchase have described purchase decisions in terms of expected utility (Friedman and Savage, 1948; Mosteller and Nogee, 1951), or a modified form of subjective expected utility (Edwards, 1955). Despite these studies, there is mounting evidence that decision-making is not perfectly accounted for by such models (Lichtenstein and Slovic, 1971; Lindman, 1971;

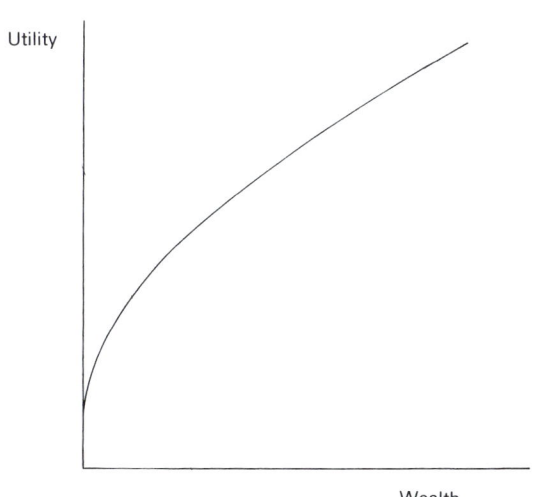

FIGURE 7.1.   Risk-taking behaviour

Slovic, 1975; Grether and Plott, 1979; Tversky, 1972). Experimental findings run counter to the model, such as: (1) that many people do not have correct information about many of the factors relevant to the expected utility model, such as information concerning fixed losses (premiums) and payoffs (deductible levels, levels of subsidization) (Kunreuther *et al.*, 1978a); (2) that even with correct information many insurance decisions are inconsistent with those which would be predicted from theory (Kunreuther *et al.*, 1978b; Slovic *et al.*, 1977); and (3) that there exists a general unwillingness to insure against low-probability, high-loss events (such as earthquakes) (Slovic *et al.*, 1977).

Several notions have been postulated to account for these findings. The first is the interference of the 'gambler's fallacy'. This notion postulates that if a low-probability hazard has recently occurred, it is unlikely to occur again soon and therefore can be treated as a zero-probability event (Slovic, Kunreuther, and White, 1974). The 'gambler's fallacy' seems to affect those individuals who have had personal experience with a severe loss with a low probability; rather than increasing the occurrence of insurance purchase, it has been found that insurance purchase is decreased under the assumption that there will be no recurrence of the event over the short run. In the case of flooding, once the '100-year flood' has occurred, households appear to feel they can occupy the floodplain with impunity for the next 99 years; in the case of a damaging earthquake, however, it is not clear what popular conceptions of recurrence are likely to be.

A second explanation for the empirical observation of a seemingly convex utility function, implying that marginal utility decreases with an increase in losses (Kahneman and Tversky, 1979), is the existence of a probability threshold. In this explanation, it is expected that people will take risks (for instance, refuse to buy insurance) if the probability is extremely low, despite the possibility of very high losses. Probabilities below some minimum threshold are treated as if they were zero (Slovic *et al.*, 1977). It should be noted that special studies zones do not have any given probability of damage associated with them, but even where these have been estimated and made public, it is possible that the probabilities might fall below the threshold at which risk is attended to. If this is the case, then disclosure would still be expected to have little effect on buyer behaviour since the probability of individual loss would be low.

Finally, some have hypothesized that it is the context of the decision which affects behaviour under conditions of risk. In the case of insurance sales, it has been noted that commission structure can have a great effect on the purchase of insurance rather than the objective determination of utilities on the part of consumers (Kunreuther *et al.*, 1978a; Pashigian, Schkade, and Menefee, 1966). Similarly, since major decisions such as the purchase of insurance or a home are made in the context of a larger set of decisions not analysed by the researcher, it is possible that individual decisions may not fit the utility maximization model, but that the conjunction of all related decisions would fit this model. This suggests the difficulty of analysing the home purchase decision, and particularly that aspect of it dealing with environmental uncertainties, apart from the rest of the constraints and utilities of the household (Pashigian, Schkade, and Menefee, 1966). Related to this issue is the empirical demonstration that the utility function and its functional form is affected by the context of the decision, and that this is particularly true where probabilities and outcomes are not known with certainty (Hershey and Schoemaker, 1980; Schoemaker and Kunreuther, 1979). The pervasiveness of the effects of context on risk-taking behaviour imply that utility functions can only be constructed within a particular decision context, and possibly the attempt to derive a general utility function for decisions under risky conditions should be abandoned. In any case, such findings weaken the applicability of a general expected utility model to expectations concerning the response of home-buyers to disclosure of earthquake hazards information.

THE IMPACTS OF INFORMATION ON ATTITUDES AND BEHAVIOUR

An entirely separate perspective on information provision and behaviour change has been developed within the fields of social psychology and communication. In these research efforts, one framework has been frequently used as at least a starting-point for hypothesis testing. This model was developed as part of a research project on communication and persuasion within the Yale Communication Research Program (Hovland, Janis, and Kelley, 1953; Hovland and Janis, 1959; Sherif and Hovland, 1961). In the general model, independent variables included *source factors* (such as the expertise of the source, its trustworthiness, its likeability, its status, and its personal characteristics such as race and religion), *message factors* (the order in which arguments were presented, the effects of presenting one-sided versus two-sided arguments, the type of appeal [emotional, logical, informational versus insight, fear], and whether the message included an explicit or an implicit conclusion), and *audience factors* (its persuasibility, its initial position with respect to the message, its level of intelligence, its level of self-esteem, and other personality characteristics). To assess the combined effects of source, message, and audience factors, responses (attitude change) were measured including changes of opinion, changes of perception, and changes in intentions or behaviour. The effect of any message would be mediated by the extent to which it was attended to, comprehended, and accepted (Figure 7.2).

Some of the specific findings as applied to manipulative communication or persuasion can be summarized as a set of expectations concerning the likelihood that information will result in opinion or attitude change (McGuire, 1969; Zimbardo and Ebbesen, 1970). With respect to the source factors (in our study, the real estate agent), it is likely that there will be more impact if: (1) the real estate agent has high credibility, a function of his expertise (the ability to provide

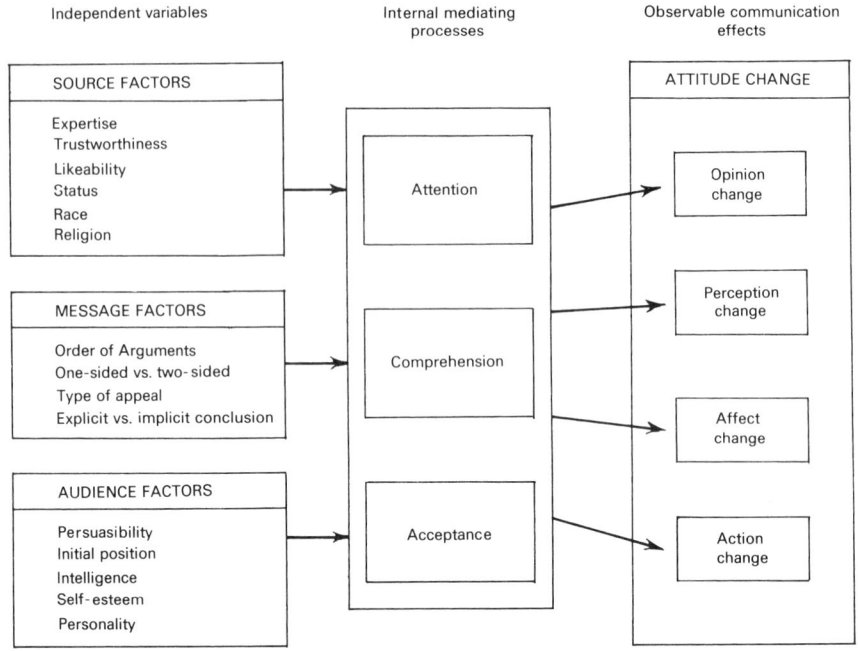

FIGURE 7.2.   Study of communication and persuasion. (*Source*: Fishbein and Ajzen, 1975, p. 45)

knowledge on a given subject) and his trustworthiness (based on his motivation to present information without bias); (2) if the information and opinions he expresses are also shared by the audience (the home buyers); and (3) the source demands some extreme opinion change (the greater the discrepancy between the communicator's and the recipient's initial positions, the greater the attitude change). Findings concerning message factors have been codified as a series of statements on 'how to present the issues' if attitude change is desired. Attitude change is greatest when: (1) if the audience is friendly, and the communicator's message is the only one to be presented, he presents only one side of the argument; (2) when the audience is initially unfriendly, and will hear the other side from someone else, he presents both sides of the issue; (3) two messages are presented, the last one has greater impact; (4) conclusions are explicitly stated rather than letting the audience draw their own conclusions; (5) when intense fear arousal is present, recommendations for action are made explicit and are possible. Audience factors also affect the success of a persuasive message. Specifically, the effectiveness of messages is: (1) variable depending on the level of intelligence of an audience; (2) increased when the individual's self-esteem is low (individuals are more susceptible to persuasion and more easily influenced when they are of low rather than high self-esteem); and (3) increased when the message is presented actively, for example in a role-playing situation. In addition, group memberships affect the likelihood of the effectiveness of communication, since they may reinforce or counteract the new information.

Two major modifications of this research model have been proffered. McGuire (1968; 1969) has developed a two-factor model involving both the reception of the information and the 'yielding' to what is understood. Because the audience must both understand and yield to the message, no linear predictions can be made about personality characteristics such as intelligence on the probability that information will be converted into attitude (and behaviour) change; in this example, because highly intelligent people may more easily comprehend the message, but are more unwilling to yield to it, there may be no straight-line correlation between intelligence and response to a given message. In addition, McGuire suggested that persuasion involves five steps: attention, comprehension, yielding, retention, and action. Each of the later steps depends on the successful occurrence of the previous steps, and it is important to note that several of the steps cannot be measured directly.

Fishbein and Ajzen (1975) have made major modifications in the model of persuasive communication in emphasizing (1) the beliefs and feelings about engaging in particular behaviours rather than their beliefs about particular objects (for example, it is less important to stress the home-buyer's attitudes to earthquakes than it is to investigate their attitudes towards particular behaviours such as insurance purchase or cost bargaining in an earthquake prone region), and (2) the specification of other variables which should be measured along with attitude change under study to increase behavioural prediction, the effects of what they term 'external beliefs' on the communication process. Non-attitudinal variables such as personal and social norms may influence behaviour, and therefore must be incorporated into the model.

Despite these modifications, several studies have expressed concern that the logic of incorporating 'other variables' into general models linking attitudes and behaviour may be formidable (Bentler and Speckart, 1979; Schwartz and Tessler, 1972). Weigel (1979, p. 23) has summarized these concerns: "It seems reasonable to ask whether or not the attitude concept has become somewhat sterile in evolving from a concept representing a relatively stable underlying disposition capable of mediating a variety of object-related behaviours to a concept which seems to equate attitudes and actions under specified situational circumstances'. The same author, however, has argued that some studies have shown that attitude measures can be used to predict behaviour *patterns,* even if they fail to predict particular single behaviours (Weigel and Newman, 1976). Finally, Weigel (1979, pp. 33–34) summarizes the likelihood that exposure to new knowledge will influence subsequent behaviour, assuming that the audience has attended to, retained and been persuaded by the new information, is a function of '(1) the degree to which behaviour-relevant information is incorporated into the knowledge synthesis, (2) the degree to which the new knowledge is consistent with other attitudes and perceived as instrumental to the attainment of valued goals, and (3) the degree of institutional support . . . '.

Implications of attitude-behaviour and communication research

The social psychology and communication research on persuasive messages suggests several expectations concerning the response of home-buyers to information about earthquake hazards zones. Responses of home-buyers should vary according to:

(1) the credibility and trustworthiness of the real estate agent;
(2) the correspondence between the information provided by the agent and the previous beliefs and attitudes of the home-buyers;
(3) the method (timing and materials used) by which the message is presented;
(4) the extent to which disclosure (a fear message) is presented with accompanying specific mitigation suggestions;
(5) the extent to which the home-buyer can comprehend the significance of the disclosure;
(6) the impacts of possible external attitudes and beliefs on the response, such as the perceived lack of optional locations, or the belief that there is little an individual can do to prevent death, injury or damage from an 'act of God', if 'one's number is up';
(7) the degree to which the disclosure is consistent with other attitudes and perceived of as significant with respect to the attainment of goals such as safe and secure housing.

Although the notion of 'expected utility' is not explicitly introduced in the work of psychologists and communications researchers, it can be seen that some of these formulations are a more detailed representation of the factors that comprise a given 'utility', and others go further to anticipate the conditions which could interfere with the predictive abilities of a strict utility model.

Combining the two methods of analysis, we should expect the provision of information concerning the special studies zones to result in a change in behaviour because individuals tend to optimize or at least 'satisfice' in residential decision-making, and more information enables them to evaluate better their alternatives, and people tend to be risk-averse, responding to the introduction of information concerning hazards with avoidance or mitigation. The extent to which such information is not converted into a behavioural response will be a function of: (1) the impacts of a multidimensional stimulus (housing purchase) on the utility calculation for a single element (special studies zones location); (2) the possible underestimation of low-probability events; (3) the interference of the so-called gambler's fallacy; (4) the inability to estimate probabilities and therefore compute expected utility because of the lack of clarity of the information presented; (5) characteristics of the source of information interfering with the degree to which it is attended to, comprehended and accepted; (6) characteristics of the message itself—its presentation format and the accompaniment of specific mitigation suggestions; (7) characteristics of the home-buyers—for example, the degree to which they can be persuaded of the importance of the message; (8) the possible irrelevance of the information to the decision at hand; and (9) the possible inappropriateness of behavioural-level modelling—the constraints placed on the individual by the political-economic system may make response impossible in any case.

In order to assess the existence of a behavioural response to the disclosure of special studies zones locations, it is necessary to postulate a range of possible actions which prospective buyers might take. The empirical study could then test to see if any of these responses were present, to assess the impacts of the disclosure on buyer behaviour.

MEASURABLE RESPONSES TO DISCLOSURE

There were two major ways in which home-buyers could respond to the disclosure that the property they were considering purchasing was located in a special studies zone which would indicate an awareness that this message connoted increased risk of financial or personal losses or damage. The first would involve the avoidance of the area—either through a refusal to buy within the special studies zone, or the insistence of a compensation within the selling price which would act as a kind of incentive to assume the increased risk of property damage in exchange for a lower sales price. If home-buyers choose this type of response, the researcher should find evidence of this response in: (1) the testimony of recent home-buyers *within* the special studies zones—such buyers should have responded to disclosure by seeking to negotiate more favourable sales terms; (2) the testimony of recent home-buyers *outside* the special studies zones—here one should find home-buyers who had considered houses within the special studies zones, but were dissuaded by the disclosure; (3) testimony of real estate agents actively selling houses within the special studies zones (either their own listings or those of other agents)—these agents should be able to indicate the approximate numbers of clients who had been dissuaded from purchasing houses within the special studies zones by the disclosure; (4) relative length of time the house was on the market and the relative listing to selling price—houses in the special studies zones should be more difficult to sell and therefore should be on the market for a longer average period of time; in addition, there should be more discrepancy between listing and selling price since there would be more latitude for seller–buyer negotiation (although this effect might be quickly eliminated as real estate agents appraising the likely possible selling price would adjust to known market conditions); (5) house-price trends—*ceteris paribis*, houses within the special studies zones should command lower selling prices than those in comparable neighbourhoods outside the zones.

A second form of response would be the purchase of the special studies zone home, but subsequent mitigation measures to attempt to minimize losses from fault rupture. The decision to take mitigation measures would be comparable to the more general decision to purchase insurance discussed in the review of economics research on response to uncertainty. According to the expected utility model, the home-buyer should be expected to expend a certain portion of income on insurance in exchange for a guarantee of a minimum income level (a maximum possible loss): as Friedman and Savage (1948) have expressed it, if $\bar{I}$ is the actuarial value of alternative A, and I^* is the certain income that has the same utility as A, then the risk-averse consumer may be willing to pay a maximum of $\bar{I} - I^*$ to insure the minimum I^* income level. According to this model, the home-buyer should be willing to expend this amount in a combination of measures which would mitigate against major property losses.

Mitigation measures include everyday actions such as the possession of a working flashlight or battery radio as well as more formal and purposeful actions such as structural reinforcements on the house, the storage of food or water in preparation for a widespread disaster, institutional and family arrangements such as community contingency plans, plans for family reunions after an earthquake, plans for emergency procedures to be taken at the residence, and plans for neighbourhood activities during and following the earthquake, or the purchase of earthquake insurance. Since a major study of the mitigation measures adopted by a random sample of Los Angeles County residents was available, covering the period immediately prior to the current study (Turner *et al.*, 1979), it was possible to compare the responses of special studies zones residents in the Bay Area with a sample of the total population of Los Angeles. It would be expected that a survey sample limited to those residents of the special studies zones who had recently had a disclosure and comprehended the meaning of this information should have *higher rates* of adoptions of mitigation measures than the general Los Angeles population. If mitigation measures are taken by approximately the same or fewer special studies zones residents, then one would have to conclude that this index did not provide evidence of a measurable response to the disclosure.

OBSERVED CONSEQUENCES OF MANDATED DISCLOSURE

To assess empirically the responses home-buyers may have taken to special studies zones disclosure, two California housing submarkets were selected for intensive study. It should be noted that although special studies zones cover only a small portion of the residential property in the state, they are present in virtually every large metropolitan area (Figure 7.3). These zones include a wide range of property and social areas, from relatively low-cost housing in San

PHOTO 7.1

Fernando (near Los Angeles) and Antioch (near San Francisco) to high-cost housing in south Pasadena (near Los Angeles) and Portola Valley (near San Jose). They pass through smaller towns and cities such as Santa Rosa and Hollister, as well as through major densely populated portions of Los Angeles and the Bay Area. They include neighbourhoods populated by whites, Hispanics, and blacks and contain property with good views and high air quality as well as areas of dense development on flat land with poor air quality.

The two areas selected for intensive surveys of residents were the Board of Realtor's regions of Berkeley and central Contra Costa County. These areas were chosen to minimize social and economic variation, while contrasting physical characteristics of site and organization of local real estate practices. The study areas have been previously established as separate housing submarkets (Palm, 1976; 1979), although they are both suburban to San Francisco. The special studies zones within the study areas are generally inhabited by white, upper-middle class households, and housing is predominantly composed of single-family detached dwellings. The areas differ in that they are located on different fault traces; Berkeley is on the Hayward fault and central Contra Costa County contains several fault traces, most important of which is the Calaveras fault. These faults have had different activity and there is more visible damage from fault creep to the retaining walls, houses, and curbs in Berkeley (Photo 7.1).

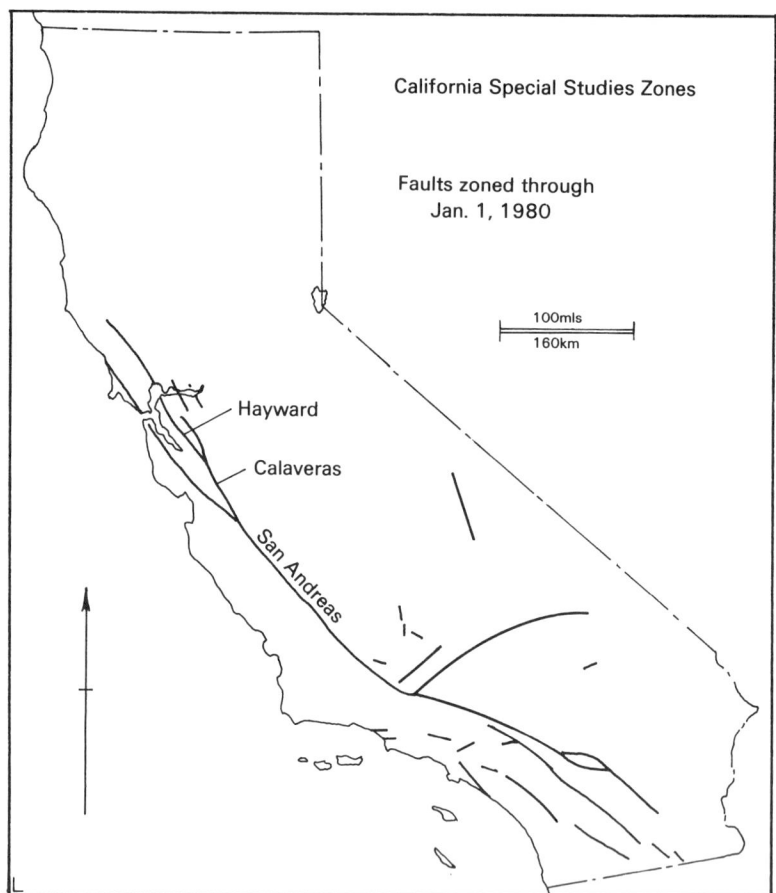

California Special Studies Zones

Faults zoned through
Jan. 1, 1980

100mls
160km

Hayward

Calaveras

San Andreas

FIGURE 7.3.   The California special studies zones

Three groups of people were surveyed. The first was the set of home-buyers within the special studies zones in Berkeley and central Contra Costa County that had purchased homes within the 6 months prior to the interviews, from August 1978 to January 1979. The second study population was those home-buyers that had purchased houses within 4.8 km (3 miles) of the special studies zones. This population was interviewed to examine any differences in attitudes between those who move to the special studies zones despite disclosure, and those who move to virtually identical areas lying outside the zones. It was expected that this second population might include those who had been discouraged from moving within the zones by disclosure. A third study population was the real estate agents responsible for recent disclosures. This population was identified by asking the special studies zones buyers to name the real estate agent who had 'helped them with their home purchase'. The survey of real estate agents excluded persons merely holding real estate licences but not actually selling real estate, or those not familiar with disclosure because no special studies zones are within their sales territory. Response rates for the home-buyer populations were about 85 per cent, and for the identified real estate agents were about 90 per cent.

Survey results

In general, home-buyers either within or near the special studies zones attached little importance to earthquake hazards in their decision to buy a house. Home-

TABLE 7.2. Rating of 15 factors according to their significance in the home purchase decision[1]

Factor		Very important	Somewhat important	Not important	Did not consider
Investment potential or	B[2]	25	9	4	1
resale	CC[3]	131	22	3	1
Price	B	23	15	1	0
	CC	110	50	6	0
Beauty of the area	B	24	13	1	1
	CC	82	57	6	1
Number of bedrooms	B	18	13	6	2
	CC	71	70	25	0
Views	B	15	21	2	1
	CC	53	83	26	1
Distance to work	B	13	17	7	2
	CC	56	62	39	9
Social composition of	B	11	20	5	2
neighbourhood	CC	49	74	31	12
Reputation of crime rate in	B	11	15	5	8
neighbourhood	CC	51	71	30	13
Air quality	B	5	13	9	12
	CC	57	53	29	27
Quality of local public	B	5	10	14	10
schools	CC	59	37	38	32
Closeness to schools	B	7	8	17	7
	CC	49	40	46	31
Closeness to friends or	B	11	12	10	6
relatives	CC	16	45	64	21
Access to public transport-	B	2	10	13	14
ation	CC	13	26	81	46
Distance from an active	B	2	6	20	11
earthquake fault	CC	14	23	63	66
Location out of a	B	0	4	8	27
floodplain	CC	21	35	36	73

[1] Rate each of the following factors according to its importance with respect to your decision to buy your home (presented in order of importance to buyers).
[2] Berkeley
[3] Contra Costa

TABLE 7.3. Rating of 'distance from an active earthquake fault' in purchase decision

	Within zone Berkeley		Adjacent Berkeley		Within zone Contra Costa County		Adjacent Contra Costa County	
	no.	%	no.	%	no.	%	no.	%
Very important	2	5.1	3	8.6	14	8.4	2	4.9
Somewhat important	6	15.4	13	37.1	23	13.9	5	12.2
Not important	20	51.3 ⎫ 79.5		10	28.6 ⎫ 54.3		63	37.9 ⎫ 77.7		10	24.4 ⎫ 82.9
Did not consider	11	28.2 ⎭	9	25.7 ⎭	66	39.8 ⎭	24	58.5 ⎭
	(no significant difference at 0.05)		(no significant difference at 0.05)		(no significant difference at 0.05)		(no significant difference at 0.05)	

buyers within and near the special studies zones were asked to rate 15 factors according to their significance in the home purchase decision. In both Berkeley and Contra Costa County, most home-buyers ranked 'distance from an active earthquake fault' as 'not important' or 'not considered' in the home purchase decision (Table 7.2); indeed, only 22 per cent of these home-buyers ranked this factor as either very important or somewhat important. Similarly, home-buyers who had purchased houses outside the special studies zones did not give particular consideration to the location of fault traces. In the two study areas only 30 per cent of the buyers in areas adjacent to the special studies zones evaluated distance from an active earthquake fault as either very important or somewhat important (Table 7.3). A similar lack of concern was expressed toward other features of the physical environment such as air quality and floodplain location. In contrast, in all study areas home-buyers placed particular importance on investment potential, price, size of the dwelling unit, and overall beauty of the neighbourhood. Given this general attitude among home-buyers, it will not be surprising that little evidence either of buyer avoidance or mitigation measures adopted was found.

Buyer avoidance

One of the two prime responses which might be expected if disclosure was having a measurable effect on buyer behaviour was some type of avoidance of the special studies zones. Several types of evidence were analysed to determine the existence of buyer avoidance. The first was the response of recent home-buyers within the special studies zones to disclosure. If disclosure affected the transaction, home-buyers should have reported that they responded to the disclosure by attempting to change the purchase contract — to break the contract and move elsewhere, or to negotiate for more favourable sales terms. Respondents were first asked about their awareness of their location with respect to the special studies zone. Of 207 households within the special studies zones, only 94 responded that they were aware their house was located within such a zone. Households were asked, 'Is your present home in a special studies zone?' If the question received a negative response, they were asked, 'As far as you know is your home located in a specially designated earthquake-prone area as defined by state or federal law?' If this question received a negative answer, there was a third attempt to jog their memories: 'When you first signed a contract offering to buy the house you are living in, do you recall the real estate agent providing you with a form or an addendum to the contract indicating anything special or particular about the location of the house?' In other words, the survey attempted to ascertain if the home-buyers remembered the term 'special studies zone,' the concept of such zonation, or the act of disclosure itself. If they answered all three questions negatively, one could assume they were not aware that they had bought a house within a special studies zone. The finding that less than half of the respondents recalled a disclosure within 6 months after it was supposed to have taken place might mean either that the disclosure was of little significance to them (they did not understand or heed it), or that no disclosure was made. Of the minority of households which did indicate a recollection of the disclosure, only 18 (8.5 per cent) responded that the special studies zone location made any difference in the decision to buy the house. Of these about a fourth (5) attempted to obtain more favourable contract terms or seek a lower selling price. Although disclosure did affect the behaviour of a few home-buyers, more than 90 per cent were either unaware the disclosure had taken place, or were not affected by the disclosure.

A second indicator of the effect of disclosure was the response of recent home-buyers who had purchased houses near but *outside* the boundaries of the special studies zones. It was expected that these buyers might have different attitudes about the significance of earthquake hazards, and that more of them would have responded that location of hazard zones made some difference in their purchase decision. These expectations were not borne out by the survey results. First, there was no significant difference between the importance attached to 'distance from an active earthquake fault' by home-buyers within and outside of the special studies zones. Second, there was no difference in the general awareness of the term 'special studies zone' or 'Alquist–Priolo zone' between the 'within zone' and 'adjacent buyers' (Table 7.4), with about 53 per cent having previously heard of the term despite no mandated disclosure for their homes. Although almost half of the Berkeley 'adjacent buyers' indicated that the location of earthquake hazard zones made a difference in their home purchase decision, less than 10 per cent of the Contra Costa County buyers indicated that the zones affected their decisions. Although there was no statistically significant difference between the response of 'within zone' and 'adjacent buyers', there were sharp differences between the two study areas; Berkeley home-buyers were far more likely to indicate that the existence of the zones made a difference in their home purchase decision (Table 7.5). This would suggest that if there was to be any 'softening of the market', any impact of the special studies zones on either length of time on the market or house prices, it should appear in Berkeley rather than in Contra Costa County. To test for such effect, three more pieces of information were gathered;

TABLE 7.4.   Awareness of the term 'special studies zone' or 'Alquist–Priolo zone'

	Within zone Berkeley	Adjacent Berkeley
Yes	34	28
No	7	11
	(no statistically significant difference at 0.05)	
	Within zone Contra Costa County	Adjacent Contra Costa County
Yes	45	13
No	120	25
	(no statistically significant difference at 0.05)	

TABLE 7.5. 'Did location of earthquake hazard zones make any difference in your decision to buy this particular house?'[1]

	Within zone Berkeley	Adjacent Berkeley
Yes	9	12
No	28	23
	(no significant difference at 0.05)	
	Within zone Contra Costa County	Adjacent Contra Costa County
Yes	9	3
No	50	34
	(no significant difference at 0.05)	
	Within zone Berkeley	Within zone Contra Costa County
Yes	9	9
No	28	50
	(difference significant at 0.05)	

[1] This question was asked to the within zone buyers only if they indicated that they knew they were located in a special studies zone.

the testimony of real estate agents as to the response of clients to disclosure, the relative length of time housing remained on the market, and house price trends.

Although real estate agents were not particularly enthusiastic about mandated disclosure, few responded that disclosure had any adverse effect on their business. When asked, 'Have you ever had a client decide not to buy a home after being informed the property was in an Alquist–Priolo special studies zone?', less than a third of the respondents said yes. Only one indicated that more than three clients had refused to buy a home after disclosure. Stated another way, 54 of the 74 real estate agents interviewed had *never* had a client refuse to purchase following disclosure, a response indicative of a lack of concern (or understanding) of buyers upon receiving the disclosure. There was no difference between the Berkeley and the Contra Costa County real estate agents in the measured responses of home-buyers (Table 7.6), indicating that, at least from the point of view of the real estate agents, there was no more 'softening' of the market in Berkeley than in Contra Costa County despite the responses of the home-buyers.

A weak test of the effects of special studies zones locations on length of time on

TABLE 7.6. Real estate agents whose clients refused to buy the house after special studies zone disclosure made—[1]

	Berkeley	Contra Costa County
Yes	5	15
No	7	47
	(no significant difference at 0.05)	

[1] 'Have you ever had a client refuse to buy the house after disclosure?'

the market was conducted in an earlier study on the impacts of zonation on the Berkeley housing market (Rosenthal, 1978). This test simply compared the number of days on the market (as reported in the comprehensive sales books of the Berkeley Board of Realtors) for houses within the special studies zones as compared to those outside the zones, with no other controls for the effects of, for example, sales price on length of time on the market.[2] Although houses in the special studies zones stayed on the market slightly longer than those outside the zones (116 compared to 108 days), the standard deviations were very large, and a t-test showed no significant difference between the two zones.

A far more comprehensive test compared house price levels in the houses within, adjacent to, and outside the special studies zones in the two study areas. In addition, a third study area, southern Alameda County, was added to attempt to further generalize the impacts of zonation on house prices (Figure 7.4). Hedonic price indices were calculated for house price levels in 1972, before the

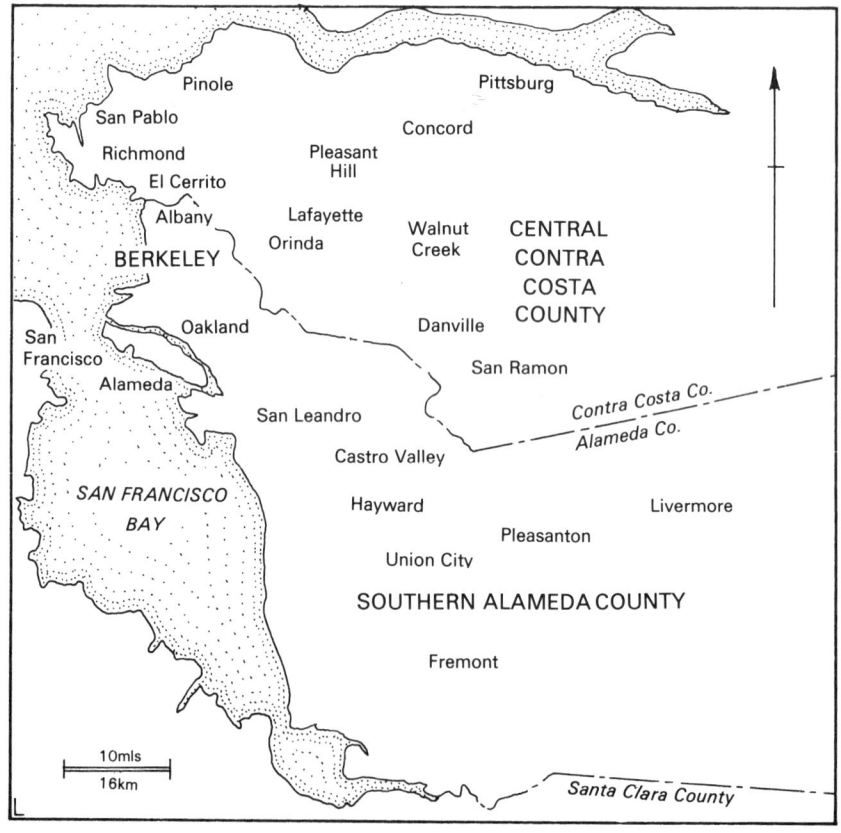

FIGURE 7.4. Study areas

disclosure legislation was in effect, and in 1977, after disclosure was in force. Data on properties sold in the three study areas were obtained from the appraisal reports filed with the Society of Real Estate Appraisers, and included information on square footage of dwelling space, age of the house, quality of the house, condition of the house, size of the lot, and the presence of such contributors to price as a swimming pool, fireplace, or 'view lot'. Data on the economic status of the area (percentage professional-managerial occupations among residents of the census tract), and housing stock composition (percentage of single-family dwelling units in the census tract) were added based on the 1970 Census of Population. Location with respect to the special studies zones was coded as a dummy variable; the property was considered to be within the special studies zone, close to (within 1.6 km (1 mile) of) the zone, or outside (beyond 1.6 km (1 mile)). The research hypothesis stated that: in 1972 location in the special studies zone was unrelated to house price (the coefficient should be close to zero), but in 1977 should be negatively related. In addition, in 1977, location near the special studies zone should have a positive regression coefficient because of a build-up of demand for housing near but not actually in the zones and location outside the zones should continue to have no effect on house prices.

The results of a set of single ordinary least squares equations for the three study areas are complex and demand some explanation (Table 7.7). For the central Contra Costa County area, when location within, adjacent to and outside the special studies zones was entered into the single-step regression equation, the results were nearly exactly as hypothesized. Although in 1972 location within a special studies zone had a negative partial effect on house prices, this effect was so variable that its coefficient was not statistically significant at the 0.10 level. However, in the 1977 equation, location in a special studies zone reduced the house price level by $4182, and the partial regression coefficient was significant at the 0.001 level. Locations within 1.6 km (1 mile) of the special studies zone, which had a slightly negative effect on the 1972 equation (although not significant at the 0.10 level), had a positive effect on 1977 prices at the 0.05 level. Similarly, locations beyond 1.6 km (1 mile) of the zones change from negative (though not statistically significant) to positive and significant at 0.01. These results are surprising in light of the general lack of awareness of the existence of special studies zones on the part of both inzone and adjacent residents, and the lack of salience which proximity to an earthquake fault has for all home-buyers. However, these equations suggest that the few people who are concerned with proximity to an active fault may have been a sufficient force in the marketplace to weaken prices within the zones, and boost them in outlying areas.

House prices in the other two study areas did not perform as hypothesized. In southern Alameda County, prices within the special studies zones were lower than elsewhere (that is, the partial effect of the inzone variable was negative), though the significance was weakened between 1972 and 1977. By 1977 the partial effect was not significant at 0.10, and therefore the effect of zonation can

TABLE 7.7 Effects of location in special studies zones on house prices

	Southern Alameda County		Berkeley		Central Contra Costa County	
	1972	1977	1972	1977	1972	1977
Inzone						
Unstandardized regression coefficient	741	−243	2617	9618	912	−4182
(significance)	(0.166)	(0.807)	(0.000)	(0.092)	(0.307)	(0.000)
Adjusted multiple r^2 for all variables except location	0.654	0.710	0.826	0.753	0.521	0.638
Adjusted multiple r^2 for all variables	0.736	0.741	0.833	0.750	0.549	0.666
Hypothesized effect	none	negative	none	negative	none	negative
Observed effect	none	none	positive at 0.01	positive at 0.10	none	negative at 0.01
Adjacent						
Unstandardized regression coefficient	807	1602	1162	9118	473	1500
(significance)	(0.030)	(0.101)	(0.061)	(0.092)	(0.620)	(0.048)
Adjusted multiple r^2 for all variables except location	0.654	0.710	0.826	0.753	0.521	0.638
Adjusted multiple r^2 for all variables	0.737	0.742	0.829	0.750	0.548	0.660
Hypothesized effect	none	positive	none	positive	none	positive
Observed effect	positive	none	positive at 0.10	positive at 0.10	none	positive at 0.05
Outside						
Unstandardized regression coefficient	−422	1121	3121	1315	623	1705
(significance)	(0.234)	(0.078)	(0.000)	(0.004)	(0.377)	(0.007)
Adjusted multiple r^2 for all variables except location	0.654	0.710	0.826	0.753	0.521	0.638
Adjusted multiple r^2 for all variables	0.736	0.742	0.837	0.769	0.548	0.661
Hypothesized effect	none	none	none	none	none	none
Observed effect	none	positive at 0.10	negative at 0.01	negative at 0.01	none	positive at 0.01

be considered to be nil. Location adjacent to the special studies zone reversed its predicted sign; in 1972 (when it should have been neutral) it was positive, but in 1977 (when it should have been positive) it had become negative. Again, however, the variation in effects causes the coefficient not to be significant at the 0.10 level. Areas distant from the zones took on a positive partial correlation with house prices.

The Berkeley equations reflect the overwhelmingly positive effects of the hills neighbourhood on house prices, even after 'view' is taken into account, and despite the existence of fault traces and other geological problems in the area. In both 1972 and 1977, location in the special studies zone was *positively* related to house price levels, although with a slight increase in the variability of this relationship in 1977 (a reduction of the significance level). Location adjacent to the zones also had a positive relationship in both years, although the strength of the partial regression coefficient was slightly less than that of location within the zone. In both years, location outside the zones had a *negative* impact on house price levels, a reflection of generally lower values attached to the smaller houses on the flat lands closer to the Bay. Although one should not interpret these equations as reflecting a positive preference for special studies zones in Berkeley, it can nonetheless be said with confidence that the disclosure legislation was not reflected in any apparent weakening of demand in the zones.

To summarize, the house price equations are somewhat contradictory. In the area in which buyers show most concern over earthquake faults and most knowledge of the meaning of special studies zones, there was the weakest effect of location within the zones on house price levels; conversely in precisely the area with the largest number of buyers who did not remember a disclosure and where there was the least concern with earthquake fault location, there seemed to be a strong effect of zonation on price levels. It would certainly be inappropriate to generalize from the central Contra Costa equation that throughout California house prices were negatively impacted within the zones by the emplacement of mandated disclosure, for the behaviour of house prices in two areas with more active fault creep shows just the reverse effect on house prices. Rather, it is probably that it is not the zonation itself that has effected house prices, but some correlated neighbourhood characteristics omitted from the equation. This point needs further empirical corroboration, but it appears likely, on the basis of price equations for two of the three study areas, that the disclosure of zonation has not had a negative impact on house price levels.

From the combination of survey evidence and analysis of market behaviour, it can be concluded that there is only slight evidence that buyers have avoided purchases within the special studies zones despite mandated disclosure. Real estate agents rarely report buyer reluctance to consummate sales after disclosure, buyers report little concern with earthquake hazards and virtually no impact of the disclosure on their final purchase decision, and market data show little if any weakening of demand (and lowering of price) within the zones. If buyers have generally not avoided purchasing houses in special studies zones, they still could respond to disclosures by taking mitigation measures *in situ*. In the following section the strength of this response is explored.

Mitigation measures

A variety of mitigation measures is available to residents of earthquake-prone areas, varying in cost and the time commitment. It can be hypothesized that each of these measures, particularly if undertaken primarily in response to earthquake hazards, involves a sequence of decisions suggested for the insurance purchase decision (Kunreuther *et al.*, 1978b). These steps involve: (1) the evaluation of the hazard as a problem; (2) the learning of the availability of a particular mitigation measure; and (3) the decision concerning the adoption of a particular measure. Since disclosure was by no means usually accompanied with a set of suggestions for hazard mitigation, it should not be assumed that the adoption of mitigation measures would be directly and automatically linked to disclosure. However, it is of interest to test whether those who had received a disclosure were any more likely to adopt mitigation measures than the general population, since such behaviour could serve as a measurable response existing virtually outside the framework through which market responses are measured.

It should be noted that each type of mitigation strategy involves a different set of constraints and considerations in the adoption process. It is useful to consider some of the conclusions drawn concerning the relative market failure for adopting earthquake insurance in California (Kunreuther *et al.*, 1978b). Among the reasons the research team found for low earthquake insurance sales were the low degree of concern with the earthquake hazard and the role of the insurance agent. The first point probably needs no further elaboration, in that it is merely a restatement of the now-frequent finding that earthquake hazards are relegated a low everyday salience by residents of earthquake-prone areas. The second point, however, is more complex. The Kunreuther group found that one reason why prospective purchasers were not buying insurance was a lack of interest on the part of the sales agent (1978b, p. 252): 'Today the agent has a limited economic incentive to initiate personal contact with his clients. Commissions are based on an amount proportional to the total premium, which, in the case of earthquake and flood insurance, is usually a small amount.' It was not in the agent's personal business interests to expend large amounts of time explaining the earthquake addendum to the home-owner's policy, since the financial rewards for such activity were seen to be small. Home-owners, and particularly those who had moved to the area from out of the state, were therefore not only unlikely to have heard of earthquake insurance, but were unlikely to learn about such policies either from the home sales agents or the insurance agencies. Since information about the mitigation measures must be acquired for its adoption, and since advertisements in the mass media have had mixed success, at best, in alerting people to hazards and mitigation measures (Robertson, 1975; Roder, 1961), it is essential to consider the role of the individual change agent—real estate salesperson, insurance salesperson, neighbour, friend, or relative—in the diffusion of mitigation measures.

The objective of the next stage of the research was a comparison of the mitigation measures adopted by special studies zones residents who had received a disclosure with the general California population recent home-buyers. The Berkeley and Contra Costa County home-buyers who had indicated in the previous interview that they were aware they lived in a special studies zone were recontacted through a mail survey. Of the 94 original respondents, 58 replied to the mail questionnaire, 17 from Berkeley and 41 from central Contra Costa County. It was this population which was taken to represent home-buyers who

TABLE 7.8.   Mitigation measures

	Have done primarily because of earthquake threat		Total percentage who have done	
	Bay Area	Los Angeles	Bay Area	Los Angeles
Inquired about earthquake insurance	41.4%[1]	23.1%	41.4[1]	23.1
Bought earthquake insurance	24.1[1]	12.8	24.1[1]	12.8
Instruct children what to do in an earthquake	20.0	47.6	22.2	50.4
Emergency procedures at residence	15.6	26.1	25.4	34.1
Family plans for reunion after earthquake	14.0	19.0	16.0	22.1
Replace cupboard latches	13.8[1]	4.5	22.4[1]	10.2
Have a working battery radio	8.6	11.1	53.4	54.6
Structurally reinforce home	8.6[1]	4.7	13.8[1]	11.1
Have a working flashlight	6.9	10.8	86.2[1]	71.5
Rearrange cupboard contents	5.2	9.7	12.1	16.3
Contacted neighbours for information	3.4	9.8	15.5	19.5
Have first-aid kit	3.4	6.0	68.9	50.1
Store food	1.7	8.0	20.7	26.8
Store water	1.7	8.0	5.1	17.1
Set up neighbourhood responsibility plans	1.7	4.0	12.0	12.2

[1] Bay Area respondents exceed Los Angeles respondents.

both received and recalled a disclosure that their property is within a special studies zone. It should be noted that this population is *not* representative of all those who should, by law, receive disclosures, in that it has both higher educational and income levels and also probably greater awareness and concern with the earthquake hazard. Adoption of mitigation measures within the general population was measured in a major survey of residents of Los Angeles County over the 1977–78 period (Turner *et al.*, 1979). A survey of 1450 Los Angeles County households, both within and outside special studies zones, and including recent as well as long-term residents, asked about the adoption of 15 mitigation measures. Although it can be argued that this sample, while representative of the Los Angeles population, may reflect neither the attitudes of other state residents nor more particularly those of Bay Area residents, nonetheless it is probably the best reflection of current attitudes and responses to earthquake threat by a cross-section of income and ethnic groups in the largest California city. The responses to the Los Angeles survey were compared directly to those of the Berkeley/Contra Costa survey of recent home-buyers in special studies zones who were aware of the meaning of this location. It was hypothesized that since the Bay Area home-buyers were more concerned with earthquake hazards, of higher average income and education than the general population and had received a disclosure concerning the location of their home in a special studies zone, they would have a greater propensity to adopt a variety of mitigation measures than the Los Angeles sample. This hypothesis was not borne out by the survey findings (Table 7.8).

Respondents were asked to indicate not only had they adopted a particular measure, but also had this adoption been primarily because of earthquake threat or for other reasons. What is perhaps most striking about the percentages adopting various mitigation strategies is the fact that only a minority of residents, either of the special studies zones or of Los Angeles County, have taken any of the measures. Of the 15 mitigation measures, the only ones adopted by a majority of respondents are the possession of a working battery radio, a flashlight, and a first-aid kit. It should be noted that in all three cases most respondents had taken this measure for reasons other than earthquake hazard.

The special studies zones residents had most frequently enquired about earthquake insurance (41.4 per cent), but only one in four households had actually purchased it. Between 14 and 20 per cent of the special studies zones residents had instructed children what to do in the event of an earthquake, established emergency procedures at the residence and made plans for a family reunion after the earthquake, but these percentages were lower than those of the Los Angeles respondents. Indeed, the special studies zones respondents exceeded the general population of Los Angeles only in the areas of earthquake insurance, replacement of cupboard latches, structural reinforcements, and possession of a working flashlight. In all other measures, special studies zones residents had less frequently adopted the mitigation measure with sometimes marked differences (as in the case of instruction to children and emergency procedures). A possible explanation for this finding is the combination of a fairly recent experience with a major damaging earthquake in the Los Angeles area (1971) and the discussion surrounding the so-called Palmdale bulge as a precursor of major movement along the southern portion of the San Andreas fault running through Los Angeles. But whatever the explanation for these frequencies, it is obvious that disclosure, even when understood and remembered, did not increase the likelihood of the adoption of mitigation measures.

Mandated disclosure has not resulted in measurable responses on the part of home-buyers. The majority of home-buyers do not even recall a disclosure within 6 months of the home purchase. Even for those who do recall the disclosure and who understand its meaning, few have responded with purchase term nego-tiations, avoidance of the area, or subsequent hazard mitigation measures in their new homes. In the final section, the problems with the current legislation will be discussed.

PROBLEMS WITH DISCLOSURE LEGISLATION

There are several major impediments to the process of mandated disclosure being translated into measurable buyer response. Three of these factors merit some attention if the current legislation is to be translated into a more effective form.

A first major factor is the role of the 'change agent', the real estate agent. To be effective in presenting environmental information, the real estate agent should have a generally high degree of credibility to the home-buyers; buyers should be willing to give their trust to what he has to say and his evaluation of what might be an ambiguous problem. Although there has been prior research on those aspects of the sale which are most influenced by the real estate agent (Hempel, 1969), and the general role of the real estate agent within society (House, 1977), we know little about the level of confidence which buyers in general place in real estate agents. On the other hand, there is a generally held belief that buyers might not trust real estate agents, a wariness which may be partly attributed to the uncertainty on the part of the buyer as to whom the real estate agent is representing when a house is shown. Since the more knowledgeable and experienced buyers and sellers realize that it is the seller who actually pays the real estate agent commission, such wariness on the part of buyers is not completely unwarranted. The fact that the real estate agent does not operate with the same level of trust and confidence as, say, a family doctor or lawyer, suggests that buyers might not change their behaviour or beliefs solely on the basis of information provided by the real estate agent.

Related to this notion is the fact that real estate agents might provide misinformation concerning the special studies zones, or reinforce wishful thinking on the part of the buyer that such zones are not meaningful. The misinformation provided by real estate agents may be attributed to a simple lack of understanding about what the special studies zones mean. In the survey of real estate agents in Berkeley and Contra Costa County who had recently sold homes in special studies zones, one question asked, 'What do you usually tell your client is the meaning of a special studies zone?' Although most of the real estate agents made the association between the zones and earthquake hazards, a full 14 per cent responded that the zones define areas susceptible to flooding or slated for transportation surveys. It almost goes without saying that if the real estate agents themselves are not fully aware of the meaning of the special studies zones, it is not surprising that buyers dealing with these agents will not understand their meanings.

The reinforcement of wishful thinking is more subtle. Since real estate agents routinely present the special studies zones disclosure at the time the purchase contract is signed (after 'the wife has mentally arranged the furniture in the living room' and a psychological commitment has been made to purchase the house), the buyers will not at this point be looking for reasons to reject the house. Instead the psychological commitment is accompanied by a desire to have the decision reinforced by information on the advantages of the property. Real estate agents may (sometimes sincerely) pander to this desire by downplaying the importance of a special studies zone location. The survey of real estate agents showed that most are not convinced that the zones are particularly important or meaningful. For example, only about a third of the real estate agents believe that people living within the zones are more likely to suffer physical injuries or financial losses attributable to earthquake damage than those who live elsewhere. Given this general attitude, the real estate agent may sincerely both comply with the disclosure law, and yet minimize the impact of the disclosure by downplaying its importance: 'This is just another government regulation', or 'I've lived [in this city] for 25 years. There has never been an earthquake [in this area] in human history!' or 'We don't get damage from earthquakes [in this area]'.

Since most real estate agents are not convinced that the special studies zones outline particularly hazardous areas, they can reassure the prospective buyer and reinforce the likelihood of the sale, while still meeting the legal requirements of disclosure. When this practice is combined with the possible misinformation about the meaning of special studies zones, and the overall lack of credibility of the real estate agent, it can be concluded that there are many opportunities for information to be provided in such a way that responses would be minimized.

A second problem with current disclosure legislation is that methods and timing were not specified in the law. The standard procedures which have been adopted by most of the members of the California Association of Realtors minimize the impact of disclosure both through timing and method. Timing of disclosure is important since it can have a strong effect on the purchase decision. Previous research indicates that the timing of the presentation of information about vacancies can affect both the length of search and the home purchase decision (Clark and Smith, 1979). Where negative information must be presented, it is best presented after a commitment to purchase has been made—that is, when the household has made a fairly firm commitment to buy a particular house, when the purchase contract is signed. The most sensitive time for negative information is when the house is actually being shown to the buyers and they are noting positive and negative aspects of the house. Thus, if real estate agents wish to minimize the impact of special studies zones disclosure, they should make the disclosure at the time the purchase contract is signed and certainly not during the first showing of the house. This is precisely what is currently being practised. When real estate agents were asked *when* they routinely made a disclosure, 90 per cent said they made the disclosure at the time of contract signing, and only 9 per cent at the time the house was being shown.[3]

Standard disclosure methods also minimize its impact on buyers. The three standard formats used are the information in the Multiple Listing Service pages (used by 30 per cent of the real estate agents interviewed), a map of the area with special studies zones drawn in (used by 70 per cent) and a contract addendum (used by 91 per cent of the respondents). The Multiple Listing Service form presents little information to the buyer. In Berkeley, disclosure on this form is simply a typed line stating 'in Alquist–Priolo zone' or 'in Alquist–Priolo district'. To the uninitiated buyer, such a statement might mean anything, most probably the names of the state legislators for the area. In Contra Costa County, the form includes a line stating 'special studies zone' and a box marked 'yes' or 'no'. This disclosure tells the buyer nothing about the *meaning* of the zones. The map, used particularly in Contra Costa County at the time of the survey, is a detailed street map of the region with the 1 per cent floodplain in blue, the special studies zone in yellow, and areas of combined hazard in green. Terms are not defined on the map, and the districts *can* be used by the real estate agents to demonstrate to the prospective buyers that many other properties share the same characteristics, and that therefore such a zonation cannot be very important since so many houses are at risk. The third disclosure method is the signing of a contract addendum. This addendum, until recently, stated that 'the property *is or may be* situated in a Special Studies Zone' (emphasis added). No definition of the special studies zone is presented, although the form does note that construction for human occupancy on the property may be subject to the findings of a geological report unless such buildings are single-family wood-frame dwellings or were in existence prior to 4 May 1975. The words 'seismic', 'earthquake', or 'fault' are nowhere mentioned in the contract addendum.

Although the specification of timing and methods would not guarantee that disclosure would be heeded, it is possible that changes in these elements might increase the memorability of the disclosure process. At present, real estate agents are disclosing at the least sensitive time, and using methods which convey the least amount of information about special studies zones. It is suggested that legislative attention to these simple notions might yield important results in increasing buyer response to mandated disclosure.

A third problem with the current legislation lies in the nature of the zones themselves. Not all of the fault traces are easily defined at every point and trenching is not feasible in all areas, particularly those in densely built-up neighbourhoods. Maps at the scale used by Boards of Realtors may therefore be inaccurate, and in any case often cannot distinguish whether border properties are actually within or outside the zones. The problem of accurate portrayal of individual parcels has become so severe that Boards of Realtors have been urged not to make assessments of the location of individual parcels but rather to recommend a geological survey (Prendergast, personal communication, 1980). Furthermore, the Contra Costa County Board of Realtors, fearful of legal repercussions involved with inaccuracies in their map, has ceased distributing special studies zones maps to member realtors or their clients.

Even more serious is the fact that the zones themselves were defined for one purpose and have been interpreted to cover a far wider range of hazards. The zones outline areas containing traces of active faults, but they were not designed to include all of the areas susceptible to damage from earthquakes, nor do they include those most susceptible to damage. For example, although the 1906 earthquake in San Francisco is recalled as particularly severe and damaging, no special studies zone runs through the city of San Francisco. The zones do not include areas susceptible to damage for liquefaction, shaking or ground failure, since these related to bedrock conditions rather than proximity to the fault itself. They only include areas more susceptible to damage from rupture and fault creep. For this reason the rare sophisticated buyer, who knows that his house is near a fault but not directly on one, may be correct in an assessment that the purchase of a house in a special studies zone does not increase his liability to damage or injury. This buyer may be fully aware that the bedrock conditions make his particular house less susceptible to damage than those built on unstable slopes or landfill. Although the special studies zones were legislatively simple to define (areas an eighth of a mile (70 m.) on either side of a designated fault trace regardless of bedrock conditions), their simplicity is a disadvantage as well as an advantage. It is essential that if buyer response to disclosure is deemed important, then the governmental units (state and county) must take more responsibility in identifying the truly hazardous zones so that home-buyers are more completely informed about the range of possible damage associated with earthquake activities at a variety of sites.

CONCLUSIONS

Despite state legislation mandating disclosure that built-up parcels lie within areas susceptible to damage from fault rupture or creep, the problem of the disposal of developed areas has not been effectively handled. Buyers have had little response to mandated disclosure for several reasons. First, the information agent (the real estate agent) has serious problems of credibility and role conflict; since it is not in the best business interests of the real estate agent to make a disclosure 'too effective', and since he is legally representing the seller, he has difficulty in presenting such negative information to the prospective home-buyer. In addition, some real estate agents are not well informed as to the nature of the special studies zones, how they have been defined, and the hazards they encompass. A second reason for low buyer response lies in the value system of home-buyers. Earthquake hazards (as well as other environmental disamenities) are ranked very low in the priority system of home-buyers. Instead the primary motivation of home-buyers is to minimize the price they pay for a dwelling unit of given characteristics and to maximize its potential resale value. The house is thus treated as an economic investment, a notion suggested by Perrin (1977), and buyers are not making long-term commitments to either house or neighbourhood with the purchase of a given property. Indeed, since buyers usually intend to stay in the house for a relatively short time (3–5 years), and since it is relatively unlikely that a major damaging earthquake will occur in that period, they do not hesitate to buy a home in a special studies zone as long as they believe it has a good potential resale value. Furthermore, they do not believe it is economically rational to take costly mitigation measures such as structural reinforcements or the purchase of earthquake insurance since these expenses cannot be recouped in a subsequent house sale. The short term decision to move to a special studies zone or other hazard district and to forego mitigation measures is seen as rational from an individual viewpoint, regardless of how this may seem to policy-makers or those viewing the potential for disaster at a statewide level. Unless environmental hazards become translated into economic risk to individuals, hazard warnings not followed by severe disasters will probably not be heeded.

An additional factor which may lessen buyer response to disclosure is the belief on the part of home-buyers that there are few real alternatives. It is stated many times by buyers and real estate agents that 'all California is earthquake country'. What this means is that micro-zonation within a metropolitan area is meaningless, since all neighbourhoods will be equally susceptible to destruction when a major earthquake occurs. When this general belief is combined with the existence of a 'seller's market' for real estate (few vacancies, excess of demand over supply), buyers have little choice but to purchase a home they can afford whenever and wherever it becomes available. These supply constraints are very real to home-buyers, and may account for some of the responses of buyers within special studies zones who said that the zones did make some difference in their purchase decision, but were unable to translate this attitude into market behaviour.

The findings of this study suggest several legislative needs. First, the legislature has to attempt to deal with the full range of hazards, natural and human-made, which face state residents. If earthquake hazards are truly deemed more important than some others, and if the legislature wishes to take effective action to mitigate these hazards, it must deal with a more comprehensive definition of earthquake hazards, and reconsider legislation which would better inform residents about the hazards and possible mitigation strategies. Although taking such action may sound feasible and perhaps even simple, it will involve the courage to face the inevitable lobbying by real estate interests whose property investments might be impaired if home-buyers were made fully aware of associated geological risks. Second, to cope with hazardous areas which have already been densely developed in residential uses, the state might institute a systematic scheme to purchase these areas, or to rezone them such that property improvement would be limited. This type of action may seem draconian, and is probably not a politically feasible option, but if such action were attempted and well-publicized, the home-buying public might be made more aware of the seriousness of the environmental hazards with which they are living.

It is possible that land-use regulation would not be necessary if the financial community—mortgage lenders and investors—were made aware of the risk involved over the long term to property located in particular hazardous areas. If mortgage lenders were to translate their understanding of this risk into additional charges for mortgage loans or were even to refuse loans in areas designated as geologically hazardous, a very effective means of 'disclosure' would be put into place. In short, the self-interest of mortgage lenders and investors would be made to work in the public interest with respect to changing the market in geologically hazardous portions of California. Even this scheme, however, is not free from problematic social consequences, which might involve a new concentration of impoverished people in upgraded but lower-cost housing—making the low-income household far more susceptible to environmental hazards than it already is.

Unfortunately there is no clear-cut answer to the dilemma of the disposal of areas susceptible to severe earthquake damage. At present the problem has not been dealt with effectively and it is very important that policy-makers at the state and federal level not delude themselves into thinking that the present disclosure law has in any way contributed to hazard mitigation or consumer protection.

NOTES

1. The following section is based on the report issued by the Joint Committee on Seismic Safety (1974).
2. It should be noted that this is no small omission since houses within the zones had higher average listing prices and selling prices ($131 290 and $127 058) compared with those outside the zones ($115 568 and $111 310 respectively) during the study period. Since length of days on the market is positively correlated with sales price, it was to be

expected that all other things being equal the areas with higher selling prices would have also been those with longer market periods.
3. Here 32 per cent indicated they introduced the buyer to special studies zones before any houses were shown, during the office interview when buyer preferences are first expressed and the real estate agent 'qualifies' the buyer (makes an estimate about the maximum the buyer can afford to spend on housing). Percentages do not sum to 100 because some real estate agents indicate that they make the disclosure at more than one time during the sales process.

REFERENCES

Bentler, P. M. and Speckart, G. (1979). Models of attitude-behavior relations. *Psychological Review*, **86**, 452–464.

Bernoulli, D. (1738). Specimen theoriae norae de mensura sortis. *Comentarii Academiae Scientiarum Imperiales Petropolitanae, Vol. 5*, pp. 175–192 (translated by L. Sommer in *Econometrica*, **22**, (1954), 23–36).

California Association of Realtors (1977). *Disclosure of Geologic Hazards*, California Association of Realtors, Los Angeles.

Clark, W. A. V. and Smith, T. R. (1979). Modelling information use in a spatial context. *Annals of the Association of American Geographers*, **69**, 575–588.

Edwards, W. (1955). The prediction of decisions among bets. *Journal of Experimental Psychology*, **50**, 201–214.

Fishbein, M. and Ajzen, I. (1975). *Belief, Attitude, Intention and Behavior: An Introduction to Theory and Research*, Addison-Wesley, Reading, Mass.

Friedman, M. and Savage, L. J. (1948). The utility analysis of choices involving risk. *Journal of Political Economy*, **56**, 279–304.

Gillies, D. (Vice President, Governmental Relations, California Association of Realtors) (1980), Personal communication.

Grether, D. M. and Plott, C. R. (1979). Economic theory of choice and the preference reversal phenomenon. *American Economic Review*, **69**, 623–638.

Hempel, D. (1969). *The Role of the Real Estate Broker in the Home Buying Process*, Department of Marketing, University of Connecticut, Center for Real Estate and Urban Economic Studies, Storrs, Conn.

Hershey, J. C. and Schoemaker, P. (1980). Risk taking and problem context in the domain of losses: an expected utility analysis. *Journal of Risk and Insurance*, **47**, 111–132.

House, J. D. (1977). *Contemporary Entrepreneurs: The Sociology of Residential Real Estate Agents*, Greenwood Press, Westport, Conn.

Hovland, C. I. and Janis, I. L. (Eds.) (1959). *Personality and Persuasibility*, Yale University Press, New Haven, Conn.

Hovland, C. I., Janis, I. L., and Kelley, H. H. (1953). *Communication and Persuasion*, Yale University Press, New Haven, Conn.

Hurst, B. (Former legislative assistant to state senator Alfred Alguist) (1980), Personal communication.

Iacopi, R. (1971). *Earthquake Country*, 3rd edition, Lane Books, Menlo Park, Cal.

Joint Committee on Seismic Safety (1974). *Meeting the Earthquake Challenge: Final Report to the Legislature of the State of California*.

Kahneman, D. and Tversky, A. (1979). Prospect theory: an analysis of decision under risk. *Econometrica*, **47**, 263–291.

Kockelman, W. J. (1980). *Examples of the Use of Earth-science Information by Decision-*

makers in the San Francisco Bay Region, California, USGS Open File Report No. 80–124.

Kunreuther, H., Ginsberg, R., Miller, L., Sagi, P., Borkin, B., and Katz, N. (1978a). *Limited Knowledge and Insurance Protection: Implications for Natural Hazard Policy*, John Wiley and Sons, New York.

Kunreuther, H., with Ginsberg, L., Sagi, P., Slovic, P., Borkan, B. and Katz, N. (1978b). *Disaster Insurance Protection: Public Policy Lessons*, John Wiley and Sons, New York.

Liberator, J. (California Department of Real Estate) (1979), Personal communication.

Lichtenstein, S. and Slovic, P. (1971). Reversals of preference between bids and choices in gambling decisions. *Journal of Experimental Psychology*, **89**, 46–55.

Lindman, H. R. (1971). Inconsistent preferences among gambles. *Journal of Experimental Psychology*, **89**, 390–397.

March, J. G. and Simon, H. A. (1958). *Organizations*, John Wiley and Sons, New York.

McGuire, W. J. (1968). Personality and susceptibility to social influence. In E. F. Borgatta, and W. W. Lambert (Eds.), *Handbook of Personality Theory and Research*. Rand McNally, Chicago, pp. 1130–1187.

McGuire, W. J. (1969). The nature of attitudes and attitude change. In G. Lindzey and E. Aronson (Eds.), *The Handbook of Social Psychology*, 2nd ed., vol. 3. Addison-Wesley, Reading, Mass, pp. 136–314.

Mosteller, F. and Nogee, P. (1951). An experimental measurement of utility. *Journal of Political Economy*, **59**, 371–404.

Mukerjee, T. (1971). *Economic Analysis of Natural Hazards: A Study of Adjustments to Earthquakes and Their Costs*, Natural Hazards Research, Working Paper No. 17, University of Toronto, Toronto.

Palm, R. (1976). *Urban Social Geography from the Perspective of the Real Estate Salesman*. Center for Real Estate and Urban Economics, Berkeley.

Palm, R. (1979). Financial and real estate institutions in the housing market: a study of recent house price changes in the San Francisco Bay Area. In D. T. Herbert and R. J. Johnston (Eds.), *Geography and the Urban Environment*, Vol. 2. John Wiley and Sons, Chichester, Sussex.

Pashigian, B. P., Schkade, L. L., and Menefee, G. (1966). The selection of an optimal deductible for a given insurance policy. *Journal of Business*, **39**, 35–44.

Perrin, C. (1977). *Everything in Its Place: Social Order and Land Use in America*, Princeton University Press, Princeton, NJ.

Prendergast, J. C. (JCP Consulting Geologists) (23 July, 1980). Personal communication.

Robertson, L. (1975). The great seat belt campaign flop. *Journal of Communication*, **26**, 21–25.

Roder, W. (1961). Attitudes and knowledge on the Topeka floodplain. In G. F. White (Ed.), *Papers on Flood Problems*. Department of Geography Research Paper 70, University of Chicago.

Rosenthal, M. (1978). The effects of the 'Alquist–Priolo zone' notification Act on the Berkeley housing market. Unpublished Paper prepared for *Business Administration*, **284**, University of California, Berkeley.

Schoemaker, P. J. H. and Kunreuther, H. C. (1979). An experimental study of insurance decisions. *Journal of Risk and Insurance*, **46**, 603–618.

Schwartz, S. H. and Tessler, R. C. (1972). A test of a model for reducing measured attitude-behavior discrepancies. *Journal of Personality and Social Psychology*, **24**, 225–236.

Sherif, M. and Hovland, C. I. (1961). *Social Judgment: Assimilation and Contrast Effects in Communication and Attitude Change*, Yale University Press, New Haven, Conn.

Slovic, P. (1975). Choice between equally valued alternatives. *Journal of Experimental Psychology: Human Perception and Performance*, **1**, 280–287.

Slovic, P., Kunreuther, H., and White, G. F. (1974). Decision processes, rationality and adjustment to natural hazards. In G. F. White, (Ed.), *Natural Hazards: Local, National and Global*, Oxford University Press, New York.

Slovic, P., Fischhoff, B., Lichtenstein, S., Corrigan, B., and Combs, B. (1977). Preference for insuring against probable small losses: insurance implications. *Journal of Risk and Insurance*, **44**, 237–258.

Turner, R., Nigg, J., Pas, D., and Young, B. (1979). *Earthquake Threat: The Human Response in Southern California*, University of California, Institute for Social Science Research, Los Angles.

Tversky, A. (1969). Intransitivity of preferences. *Psychological Review*, **76**, 31–48.

Tversky, A. (1972). Elimination by aspects: a theory of choice. *Psychological Review*, **79**, 281–299.

US Office of Emergency Preparedness (1972). *Disaster Preparedness*, Vol. 3. Executive Office of the President, Washington, DC.

Visvader, H. and Burton, I. (1974). Natural hazards and hazard policy in Canada and the United States. In G. F. White (Ed.), *Natural Hazards: Local National, Global*. Oxford University Press, New York, pp. 219–231.

Weigel, R. H. (1979). The behavioural implications of knowledge: lessons from the attitude-behavior controversy. Unpublished paper prepared for the National Institute of Education.

Weigel, R. H. and Newman, L. S. (1976). Increasing attitude-behavior correspondence by broadening the scope of the behavioral measure. *Journal of Personality and Social Psychology*, **33**, 793–802.

Zimbardo, P. and Ebbesen, E. B. (1970). *Influencing Attitudes and Changing Behavior*, Addison-Wesley, Reading, Mass.

Geography and the Urban Environment
Progress in Research and Applications, Volume V
Edited by D. T. Herbert and R. J. Johnston

Chapter 8

Negotiating Urban Risk

John E. Seley and Julian Wolpert

INTRODUCTION

In his prologue to an international conference on social risk assessment, Lowrance (1980) identifies six classes of hazard. These are: (1) infectious and degenerative diseases; (2) natural disasters, such as floods, earthquakes and tornadoes; (3) failure of large technological systems, such as dams, power plants, airplanes, and ships; (4) discrete small-scale accidents, such as car crashes, workplace incidents, or sports injuries; (5) low-level, delayed-effect hazards, such as asbestos poisoning, radiation, noise pollution, and psychological stress; and (6) sociopolitical disruption, such as terrorism, nuclear weapons proliferation, and an oil embargo. Each of these potential hazards is, in itself, of grave consequence. However, an increase in technological and societal complexity has led to the possibility of exposure to new and multiple hazards, especially in our urban areas. Multiple-risk exposure is the compounding which results from actual hazards perceived to be managed hazardously, unjustly, or inequitably. Both direct and spillover effects can be expected in greater magnitude and scope than for isolated hazards in rural areas. For example, high densities and congestion suggest that hazards will take a higher toll and the management of hazards and their aftermath will be more complex and more subject to error. Thus, impacts will be potentially more devastating of lives and property.

An additional component of this urban differential relates to the greater experience with the *process* of implementing and administering large-scale projects. Urban communities have been more severely affected over a longer period of time with the threat of disruption, household relocation, and other forms of erosion of quality of life than have smaller cities or towns. With these disruptions have come a large measure of distrust of the implementation strategies and motives of private and public developers. Suspicions have been fuelled by several decades of closed planning processes and rule by 'experts'. Neither the private sector nor public officials have much credibility in the management of risky enterprises or programmes, partly related to agendas which are different from the public interest (Clarke, 1973). Experiments in citizen participation provide some promise of a more open process in the assessment of hazards and their distributional impacts. Urban participants, like those actively involved in the environmental movement, have developed a reservoir of skills amenable to a negotiating process on issues of hazards and their management.

Since the topic of this paper is a relatively new concern for planners and citizens, our focus is on identifying general issues. It remains for geographers and others to conduct the specific research necessary to give these issues specificity for policy application. We start with some general considerations, including existing risk assessment methodologies and the process of choosing hazardous projects or programme; the focus here is upon commonalities across types of hazard. Next we examine some of the recent experience with citizen involvement in large-scale technological change—in the decisions to locate highways in urban areas and in the controversies surrounding the development and siting of nuclear power plants. It is through such controversies that we have begun to discover the significance of safety (broadly defined) to impacted populations, as well as some directions for clarifying acceptable risk. Next we explore some of the particular limitations on decision-making for complex technological or institutional changes which pose risk to the urban environment. This leads into a discussion of several proposed methods for resolving the fact and process conflict between scientists and citizens, including the science court, the public board of inquiry, and the siting jury. We also briefly examine mediation and arbitration as methods for resolving citizen–policy-maker conflicts. Next we explore some of the problems of management, or how to monitor hazards. Finally, we outline next steps in an agenda, including legislative and regulatory considerations, as well as more general decision-making concerns.

RISK ASSESSMENT

Rather than repeat the litany of problems with hazard identification, prediction, measurement and control, our main concern is with a range of hazards which has been relatively underemphasized though this does involve learning from risk assessments of hazards which have received more considerable study. The class of hazards which concern us are those which result from social or technological events that affect urban environments. Whereas the focus of our research is the United States, the experience of other countries does not seem different and our findings may have generality.

Natural hazards

Risk assessment, or the identification of hazards, the estimation of risk, and the assignment of social value to the hazard, is a growing field of study. An international symposium (Schwing and Albers, 1980), United States Congressional hearings (US House of Representatives, 1980), reports sponsored by prestigious scientific institutions (Whyte and Burton, 1980), and even a Society for Risk Analysis all attest to its increasing importance. Yet, despite much interest and the fact that most risk assessments confine themselves to natural hazards or discrete scientific concerns (food additives, carcinogens, direct toxicity, for example), many issues remain.

One of the most significant of these lies in the empirical analysis of hazard, or the attempt to identify the presence of hazard and its magnitude. Screening, monitoring, and diagnosis still rely heavily on intuition or obvious indicators of harm (Kasperson and Kates, 1980). For example, 'seepage', or delayed-effect hazard, is less identifiable than sudden events. Yet, identification of hazards is more advanced than our ability either to estimate the range and likelihood of risk or to identify priorities for policy (Kasperson and Kates, 1980; Lowrance, 1980). More specifically, our ability to recognize physical health and ecological effects is much greater than our ability to isolate sociological, psychological, political, or even economic effects. Just within the narrow range of food and consumer goods, the number of new products in any given year already taxes the capacity of a number of government agencies established for their regulation and, as the Director of the National Institute for Occupational Safety and Health notes, 'Research often becomes a way to delay action, not promote it. Note how the debate about thresholds has been used to stall action on asbestos' (Robbins, 1980, p. 348).

Second, third, and higher-order impacts simply defy current risk assessment capabilities (Ashford and Hattis, 1980, pp. 320–328; Massam, 1980) Yet, as Clark (1980) notes, inability to predict system-wide or long-term impacts may prove problematic. Efforts in the United States to control forest fires, for example, were so successful that they led to accumulations of brush and scrub in amounts which made catastrophic fires more likely and resulted in conflagrations of a size and intensity far beyond prediction.

The desire to define hazards as simple and controllable has its origins in the policy arena. Citizens as well as policy-makers demand certainty in the face of potential catastrophe; developers of new technologies feel compelled to provide assurances (Kasper, 1979). This has led observers to point out that some risk is inevitable and that the focus on certainty is inappropriate and, ultimately, inefficient. Once we recognize risk as a continuum, it will be easier to accept it.

Manmade risks in the urban environment

Unlike natural hazards, the threat from urban, manmade sources like power plants, toxic waste dumps, and highways, is generally of low probability and high impact. As Wolpert has argued elsewhere (Wolpert, 1980), the relative lack of attention to the risks from such events has led to an inability to predict or control incidents; indeed, many such sources are not perceived as hazardous until control becomes a serious problem.

Yet, a form of risk assessment—social impact assessment (SIA)—has existed for urban projects in the United States since passage of the National Environmental Policy Act of 1969. This act mandated environmental impact statements for all actions, funded or conducted by the federal government, which significantly affect the environment. The resulting interest in and growth of the field of social impact assessment extended the concept of environmental impact to social, political, economic, health, aesthetic, and psychological concerns, particularly in the effort to insure the protection of social units (as opposed to natural environments) from adverse consequences of public actions (Finsterbusch, 1980). These social units include individuals, households, organizations, neighbourhoods, and communities.

Aside from political constraints on the design and use of social impact assessments and severe methodological problems (Kates, 1977), there are two conceptual limitations to such efforts which allow much of the risk of high impact, manmade rare events to escape detection or serious consideration. First, the case method (encouraged by the decision process) ignores cumulative or aggregative impact (Massam, 1980). What is the effect of one *more* facility on a community? What is the effect of a fifth highway in a given urban area, or a third methadone clinic in an inner city neighbourhood? Second, the emphasis on one project at a time ignores the possibilities of alternative locations or alternative forms of achieving the same societal goal. Thus, individual highways are assessed for their impact on local communities. The possibility of other locations for the highway, or mass transit in its stead, are often not considered by social impact assessments. The argument is that it is not the role of the impact assessor to compare highway locations or to suggest alternatives—that is the purview of the planning process. Unfortunately, the practical reality is that the cost and effort involved in impact assessments often means that more than one assessment is not conducted; alternatives are generated only on drawing-boards or in political backrooms, where assessment is a very small part of the picture. Indeed, there is no built-in mechanism for considering impact of the building of a highway for its potential to cause catastrophe.

The inability of the planning, decision-making, and assessment processes to consider low-risk, high-impact consequences of failure has implications, as well, for the way a facility is monitored and run. Operators will try to avoid high probability, low-impact incidents (radioactive leaks), while ignoring low-probability, high-impact incidents (core meltdown). As one of the Nuclear Regulatory Commissioners explained after the Three Mile Island incident: 'That goes back to the point—referred to earlier—my theory that the whole system was just set to believe that accidents wouldn't happen. When you believe that, then there are things that you don't do' (Ahearne, in Curtis and Hogan, 1980, p. 17). Since Three Mile Island, there has been increased concern over evacuation planning and the United States government has recommended that new nuclear power plants be located in remote areas; yet the majority remain near urban centres with little or no comprehensive evacuation programmes. Indeed, neither nuclear proponents nor opponents seem to want discussion of evacuation plans—the former because they do not want to emphasize catastrophe; the latter because evacuation plans may create a false sense of security (Beyea, 1980). The result of inadequate understanding of rare, high-impact incidents is that if such incidents do occur, public agencies are unprepared to respond, planners and policy-makers are discredited and local communities become highly suspicious of (and less cooperative toward) other planning efforts. The question remains as to how best to anticipate or monitor incidents before they pose serious hazard and how to cope once hazard occurs.

THE CENTRALITY OF PROCESS

Experience with natural hazards and with controversial urban facilities and programmes suggest some useful directions for research. Most prominent of the concerns is process—how is the decision to employ a potentially hazardous facility or programme made? Subsets of this concern include the trade-off between fact and value, who participates, the role of experts, and who has responsibility for unwanted impacts. In order to clarify these issues further, it is necessary to examine specific aspects of the problem.

Chief among the concerns with process is the role of citizens in planning and monitoring hazards in the urban environment. Aside from any philosophical or theoretical justifications for such involvement, there are several practical considerations. First, more and more communities and organizations are demanding a say in the way their local environments look. Citizen involvement has grown exponentially in the United States over the past decade. The National Commission on Neighborhoods has identified more than 8000 grassroots neighbourhood organizations. In New York City, alone, there are more than 10 000 block associations. Recent estimates are that there are more than 450 consumer groups in the United States, 350 environmental action organizations, and 650 cases of citizen-initiated environmental legislation. There are over 850 mental health associations (Langton, 1978). A review by the Community Services Administration concluded that there were 226 federal public parti- cipation programmes by 1977, with a steadily expanding role for citizens (Rosenbaum, 1978).

Second, it is becoming more evident that the only sure way of including social value appraisal in impact (or risk) assessments is to include those most susceptible to impact in the initial generation of data and in the analysis of the data for their social meaning. Indeed, it is no longer sufficient to allow experts or policy-makers to define a problem as strictly scientific and therefore *beyond* the comprehension of the lay public. Expect for a few technical advances in chemistry, biology, or medicine, the scientific imperative no longer appears immune to debate (Ravetz, 1971; Noble, 1977). There is considerable difference between the expert's definition of acceptable risk and that defined by potential victims or a well-informed public. This implies that the role of the risk assessor may be limited to one of outlining uncertainties in clearly technical concerns, or trying to specify the outer boundaries of hazard potential.

Third, the range and scope of hazards (particularly those urban hazards which are the concern of our current research) suggest the need for monitoring, observation, screening and management on a massive scale, beyond the regulatory and oversight powers of already overworked government agencies. Some form of citizen involvement might be helpful in this process.

It is important to emphasize that we can draw a general distinction between hazards which are the result of distinct facilities or programmes (nuclear power, highways, group homes, etc.) and hazards which result from an accumulation of programmes or decisions made by many individuals (gentrification, displacement, arson, etc.). The prospects for citizen involvement and early detection are clearly greater for the former—predicting hazard from the cumulative effect of many individual decisions requires far greater precision and sophistication than currently seems available. At best, we can aspire to early detection (rather than early warning) of such hazards. Nonetheless, it is possible to explore structures which might make such detection more likely, especially if we are able to reorientate our thinking about risk to include high-impact rare events in the urban environment.

How can citizens be employed most effectively in decisions over institutional or technological hazards in the urban environment? For what decisions is citizen involvement irrelevant or inefficient? How do we move from the current antagonistic posture assumed by citizens and government or industry to a more cooperative arrangement which will make risks acceptable and safer? Since the role of citizens in the siting of large-scale projects or programmes is at the core of improving our ability to understand, predict, and control hazards in the urban environment, it is appropriate to review past experience with participation of citizens in such projects and to examine suggestions for resolving conflicts between citizens and others.

PARTICIPATION LEGACY

Over the past two decades, participation in government decision-making has expanded to include individuals and communities who have vested interests in specific projects. In some cases, participation was strictly reactive—opposing urban renewal or highways, for example. In more recent instances, participation has become more initiative—community boards advising on budget allocations, for example, or helping to evaluate the effectiveness of local services. The legacy of participation, however, is mixed. There remains no standard form of participation, either generically, or by kind of community or project. Indeed, the purpose and function of participation are controversial. Who should participate, how, why, and when all remain elusive and potentially are sources of conflict. Many still question the value of participation. In reviewing federal public participation programmes, Rosenbaum (1978) cites a number of implementation problems, including a lack of incentives for agencies to comply, incompatibility between citizen and agency objectives, lack of resources to reach diffuse publics, vague standards and disagreement over definitions of terms like 'public participation'.

If local communities are to become involved in helping to determine acceptable trade-offs between benefits and risks, it is necessary to understand the possibilities and limits of participation in such cases. In order to explore this, several examples will be helpful, as well as a more extensive discussion of participation techniques. It is important to note that the participation experience and literature emphasizes the need for decision-making in a short-term context. The continuing role of communities in monitoring and coping with rare, high-impact events has yet to be tried.

Highways

The best-known American example of the role of communities in local decision-making was a result of demands by citizens to affect highway decision-making beginning in the early 1960s. Faced with the prospect of losing homes and neighbourhoods, previously passive individuals in almost every major city in the United States banded together in a series of virulent protests. Many groups were successful and the physical vestige of their success dots the urban landscape as half-completed highways—Boston and San Francisco are notable examples. On the other hand, success in stopping or altering highway routes results in increased expenses of road building and delays in development of some industries which rely on truck transport. As sophisticated as some groups became in their efforts to oppose highway construction, there was little or no mention of the longer-term hazards of highways, particularly the rise in automobile-related deaths which were an inevitable consequence of faster speeds; a profound change in American housing and employment patterns occurred as suburbs were opened up for development.

The Federal Department of Transportation responded to highway protests by trying to incorporate 'community values' into highway decision-making (Mannheim, 1971), and to involve local groups in highway planning (Lupo, Colcord, and Fowler, 1971). By 1976, after more than a decade of rancorous experience, the Department hired consultants to review the participation experience and to list possible participation mechanisms. The report remains one of the most comprehensive reviews of specific participatory techniques, and includes 37 major methods related to 19 steps in the transportation planning process (see Table 8.1) (Jordan et al., 1976).

The role of citizens is primarily advisory. Even those techniques listed as

TABLE 8.1. Participation techniques classified by function

1. Information dissemination	4. Reactive planning
Public information programmes	Citizens' advisory committees
Drop-in centres	Citizen representatives of policy-making boards
Hot lines	Fishbowl planning
Meetings—open information	Interactive cable TV-based participation
2. Information collection	Meetings—neighbourhood
Surveys	Neighbourhood planning councils
Focused group discussions	Policy capturing
Delphi	Value analysis
Community-sponsored meetings	
Public hearings	5. Decision-making
Ombudsman	Arbitrative and mediative planning
	Citizen referendum
3. Initiative planning	Citizen review board
Advocacy planning	Media-based issue balloting
Charrettes	
Community planning centres	6. Participation process support
Computer-based techniques	Citizen employment
Design-in and colour mapping	Citizen honoria
Plural planning	Citizen training
Task Force	Community technical assistance
Workshops	Coordinator or coordinator/catalyst
	Game simulation
	Group dynamics

Source: Jordan et al. (1976), p. 19.

'decision-making' are designed 'not . . . as replacements for the responsibilities of elected officials, nor are decisions made with these techniques final' (Jordan et al., 1976, p. 21). Rather, the consultants note that 'transportation implementation decisions are legally delegated to elected or appointed officials' (Jordan et al., 1976, p. 21). In addition, the actual transportation alternatives are created by professional staffs, over whom citizens may or may not exert influence. As they point out, 'In the unusual case in which a transportation decision appears on a ballot as a REFERENDUM, the citizens do make the decision, but they still do not shape the alternatives' (1976, p. 21). They conclude that, 'Finally, citizens who are drastically aggrieved may still challenge decisions formally through the courts and informally through the political process' (1976, p. 21).

Ironically, after years of litigation and efforts to find alternative means of decision-making in transportation which would avoid the cost and conflict of litigation, the conclusion is that, if citizens want to *choose* the alternatives (rather than simply be *guided* by professional staffs), they may find themselves in court, once again, and there is still no mention of the 'no-build'/no risk option. The only implementation and post-construction mechanisms proposed for citizens are reactive planning procedures or a citizen review board. It may be that the greatest risk from highway planning was, indeed, the possible disruption of neigh-bourhood, for which the existing and proposed participatory mechanisms were inadequate. However, it was not until conflicts occurred over nuclear power plant siting that the tradeoffs between economic gain and human risk became part of the open debate.

Nuclear power plants

Opposition to nuclear power plant siting has now spread worldwide, involving many thousands of demonstrators in Germany, France, Switzerland, and the United States. Stever (1980, p. 1) observes that opposition falls into two general categories—'that which is concerned with environmental or economic, social, and land use impacts of a particular facility, and that which is related to safety, in the sense of concern over radiation generated as a consequence of the nuclear fuel cycle'. In the United States, opposition based on environmental and other site-specific issues is organized and legal. Opposition based on safety is extra-legal. This distinction is important, and reflects the fact that regulations and laws governing siting criteria focus on the narrower definitions of social impact assessment and participation. One result, as Stever (1980, p. 2) notes, is that 'there are signs that increasing numbers of people are abandoning the licensing arena for civil disobedience'.

Both the general regulations specified in the National Environmental Policy Act of 1969 and the specific actions of the Nuclear Regulatory Commission focus attention on site-specific criteria for power plants. Standards for safety are unclear, but tend to take a moderate view of probable risk. Part 100 of the Nuclear Regulatory Commission regulations (issued in 1962) attempted to establish general criteria for the location of nuclear reactors as related to population clusters. More specifically, Section 100.3(c) defines the concept of 'population centre distance' (PCD) as being 'the distance from the reactor to the nearest boundary of a densely populated center containing more than about 25 000 residents' (cited in Stever, 1980, p. 59). The functional meaning of the PCD is not clear. The well-known siting case at the Seabrook, New Hampshire, power plant was resolved in favour of a theoretical definition of risk which was confined to 'postulated' or 'credible' accidents. Such 'postulated' accidents are those accidents for which safety systems are designed and are of less magnitude than other possible but less probable ('incredible') accidents, such as a core meltdown (Stever, 1980, pp. 63, 68). Stever concludes (p. 68) that 'It is . . . clear that no consideration whatever is being given to 'catastrophic' accidents, even though the potential occurrence of such an accident is at least in part behind the development of the PCD concept'.

Despite different legal systems (Roman versus civil law, for example) other countries have sometimes allowed their courts to focus on the safety issue. Most prominent is Germany, where, since 1972, the courts have interpreted the Atom Law to mean that safety must take precedence over economic development and promotion of nuclear power (Nelkin and Pollack, 1980a). The Brokdorf decision of 1977 suspended work on nuclear power plants based, in part, on the inadequacy of waste disposal planning. Later the same year, a higher court in Whyl made the important connection between *degree* of potential harm and extent of precautions. Nonetheless, this issue remains undecided—other courts have ruled that a worst-case scenario is not relevant; that safety within the bounds of existing technology is sufficient justification for construction (Nelkin and Pollack, 1980a). In any case, the German experience has opened the door to a degree of judicial review and consideration of risk that has not yet been evident in the United States.

The minimalist view of potential hazards from nuclear reactor accidents in the United States is reflected, as well, in the structuring of insurance against such accidents. The Price–Anderson Act, originally passed in 1957 and now renewed until 1987, provides a maximum of $560 million accident coverage per reactor accident (a figure which has not been changed in 24 years). The estimated cost of an accident as specified in the 1957 WASH-740, or Brookhaven Report, was $7 billion in property damage alone. Recent estimates of the cost of damages due to the Three Mile Island accident far exceed the maximum amount, including $24 million per month being paid by the utility's customers just for replacement power supplies. In addition, the Price–Anderson Act places a 10-year limit on liability, thus implicitly acknowledging that cancers or other long-term diseases related to radiation exposure are not considered significant. Recently, owners of chemical dumps were required to purchase liability insurance for fires, explosions, or other accidents, and, also, against pollution of groundwater. The requirements are small–$1 million for accidents; $3 million for pollution of ground water (*New York Times*, 1981). The United States government's stance toward nuclear safety or toxic contamination clearly indicates severe discounting of the probability of major accident or long-term risk (Alliance of American Insurers, 1979).

What is problematic about both the assumptions of siting and of insurance in the case of accident is that the decision on determining the degree of risk and its subsequent compensation has been established by a regulatory agency on the one hand, and Act of Congress on the other. This removes the decision on acceptable risk from those most immediately at risk—namely, local constituents. Thus, it is clear why opposition based on safety has assumed extra-legal strategies—there is simply no provision for considerations of safety or risk to be decided by local populations.

By discounting participation on the one hand, or excluding it by definition or law on the other, the legacy of highways and nuclear power plant siting leaves little optimism for meaningful involvement by local impacted populations in the decision to locate, or in trade-offs necessary to make hazards acceptable. Nevertheless, there is a limited body of experience to suggest directions for involvement of potentially impacted populations which try to balance scientific prerogatives and social values. Before exploring some of these options, it is necessary to outline some of the other constraints on who should decide 'how safe is safe enough'.

CRITERIA FOR DECISION PROCESS

After reviewing the experience in several European countries and the United States, Nelkin and Pollack (1980b) outline the needs for a process which allows for airing and resolving opposing views on technological or institutional issues which pose risk to society. Chief among these is the definition of the problem, or the real basis for conflict, in any given case. Thus, for instance, Nelkin and Pollack (1980b) note that the nuclear issue is symbolic of concerns with governance of societies—centralization, the role of government, the role of regulation, the role of the scientist and expert, etc: 'Is opposition to a technology really based on concern about risk or is this a surrogate for more fundamental social concerns?' Nelkin and Pollack, 1980b, p. 243) Informational or advisory strategies, by focusing narrowly on local concerns or questions of fact divorced from social values, ignore issues of long-term hazard (disruption; death) and ethics.

Other critical needs include (see Krinsky, 1979; Nelkin and Pollack, 1980b):

(1) careful consideration and the weight granted to social and political concerns;
(2) clear delineation of the involvement of affected interests, including a role for impacted populations and public interest groups;
(3) unbiased management of the dispute;
(4) fair distribution of expertise, including money available for technical advocates;
(5) real choice (including the no-build alternative);
(6) a clearly defined decision process, including entrance points for citizen involvement and forms of citizen involvement.

Scientific prerogative and normative evaluation

Several other issues are peculiar to decisions which involve complex technical or institutional change, such as nuclear energy development, genetic research, weapons production, supersonic transport, etc. Scientists are reluctant to give up what is seen as their traditional prerogative to pursue whatever scientific advance they feel appropriate. Politicians, too, often assume that experts should be left to 'tinker'; and that they alone know the potential of serendipitous research and 'following one's nose'. When it comes to decisions over technological issues, it is necessary to ask whether citizens can judge the value of scientific research; or whether it is necessary to use other scientists as judges (even those with no vested interest in a particular project). The scientific prerogative is compounded by government decision-making, which is frequently obscure or ambiguous. Bureaucracies guard their decisional terrain.

Finally, there is a great deal of confusion over the relationship between scientific fact and normative evaluation. This is a result of the 'naturalistic fallacy', which Shrader-Frechette (1980) defines as the use of inappropriate evidence to substantiate an ethical or policy conclusion. The naturalistic fallacy takes a number of forms, which include: (1) replacing ethics with norms relevant to the natural sciences; (2) deriving 'ought (evaluative, normative, emotive, or prescriptive)' statements from 'is (non-evaluative, descriptive, or factual)' statements; and (3) failing to consider the 'open question' (Shrader-Frechette, 1980, p. 136).

The first error involves the use of scientific reasons alone to justify ethical beliefs. This is often done in the nuclear debate, when a very low risk of death is equated with the acceptability of taking the risk. The second error flows from the erroneous equation of something which is desired with something which is desirable. In other words, simply because many people watch television does not mean that they *ought* to watch it. The third error comes from the attempt to define something which is good without asking *why* it is good. Definition as good does not *make* it good.

Shrader-Frechette's exploration of these problems leads her to conclude that future evaluations of technology ought to focus on:

(1) the moral acceptability, rather than merely on the magnitude, of technological benefits and risks;
(2) the ethical constraints operative in deciding to implement an involuntarily-imposed (as opposed to a voluntarily chosen) technology;
(3) the moral significance of 'statistically insignificant' increases in technology-induced fatalities; and
(4) the value presuppositions hidden in employing what is 'normal' or 'necessary' as a criterion for acceptable policy regarding technology (Shrader-Frechette, 1980, pp. 156–157).

It is not necessary for risk assessments in the urban environment to include all of the criteria suggested by our review of the experience with highways and nuclear power plants, or the suggestions of Nelkin and Pollack and Shrader-Frechette. Nonetheless, the criteria, by focusing on the potential hazard of low probability, high-impact incidents, provide a valuable checklist. At the least, the reasons for *not* including social and political considerations, fair distribution of experts, or ethical constraints, for example, should be clear. We explore some of the practical applications of a 'checklist' in the next section.

ACCEPTABLE RISK AND THE SCIENCE COURT

The most direct attempt thus far to include considerations of safety from a citizen perspective in the decision to pursue technological change is the science court. Originally proposed as a panel of 'scientist judges' (Task Force, 1976) presided over by a disinterested referee, the concept evolved into a panel of lay judges in an adversary hearing in which expert proponents of opposing scientific positions argue their cases (Kantrowitz, 1977), and finally into a broad-based review of safety issues involved in the pursuit of scientific research (US Department of Commerce, 1977).

The best-known example of a science court procedure is the Cambridge Experimentation Review Board, which examined the safety of proposed recombinant DNA research at Harvard and MIT. Citizens, chosen by the City Manager of Cambridge, Massachusetts, were given a broad mandate. They were asked to: (1) review methods of physical and biological containment; (2) review methods for monitoring compliance with applicable procedural safeguards; (3) review methods for monitoring compliance with safeguards applicable to physical containment; (4) review procedures for handling accidents; and (5) advise the Commissioner of Health and Hospitals on the reviews, findings, and recommendations of the Board (Cambridge Experimentation Review Board, 1977).

The Cambridge Review Board read all relevant documentation (academic, government, popular press), heard over 75 hours of testimony from more than 35 individuals representing both sides of the controversy, attended a forum in which opponents and proponents were questioned by an audience, and conducted open-line telephone conversations with interested parties outside the state. In addition, the Board conducted a 5-hour marathon mock courtroom with cross-examination of witnesses by advocates, and visited the laboratories where research would be performed. This research demonstration included a mock experiment duplicating the stages of recombinant DNA research. To aid in understanding documents, a technical assistant was available and experts were asked to phrase technical concepts in laymen's terms (Cambridge Experimentation Review Board, 1977; Krimsky, 1978).

The results of the Cambridge experience were that the Board voted unanimously to allow recombinant DNA research, but with certain amendments to the National Institute of Health guidelines for such research. Specifically, the Board wanted more assurance than it felt was provided by the general federal guidelines. It was satisfied with protections against any *reasonable likelihood* of a biohazard, but was not satisfied with protection against *extremely unlikely* possibilities. The recommendations include a manual and formal training on laboratory safeguards, monitoring safety procedures and potential hazardous releases and establishment of a Cambridge Biohazards Committee (CBC). The CBC consists of the Commissioner of Public Health, the Chairman of the Health

Policy Board and three members appointed by the City Manager, the executive in charge of city government. The CBC was designed to insure compliance with those concerns expressed by the Review Board, including all specific proposals for research, developing a procedure for those involved in research to report violations without retribution, conducting site visits, and modifying recommendations to reflect future developments.

Critique of the science court

The experience of the Cambridge Experimentation Review Board reflects several important innovations. First, lay citizens were shown to be capable of understanding and evaluating potential hazards from highly technological research (McAllister, 1980). Indeed, their understanding went so far as to enable them to recommend specific guidelines for overseeing and monitoring research procedures; that is, system hazard as well as construction hazard. Second, the Board was able to introduce into the issue of scientific research a degree of concern with low-risk, high-impact events ('extremely unlikely possibilities'), whereas previous government concern had focused primarily on high-risk, low-impact events ('any reasonable likelihood'). Third, the Board introduced a concern with continued monitoring, including a recommendation to the federal government that it make health monitoring programmes a requirement for funding recombinant DNA research. Finally, citizens were able to introduce a concern not only for the surrounding environment in which research is to be conducted, but for those actually doing the research. Written manuals, a training programme, and a federal registry of all workers involved in such research for the purpose of conducting long-term epidemiological studies, were all part of the recommendations. In short, the Review Board was able to take a broader and more long-term view of recombinant DNA research than government guidelines or those involved in the research seemed willing to do.

Yet, despite the important concerns which the Board was able to address and for which it offered specific recommendations, some nagging questions remain. These relate primarily to the way in which the science court was conducted, leading one to wonder whether some issues were not considered, or considered in a manner which belied citizen concerns.

The Experimentation Review Board consisted of eight people. They met over a period of 7 months, on an average of twice weekly, for at least 2 hours each time, not counting time spent reviewing materials. Aside from the obvious issue of how Board members *should* be selected, it is clear that those involved must be highly dedicated and must have considerable time and intelligence to participate. This is not a simple problem for a heterogeneous society, in which much of the impact of hazardous or threatening facilities may be felt by low-income populations with neither the time nor the education to participate fully. Cambridge, Massachusetts, is perhaps the most highly educated community in the United

States, and leaves one to wonder whether the science court could be duplicated elsewhere. In addition, the science court allows both proponents and opponents to present their views. This assumes that the sides are well developed, articulated, and have equal resources. This is almost never the case, especially when the issue involves highly technological concerns which demand elaborate and expensive scientific procedures or experimentation. As Turner (1977) notes, millions of dollars were spent on legal and scientific activities in support of the use of cyclamates in the general food industry. Its critics had virtually no resources and could only raise general questions as to its safety.

Finally, by its own admission, the Review Board did not consider philosophical, ethical, or social considerations involved in the conduct of recombinant DNA research. Thus, although it did expand the issue to consider low-risk, high-impact events, it is possible that it overemphasized the degree to which safety can be narrowly confined to technical considerations. Social or ethical considerations might include the psychological impact on local communities of conducting hazardous research nearby, as well as the more general implications for society of doing such research. The 'resolution' of the safety issue, narrowly conceived, begs the question of the conduct of such research, to begin with. That issue was not questioned.

As was discovered in highway cases, even the most ardent supporter of highways would be hard pressed to decide between the highway programme, as a whole, and the destruction of his home. In an analogous situation, supporters of the *idea* of defence became vehement opponents of the MX missile system when it threatened their land and livelihood (Albrecht, 1981). Thus, to ignore all but the specific safety issue is to ignore, perhaps, critical issues which override the safety issue in scope and magnitude (the definition problem). Indeed, on most of the points on a decisional checklist, the science court leaves many questions unanswered and yet, despite its disadvantages, the current interest in the science court concept means it is appropriate to ask whether its continued use would be of any value in the resolution of other technical issues and whether it is a substitute for, addendum to, or contradiction to other forms of citizen participation.

First, it is important to understand that the science court is probably a misnomer. It is not a court, *per se*, because it does not render a final decision; nor is there an appeals process; nor are the rules and operations established in any formal sense. Other terms have been proposed—'technical board of inquiry' appearing to be the most descriptive. Second, as Turner (1977) points out, it is important to distinguish between the concepts of truth and justice and their relationship to a science court. The function of the science court is to establish truth. The truth which is established is then injected into an administrative or political or legal process which attempts to establish justice. Thus, for instance, the science court should not consider whether food additives are necessary to feed the underdeveloped world; only to provide the parameters for the use of food additives—in other words, to indicate that food additives will preserve food and, also, perhaps cause hypertension. The more specific the court can be in delineating the exact benefits and costs, the more helpful will be the result for policy making. Which raises another critical point. In almost all cases involving risk, there is an issue of *degree*—thus, 'how safe is safe enough?' Policy demands an either/or conclusion from the science court, whereas the court may be most appropriately used to delineate the range of risks and uncertainties (Holdren, 1977).

PUBLIC BOARD OF INQUIRY

Recognizing the role of scientific inquiries like the science court as a method of delineating the range of scientific fact, the Food and Drug Administration established a Public Board of Inquiry to examine the issue of food additives. The explicit intention of the Board was to speed the process toward federal court, not to avoid legal issues.

The FDA's Public Board of Inquiry was chosen by the Commissioner from among names submitted by interested parties on different sides of the issue—in the food additive case, one each from opposite sides, and one from the Commissioner's staff. These three persons are scientists qualified in the particular area under consideration, and their work is defined by the interested parties as a specific set of issues to be addressed and resolved. Once the Board and issue are determined, the sides are presented (Turner, 1977). The Board of Inquiry considers both scientific and social policy questions; it makes a statement on the facts involved (truthfulness and range of truthfulness) and recommends action(s) to be taken by the Commissioner (adopt additives; do not adopt; adopt with modifications). The Commissioner has the final decision, except, of course, if the federal court becomes involved.

The critical difference between a board of public inquiry and a science court (or board of technical inquiry) is that, in the former case, the procedure for resolving social policy questions is well established. In this case, the board of inquiry is designed to make sure that the procedure allows for all parties to gain input. On the other hand, a science court is designed for those issues in which the procedure for resolving the problem of safety, for example, is not well established. Indeed, even the facts are in question. Thus, the science court is supposed to revolve around the issue of establishing what is factual, what is not factual, and what is partially factual. Thus, the science court is one step removed from the process of deciding acceptable risk—it can only identify the range of risk which will exist under different parameters of scientific behaviour and environmental situations. It parallels the distinction of the naturalistic fallacy between is and ought.

What is suggested, then, is that the science court can be a critical part of a process, but that the necessity of designing a process which includes all parties to an issue is still unresolved. A board of inquiry can be the second stage of a science court—once facts are understood, the board of inquiry can try to understand the *relevance* of the facts for policy; in other words, the significance which different parties put on the facts. Is *x* degree of risk acceptable? What are the outer limits of uncertainty in risk?

Even if the Board of Inquiry can determine the answer to such tricky questions, it still is not the end of a process of siting or building facilities which pose potential risks. As in the case of the food additive controversy, a further process must exist for challenges to decision-making by established authorities, or for more input into the decision process.

Further problems with a science court or public board of inquiry

There are more substantive reasons for the inadequacy of a science court procedure or public board of inquiry to apply to an issue like nuclear power. A central problem is that for such procedures to work, the sides have to agree on the major issues to be addressed, the propriety and authority of the mechanism which has been established, and the process of resolution of continued disagreements. The nuclear power debate does not satisfy any of these criteria. Most importantly, the disagreements in the nuclear debate do not centre on technical facts, but on the diversity of issues, their relative importance, and the process for resolution (Holdren, 1977). Holdren's list of critical issues, in order, includes fear of the spread of nuclear weapons, theft, sabotage, and routine emissions. He points out that his list is ranked inversely to the size of the technical component of the issue. In particular, the human factor—in theft or sabotage, as operating error, or in policy-making toward weapons development—far outweighs individual technical issues like amount of emissions. Similarly, opposition to the proposed mobile MX nuclear weapons system centres on the feeling by local residents that the system is being imposed on them, on the lack of adequate consideration of alternatives, on the ultimate usefulness of the proposed system, and on economic and social hardships which the system would inflict on the local area. Again, attitudes and process dominate the reasons for opposition.

The other major objections which Holdren raises to a science court in the nuclear power debate are related to the difficulty of obtaining appropriate information. These difficulties include relevant information that simply does not exist, inaccessible information (suppressed information is common in the nuclear debate, for both defensible and indefensible reasons), obscure information, information which is unverifiable, and information which is impenetrable (too technical or too ambiguous, for instance). Holdren recommends that the science court should de-emphasize single valued answers in favour of outlining the magnitude and implications of uncertainty; thus, it should be able to say: 'With this technical problem the magnitude of technical uncertainty is this much. Put that into your decision process. Do you want to buy this bag of uncertainties in exchange for this bag of benefits?' (Holdren, 1977, p. 177). He concludes that the nuclear issue is too intricate for a science court—that simply trying to decide on which issues to address in such a court is too value-laden to make the use of a court appropriate. Politics enters too early and carries too much import to make the science court useful.

We have indicated that the science court and the public board of inquiry do not address the issues raised in a preliminary checklist of decision criteria for such issues as the siting of nuclear power plants. Before turning to issues of management and coping, as well as some more general conclusions about risk in urban environments, it will be useful to review two more examples of ways of dealing with a complex technical and institutional issue—a siting jury for a nuclear waste repository, and mediation/arbitration in environmental disputes.

SITING JURY

Another mechanism proposed specifically for the nuclear waste issue is the siting jury. Lee (1980), its originator, argues that the notion of 'consultation and concurrence' embedded in current legislation is vague and ambiguous, and therefore demands clarification. His 'siting jury' to strengthen concurrence envisages States as third parties in the conflict which he perceives as occurring primarily between the federal government (pronuclear) and a series of environmentalists, local governments, and nuclear activists (antinuclear). The siting jury would consist of five elected State and local officials randomly selected from recommendations by various national associations. The jurors make their recommendation to the President of the United States, who has ultimate authority for site selection.

There are a number of unresolved problems with the siting jury concept. Most problematic is the final authority granted the President. After admitting that the federal government has been the nuclear industry's advocate for further nuclear development, Lee suggests that the final decision rest with the federal government. This leads to further problems. It is not clear that *any* nuclear opponent would either be chosen for or agree to sit on a siting jury. It is possible, for instance, that the selectors (governors, state legislatures, congressmen, and local officials) will all come from the same political party as the President. If the President, in turn, is strongly pronuclear, the party members would be reluctant to make appointments that would jeopardize their party affiliation, or need for federal support for other projects. A great deal of political bargaining may occur—with certain appointments (assuring siting) leading to increased federal revenues for states. One possible solution is to have the jury elected, and to insure that those who represent both sides are involved in running and voting. This, of course, presents its own problems, but at least avoids the traditional hazards of political influence. In addition, the role of environmentalists and activists is unclear. Given their involvement in the nuclear issue, should their presence be assured on a siting jury?

Once a jury is selected, Lee indicates that they will have a chance to master the complex scientific, managerial, and technical problems of nuclear waste siting but does not show how this will be achieved. As Holdren (1980) argues in his analysis of the science court, control of information, research and public relations has been lopsided in the nuclear debate due to the money and influence of the nuclear industry. The federal government has supported the industry through their vast array of consultants and other technical experts on the payroll. The antinuclear activists, on the other hand, lack research support and have mounted attacks based primarily on re-reading or interpretation of government-generated information (when available), and on generating fear. To expect lay jurors to comprehend and analyse information (even technical information made 'readable') is clearly not realistic, and certainly not what Lee has in mind. But the alternative is to conduct something akin to a science court, whose problems have already been raised. Indeed, the entire siting jury process may collapse under the weight of the problem facing science courts—how to judge technical issues—even before equally complex political and managerial concerns can be considered.

Finally, the siting jury is not a jury at all. With the ultimate decision in the hands of the President, it is more appropriately called a 'siting advisory board'. Aside from the problems of representativeness, technical competency, specific questions to be addressed and actual mode of operation, it ignores the 'weighted impact' problem, namely the importance of giving greater weight to those most at risk (Hershberger, 1980). Should not local communities have greater representation than an advisory board consisting of only one representative at an advanced stage in the process? Again, what of those along transport corridors? By not considering such questions, Lee's siting jury underemphasizes the fundamental issues of who is at risk and what the magnitude of the risk is.

None of the problems with the siting jury which have been raised argue that it is worse than the existing mechanisms to involve state and local authorities in the traditional political system. Indeed, it goes a long way toward clarifying and concretizing 'consultation and concurrence' in the siting of a waste repository. Nonetheless, it does not resolve the problems raised more generally by the set of decision criteria for low-probability/high-risk events—problems which, from our review, seem beyond the means of any one existing or proposed political solution.

MEDIATION/ARBITRATION

If mechanisms for including risk considerations in the decision to proceed with a given programme or project are inadequate, it is perhaps because they are not flexible enough, or because the ultimate decision of whether to proceed with the project is not shared by at-risk populations and policy makers. Variants of mediation or arbitration are designed to address the problems of flexibility and ultimate responsibility.

Mediation defies clear definition, in part because mediation mechanisms are, by definition, evolutionary. Yet, certain informal ground rules have been identified. These include voluntary participation by affected interests and policy-makers; some power balance between the various parties (including assurance that solutions will be implemented); a mediator with no vested interest in the issue, and resolution only when agreement is reached by all parties (Greene, et al., 1980).

Mediation

It is in the last proviso that mediation and arbitration differ. In mediation, the mediator(s) does not have the authority to impose a solution; rather, solutions are dependent upon mutual agreement. The mediator's role is 'to insure that all positions are heard and included in whatever solution is reached' (Greene et al., 1980). Two types of mediation have been used in environmental issues—participation-oriented and settlement-oriented. They can be sequential. Participation-oriented mediation is essentially an information and communication process, whereby the parties involved are informed of the facts of a given case and mediation is designed to structure or organize issues (Abrams and Berry, 1977). Solution to the siting problem is neither desirable nor helpful at this stage. Settlement-oriented mediation is designed to come to some resolution after the parties involved have come to an impasse. Greene et al. (1980) point out that it is necessary for the issues in mediation to be spelled out and defined clearly. If participation-oriented mediation is not effective, settlement is unlikely. This implies an ability to communicate; and, more importantly, to come to agreement on the facts. Yet, perception of risk, as was noted for the science court, may not be a factual problem. In addition, unless the relationship between mediation and policy-making is clear, the mediation process may be superfluous.

Thus, mediation leaves many questions unresolved. For instance, what kind of mediation is appropriate? At what stage? Who should participate? Who will manage the mediation effort? What will be done with the results? Who will fund mediation? Notwithstanding questions of this kind, the experience with mediation suggests that it is helpful in emphasizing and addressing some critical issues, such as the importance of ensuring representation of all interests, the need for neutral technical support, the need for mutually acceptable resolution to problems, and the importance of ensuring the implementation of solutions.

Arbitration

Arbitration is designed to allow for the advantages of openness and communication characteristic of mediation, with a formal provision for ensuring resolution. This is done by granting the arbitrator(s) the power of imposing a solution. As in the public board of inquiry, the parties involved agree to the selection of a board or individual arbitrator. They also agree to abide by the decision of the arbitrator. As in mediation, an arbitration proceeding is dependent on the involvement of all critical parties and their satisfaction that the proceeding pre-empts other political processes. If one party is not satisfied with the solution chosen by the arbitrator, for example, it is assumed that party will not resort to other political or legal mechanisms. If this occurs, the advantage of the arbitration process is lost—resolution is again open to debate and change.

Unfortunately, arbitration is subject to the same practical and theoretical constraints as other approaches to conflict resolution for risk-producing projects. These include confusion of issues, complexity of decision-making, multiple parties, and contradictions between technical facts and public perception. Arbitration, however, has the advantage that solutions are binding to the degree that challenge is difficult and undertaken reluctantly. If arbitrators are carefully chosen and the process of arbitration is meticulously delineated, arbitration can work. However, because of the relatively primitive state-of-the-art of risk assessment for urban hazards, the ability to define issues or analyse them may simply be beyond the promise of arbitration as presently contemplated.

MANAGEMENT OF RISK AND RESPONSE TO HAZARD

If the potential for risk is always uncertain to some degree and if participation or planning cannot possibly anticipate all risks (especially those which are most catastrophic), then an important part of the decision to build or proceed with a programme is related to the effectiveness with which management structures will monitor, observe, and react to risks as they occur. Clark (1980) has argued for adaptive risk management which recognizes the uncertainty and surprise inherent in new technologies. Others have argued for the application of 'human engineering' in the design of technologies, to facilitate monitoring of errors during operation (Rogovin, 1979) and much greater attention to detail in construction and operation (Gilinsky, 1980).

It seems apparent that the design of bureaucratic or other mechanisms for responding to uncertainty or hazard will be subject to many of the political and sociological constraints which hamper risk prediction and planning. Thus, for instance, Davis and Seitz (1980) point out that the definition of disaster and the response to disaster, particularly in developing countries, is influenced by the needs of political regimes to procure outside aid or to reinforce their authority. Clark (1980) argues that regulatory or legislative response to hazard is inappropriate and only serves to reinforce the rigidity which might have caused or escalated the hazard to begin with. Ironically, as more and more regulations and regulatory authorities are created to cope with risk, the ability to respond in new, more appropriate ways seems to diminish (Clark, 1980). As is evident in the nuclear power debate, nuclear proponents seek to justify more nuclear power by minimizing perception of risk than by exploring creative alternatives (Kasper, 1979).

Others have argued that the fact that failures are penalized more than successes are rewarded leads to an avoidance of new technology deployment by public sector decision-makers (Feller, 1981). It is easier to blame failure on inappropriate use of existing means than on incorrect choice of a new approach. This implies that before new structures or procedures are devised for risk management, it is necessary to identify and overcome existing constraints on creating imaginative responses to hazard.

Since it is unlikely that regulatory approaches will be altered dramatically, or that new structures will be devised in their stead, it is appropriate to ask whether there might not be an existing structure through which hazard information and planning could be channelled other than regulatory agencies. For infrastructure hazards, a couple of decades of decentralization experiments in planning suggest a range of possibilities. Among these are zoning boards, community planning boards, citizen review committees, neighbourhood planning councils, and local development corporations. Each of these is, in some sense, close to the needs of potentially affected parties in the urban environment. Yet, each also operates within the constraints of vested interests and organizational goals. Zoning boards, for instance, are often controlled by those who want to preserve the *status quo* within a narrow definition of what is good for a local area. The result has been the exclusion of non-white, low-income populations from the majority of suburban locales. Community planning boards, although less subject to concentrated political influence and elitism, display their own forms of insular behaviour when it comes to accepting change in local areas. Local development corporations, by focusing on industrial or commercial development, may sacrifice community for profit and, therefore, underemphasize potentially hazardous facilities.

Issues of bureaucratic stagnation and avoidance of new solutions and the inadequacy of existing citizen forums to monitor risk suggest the need for new mechanisms to manage and cope with hazard. At a minimum, operating and coping functions need to be separated. Management structures should allow for flexibility while accounting for independent citizen participation.

CONCLUSIONS

We have suggested that there are a range of technological or institutional issues which impact on the urban environment that require study. These manmade rare events affect the daily lives of many of our cities' dwellers.

Assessment

The first item on a proposed agenda for dealing with such hazards is to identify their presence and estimate their scope, magnitude, and severity. This is no simple task. The cataloguing of hazards alone will probably require a major commitment by government agencies and researchers, akin to efforts in natural hazard research. Complex methodological issues will have to be resolved, or at least advanced beyond existing primitive capabilities.

Citizen participation

A second item for an agenda might include delineation of a decision process for selecting and siting hazardous projects or programmes which recognizes the import of affected interests and the acceptance of risk. We have argued that the involvement of citizens in early detection, siting, and monitoring of potentially hazardous technological or institutional changes in the urban environment can be both useful and necessary. Unfortunately, the legacy of participation is such that policy-makers are concerned about their own prerogatives and citizens are equally concerned about cooptation. This is primarily due to narrow and ill-conceived experiences with participation, and the lack of participatory strategies which respond to the demands of decision criteria. Such criteria can delineate the role of citizens while making policy-makers more comfortable with citizen involvement. None of the existing or proposed schema—science court, public board of inquiry, siting jury, mediation, arbitration—alone satisfy all of the basic criteria, although some combination might prove satisfactory.

Any effort to involve citizens, no matter how worthy in theory, must confront the reality of decision-making. The discrete nature of decisions for particular facilities (highways, power plants) makes involvement by citizens more likely. The constraints on such involvement are strong, but the ball park is defined. For other changes in the urban environment which are more diffuse in decision-making or scope, such as displacement due to gentrification, or arson, the monitoring role seems more easily adopted for citizens. Nonetheless, even if decisions are made by many individuals rather than one government agency, the effect of hazard can be just as severe for those displaced or who lose their jobs. In such circumstances, monitoring is critical; but some means of aggregating the separate incidents must exist.

Legislation and regulation

A third item on the agenda for change is revision of legislative and regulatory processes to recognize the significance of risks in the urban environment. This should include extending the discussion of safety beyond immediate impact, perhaps involving a modification of the traditional social impact assessment. Experience does not give much hope for believing that existing regulatory processes will anticipate hazard before it occurs. A recent congressional committee in the United States concluded, for instance, that the existing federal inspection system for nuclear power plants 'is not capable of offering genuine assurance that the nuclear power industry is being safely operated' (Molotsky, 1981, p. 1). A growing list of power plant accidents attests to their findings.

Management

The same congressional committee which examined the federal inspection system also observed that, 'there are serious and widespread management failings in the nuclear industry' (Molotsky, 1981, p. 44). Toxic waste disposal is virtually unregulated (Blumenthal, 1981). Thus, a fourth agenda item is improvement in the management of potentially hazardous projects and programmes to ensure better early-warning procedures and the ability to respond to hazard. This will involve overcoming many bureaucratic stumbling blocks, including resistance to change and antagonism towards outside review. It may even necessitate altering the profit motive to reward accountability and competence rather than strict economic efficiency (Clarke, 1973).

Liability

A fifth item on the agenda is the issue of liability or responsibility for error. This involves at least two concerns. First is the ability to determine what went wrong and who is responsible. The failure of the DC10 aircraft over Chicago seems to have been the result of a complex of management mistakes and regulatory oversight for which one person or agency cannot alone be blamed (Lowrance, 1980).

A second concern with liability is who will pay for error. As indicated, the federal government has assumed the greatest burden of responsibility for nuclear accidents, under an agreement that includes use of tax monies as well as more standard insurance arrangements; but the definition of insurable impacts is highly controversial. The United States government has also provided a 'Superfund' for chemical spills and toxic waste dumps and mandatory insurance for handlers and disposers of hazardous wastes (other than nuclear). Nonetheless, no such insurance exists for risks in the urban environment.

Insurance against *all* such risks would be prohibitive, for both insured and insurers. Yet, the range of insurance possibilities might be extended. At the least, some examination of the possibilities for insurance should be part of an agenda, especially as the identification of responsibility becomes more elusive. The trade-off between societal obligation and individual obligation should be part of such considerations. The shift of insurance concepts from sudden occurrences to 'seepage' events (like radiation exposure) also requires more examination for urban phenomena.

Burden of proof

Underlying most of these agenda items is the implicit moral criterion that the burden of proof lies on those who want to increase hazard in the urban environment. We have argued that increasing risks suggest that it is time to apply this criterion to practical considerations of risk identification, improved decision processes, more effective legislation and regulation, improved methods of hazard management, provision of insurance, and response to hazard. Hopefully, we have provided some direction and an agenda which can enhance these efforts.

REFERENCES

Abrams, N. E. and Berry, R. S. (1977). Mediation: a better alternative to science courts. *Bulletin of the Atomic Scientists*, **33**, 50–53.

Albrecht, S. L. (1981). *The MX Missile: An Analysis of Community Response*, Brigham Young University, Utah (mimeo).

Alliance of American Insurers (1979). *Nuclear Power, Safety and Insurance Issues of the 1980s: The Insurance Industry's Viewpoint*. New York (mimeo).

Ashford, N. A. and Hattis, D. B. (1980). *The Limitations of Comparative Risk Assessment in Decisions Concerning Health, Safety, and the Environment*, Testimony in US House of Representatives, Committee on Science and Technology, Hearings on Comparative Risk Assessment, Washington, DC, pp. 320–328.

Beyea, J. (1980). Emergency planning for reactor accidents. *Bulletin of the Atomic Scientists*, **36**, 40–45.

Blumenthal, R. (1981). Jersey registration law for waste haulers largely ignored. *New York Times*, **130**, B2.

Cambridge Experimentation Review Board (1977). The Cambridge Experimentation Review Board. *Bulletin of the Atomic Scientists*, **33**, 23–27.

Clark, W. C. (1980). Witches, floods, and wonder drugs: historical perspectives on risk management. In R. C. Schwing, and W. A. Albers Jr (Eds.), *Societal Risk Assessment*, Plenum Press, New York, pp. 287–318.

Clarke, C. W. (1973). Profit maximization and the extinction of animal species. *Journal of Political Economy*, **81**. 950–961.

Curtis, R. and Hogan, E. (1980). *Nuclear Lessons*, Stackpole Books, Harrisburg, Penn.

Davis, M. and Seitz, S. T. (1980). Disasters and Government: A Theory and Some Data, paper presented at International Congress of Arts and Sciences of the World University, Cambridge, Mass.

Feller, E. (1981). Public-sector innovation as 'conspicuous production'. *Policy Analysis*, **7**, 1–20.

Finsterbusch, K. (1980). *Understanding Social Impacts*, Sage Publications, Beverly Hills, Cal.

Gilinsky, V. (1980). The impact of Three Mile Island. *Bulletin of the Atomic Scientists*, **36**, 18–20.

Greene, M. R., Lindell, M. K. Nealey, S. M. and Drexler, J. A. Jr (1980). *Nuclear Waste Management and Environmental Mediation: An Exploratory Analysis*, Battelle Memorial Institute, Human Affairs Research Centers, Seattle, Washington.

Hershberger, J. (1980). *A Comparative Assessment of Repository Siting Models with Respect to Intergovernmental and Public Relations*, Institute of Governmental Studies, University of California, Berkeley, Cal.

Holdren, J. (1977). The Nuclear Power Controversy, in US Department of Commerce. *Proceedings of the Science Court Colloquium*, Leesburg, Va, pp. 170–178.

Jordan, D., Arnstein, S. Gray, J. Metcalf, E. Torrey, W. and F. Mills. (1976). *Effective Citizen participation in Transportation Planning* (2 volumes), US Department of Transportation, Federal Highway Administration, Washington, DC.

Kantrowitz, A. (1977). The science court experiment: criticisms and responses. *Bulletin of the Atomic Scientists*, **33**, 44–50.

Kasper, R. (1979). 'Real' versus perceived risk: implications for policy. In G. T. Goodman, and W. D. Rowe (Eds.), *Energy Risk Management*, Academic Press, Washington, DC, pp. 87–95.

Kasperson, R. and Kates, R. (1980). *The Management of Technological Hazards*, Center for Technology, Environment, and Development, Worcester, Mass. (mimeo).

Kates, R. (1977). Summary report. In R. Kates, (Ed.), *Managing Technological Hazard: Research Needs and Opportunities*, Institute of Behavioural Science, University of Colorado, Boulder, Col.

Krimsky, S. (1978). A citizen court in the recombinant DNA debate. *Bulletin of the Atomic Scientists*, **34**, 37–43.

Krimsky, S. (1979). Citizen participation in scientific and technological decision-making, part II. In S. Langton, (Ed.), *Citizen Participation Perspectives*, Lincoln Filene Center for Citizenship and Public Affairs, Medford, Mass., pp. 181–186.

Langton, S. (1978). Citizen participation in America: current reflections on the state of the art. In S. Langton, (Ed.), *Citizen Participation in America*, Lexington Books, Lexington, Mass., pp. 1–12.

Lee, K. (1980). A federalist strategy for nuclear waste management. *Science*, **208**, 679–684.

Lowrance, W. W. (1980). The nature of risk, in R. Schwing, and W. A. Albers, Jr (Eds.), *Societal Risk Assessment*, Plenum Press, New York, pp. 5–17.

Lupo, A., Colcord, F. and Fowler, E. P. (1971). *Rites of Way: The politics of Transportation in Boston and the US City*, Little, Brown and Company, Boston.

Manheim, M. (1971). *Community Values in Highway Location and Design: A Procedural Guide*, MIT Urban Systems Laboratory, Cambridge, Mass.

McAllister, D. M. (1980). *Evaluation in Environmental Planning*, MIT Press, Cambridge, Mass.

Massam, B. H. (1980). *Spatial Search*, Pergamon Press, Oxford.

Molotsky, I. (1981). A US panel faults nuclear inspection. *New York Times*, **130**, 1 and 44.

Nelkin, D. and Pollack, M. (1980a). French and German courts on nuclear power. *Bulletin of the Atomic Scientists*, **36**, 36–62.

Nelkin, D. and Pollack, M. (1980b). Problems and procedures in the regulation of technological risk, In R. Schwing, and W. A. Albers, Jr (Eds.), *Social Risk Assessment*, Plenum Press, New York, pp. 233–253.

New York Times (1981). US gives owners of waste dumps 6 months to insure against hazards, **130, 2 January**, A12.

Noble, D. (1977). *America By Design*, Oxford University Press, Oxford.

Ravetz, J. R. (1971). *Scientific Knowledge and Its Social Problems*, Oxford University Press, New York.

Robbins, A. (1980). *Risk Assessment—Too Complex—Too Soon*, Testimony in US House of Representatives, Committee on Science and Technology, Hearings on Comparative Risk Assessment, Washington, DC, pp. 347–349.

Rogovin, M. (Ed.) (1979). *Three Mile Island, Vol. 1*, Nuclear Regulatory Commission, Special Inquiry Group, Washington, DC.

Rosenbaum, W. A. (1978). Public involvement as reform and ritual: the development of federal participation programs. In S. Langton (Ed.), *Citizen Participation in America*, Lexington Books, Lexington, Mass., pp. 81–96.

Schwing, R. C. and Albers, W. A. Jr (1980). *Societal Risk Assessment*, Plenum Press, New York.

Shrader-Frechette, K. S. (1980). *Nuclear Power and Public Policy*, D. Reidel, Boston.

Stever, D. W., Jr. (1980). *Seabrook and the Nuclear Regulatory Commission*, University Press of New England, Hanover, NH.

Task Force of the Presidential Advisory Group on Anticipated Advances in Science and Technology (1976). The science court experiment: an interim report. *Science*, **193**, 653–656.

Turner, J. S. (1977). The food additive controversy. In US Department of Commerce. *Proceedings of the Science Court Colloquium*, Leesburg, Va. pp. 161–169.

US Departement of Commerce, Commerce Technical Advisory Board. (1977). *Proceedings of the Colloquium on the Science Court*, Leesburg, Va.

US House of Representatives, Committee on Science and Technology, subcommittee on Science, Research, and Technology (1980). *Hearings on Comparative Risk Assessment*, Washington, DC.

Whyte, A. and Burton, I. (1980). *Environmental Risk Assessment*, John Wiley and Sons, New York.

Wolpert, J. (1980). The dignity of risk. *Transactions, Institute of British Geographers*, **5**, 391–401.

Geography and the Urban Environment
Progress in Research and Applications, Volume V
Edited by D. T. Herbert and R. J. Johnston
© 1982 John Wiley & Sons Ltd.

Chapter 9

Crime, Criminal Justice Policy and the Urban Environment*

John Lowman

INTRODUCTION

The relation of crime and justice

One of the more problematic characteristics of geographical perspectives of crime as they have developed to date concerns the analytic separation of crime from both law and justice. In some studies this separation is only analytically implicit: Keith Harries' *Geography of Crime and Justice* (1974) examines both spatial variations in the incidence of crime (as measured by the official statistics) and spatial variations in the judicial response to crime but the possible relationship of the two is never considered. Daniel Georges (1978, p. 2) makes the separation explicit by suggesting that the geography of justice lies beyond the scope of a geography of crime. Even in Harries's most recent work *Crime and the Environment*, where he acknowledges that the effects of the criminal justice environment in the patterning of crime 'should not be entirely overlooked', such considerations lie entirely beyond the range of his discussion (1980, pp. 63–64, 116). Although Harries' publishers claim that 'this monograph focuses on the relationships of human and physical environments to the origin of criminal behaviour . . . the emphasis is on the broad set of conditions and interactions in which people find themselves, whether they involve cities, neighbourhoods, neighbours, or some aspect of physical conditions', nowhere is there any systematic consideration of what must surely be one of the most important dimensions of the social environment relating to crime: the law itself.

David Herbert represents an exception to the geographical mainstream by suggesting in two recent papers (Herbert, 1977; 1979) that the social processes underlying crime patterns are of key significance, but only to lament that while the possibility of research into the antecedents of crime patterns has been identified, their importance remains untested. Yet there are examples of the impact of the sociolegal context on crime and crime patterns reported in a wide-

* The comments of David Ley on a Postdraft of this chapter are appreciated.

ranging but often unconnected literature. Much of this concerns the social impact of criminal justice policy, and as a result there has not been much of an interest in the way in which what Harries calls the 'criminal justice environment' influences crime or criminal residence patterns. Indeed much of the criminological literature is remiss in its lack of consideration of the subtle relations between law and crime in general (aside from the deterrent effect of law, and the deviance amplification process associated with criminal labelling). Recognizing these deficiencies, the purpose of this paper is to begin to organize the fragmentary evidence describing how crime control policy (especially law enforcement protocol, both formal and informal) conditions crime in general, and crime occurrence and criminal residence patterns in particular. For the most part the paper deals specifically with criminal justice/legal policy, but some consideration is also given to related social control and crime control measures. The discussion focuses on two dimensions of the effects of social control and criminal justice policy on crime: firstly, their influence on public and scientific images of crime and criminals and, secondly, their influence on actual behaviour patterns. The chapter is thus divided into two parts: crime control and the perception of crime, and crime control and actual behaviour.

Crime control and the perception of crime

The first sense in which crime control policy conditions crime patterns (and, by implication, criminal residence patterns also) lies in the meaning attributed to official crime statistics. The issue is whether such statistics represent the actual incidence of crime, or whether they represent an image of crime – an image which serves as a self-fulfilling prophecy in the way crime statistics are produced. At issue is the nature of the 'dark figure of crime', that not actually reported to the police. The usual geographical interpretation suggests that criminal incidence statistics represent an unbiased sample of the true population. In this interpretation, bias is conceived of as 'instrumental', located in such factors as the poor and uncoordinated reporting practices of different police jurisdictions.

Alternative epistemological positions, however, suggest that the bias of official statistics is uneven; that either (1) systematic differences occur in the reporting rates of different social groups, and for different kinds of crime; and/or (2) police discretionary powers operate differentially to produce different rates of criminalization of different social groups or classes. In this interpretation of statistical bias as 'essential' rather than 'instrumental' the meaning of statistics is problematic in terms of *what* they represent rather than *how* they are represented. By casting the problem in a wider theoretical literature we raise the possibility that there is an important ideological element in the official crime reports and that a crime incidence map may tell us as much about the mental and moral images of the researcher and judicial agencies as it does about the actual incidence of crime. Conflicting claims regarding these influences will be examined.

This chapter begins by considering the problems of interpreting official statistics and the relations between crime rates and law enforcement strategy, particularly in terms of police patrol methods. Together these discussions suggest how our image of crime may be systematically distorted both in theory and in practice.

Crime control and actual behaviour

The second sense in which the social control/criminal justice environment conditions crime is its actual impact on behaviour. In very fundamental ways criminal law structures social activity. Law not only defines appropriate behaviour, but also helps to define social groups. Certain groups are formally consolidated by legal definition, others are informally consolidated as a result of differential law enforcement; a seemingly ubiquitous criminological assertion is that lower-class persons are the most likely to be criminalized (Hood and Sparks, 1970, p. 54).[1] Law structures the relationship between certain groups by providing rules for resolving conflict and generally specifies the very conditions of social change itself (although social change, it should be noted, is often affected before these conditions are delineated, and sometimes in spite of them). In a general sense, law is a system of social engineering. Geographers have rarely evinced much concern over the impact of law beyond its deterrent effect (see, for example, Pyle, 1976). Until the development of the labelling perspective, criminologists and sociologists had become singularly deterrence-minded in their vision of the social impact of law. This perspective suggested that rather than deterring crime, the criminal labelling process might in some ways serve to amplify deviance. But in identifying a deterrence–amplification continuum, some of the important relations between crime control policy and social behaviour are lost. This paper considers these relations by examining the unintended or unanticipated consequences of a range of social control policies, particularly criminal justice policy.

The importance of the labelling perspective in criminology has been to suggest that the consequence of criminal labelling is sometimes the very opposite of its purpose. The amplification of deviance is the unintended consequence of the effort to contain it. The intention of criminal justice policy is not always consonant with its effect in practice, particularly if laws are differentially enforced. We may thus start to appreciate more fully the social impact of crime control policies in terms of their unanticipated consequences. The notion of unintended consequences serves as the main organizational thread of the second part of the paper. A general discussion of these effects serves to introduce a geographical perspective for probing the relations between crime control policies and social behaviour. The geographical perspective is organized around a concept of displacement—the movement of people in direct response to legal, judicial or other forms of social control policy. Although largely concerned with the effects of formal policy, we must also acknowledge the impact of informal protocols, particularly in terms of differential law enforcement practices. For example, it maybe the informal 'policy' of law enforcement personnel which leads to an uneven bias in official statistics.

It is to this and to the problem of interpreting official crime and delinquency statistics that we now turn.

CRIME CONTROL AND THE PERCEPTION OF CRIME: THE MEANING OF OFFICIAL STATISTICS

Geographers have been particularly single-minded in their importation and adaptation of criminological theory in developing geographical perspectives of crime. Three elements of criminological theory have been consistently adopted by geographers: a consensus model of society and law; a positivist interpretation of legal categories (that is, legal categories correspond to a discrete behaviour); and a correctionalist purpose (many geographical studies produced in this period of allegedly soaring crime rates are prefaced by a desire to do something about crime). Because of the consensual model of law formation, geographers have largely focused on the criminal—the person who defies a putative consensus (thus missing the subculturalist point that law-breaking is often norm-conforming behaviour). The literal interpretation of statistics follows a positivistic epistemological imperative separating facts from values—crime categories are part of an observational language, not a theoretical one. When combined, these ontological and epistemological claims (even though only implicit) produce a moral imperative which gears academic analysis to the eradiction of crime. In this programme, a critique of law or law enforcement has been effectively denied. This denial is in part a reflection of the image of law as consensual and discrete. A very different picture emerges if the meaning of law is made problematic, particularly if it is seen to emerge from social conflict rather than consensus, and as sometimes representing vested rather than social interests. A different image of the bias in official statistics also emerges, but geographers have ignored the alternative interpretations of criminologists and sociologists which arose mainly as a reaction to (and sometimes in direct opposition to) positivistic epistemology; to date geographers have missed the *theoretical* implications of 'hidden' crime.

The geography of crime has generally followed a positive interpretation of official statistics, assuming that crime categories correspond to discrete behaviour types. Geographers interested in crime have usually taken the position that problems of interpretation occur because jurisdictional procedures sometimes distort the accuracy of data for index purposes. Because reporting systems are often imperfectly developed and subject to change, comparative analyses are problematic. But they are not as problematic as they might be, were it not for a convenient tactic; analysis typically begins with a warning about the difficulties associated with interpreting crime statistics, but then proceeds unabashedly as if the statement of the problems resolved them (see, for example,

Harries, 1974; Georges, 1978; Pyle *et al.*, 1974). While this strategy is convenient it is also unsatisfactory, particularly when the results are further compromised if the source of bias in the official statistics is uneven (that is, socially differentiated).

Geographers have not considered the theoretical implications of the sociological literature which suggests that other sources of bias are contained in the official statistics beyond their instrumental imperfection (Briar and Piliavin, 1964; Kitsuse and Cicourel, 1963; Short and Nye, 1957). Short and Nye, for example, suggest that self-report studies of delinquency indicate that the higher probability of delinquent behaviour occurring among lower socioeconomic groups tells us more about the criminal labelling process than it does about the criminal propensity of different social strata. A comparison of the self-reported delinquent behaviour of juveniles in different socioeconomic categories finds few statistically significant differences in the incidence of such behaviour (Short and Nye, 1957, p. 208). But these studies do confirm certain findings predicated by official statistics; males do commit more delinquent acts than females in almost every delinquency category. Thus the problem remains as to which categories are biased, and to what degree (Short and Nye, 1957, p. 210).

Although geographers have considered the quantitative aspects of statistical bias, they have not considered the qualitative aspect that remains—in so doing, they may well misconceive the quantitative bias. For the purposes of this discussion the qualitative element of the bias is termed 'essential' bias, and refers to the systematic effects of socially differentiated structures of meaning on the signification of behaviour as criminal. Whereas essential bias arises from the way behaviour is interpreted as being delinquent or criminal, instrumental bias arises from the way that this information is subsequently recorded.

The most important conceptual lesson to be learned from these observations about crime categories is that crime and delinquency are not necessarily discrete behaviours with a clear meaning. The explanation of who is caught and who is prosecuted becomes as important in the explanation of crime as the circumstances conditioning or generating certain types of behaviour. Social status may sometimes be a more important predictor of the attribution of a criminal label than is a particular kind of behaviour. But the prevailing tendency of spatial studies of crime has been to view crime and delinquency as monolithic categories.

In order to overcome the instrumental biases of official statistics and the inferential problems of areal aggregate statistics, a number of studies have attempted to use official measures of crime residence to identify areas for more intensive research. The problem of the ecological fallacy may be overcome by gathering more detailed measures to circumvent the problem of making specific inferences about individual behaviour from aggregate statistics (Baldwin, Bottoms and Walker, 1976). While this strategy may help overcome the instrumental biases of official statistics and the problem of the ecological fallacy, it makes no allowance for essential bias. Thus when Shaw and McKay

(1931, 1942) used official statistics to identify delinquency areas for a more intensive analysis of the causes of delinquency, the aetiology they provided failed to take into account the delinquent behaviour which self-report studies might have identified in other types of area. The literal interpretation of delinquency reports thus importantly shaped the theoretical formula emerging from it/and may be partly responsible for the circular argument contained within it; while social disorganization is offered as the principal explanation of delinquency, delinquency rates themselves are used as the principal indicator of social disorganization.

Sociological interpretations of essential bias

The critique of official statistics dates back (at least) to Shirley Robison's *Can Delinquency Be Measured* (1973), a critique of Shaw and McKay's ecological studies of delinquency. The data presented in this study 'definitely indicate that for the field of delinquency index-making is at present not feasible' (Robison, 1937, p. 209). This conclusion follows from her observation that 'delinquency and non-delinquency are not mutually exclusive. The label delinquent depends on many subjective factors in the observer and the observed' (Robison, 1937, p. 195). Although this statement seems to have become an indefatigible sociological axiom, its subsequent adherents do not always recognize its pedigree.[2] Nor did its original statement by Robison stem the tide of areal studies of crime based on official crime rates. Short and Nye's (1957) finding mentioned above suggested that, when measured by self-report indexes, the socioeconomic differences in delinquency rates implied by the official statistics largely disappeared. Similarly, Briar and Piliavin's study (1964) of police encounters with juveniles suggested that social status was as important a criterion as behaviour in the police's decision to arrest and signify a juvenile as delinquent.

The theoretical implications of these findings were developed by Kitsuse and Cicourel (1963) who warn against viewing bias simply as a technical and organizational problem. Rather, they assert, the problem concerns differentials in the definition of deviant behaviour (p. 134). Current geographical theory sounds very much like the traditional theory forming the target of their attack—traditional deviancy inquiry treated forms of behaviour as independent variables. In contrast, Kitsuse and Cicourel (1963, p. 135) treat rates of deviant behaviour as dependent variables: 'the theoretical conception which guides us is that the *rates of deviant behaviour* are produced by *the actions taken by persons in the social system* which define, classify and record certain behaviours as deviant'.

In this way the concerns of the deviancy theorist include not only how acts officially or unofficially defined as deviant are generated, but also how different forms of behaviour come to be defined as deviant, and how individuals manifesting such behaviours are organizationally processed to produce rates of deviance.

The ethnomethodological critique

In a later work, *The Social Organization of Juvenile Justice*, Cicourel (1968) utilizes an ethnomethodological programme to question the scientific 'fact' of juvenile delinquency. Ethnomethodology examines the conventionality of the commonsense world, suggesting that social reality is an ongoing practical accomplishment of the concerted activity of everyday life. In Cicourel's language (1968, p. 7): 'Ethnomethodological studies analyse everyday activities as members' methods for making those same activities visibly rational and reportable for all practical purposes ie. 'accountable' as organisations of commonplace everyday activities'. He replaces the usual sociological complaint about 'bad' statistics and distorted bureaucratic record-keeping by making the procedures producing 'bad data' an object of study.

Cicourel's study shows how the 'problem of delinquency' is generated by the everyday activities of professionals and laymen in contact with juveniles. The decision-making activities that produce the social problem called delinquency are important because they highlight fundamental processes of how social order is possible (1968, p. vii). Thus the study of delinquents tells us as much about the articulation of notions of legality and justice as it does about delinquency. Furthermore 'the interaction of legal and non-legal rules implies that what is considered deviant by some members of the community (including the police) is not always obvious to the suspect or his supporters, and that what ends up being called justice is negotiable within the boundary conditions of established organisations' (Cicourel, 1968, p. 22).

Cicourel, in following the ethnomethodological perspective, directs his attention to theories of delinquency employed by laymen (particularly police, court and probation officers) when deciding the existence of delinquency. It is a study of the 'background expectancies' of the officials who channel juveniles in and out of the justice system. Criminological theory, Cicourel suggests, has followed commonsense definitions of delinquency and crime in general, and has only questioned official statistics to the extent that they may grossly under-estimate crime. For Cicourel *official statistics embody a theoretical problem*; they gloss over the process by which official categories of deviance are endowed with meaning and consequently miss that meaning.

The explanatory power of traditional delinquency theories is thus contained in their neatness in providing retrospective accounts which fit both popular conceptions about how juveniles become delinquent, and how official de-linquency rates are distributed (Cicourel, 1968, pp. 26–27). According to Cicourel, an adequate description depicting how persons come to be defined and processed as delinquent is as follows (1968, p. 27):

The data for demonstrating the cogency of the sociologists' program consists of his and members' descriptions of observed events, an account of the environment of objects attended, and the progressive transformations that can be affected by initial encounters between suspects and victims, suspects and the police, the writing of an official report based on interrogation and observation, subsequent probation interviews and reports, court performances and the like. The analysis of oral and written material presupposes a seldom mentioned contextual relevance based on linguistic and practical reasoning principles as they are used in different social groupings.

Oral and written reports prepared by officials continually simplify or 'round', abstract, and reinterpret the original act so that it fits the kind of logic used by officials accustomed to standardized recipes for explaining relationships between legal rules and social conduct (Cicourel, 1968, p. 28). The major thrust of Cicourel's argument is that legal categories (such as 'delinquent') do not correspond to the positivistic type system where the category represents some actual object. Rather, he argues, these categories are given meaning through social interaction.

Cicourel (1968, p. 45) demonstrates that the juvenile justice system selectively assembles juveniles in the process of their being labelled delinquent: 'Persons involved in deciding matters of legality and justice carry with them a stock of knowledge about social types they encounter in different situations in the community, and their social actions reflect conceptions of what is normal strange, acceptable, safe, likely, usual etc.'

Part of Cicourel's empirical research attempts to examine the extent to which official records revealed or did not reveal the incidence and form of middle/upper-class delinquency as compared with lower-income groups. In the study of a Chicago suburb he found a fairly high incidence of delinquency, much higher than suggested by the official statistics (1968, pp. 32–33). In the comparison of two unidentified cities he also notes the influence of police organizational procedures on differences in the overall rates of deviance in the two cities and in the same city at different times.

Cicourel uses these empirical findings to indicate the 'indexical' nature of the label 'delinquent' and to show how rates of delinquency are officially produced; each instance of invoking the label 'delinquent' requires decisions which transform a truncated behavioural description of 'what happened' in a particular incident into some precoded but almost never unidimensional category that enables police to invoke legal language. This invocation is often more a reflection of a juvenile's status or demeanour than his behaviour. The construction of official statistics can consequently be seen to employ improvised or *ad hoc* procedures for obtaining, labelling and presenting their information. Such procedures produce technical errors that can be controlled. But more problematically these procedures are integral procedures for arriving at and interpreting the end-product, and cannot be corrected, in Cicourel's view, by statistical estimates of error.

It is in the validity of this claim that the ethnomethodogists base their critique of official statistics. In the case of juvenile delinquency, what this means is that official files on juveniles cannot be understood without recourse to an understanding of the normal rules and theories utilized by officials assigning cases to the category delinquent. As Cicourel sees it, the task posed for the researcher is to examine the socially organized ways in which juvenile activities are translated into types of delinquency, an analysis which produces a very different picture to the one provided by a positivistic type analysis of police statistics. What the latter does not recognize is that all legal categories and procedures are bargained or negotiated. Knowledge of how statistics are assembled is needed to transform the formal report descriptions into processual statements about the public and private ideology of law enforcement agencies. If the researcher ignores these constructions, he imposes a system of measurement by *fiat*, treating official reports as a literal depiction of 'what happened'.

Limitations of the ethnomethodological critique

Cicourel's (1968) study shows that delinquency is not a behaviour in its own right. But is this the case with all crime categories? The central problem that the critique raises concerns the *meaning* of law, the neglected part of the equation in the geographer's approach to crime. Following an ethnomethodological programme Cicourel shows how the commonsense rules of everyday life dictate the interaction between police and public in deciding who the delinquents are. But such a view ignores the way more widely pervasive ideological beliefs mould this process. Indeed, ethnomethodology has been criticized in general for failing to incorporate an understanding of ideology (see, for example, Beng-Huat Chua, 1977; Freund and Abrams, 1976).

Ethnomethodology leaves the impression that meaning is constructed solely through the process of immediate social interaction and has thus been criticised as offering an unwarranted and highly relative pluralism with an inadequate grasp of the relation between knowledge and social structure (see, for example, Taylor, Walton, and Young, 1973, pp. 193–208).[3] Thus Young (1975, p. 87) takes the position that it is only in atypical situations that the idiosyncratic values and ideologies of particular social control agencies assume *paramount* importance however dubious the positivistic acceptance of the criminal statistics, their wholesale rejection would be equally cavalier. The social actors faced with the task of assigning criminal labels may often have a very clear understanding of the kind of activity a particular law prescribes. Barry Hindess (1973) highlights the unstated problem of classification by *fiat* this way (p. 18): 'With respect to which categories do these difficulties arise? What proportion of cases must be decided in this fashion: 0.01 per cent, 5 per cent, 95 per cent? If it is the last then the final tabulation is obviously worthless; if the first, then classification by fiat may be ignored as a source of error in the tabulation in question.'

316 of this neglect

The result of this neglect is that ethnomethodology has demonstrated only the incompleteness of any set of categories and instructions. Hindness suggests that a positivistic critique of official statistics could be developed which would be perfectly consistent with the claims of ethnomethodology. In fact the ethno-methodological programme is highly positivistic, Hindess suggests, directed at the absence of a set of correspondence rules linking legal categories and actual phenomena. (Tudor (1976) makes a similar point.) Thus Hindess suggests that the problem of statistics is instrumental not epistemological. But in noting the similarity of positivism and ethnomethodology, Hindess tends to minimize their differences. This may reflect his desire to offer an alternative rationalist model in which he sees the problem of classification by *fiat* as only involving what he calls 'alien' or ambiguous categories; to this extent the problem of what the statistics mean is an instrumental problem. But in making this argument, Hindess nevertheless suggests that official categories cannot be taken-for-granted by the researcher. The most important hallmark of positive criminology, according to David Matza (1964, 1969), is its analytical separation of crime and justice. The tendency to focus on the criminal and not the law has important consequences for the type of explanation offered, and thus the problem is, at least in part, epistemological (the method of inquiry structures the type of explanation possible). The difference between positivism and ethnomethodology that Hindess largely ignores is the latter's focus on meaning, particularly in-tersubjective meaning.

The important point is that the meaning of legal categories in the ethnometho-dological programme is socially negotiated. In the positivist programme, as it is characterized here, the meaning of legal categories is pregiven. Again, the important point emerging from these insights is that crime is not all of a piece—crime is not a monolithic behavioural category. (Indeed, it would be a mistake to see a *single* crime category as being necessarily discrete.) For some crime categories the problem of classification by *fiat* is paramount. In Hindess' sense the category 'delinquent' is more alien than the category 'murderer' (although even the classification of the taking of a human life is dependent on the social context in which it occurs—hence the dispute over the definition of Lieutenant Calley's behaviour at My Lai in Vietnam in 1971 as an act of war or an act of murder).

The interpretation of bias has profound implications for the explanation of a delinquency rate map. Because the decision to process juveniles is often based on their social status, the rate map may be interpreted as the product of a self-fulfilling prophecy reflecting the beliefs of social control personnel as to where society's delinquent populations are located. In this sense it may be best thought of as a mental map, an *interpretation* of behaviour rather than a *description* of it.

A number of criminologists have suggested that social privilege structures determine the type of populations to be controlled, both formally and informally (Taylor, Walton, and Young, 1973; Chambliss, 1979; Krisberg, 1975; Quinney,

1974), and Sutherland (1949) notes that 'white-collar' offences generally fall under civil rather than criminal law and that very little time is spent uncovering those white-collar infractions which could be considered criminal. The task of 'exposé' criminology 'is thus to reassert that crime is problematic in all social groups, not just the lower orders' (Taylor, Walton, and Young, 1973, p. 24) and quite possibly that the crimes of the powerful are the most socially injurious. Alleged oil company rip-offs and various breaches of environmental pollution law come to mind in this respect. Thus the differential activity of law enforcement agencies in enforcing various laws also comes into play in the process of constructing popular images of criminogenic or 'problem' population groups. David Matza expands this theme in an attempt to show how privilege structures shape the process of criminal signification.

Methodical and incidental suspicion: the influence of privilege

David Matza (1969), in discussing the implications of the statistical bias of official crime reports, lays a foundation for the understanding of an ideological element of bias. He suggests that the major source of systematic bias arises from the method of suspicion routinely utilized by the police when investigating crimes (1969, pp. 180–195).

However important the promise of protection by civil rights, the most important way in which a citizen's rights are protected is the expectation that under ordinary circumstances he or she will remain above police suspicion (1969, p. 182). To fall under suspicion, most members of society would have to go out of their way. But, conspicuously, this is not the case for certain groups. To illustrate this assertion, Matza draws a distinction between 'incidental' and 'methodical' suspicion.

Most people are subject to police attention only under special circumstances, particularly traffic offences and, exceptionally, murder. In these cases the method of suspicion is incidental. It is suspicion that flows from an incident of a citizen's apparent dereliction of legal duty (1969, pp. 183–184). Certainly a bias may occur in such cases, but it is superficial and arises from flagrant discrimination. But this is not the usual method of suspicion used by police in their routine criminal investigations. 'Methodic suspicion' is the customary mode, Matza asserts, one which leads to the most profound source of *systematic* bias in the official statistics. This method of suspicion employs police knowledge of known criminals to expedite their apprehension and the subsequent clearing of citizens' complaints. Rather than a specific incident evoking suspicion, suspicion arises from being 'known to the police' — 'known' in the sense that a particular identity or resemblance produces suspicion. Matza terms this 'bureaucratic suspicion' because it arises from the police need to account (to both higher officialdom and the public) for their activity. The method is 'outgoing' in that it seeks a regular suspect in the hope that any one or a whole series of uncleared offences can be settled. The method is common in burglary and larceny investigations in an attempt to clear incidents reported to the police, or in drugs and other vice areas in the form of stop-and-search tactics, but only in the stopping and searching of people who 'look' suspicious. In this sense the method of suspicion continuously sustains criminal and delinquent identity. With this analysis, Matza moves towards an understanding of the ideological dimensions of the criminal labelling process; the element which we noted above remains a striking omission of the ethnomethodological account of the social construction of meaning.

It must nevertheless be noted that Matza's work is speculative and hypothetical. The contribution of the different modes of suspicion to the clearing of offences is an empirical question. Mawby (1979) has recently suggested that criminologists have uncritically accepted Matza's conjectures—that the role of police discretion in biasing official statistics (in Mawby's study area at least) is minimal. It is to a consideration of these counterclaims that we now turn.

Policing the city: how much of a corrective?

In his *Policing the City* (1979) Mawby tackles head-on the question of how much crime rates reflect different law enforcement processes. He wastes no time in offering a conclusion (1979, p. 2):

> I anticipated that such an exercise would reveal that area differences in offence and offender rates were to a large extent due to different police styles, and the differential involvement of the police, in contrasting areas of the city. . . . In fact I found no such thing. An area analysis of policing patterns revealed that there was little or no evidence that differential policing affected the relative offender rates of contrasting residential areas. Similarly, although there was some suggestion that offence rates may have been affected by the extent of police presence, the distinctions found were between residential and other areas, rather than between different types of residential area.

Mawby draws this conclusion from an analysis examining four elements of the criminal labelling process: the discovery and reporting of crime; the detection process; police recording processes; and the handling of identified offenders. Mawby correctly criticizes Matza for offering no empirical evidence to back up his theoretical work on methodic and incidental suspicion and questions the extent to which the method of suspicion comes into the detection process. Here he stresses the role of the public in the discovery of crime (1979, p. 18–22).

Of the amplification hypothesis in general Mawby concludes:

> . . . the most striking conclusion . . . is that the role of the police in the discovery of crime in these residential areas is minimal, and that variation between areas does not fit the amplification hypothesis (p. 98). . . . It . . .

appears that whether we consider offence or offender data, all reported offences, all detected offences, or only police detections, there is no evidence to suggest (let alone demonstrate) that police involvement in any way creates differences in crime rates between different residential areas.

What are we to make of these findings which at first glance directly contradict some of the arguments advanced above? Several criticisms can be made of Mawby's work which, when taken together, suggest that he has simply not made his case regarding the amplification hypothesis. The first of these is the most serious objection.

First, Mawby never considers the possibility that the effect of policing on residential crime rates occurred before the point in time that his study was conducted. The amplification of deviance literature suggests that the criminal labelling process can act as a self-fulfilling prophecy. To study patterns of crime incidence and criminal residence in Sheffield at one point in time may only provide a partial answer to the effect of policing. Remember that the amplification hypothesis posits an *actual* increase in crime as a response to the mobilization of the social control apparatus. It may be that differential policing was responsible for amplification of crime in the high crime-rate residential areas and that what Mawby is describing now is the *result* of this process. The effect of policing on the pattern of crime incidence or offender residence may have occurred during the period of development of certain residential areas or at some time more recently. The point of invoking a self-fulfilling prophecy is that at some time high crime-rates in certain areas may reflect policing, and then become real through the amplification process. Mawby fails to consider this possibility by virtue of dislocating the pattern of crime from its historical context. Having realized this, one is left with an amplification hypothesis that is quite consistent with Mawby's findings.

Secondly, Mawby concentrates on nine 'contrasting residential areas' in Sheffield. But just how 'contrasting' are these? It turns out that eight can be classified as 'working class' (p. 186). While these were specifically chosen because of their variation in crime rate, the differences between areas containing different social classes is ignored. Certainly one area is characterized as containing a higher social class, but on what grounds could one consider this representative? We are left with the possibility that the role of the police in distinguishing between rates in working-class areas is minimal, but may be significant if we compared areas of different social class. While Mawby does acknowledge this problem, it does not alter his conclusions. This is curious because many labelling theorists suggest that social class is one of the most poignant indicators of the differential operation of police discretion. Mawby does not really provide a way of testing this hypothesis.

Thirdly in the American studies that Mawby uses as a reactive springboard for his own findings, race is one of the most important variables in hypothetical statements about the operation of police discretion. One wonders how representative is a city like Sheffied, particularly Mawby's nine areas which do not seem to contain much of a racial mix. Mawby thus provides no means of testing hypotheses about the relationship between race and the operation of police discretion. This limitation does not seem to temper his conclusions.

Fourthly, one cannot help but get the feeling that Mawby is rather too selective with his findings. In fact, he notes, they really only apply to indictable crime (and, one would have to add, only to *certain kinds* of indictable crimes—Mawby only deals with street crime). While Mawby can find no evidence of police impact on criminal residence (and this may only be because he looked at the wrong time) he does offer a variety of examples of a police impact on crime rates, particularly of victimless crime. The amount of recorded drug use is directly related to extent and types of police activity (1979, p. 160), and of victimless crime in general Mawby acknowledges the importance of police discretion in its widest sense. He gives evidence for a relationship between enforcement and offence rates for under-age drinking, and also of a sexual bias (1979, pp. 135–136). Police involvement in the development of rates of what Mawby calls 'marginal crime' are similarly important. In this context he includes family violence, but one wonders in what sense this is 'marginal'—if anything family violence is the most common residential crime, even if it is the least reported.

There were some slight indications of area differences in cautioning rates, at least as far as some males were concerned (p. 182), but Mawby makes nothing of this. Areas also appeared to be differentiated when offender rates were based on data restricted to those receiving probationary or custodial sentences (p. 182). Surely these findings fit an amplification of deviance formula!

When individual offender variables were considered, most appeared unrelated to detection method. But, notably, police detections were most common for the 17–20-year-old group (1979, pp. 132, 178). Is an enforcement–area effect missed in this observation? If different areas have different demographic profiles, one would expect areas with a proportionately greater number of 17–20-year-olds to have higher crime rates. And, without other areas of social class with which to compare these findings, how can we tell if the police treat youths from different social groups in the same way in these police initiated encounters? Do police initiate such encounters in other areas?

There was a clear and significant difference in the proportion of offences cleared up individually according to the offender rate of the area in which the offender lived, as evidenced by a higher rate of 'indirect clearing' of offences in the high-rate areas. But there was only a slight indication that offenders from high-rate areas committed more offences than those from low-rate areas (pp. 109–110). It thus appeared to Mawby that the police were more likely to attempt to 'clear their books' when they faced offenders from disreputable areas. Again it would not be difficult to fit this finding into an amplification of deviance formula.

There are then a number of findings in *Policing the City* which do suggest a relationship between policing and crime and which are consistent with an amplification of deviance formula. While many of the findings apparently minimize the importance of police discretionary power in producing crime rates (of offenders or incidence), their wider relevance is questionable. Within the area of his study, Mawby's interpretation of the results is problematic because it largely ignores the historical dimension of the production of crime rates. While police discretionary power may not be particularly important now (the above observations should be enough to suggest that it is still of some importance) it may have been critical at some point in time in the formation of what Mawby now calls 'disreputable areas'. The wider relevance of the study is questionable on grounds of its representativeness. While labelling theory is by no means coherent (and, some would argue, is better thought of as a perspective) the operation of police discretionary power has been broadly related to three privilege structures—ethnicity, social class, and age. Mawby's study contains some information about the influence of a person's age, particularly that youth excites police attention. But his sample does not cover a range of social classes and there does not appear to be much of a telling racial mix. We have thus learned very little about the operation of police discretion in some of its most important dimensions. Mawby's work does, however, serve as a useful corrective: 'The finding that area differences in one study cannot be "explained away" suggests that differences elsewhere should be considered on a multi-dimensional level rather than being sceptically written off as due to policing practices. (1979, p. 183). By the same token, the effect of policing practices should not be sceptically written off either.

Police patrol and offence patterns

Harries (1980, p. 63) notes that the relationship between law enforcement and levels of crime has attracted a fairly substantial literature; but the literature cited deals largely with the impact of uniform patrol deployment on crime rates and thus patrol strategy (Pogue, 1975, Press, 1971; Swimmer, 1974; and Wellford, 1974, on the relation between patrol intensity and crime rates; and Chaiken, 1975; Elliot, 1973; Larson, 1972; and Sweeney and Ellingsworth, 1973 on the operational environment of law enforcement). There is no consideration of such factors as Matza's 'methodic suspicion' or the general impact of law enforcement policy in structuring and defining social activity. The suggestion made in this paper is that the impact of what Harries terms the 'criminal justice environment' is much broader than the one considered by police scientists. But even if we restrict our analysis to the police science literature we find that no consensus of opinion has been reached concerning the effect of patrol deployment on crime rates. Geographers have tended to gloss over this confusion. Carter and Hill (1979), for example, in their study of *Criminals' Images of Urban Areas* suggest that both criminal and non-criminal populations associate 'strong police protection' with 'low crime incidence'. But criminals do not associate 'hard marks' (that is, difficult targets) *so highly* with strong police protection as non-criminals. Carter and Hill suggest that this is consistent with the Kansas City study finding that different methods of employing police patrol forces resulted in no statistically significant differences in subsequent crime levels (Police Foundation, 1977). This is, of course, very convenient for the interpretation of crime rate maps since we can rest assured of the negligible impact of police patrol. But if this is so, why would Carter and Hill's criminals associate low crime rates with strong police protection? And apparently criminals do associate hard marks with strong police protection, just not as strongly as non-criminals. At second glance, then, the Carter and Hill findings do not really seem to support the Kansas City study at all. Unfortunately no definitive statement can be yet made concerning this effect, for the findings of the Kansas City study are directly contradicted by alternative sources. A comparison of the Kansas City study with 'Operation 25' (Ficklin, 1970) should make the point. The comparison also suggests a fatal methodological flaw in the Kansas City study, one which makes its findings highly questionable; in the process of assessing the effects of changing the patrol density, no members of the public were asked whether they perceived such changes. If not, then it is hardly likely that crime rates would have reflected the changing patrol strategies; the issue is complicated by the possibility of a time-lag between patrol change and perception of that change.[4] The problem is that if something is not perceived as real, it may not have real consequences.

Police patrol strategies have been based on two unproven but widely accepted hypotheses according to the Police Foundation study (1977). First, that visible police presence prevents crime by deterring potential offenders; and, second, that the public's fear of crime is diminished by such police presence. (The fear of crime has been an emerging theme in the criminological literature recently. Springer's (1974) work is unusual to the extent that he utilizes a geographical perspective to throw light on this problem. Also Ley's (1974) 'stress topography' map of Monroe, a Philadelphia neighbourhood, is generated from a questionnaire mainly designed to measure perceived crime danger.)

Between 1 October 1972 and 30 September 1973, the Kansas City Police Department conducted an experiment to measure the impact of routine preventative patrol on the incidence of crime and the public's fear of crime. The experimenters concluded that 'traditional routine preventative patrol had no significant impact on either the level of crime or the public's feeling of security'. In the experiment three types of patrol areas were designated. In one, the reactive type, there was no routine preventative patrol—officers only entered one of these areas in response to a citizen call for assistance. In the second, the proactive type, police visibility was increased by two to three times its usual level. In the third type of area the usual patrol was maintained.

In summarizing the findings thirteen points were made suggesting that no statistically significant differences could be found between the areas in terms of such measures as a victimization study of the areas, departmental crime reporting, arrest patterns, community attitudes to the police, protective security measures taken by the public, traffic accidents, and police response times in answering calls for service.

Let us compare these findings to those of a New York experiment conducted some 25 years earlier. 'Operation 25' had among its various goals the purely experimental purpose of determining what would constitute adequate policing in a busy New York precinct (Ficklin, 1970). The experiment began on 1 September and concluded on 31 December 1954. It was an example of what has been termed saturation patrol, but also included establishment of a special Juvenile Aid Bureau, a Special Narcotic Squad and increases in the regular precinct detective squad and in traffic and emergency service personnel. The precinct chosen was described as a 'crime-ridden urban area' (1970, p. 342) containing a mixed population of more than 120 000 persons of whom roughly two-thirds were non-white.

Prior to the experiment the uniformed force included 188 patrolmen. Largely by importing probationary patrolmen directly upon graduation from the Police Academy, this number was increased to 440. In place of 15 sergeants for supervision of patrol there were 33, five captains in place of one, and an additional Deputy Inspector assigned to supervise the operation. Instead of 27 men being turned out for one tour of foot and radio patrol duty, the experimental force numbered 99. The precinct's detective squad was also strengthened by the addition of two sergeants, 11 detectives, and eight patrolmen to the existing 33-man unit. Besides creation of a Narcotic Squad, a further task-force was constituted to investigate vice, gambling and liquor-law violations (Ficklin, 1970, pp. 343–346).

Results of the experiment were claimed as dramatic. During the experiment only 488 felonies were reported compared to 1102 for the same 4-month period a year earlier—a decrease of 55.6 per cent. Importantly, in New York as a whole there was only a 4.7 per cent decline in the same period. The number of misdemeanours actually rose. But the authors hide this fact by suggesting that the total number of crime complaints—both felonies and misdemeanours—declined by 27.5 per cent, or from 1757 to 1273. This statistical ploy helps to mask an increase by averaging it away; misdemeanour complaints rose from 655 to 749. The important implication this has for our discussion of crime rates is that this increase may represent a better apprehension rate rather than a change in social behaviour. This was certainly the case with the incidence of disorderly conduct, dangerous weapons and narcotic offences, those which are almost always recorded as the result of police-instigated action. Similarly juvenile referrals increased dramatically from 135 in the equivalent 4-month period in 1953 to 372 during the experimental period. Summonses for traffic offences also showed an overall increase (Ficklin, 1970, pp. 344–348).

In noting the impact of Operation 25 in reducing certain crime levels Ficklin concludes (1970, p. 351): 'Operation 25 was, in essence, a practical test of police theory, the theory being that an adequate police force properly supervised can effectively reduce crime and maintain law and order, peace, and security in an area of any kind. The experiment . . . was an unqualified success'. Compare this statement to that made by the Police Foundation (1977, pp. 118–119), from an apparently impressive list of the non-effects of patrol differentials. The Kansas City experimenters were moved to making some extravagant claims:

> The experiment (showed) that routine preventative patrol in marked police cars has little value in preventing crime or in making citizens feel safe . . . . The results of the preventative patrol experiment . . . repudiated a tradition prevailing in police work for almost 150 years . . . (making it) necessary to develop viable alternatives to the obsolescent concept of preventative patrol.

Unfortunately the experiments are not strictly comparable to the extent that the Kansas City study only concerned preventative uniform patrol. But this difference is not sufficient to explain their diametrically opposed findings. One useful insight for the geography of crime to emerge from these contradictory findings is that the importance of patrol and enforcement strategies in the configuration of crime rates cannot be ruled out. But to this point in time, geographers have not even considered them. A final example serves to stress the potential importance of enforcement differentials. Donald Rumbelow (1971), in *I Spy Blue*, illustrates some of the consequences of the piecemeal implementation of police patrol.[5] He suggests that young thieves went to great lengths to avoid 19th-century London's City Day Police, formerly the City Patrol, founded in 1784. The movement of young thieves from Whitechapel to Aldgate occurred at 8 o'clock when the Day Police went off duty. But the establishment of patrols was piecemeal. The Solicitor-General of that time noted the success of certain patrols when he introduced to Parliament the London and Westminster Police Bill. He proposed a similar plan (1971, p. 104): 'but to extend generally to every part of the town, and its environs; for if it were to be confined to the heart of the city, it would drive the robbers to the outskirts, and if it were only to be applied in the outskirts, it would bring them all to the centre'.

Rumbelow offers an example of this effect created by the structure of the jurisdictional boundaries of the various patrols. The formation of the New Police outside the City of London may have caused an increase of criminal activity within the city. A city watchman of that time suggested that an increase of 'bad characters' had occurred on his beat. Moreover:

> when there was a quarrel among them the other night, a policeman came up and drove them through the Bar, saying, 'Ye shant stand here; go into the City with you rows!' Sir Peter Laurie said that he had heard that a police magistrate

had directed the policeman to drive all bad characters into the City. If there was any truth in this, it was an imprudent—an improper observation. He desired the watchman present to drive all the bad characters out of the City instead of apprehending them in future. 'We can play at tennis-ball,' said the Alderman in an undertone (1971, p. 114).

THE IMPACT OF CRIME CONTROL POLICY: TOWARDS A GEOGRAPHICAL PERSPECTIVE

The work of Matza and Cicourel on the interpretation of official statistics represents only one element of a wider critique of criminological and deviancy theory developed in Britain and North American during the 1960s and 1970s. The main thrust of this critique suggested that criminologists, by adopting a classical scientific approach to social science (that is, a positivist position concerned with the objective discovery of the causes of crime in a deterministic explanatory framework), were missing some of the most important elements. In attempting to develop deterministic theories of crime causation researchers focused either on the psychological biological constitution of the criminal, or on the social circumstances that might compel people to law-breaking. In this programme, which takes law for granted, the process of overall social control is ignored, particularly the political and ideological elements.

In criminology the critique of positivism and the attempt to reintroduce a notion of free will to redress the excesses of mechanistic determinism has led to the development of a number of alternative perspectives. Any one of these could be used as a basis for establishing new directions for geographical perspectives of crime. In his debate with Harries, Peet (Harries, 1975; Peet, 1975) has introduced one such perspective to geographers, but his structuralist appraisal of the impact of political economy in the process or criminogenesis implicitly denies a voluntaristic element of human behaviour. But then in criminology, too, the structure/action issue remains the subject of heated debate (see, for example, Rock, 1979; Taylor, Walton, and Young, 1973).

Both in Britain and North America, one of the main developments issuing from the critique of traditional theory is a radical brand of criminology (see, for instance Taylor, Walton, and Young, 1973, in Britain; and Chambliss, 1979; Quinney, 1974; and Platt, 1975 in the United States). But the days are now past when the self-appointed mavericks of criminology were more united than divided in their common aim to eradicate positivism (Downes and Rock, 1979, p. vii). Alternative forms of conflict theory now vie for attention along with the neo-marxian versions. In Britain a generally humanistic and particularly in-teractionist splinter group has taken radical criminology (particularly Taylor, Walton, and Young, 1973;) to task on a number of grounds, especially over the issue of determinacy and the search for 'total' explanation (Downes and Rock, 1979). But in the geography of crime the positivist demon still awaits an epistemological exorcism. While some of the problems of the positivist perspective have been dealt with here, they are more fully discussed in a separate work (Lowman, forthcoming). Here we have considered the relevance of certain non-positivistic perspectives for interpreting crime rate maps, suggested the implications of a conflict model of law for interpreting crime patterns and argued that an analysis of the unfolding meaning of law is important for understanding spatial processes.

What all of this needs from geographers is a much greater emphasis on the social control system in understanding crime. To this extent we must raise the possibility that social control practices may, in some sense, condition, or even 'cause' crime. The purpose of the remainder of the chapter is to review examples of such a proposition.

The unintended consequences of purposive social action and the problem of displacement phenomena

Robert Merton (1936) noted that in some of its numerous forms the problem of the unintended consequences of purposive social action has been treated by virtually every substantial contributor to the long history of social thought, but never in any systematic way. Merton was the first to do so. A programme of structural-functional sociology emerged from this early insight explaining unintended consequences in terms of the 'latent' functions of social institutions and various sociostructural arrangements. My intention is not to introduce a programme of structural-functional sociology, however, because of the numerous problems that have been suggested involving this perspective (see Tulmin, 1965, for example). Rather, I would urge a dialectical interpretation of the process. The dialectical approach sees unanticipated consequences as stemming from the ongoing development of something—from continuities rather than breaks with it (Henshel, 1976, pp. 72–73).

Both Marx and Weber were concerned with outcomes which are the opposite of what the actors desire or intend—thus for Weber, the success of Protestant asceticism brought about its own demise. Capitalism was founded upon the Protestant work ethic, but the accumulation of wealth exerted a corrosive effect on the very puritanical aspects of the religion which made that accumulation possible (Henshel, 1976, pp. 75–77). Marx similarly saw the ultimate destruction of capitalism through its success. The development of monopoly capitalism (the logical outcome of capitalist competition according to his general law of capitalist accumulation) leads to an ever-larger unemployed surplus population. As this population grows, there are insufficient wage-earners to consume the product of capitalist industry. While this is a labour pool ready to be exploited, it also highlights the inequality of the capitalist order, thereby creating the seed of revolutionary consciousness.

In terms of the present paper, what is important about Marx's analysis is not so much the content of that analysis (the substantive aspect), but the logic by which it is achieved (the dialectic). Following Ollman (1978), and Heilbroner (1980) certain points need to be made to avoid confusion (especially because of the competing interpretations of Marx's writings that presently vie for attention). The dialectical method is not right or wrong, but a perspective for looking at the world. According to Ollman, the dialectical logic of Marx is based on a thesis of internal relations which stresses the connectedness of things, rather than their separateness, as is the case with Aristotelian categorical logic and logical positivism. The dialectic is a way of viewing things as moments in their own development in, with and through other things (Ollman, 1976, p. 52). The notion of 'relation' is at the heart of a dialectical view, relations not only between different entities, but between the same ones in times past, present and future; hence the importance of the historical dimension to marxian analysis. The dialectic is thus a prism, focusing on the nature of change, particularly change in terms of 'inner contradictions', such as those identified by Marx and Weber and mentioned above. In these terms what I shall be concerned with here is an analysis of the internal contradictions of social control as manifested by the unintended consequences of criminal justice and legal policy.

In terms of a geographical analysis we may systematize these relationships through a concept of displacement. The aim is to show how social control and social behaviour are internally related; how an understanding of criminal justice and legal policy is necessary to understand certain kinds of sociospatial behaviour, particularly criminal behaviour. Rather than the static-type analysis typical of geographical studies of crime (static in the sense that the impact of legal or judicial change is rarely considered, and even when it is, it is only in terms of deterrent effects) the focus here is dynamic, considering the impact of legal policy on behaviour patterns. These will not necessarily involve criminal behaviour to the extent that some patterns reflect adaptive strategies designed to prevent certain kinds of activity from being defined as illegal (by, for example, restricting them to private places) or from being detected as illegal. The discussion will nevertheless be restricted to activities that were, or could be, defined as illegal at some point in time. Displacement can be provisionally defined as movement which would not have occurred had some legal or criminal justice policy not been enacted (formally or informally).

Consideration of displacement phenomena is of fairly recent vintage in criminology, with a much more limited application than suggested here. Thomas Reppetto (1976) reported an introductory study of the displacement effects which may be associated with crime prevention through environmental design programmes. Given the cost of environmental redesign, such programmes are likely to be piecemeal in their implementation. Rather than prevent crime, they may merely displace it. Reppetto identified five modes of displacement which may be associated with target-hardening crime prevention programmes—spatial (the literal form of displacement from area to area), temporal (change of characteristic time of crime commission), typological (change of type of crime commission), tactical (the change of *modus operandi* rather than target), and target displacement (a shift to another target within the same area) or a combination of these (Reppetto, 1976, pp. 168–169). While there are few studies of these effects, several authors have recently suggested their importance (Harries, 1980, pp. 100–101; Mayhew *et al.*, 1976, pp. 5–6; Winchester, 1978, p. 118). Although several studies have examined displacement, none of these actually specify the criteria by which the effect can be identified. Importantly, these studies only consider displacement in terms of preventative design strategies or levels of police surveillance (Chaiken, Lawless, and Stevenson, 1974; Lateef, 1974; Press, 1971; Tyrpak, 1975; Waldt, 1975).

The contention here is that displacement phenomena are associated with a much wider range of criminal justice strategies, and other varieties of social control policy. The term displacement thus provides a guiding *concept* for developing a critical geographical appraisal of the effects of public policy in general, criminal justice policy in particular, and especially for examining the relationship between law and behaviour. In a practical sense displacement is important because it serves as an indicator of the efficacy of various anticrime programmes.

In the development of a critical analysis of law and social control, displacement effects can be viewed, at least in part, as the consequences of contradictions within law, or between the system of law and social control and other elements of society, particularly the political economy. Thus the analysis of displacement phenomena as unintended consequences is only the first step of a much broader critical approach. The analysis is designed to beg a question; how does one explain the discordance between the intended effect of legal and criminal justice policy and its actual impact (a concern very similar to that of urban impact analysis—see Clark, 1980—but with a more overtly critical intent in this case)? Conflict over the meaning, the making, and the enforcement of the law becomes central in this account.

Several criminological studies are organized around a concept of unintended consequences. Henshel (1976) discusses labelling theory in general in these terms, viewing the amplification of deviance associated with the labelling process as an unintended consequence of the effort to suppress crime. A wide-ranging literature has suggested that drug law serves to increase crime by artificially raising black market prices, thereby creating professional criminal organizations to reap the harvest produced by conditions of false scarcity (see, for example, Chambliss, 1977; Lindesmith, 1965). A further criminogenic subculture of addictive drug-users develops relying on illegally derived wealth to supply the funds necessary for maintaining a drug habit. Thus drug law, designed to deter crime, may actually *increase* it. Lawrence Gooberman (1974), in his study of *Operation Intercept*, indicates how a period of intense surveillance at the United States–Mexican border designed to stop the flow of marijuana into the United

States did have this effect. But its consequence in New York was that the users of marijuana experimented with other drugs. In Reppetto's sense, a typological displacement occurred, but it occurred differentially—white user populations largely turned to hashish, speed and certain hallucinogens while ghetto users turned to heroin. In the case of the ghetto users the control of marijuana supply (a physically non-addictive drug) led to the development of a more intractable problem—the use of an addictive drug. Gooberman interviewed a number of addicts who suggested that they first used heroin during the marijuana shortage following 'Operation Intercept'.

Letkeman (1974, p. 89) suggests that a form of typological displacement has resulted from the intensification of alarm-system usage and target-hardening strategies adopted by business establishments. His informants (Canadian penitentiary inmates) argued that the increased difficulty of burglarizing banks led to a rise in the number of bank robberies, and further, that the general widespread use of alarms has meant that the burglary of business establishments in general has given way to armed robbery. MacDonald (1975), in his work on armed robbers, suggests a slightly different reason for the proliferation of bank robberies in the United States in the early 1970s. The main reason for this increase may have been the coincidental proliferation of suburban branch banks which were typically provided with only minimal security systems (MacDonald, 1975, p. 329; Conklin, 1972, p. 40, makes a similar point).

The verification of these various arguments is, of course, likely to be the subject of debate for some time to come.

Geographical displacement: three vignettes

Whereas the possible displacement effects of crime prevention through environmental design programmes have been noted in the literature, little attention has been given to the spatial consequences of criminal justice and other types of social control policy. The vignettes presented here describe not only the displacement effects associated directly with criminal justice policy, but also the spatial impact of associated policies designed to control and contain (or sometimes disperse) what are perceived as 'problem' populations. Two of the vignettes thus describe the consequences of 19th-century social policies designed to control the 'dangerous classes'. The third vignette focuses more directly on the spatial impact of specific criminal justice policies designed to contain prostitution in a contemporary setting. While these vignettes describe the unintended spatial consequences of various criminal justice and social control policies, we must not forget that certain types of policy may consciously attempt to relocate unwanted activities as was the case with Sir Peter Laurie's informal 'tennis-ball' policy. A second point is that unintended consequences may be positive and/or negative—this will largely depend upon certain value-judgements made by the researcher and reader.

Environmental design as social engineering: a 19th century allegory?

Crime prevention through environmental design has been hailed by its practitioners as a product of the 20th century; its pedigree is usually traced back
through Newman (1972) and Jeffery (1971) to Jane Jacobs (1961). But
environmental design is, in a sense, a child of the 19th century (if not earlier)
redressed for 20th-century consumption. While the example cited here may
represent more of a parody than an allegory, it does suggest that a crude
environmentalism does little to change anything but the surface appearance of
social problems (while some types of crime may be suppressed by restricting
opportunity, crime itself may only be the epiphenomenal expression of some
deeper social malaise). Such was the case with 19th-century programmes of street
development deliberately routed through London's 'rookeries' which not only
enhanced transportation facilities but also offered the ancillary benefit of slum
clearance. But as a result slum problems, particularly crime, were simply
displaced rather than being alleviated.

According to Dyos (1957), the Commissioner of Sewers of Finsbury wrote to
the Privy Council in 1835 to say that an extension of Farringdon Street would not
only create a communication link between north and south London, but also that
such an improvement was 'far more important as relating to the health of that
part of the capital through which it would be made, by the removal of a
description of buildings that have long been a hotbed of disease, misery and
crime'. Dyos gives evidence that officials in Westminster shared such views over
the proposed development of New Oxford Street through St Giles, and this
general attitude was epitomized by the Select Committee on Metropolitan
Improvements of 1838. In their second report, the Committee did not 'confine
themselves to the single purpose of obtaining increased facilities of communication' but suggested that 'other public benefits might in some cases be
derived simultaneously with that principal object' in particular the partial
clearance of the St Giles' 'rookery' by means of an extension of Oxford Street
(Dyos, 1957, p. 262). Street improvements were thus seen as including positive
social effects, improving public health and morals. Dyos suggests that the line
taken by new streets was generally determined by their potential for clearing as
many slum dwellings as possible. Street improvement during these years was seen
as the only effective large-scale method of rectifying some of the worst features of
urban growth. But such a naive expectation conspicuously failed to obliterate
slums 'which were generally merely displaced, often in aggravated forms, to
other localities' (Dyos, 1957, p. 264).

Henry Mayhew, a 19th-century commentator (who also provides our second
example of displacement, one associated with Poor Law policy) lends support to
Dyos' hypothesis that street developments merely displaced the conditions they
were routed to alleviate. Mayhew (1862, vol. 4, p. 313) suggests: 'About twenty

years ago a number of narrow streets, thickly populated with thieves, prostitutes, and beggars were removed when New Commercial Street was formed'.

Mayhew acknowledges the value of this development as 'leaving a wide space in the midst of a densely populated neighbourhood, which is favourable to its sanitary conditions, and might justly be considered one of the lungs of the metropolis'. One thus cannot deny the impact of urban redevelopment in ameliorating physical living conditions, but, according to Mayhew, this would not effectively change the lot of the displaced population. 'The rookery in Spitalfields we proposed to visit is comprised within a space of about 400 square yards . . . and contains 800 thieves, vagabonds, beggars, and prostitutes, a large proportion of whom may be traced to the old criminal inhabitants of the now extinct Essex Street and Old Rose Lane' (1862, vol. 4, p. 313).

According to Mayhew, some 150 000 persons of 'bad character' inhabited England and Wales in 1848 and constituted what were referred to at that time as the 'criminal' classes (1862, vol. 3, p. 377). In 1857 there were some 8600 prostitutes known to the police in London, but because of the inadequacy of police statistics, he gives credence to estimates that there were 80 000 prostitutes in London at this time (p. 225). Without dwelling upon the reasons for this large surplus population, it is hardly surprising that urban cosmetic surgery failed to improve their lot. What is particularly interesting, given the theme of this chapter, is the effect the system of social control had on the movement of this population and the discrepancy between the goal of the policy and its actual effect.

Social control and migration: the effect of Poor Law policy in 19th-century England

Of the 16 million people in England and Wales in 1841 Mayhew suggests that 12 per cent (2 million) lived by pauperism, mendicancy or crime. As noted above, Mayhew suggests that 150, 000 of these constituted the 'criminal classes', excluding paupers and mendicants. While we may question this rigid classification (many beggars may also have been thieves), and the reliability of the statistics used, there did appear to be a huge unemployed underclass at this time in Britain. Significantly, many of this group were juveniles (1862, vol. 3, p. 393). In Mayhew's opinion, juvenile vagrancy acted as one of the main suppliers of the criminal class and constituted one of the most dangerous elements of society: 'That vagrancy is the nursery of crime, and that the habitual tramps are first the beggars, then the thieves, and, finally, the convicts of the country, the evidence of all parties goes to prove' (1862, vol. 3, p. 398). But vagrancy, for Mayhew, expressed a telling contradiction; the hostelries, although necessary to provide food and shelter for unemployed workers, could be seen to allow the idle to avoid labour: 'The mere fact of man's seeking work in different parts of the country may be taken as evidence that he is indisposed to live on the charity or labour of others; and this feeling, should be encouraged in every rational manner' (1862, vol. 3, p. 368).

This was the culmination of a massive period of social readjustment which made vagrancy even more prevalent in Great Britain than in certain earlier periods. The mobility of the working classes and their feudal predecessors had been controlled by the Poor Laws since the 13th century. The increasing mobility of the working classes in the late 18th and 19th centuries led to the establishment of 'casual wards', the free hostelries of the unemployed population. But in Mayhew's opinion, 'The establishment of these gratuitous hotels has called into existence a large class of wayfarers, for whom they were never contemplated' (1862, vol. 3, p. 368). Such places encouraged erratic spirits and compounded what Mayhew considered the prime cause of vagabondage; the lack of inculcation of a habit of industry.

One experiences a sense of *déjà vu* reading Mayhew's account which adumbrates many elements of modern sociological theory and popular opinion; lack of socialization has been a consistent feature in sociological accounts of deviance and the welfare bum is still subject to the wrath of the American hardhat. In suggesting 'bad companions' as one of the main causes of vagrancy (1862, vol. 3, p. 378), Mayhew offers a hint of the later development of differential association and subcultural theory.

Mayhew identified three classes of vagrant of which the smallest was considered to be those temporarily out of work. A second class was constituted by the Irish as the result of the potato famine, but this was not as criminally inclined as the remaining class, the habitualized vagrants—those for whom vagrancy had become a way of life. Whether Mayhew is correct as to the causal role of the casual wards in generating vagrancy is open to conjecture. Although not using the concept, he suggests that the intensification of vagrancy was the unanticipated consequence of the casual ward programme. He also illustrates the way that the organization and functioning of these wards moulded patterns of seasonal migration. And again this pattern effect can be interpreted as the unintended consequence of the poor relief system.

Mayhew was particularly struck by the unequal spatial and temporal distribution of vagrants throughout the Poor Law Unions of England and Wales. To explain this distribution Mayhew presents and attempts to corroborate the opinion of an experienced vagrant. According to this informant, the vagrants moved to London in large bodies at the end of December when the winter refuges opened up. The regular vagrants left London during April and early May. Mayhew's informant suggested that the movement of the vagrants was explicitly connected to casual relief policy:

A very large portion of the wandering beggars and thieves would remain in town if they were allowed to remain longer in their nightly haunts; but after the closing of the refuges, the system of not permitting them more than one night in the same union forces them to be continually on the move: so they set off immediately they have made themselves known at all the workhouses. The boys will mostly go in small gangs of two or three. Before they start, they generally pick up from some other band whom they meet in the London Wards the kind of treatment and relief they will receive at the country unions, and they regulate their journey accordingly; and they will very often go one or two days march out of their way, in order to avoid some union that has a bad character among them, or to get to some other union where the accommodation is good, and the work required of them very slight (1862, vol. 3, p. 400).

A recognizable circuit developed with young vagrants travelling through Essex and Suffolk northwards to Leeds. The Mendicity Asylum in Leeds was particularly popular because after providing a night's lodgings, boys might be given threepence, fourpence or even sixpence according to the apparent worthiness of the applicant. From Leeds they travelled in different directions, some through Durham and Northumberland, others to Manchester where a Quaker society furnished similar treatment to that received in Leeds. Those travelling north rarely entered Scotland since the vagrants fared very poorly beyond Berwick, receiving little more than barley cake. From Northumberland they travelled through Cumberland, Westmorland and Lancashire, then branching off into Cheshire and North Wales or Staffordshire and Derbyshire, and then south to Birmingham, a favoured meeting-place. In Birmingham: 'they make a point of tearing up their clothes, because for this offence they are committed to Warwick Gaol for a month, and have a shilling on being discharged from the prison. It is not the diet of Warwick Gaol that induces them to do this, but the shilling. Frequently they tear up their clothes in order to get a fresh supply.'

We realize fully the plight of those boys as Mayhew's informant described the rationale for their behaviour:

From continually sleeping in their clothes, and never washing their bodies or changing their shirts . . . they [the clothes] get to swarm with vermin, to such an extent that they cannot bear them upon their bodies . . . . I have seen the lice on their clothes in the sunshine, as thick as blight on the leaves of trees. When their garments, from this cause, get very uncomfortable to them, they will tear them up, for the purpose of forcing the perish officers to give them some fresh ones (1862, vol. 3, p. 401).

From Birmingham they travelled back through Northampton and Hertford to London. By this time the London refuges would be again opening for the winter, or if early, the boys would be forgotten in the surrounding unions, and receive benefit there. A smaller autumn circuit also existed through Sussex, Hampshire and Wiltshire. The timing of this migration coincided with the hop-picking season: 'It is not hard work, and there are a great many loose girls to be found there' (1862, vol. 3, 0.401).

The movements of the Irish vagrants conformed to a different pattern—they were mostly found on the roads from Liverpool and Bristol to London. By the end of June 'The roads must be literally covered with the Irish families tramping to London'. The Irish tramps, it was suggested by Mayhew's informant, lived solely by begging. In contrast the English tramps lived by a mixture of begging and stealing.

For these commentators the poor relief system came to exacerbate the very condition it was designed to relieve. Here Mayhew's informant was unequivocal:

> As the refuges are managed at present, I consider they do more harm than good. If there were no such places in London in the winter, of course I, and such as are like me, would have been driven to find shelter at our parishes; whereas the facilities they afford for obtaining a night's shelter—to the vagabond as well as to the destitute—are such that a large number of the most depraved and idel classes are attracted to London by them. . . . I have known many an honest, industrious, working man, however, made a regular beggar and vagrant by continued use of the casual wards. They are driven there first by necessity, and then they learn that they can live in such places throughout the year without working for their livelihood (1862, vol. 3 pp. 399–400).

In many senses Mayhew's aetiological account is grossly inadequate (see, for examples, Jones, 1971, chapter 14). With the advantage of hindsight we might conclude that the existence of the casual wards of the workhouse was not the only, or even the main factor involved with the proliferation of vagrancy. But it seems reasonable to conclude with Mayhew that the relief system was important in creating and maintaining a certain migratory lifestyle.

To do away with the workhouses would not have done away with the circumstances that made such a lifestyle more a reflection of necessity than of volition. Who, after all, would chose the workhouse given Mayhew's descriptions of it, if their freedom of choice was anything but enormously curtailed? 'No one can imagine, but those who have gone through it, the horror of a casual ward of a union; what with the filth, the vermin, the stench, the heat, and the noise of the place, it is intolerable' (1862, vol. 3, p. 402). Of the Asylum for the Houseless Poor of London—opened only in the winter and offering only bread, water and warm shelter—Mayhew wrote (1862, vol. 3, p. 428):

> It is impossible to mistake the Asylum if you go there at dark, just as the bump in the wire cage over the entrance door is being lighted. This is the hour for opening; and ranged along the kerb is a kind of ragged regiment, drawn up four deep, and stretching far up and down the narrow lane, until the crowd is

like a hedge to the roadway . . . . There they stand shivering in the snow, with their thin, cobwebby, garments hanging in tatters about them. Many are without shirts . . . . A few are without shoes; and they keep one foot only to the ground, while the bare flesh that has had to tramp through the snow is blue and livid-looking as half-cooked meat . . . . The only sounds heard are the squealing of the beggar infants, or the wrangling of the vagrant boys for the front ranks, together with a continued succession of hoarse coughs, that seem to answer each other like the bleating of a flock of sheep.

While seemingly passing harsh judgement on vagrants, Mayhew is even harsher on those who might see themselves as architects of their own good fortune: '. . . get down from your moral stilts, and confess it honestly to yourself, that you are what you are by that inscrutable grace which decreed your birth place to be a mansion or a cottage rather than a "padding-ken", or which granted you brains and strength, instead of sending you into the world, like many of these, a cripple or an idiot' (1862, vol. 3, p. 429). Mayhew was clearly not unaware of structural inequalities in society and keenly aware of the relations between social control policy and social behaviour. It is with the latter consideration in mind that we move to a study of prostitution in Vancouver.

Street prostitution in contemporary Vancouver

'The police clearly recognised RHH as the centre of the prostitution trade, and focused their patrols on the area. To them, any suggestion that such policies 'created' area differences in respect to prostitution would be treated with some amusement' (Mawby, 1979, p. 146).
While this statement may well accurately portray the influence of police activity on Sheffield's areas of prostitution, it does not necessarily follow that this relationship will hold for all places at all times. The example which follows should amply demonstrate the need to treat Mawby's general findings with caution.

A recent study of street prostitution in Vancouver (Lowman, forthcoming) offers a deliberate attempt to break sharply with the traditional practice of the geography of crime by making the law and enforcement policy the focus of analysis rather than the criminal actor. This strategy developed out of the realization that it was impossible to explain changing patterns of street prostitution in Vancouver by focusing exclusively on the criminal actor since the behaviour of prostitutes was intimately tied to the meaning of the law, court decisions, and the behaviour of law enforcers. The official statistics proved particularly problematic, suggesting an overall decline in street prostitution during the period 1975–79, when, in fact, informal observation, media accounts, and informal police impressions suggested that the amount of street prostitution was sharply increasing. This consequently necessarily became a study of crime in a legal context, suggesting certain unintentional consequences of particular law enforcement policies and demonstrating the practical implications for law enforcement of a double-standard sexual morality enshrined in prostitution law. The study also takes something of an unusual approach in relation to the geographical literature to the extent that it is concerned with the process of pattern change rather than the associational analysis of static crime patterns with other index measures (either social or physical).

The purpose of the study was to explain a change in the pattern of street prostitution in Vancouver. Until 1975, there were three areas of street prostitution all located in or bordering the central city. One was located adjacent to Chinatown and the other two in what could be described as skid-row type areas. After 1975 two new areas developed, but not in the zones of blight customarily associated with prostitution. Instead, they were in two esteemed areas of civic pride in the central business district. Why did this pattern change occur?

In 1975, the police investigation of a well-known cabaret club, prompted by the belief that its owners were living off prostitution, led to the club's closure. A second club threatened by a similar investigation burnt to the ground and was not reopened. Both of these clubs until this time (for a period of 20–25 years in the case of the one investigated by the police) flourished as protected soliciting havens for prostitutes. In this respect the general division of space into public and private spheres has had important consequences for social behaviour; while the act of prostitution is itself legal in Canada, soliciting for the purpose of prostitution publicly is illegal (but quite legal in private places). By tolerating soliciting and prostitution these clubs allowed prostitution to continue, but effectively contained it. In this respect they quite successfully, but informally, realized the prophylactic purpose of Canadian prostitution law—the containment of prostitution. In so doing, they also happened to realize their own purpose—profit maximization. The possibility was then raised that the clubs' owners lived off prostitution, an offence under a different section of prostitution law. Ultimately the owners were not convicted of any of the charges laid against them. But the clubs had closed.

The effect of the closure of the clubs was simply that the prostitutes—whose activities in the clubs were consonant with the dictates of the law—were displaced onto the (public) streets, apparently undeterred by soliciting laws which they could not longer circumvent. Both police and academics are sceptical about the deterrent effect of prostitution law which is often characterized as 'the revolving door of justice'. The levying of fines for prostitution offences looks more like an informal licensing system than a powerful deterrent and, perhaps in this light, the police devoted little attention to prostitution control after the closure of the clubs. But then a 'new social problem' in Vancouver was identified by the press and various public pressure groups (notably hoteliers and businessmen from the new areas of street prostitution which developed after the closure of the cabaret clubs). The problem concerned the visibility of prostitutes, particularly in the new area where they chose to carry out their soliciting activities: a night-club area one block from Vancouver's peak-value intersection, and the main thoroughfare of the West-End high-rise area, the most populous square mile in Canada. Prostitutes proved themselves able locational decision-makers by choosing these areas of heavy pedestrian traffic.

In response to the identification of the social problem, the police mounted a special task-force in order to intensify the laying of soliciting charges. But this very effort served to highlight the double-standard sexual morality enshrined in Canadian prostitution law which prevents a man from being defined as a prostitute, and takes the position that only a female can solicit a male in the process of making a sex–money contract. Although one male was convicted of soliciting (by virtue of pleading guilty) a second case prevented further action of this type when the sex bias of the law was interpreted literally and the man charged with soliciting was acquitted. While this effectively highlighted both the plight of the prostitute and the sexual ideology of prostitution law, the acquittal of the cabaret club-owners revealed how the closure of the cabarets had created the very problem the law is designed to contain. Law enforcement efforts designed to curb the derivative problem were rendered almost totally ineffective as landmark court decisions were made favouring prostitutes—the meaning of soliciting was reinterpreted to imply harassment, rather than just the offer of the prostitute's service and her quotation of a price. 'Public places' were defined as not including the inside of a car. Thus the police strategy of 'trolling'—cruising in a car equipped with tape-recorders and cameras in the hope of recording a prostitute's offer of service while seated in the car—was rendered defunct; and, because of the interpretation of soliciting, charges so derived would be worthless even if some other strategy was employed. From the prostitute's perspective, the legal problem presented by public soliciting disappeared. Thus not only did areas of street prostitution spread, but, as prostitutes migrated into the city to take advantage of what they now saw as a permissive legal environment, the number and density of prostitutes also increased.

Thus a police initiative to reduce crime foundered on legal interpretation and in fact had the opposite contradictory effect. Prostitution in public places emerged as an unintended consequence of law enforcement compromised by legal definition. The map of crime was in large measure a legally constructed reality. In Vancouver, the suggestion that enforcement policies created area differences in street prostitution is treated by police with everything but amusement.

CONCLUSIONS

Implicit in the approach taken in this chapter is a number of claims concerning what elements should be included in the explanation of sociogeographical criminological phenomena. For the sake of clarity I will be concise. Geographical perspectives of crime as they have developed to date are deficient in a number of respects:

(1) A historical perspective of both law and crime.
(2) A sociology of law in the explanation of crime.
(3) An epistemology concerned with the social (and scientific) production of meaning.
(4) A conflict model of society which recognizes that some values are probably largely consensual. This would include a concern with the translation of power to legal authority, and thus be concerned with the legitimacy of law.
(5) Incorporation of a critical view of society which frees the practical interests of the research from a merely correctionalist stance.

By considering such elements we may move toward a geographical perspective of social control, and a critical theory of society.

NOTES

1. We should note, however, that the validity of this relationship has been challenged at various times. Box and Ford (1971), for example, suggest that the facts do not fit the class hypothesis. The rejoinder by Bytheway and May (1971) argues that Box and Ford do not make their case. Similarly the challenge by Tittle and Villemez (1977) and Tittle, Villemez, and Smith (1978) to the class–crime relationship has been suggested as thoroughly misrepresenting the facts (Clelland and Carter, 1980).
2. Indeed in the introduction to the 1969 edition of Shaw and McKay's *Juvenile Delinquency and Urban Areas,* James F. Short sites Robison's as one of a number of studies which 'In general . . . support the findings reported in (Shaw and McKay's) earlier publication'. Curiously this is the same J. F. Short cited earlier in this paper as arguing with F. I. Nye that self-report studies find few socioeconomic differences in delinquency rates (Short and Nye, 1957).
3. It should be noted that Taylor, Walton, and Young's reading of ethnomethodology has been challenged by Coulter (1974). Coulter's defence does not adequately engage the problem created by the failure of ethnomethodology to incorporate some notion of ideology. This does not mean to say that ideology or some notion of social structure are inimical to ethnomethodology—see, for example, Freund and Abrams (1976), and Beng-Huat Chua (1977). Ethnomethodologists and interactionists would argue in defence of a contextual approach that only through a study of the processes generating intersubjective understanding and contextual meaning can any notion of social structure be warranted. Any other notion of social structure derived through abstract analysis, such as that offered by structural-functional or structural-marxist analyses, are scientific chimera (Rock (1979) makes this point in defence of a symbolic interactionist perspective, and Coulter (1974) in defence of ethnomethodology).
4. In a personal communication, Dr Patricia Brantingham has suggested that some of the reactive areas were so small that the change in patrol density would be unnoticeable within these areas anyway.
5. Thanks to Dr Paul Brantingham for bringing this example to my attention.

REFERENCES

Baldwin, J., Bottoms, A., and Walker, M. A. (1976). *The Urban Criminal*, London, Tavistock.

Beng-Huat Chua (1977). Delineating a Marxist interest in ethnomethodology. *American Sociologist*, **12**, 24–32.

Box, S. and Ford, J. (1971). 'The facts don't fit: on the relationship between social class and criminal behaviour. *Sociological Review*, **19**, 31–52.

Briar, I. and Piliavin, S. (1964). Police encounters with juveniles. *American Journal of Sociology*, **70**, 206–214.

Bytheway, W. R. and May, D. R. (1971). On fitting the 'facts' of social class and criminal behaviour: a rejoinder to Box and Ford. *Sociological Review*, **19**, 585–607.

Carter, R. L. and Hill, K. M. (1979). *The Criminal's Image of the City*, Toronto, Pergamon Press.

Chaiken, J. M. (1975). *Patrol Allocation Methodology for Police Departments*, Rand Corporation, Santa Monica, Cal.

Chaiken, J. M., Lawless, M. W., and Stevenson, K. A. (1974). *The Impact of Police Activity on Crime: Robberies on the New York Subway Systems*, New York City Rand Institute.

Chambliss, W. J. (1977). Markets, profit, labour and smack. *Contemporary Crises*, **1**, **1**, 53–75.

Chambliss, W. J. (1979). *On the Take: From Petty Crooks to Presidents*, Indiana University Press.

Cicourel, A. V. (1968). *The Social Organisation of Juvenile Justice*, New York, Wiley.

Clark, G. L. (1980). Urban impact analysis: a new tool for monitoring the geographical effects of federal policies. *Professional Geographer*, **32**, **1**, 82–85.

Clarke, R. V. G. (1980) 'Situational crime prevention: theory and practice. *British Journal of Criminology*, **20**, **2**, 136–147.

Clelland, D. and Carter, T. J. (1980). The new myth of class and crime. *Criminology*, **18**, **3**, 319–336.

Conklin, J. E. (1972). *Robbery and the Criminal Justice System*, Lippincott, Philadelphia.

Coulter, J. (1974). What's wrong with the new criminology?, *Sociological Review*, **22**, **1**, 119–135.

Downes, D. and Rock, P. (1979). *Deviant Interpretations*, Martin Robertson, Oxford.

Dyos, H. J. (1957). Urban transformation: a note on the object of street improvement in Regency and early Victorian London. *International Review of Social History*, **2**, **2**, 259–265.

Elliot, J. F. (1973). *Interception Patrol—An Examination of the Theory of Random Patrol as a Municipal Police Tactic*, Charles C. Thomas, Springfield, Ill.

Ficklin, L. R. (1970). Operation 25. In S. G. Chapman (Ed.), *Police Patrol Readings*, Charles C. Thomas, Springfield Ill.

Freund, P. and Abrams, M. (1976). Ethnomethodology and marxism: their use for critical theorizing. *Theory and Society*, **3**, 377–393.

Georges, D. (1978). *The Geography of Crime and Violence*, Resource Papers for College Geography, No. 78.1.

Gooberman, L. A. (1974). *Operation Intercept: The Multiple Consequences of Public Policy*, Pergamon Press Inc., New York.

Harries, K. D. (1974). *The Geography of Crime and Justice*, McGraw-Hill, New York.

Harries, K. D. (1975). Rejoinder to Peet: the geography of crime: a political critique. *Professional Geographer*, **27**, 280–282.

Harries, K. D. (1980). *Crime and the Environment*, Charles C. Thomas, Springfield, Ill.

Heilbroner, R. L. (1980). *Marxism: For and Against*, W. W. Norton and Co., New York.
Henshel, R. L. (1976). *Reacting to Social Problems*, Longman, Toronto.
Herbert, D. T. (1977). Crime, delinquency and the urban environment. *Progress in Human Geography*, **1**, 208–239.
Herbert, D. T. (1979). Urban crime: a geographical perspective. In D. T. Herbert and R. J. Johnston (Eds.), *Social Problems and the City: Geographical Perspectives*, Oxford University Press, pp. 117–138.
Hindess, B. (1973). *The Use of Official Statistics in Sociology: A Critique of Positivism and Ethnomethodology*, Macmillan, London.
Hood, R. and Sparks, R. (1970). *Key Issues in Criminology*, McGraw-Hill, New York.
Jacobs, J. (1961). *The Death and Life of Great American Cities*, Vintage Books, Random House, New York.
Jeffery, C. R. (1971). *Crime Prevention Through Environmental Design*, Sage Publications, Beverly Hills.
Jones, G. S. (1971). *Outcast London: A Study in the Relationship Between Classes in Victorian Society*, Clarendon Press, Oxford.
Kitsuse, J. I. and Cicourel, A. V. (1963). A note on the uses of official statistics. *Social Problems*, **11**, 131–139.
Krisberg, B. (1975). *Crime and Privilege*, Prentice-Hall, Englewood Cliffs, NJ.
Larson, R. C. (1972). *Urban Police Patrol Analysis*, MIT Press, Cambridge, Mass.
Lateef, B. A. (1974). Helicopter patrol in law enforcement—an evaluation. *Journal of Police Science and Administration*, **2**, 62–65.
Letkeman, P. (1974). *Crime as Work*, Prentice-Hall, Englewood Cliffs, NJ.
Ley, D. (1974). *Black Inner City as Frontier Outpost: Images and Behaviour of a Philadelphia Neighbourhood*, Association of American Geographers, Monograph 7, Washington, DC.
Lindesmith, A. (1965). *The Addict and the Law*, Indiana University Press, Bloomington.
Lowman, J. (forthcoming). Geographical Perspectives on the Relationships Between Law and Criminal Behaviour, Department of Geography, University of British Columbia, PhD dissertation.
MacDonald, J. M. (1975). *Armed Robbery: Offenders and Their Victims*, Charles C. Thomas, Springfield, Ill.
Matza, D. (1964). *Delinquency and Drift*, John Wiley and Sons, London.
Matza, D. (1969). *Becoming Deviant*, Prentice-Hall, Englewood Cliffs, NJ.
Mawby, R. (1979). *Policing the City*, Saxon House, Farnborough, Hants.
Mayhew, H. (1862). *London Labour and the London Poor*, Volumes 3–4, Griffin, Bohn and Co. London.
Mayhew, P. *et al.* (1976). *Crime as Opportunity*, Home Office Research Study No. 34. HMSO, London.
Merton, R. (1936). The unanticipated consequences of purposive social action. *American Sociological Review*, **1**, 894–904.
Newman, O. (1972). *Defensible Space*, Macmillan, New York.
Ollman, B. (1978). *Alienation: Marx's Conception of Man in Capitalist Society* (2nd Edition), Cambridge University Press.
Peet, R. (1975). The geography of crime: a political critique, *Professional Geographer*, **27**, 277–280.
Platt, T. (1975). Prospects for a radical criminology in the USA. In I. Taylor, P. Walton, and J. Young (Eds.), *Critical Criminology*, Routledge and Kegan Paul, London.
Pogue, T. F. (1975). Effect of police expenditures on crime rates. *Public Finance Quarterly*, **3**, 14–44.
Police Foundation. (1977). The Kansas City preventative patrol experiment. Reprinted in L. Radzinowicz and M. E. Wolfgang. *Crime and Justice*, 2nd edition, Volume 2, Basic Books, New York, pp. 118–128.

Press, E. J. (1971). Some Effects of an Increase in Police Manpower in the 20th Precinct of New York City, The New York City Rand Institute.

Pyle, G. F. et al. (1974). The Spatial Dynamics of Crime, University of Chicago, Department of Geography, Research Paper No. 159.

Pyle, G. F. (1976). Geographic perspective on crime and the impact of anti-crime legislation. In J. S. Adams (Ed.), Urban Policymaking and Metropolitan Dynamics, Ballinger, Cambridge, Mass., pp. 257–291.

Quinney, R. (1974). Critique of Legal Order, Little Brown and Co., Boston.

Reppetto, T. A. (1976). Crime prevention and the displacement phenomenon. Crime and Delinquency, 22, 166–177.

Robison, S. (1937). Can Delinquency Be Measured?, Columbia University Press, New York.

Rock, P. (1979). The sociology of crime, symbolic interactionism and some problematic qualities of radical criminology. In D. Downes and P. Rock, Deviant Interpretations, Martin Robertson, Oxford.

Rumbelow, D. (1971). I Spy Blue: The Police and Crime in the City of London from Elizabeth 1st to Victoria, Macmillan, London.

Shaw, C. R. and McKay, H. D. (1931). Social Factors in Juvenile Delinquency: A Study of the Community, the Family and the Gang is Relation to Delinquent Behaviour, US Government Printing Office.

Shaw, C. R. and McKay, H. D. (1942). Juvenile Delinquency and Urban Areas: A Study of Rates of Delinquency in Relation to Differential Characteristics of Local Communities in American Cities, University of Chicago Press.

Short, J. F. and Nye, F. I. (1957). Reported behaviour as a criterion of deviant behaviour Social Problems, 5, 207–213.

Springer, L. M. (1974). Crime perception and response behaviour: two views of a Seattle community, PhD dissertation, Penn State Department of Geography.

Sutherland, E. (1949). White-collar Crime, Dryden Press, New York.

Sweeney, T. J. and Ellingsworth, W. (1973). Issues in Police Patrol, Kansas City Police Department and the Police Foundation.

Swimmer, G. (1974). The relationship of police and crime—some methodological and empirical results. Criminology, 12, 293–314.

Taylor, I., Walton, P., and Young, J. (1973). The New Criminology: For a Social Theory of Deviance, Routledge and Kegan Paul, London.

Tittle, C. R. and Villemez, W. (1977). Social class and criminality. Social Forces, 56, 474–503.

Tittle, C. R., Villemez, W., and Smith, D. (1978). The myth of social class and criminality: an empirical assessment of the empirical evidence. American Sociological Review, 43, 643–656.

Tudor, A. (1976). Misunderstanding everyday life Sociological Review, 24, 479–503.

Tulmin, M. (1965). The functionalist approach to social problems. Social Problems, 12, 379–388.

Tyrpak, S. (1975). Newark High-Impact Anti-Crime Program: Street Lighting Project Interim Evaluation Report, Office Criminal Justice Planning, Newark, NJ.

Waldt, L. G. (1975). Residential Burglary Prevention Program—Final Report, King County Department of Public Safety, Seattle, Washington.

Wellford, C. R. (1974). Crime and the police: a multivariate analysis. Criminology, 12, 195–213.

Winchester, S. W. C. (1978). Two suggestions for developing the geographic study of crime Area, 10.

Young, J. (1975). Working-class criminology. In I. Taylor, P. Walton and Young, J. (Eds.), Critical Criminology, Routledge and Kegan Paul, London, pp. 63–94.

Geography and the Urban Environment
Progress in Research and Applications, Volume V
Edited by D. T. Herbert and R. J. Johnston

Chapter 10

Revitalizing Downtowns:
by whom and for whom?

Roman A. Cybriwsky and John Western

The 1980s have been heralded as a decade of urban revival in the United States (Allman, 1978; Sutton, 1978). This follows many years of continual decline and, for the first time in a number of generations, has engendered optimism among many observers of the urban scene. Even though decentralization of people and economic activity continues as the dominant trend in America's metropolitan areas (Muller, 1981), there is now considerable evidence of a countervailing trend. In Baltimore, Chicago, San Francisco and countless other cities, there is a new enthusiasm for the so-called 'urban renaissance': each city has its 'new downtown', with shiny office towers, landscaped plazas and showy shopping malls; surrounding these are suddenly fashionable residential neighbourhoods, recently reclaimed from blight and decay, and widespread in the urban core are signs of a consciously city-focused, urbane way of life, allegedly contrasting with the stereotypical suburban style of the postwar era. It is no mere chance, then, that James W. Rouse, one of America's largest developers of the urban fringe, asserted that inner-city locations would be so attractive by the turn of the century that 'the suburb will be the obsolete place to live' (Rouse, 1978, p. 44).

But this much-touted renaissance is at best a partial picture. Important questions obtrude. Just how significant is this trend in the overall evolution of American cities? Will it eventually spill over from the core to all parts of the urban area? May we anticipate that the 'urban crisis' of conventional wisdom will go away? Will the benefits of a revivified city be equitably shared among all citizens?

This paper addresses selected aspects of these questions as they are revealed in Philadelphia, Pennsylvania. This city contains remarkable examples of the urban crisis at its worst, juxtaposed with a much-extolled urban renaissance. In the city's landscape and in the lives of its citizens, the contrasts are strikingly clear. We intend to delineate the contours of a shifting social geography in Philadelphia, and then to focus upon its various implications for the city's many diverse social groups. Specifically, we want to explore the impact of the recent renewal of Philadelphia's core on other areas of the city and to identify the means by which an improved Philadelphia is being achieved. Certain sociocultural values held by specific social groups seem to have become dominant in the remoulding of Philadelphia's core; by the same token, other groups' volitions have been in large measure discounted.

THE STUDY OF INNER-CITY REVITALIZATION

The questions we have raised are of some moment, in part because of their obvious implications for urban policy. Not surprisingly, an extensive literature has been emerging, both within and outside academia. Nor is it surprising that contrasting positions have arisen on certain specific points; hence a vigorous debate.

A first facet of this debate concerns the very magnitude of recent central city revival at a countrywide scale. Does the change hold for all cities, or only for a particular subset? Is this indeed a secular development, or will it prove to be a shortlived phenomenon, trivial over the long-term? We cannot claim to have definite answers, in part because 1980 census materials are not yet available in the detail that would permit appropriate analyses. However, some previous studies, the majority of which might be considered somewhat tenuous because of the unsatisfactory data they are based on, indicate that the trend seems widespread. Lipton (1977), for example, found that from 1960 to 1970, in at least ten of the 20 largest SMSAs, family income and educational attainment statistics 'improved' in or near the central business districts. This, he concluded, pointed to a measure of central city revival. So too, from their broadly based surveys of housing rehabilitation activity in central cities across the United States, both Black (1975) and James (1978) concluded that a marked upturn is evident in numerous older neighbourhoods. Clay (1978, 1979) found evidence of revitalization, though in differing degrees, in more than 100 neighbourhoods, at least one in each of the country's 30 largest cities.

By contrast, Sternlieb and Hughes (1979, 1980) have uncompromisingly argued, based on aggregated census data for 1960, 1970 and 1977 (estimates), that 'it is premature to extrapolate from isolated success stories a wide-ranging "back-to-the-cities" movement. There has been little, if any, abatement in the broader centrifugal forces depleting the urban arena' (1979, p. 634). Similarly, in their analysis of the 20 largest SMSAs, Long and Dahmann (1980, p. 19) concluded that 'for the mid- to late 1970s, [there is] little evidence of a systematic narrowing of family incomes in cities and suburbs, as might be expected [in the context of a] back-to-the-city/stay-in-the-city trend'.

As a result of the existence of such diverse opinions about the magnitude of central city improvement, and because of the obvious lack of comparability between these and yet other studies, Sumka (1979), in his review of the question at hand, offers the patently unsatisfactory conclusion which we admit can be little different from ours; 'the totality of the evidence indicates clearly that something is occurring in many urban areas . . . ' (1979, p. 482). But we note that even if the 1980 census does lead to agreement on the degree to which there has been a revival in central cities, there will doubtless still be debate over the degree to which the trend will continue.

What is perhaps of greater importance than the precise lineaments of these trends at a national scale, however, is the fact that in many cities there has been massive impact upon particular neighbourhoods. Aggregated statistics may frequently be masking such changes owing to continuing decentralization trends in much of the cities' territory. However, numerous specific studies, for example O'Loughlin and Munski (1979) on Lower Marigny and Algiers Point in New Orleans, Winters (1979) on parts of New York, San Francisco, Boston and Washington, DC, Levy (1978) on Queen Village in Philadelphia, and Barnekov and Caron (1980) on Quaker Hill in Wilmington, Delaware, as well as the case studies from Washington, New Orleans, Philadelphia, Columbus (Ohio), Charleston (South Carolina), Seattle, and Atlanta, contained in the volume *Back to the City* edited by Laska and Spain (1980), all incontrovertibly document often total transformation of neighbourhood social and physical texture. Yet, a recent careful case study by Hodge (1981) purports to show that 'the processes of inner-city revitalization and . . . displacement . . . occurring in Seattle are not geographically restricted. Although revitalization is more active in some neighbourhoods than in others, the effects are felt throughout the entire city' (p. 195).

A major emphasis of these studies is the matter of social costs, especially those of displacement, inherent in rapid neighbourhood revival. Some scholars (such as Clay, 1979) have chosen to distinguish between two modes of 'upward' neighbourhood transformation. 'Incumbent upgrading' refers to the physical improvement of a neighbourhood's housing stock with no significant change in the socioeconomic status of the inhabitants—in other words, the appearance of the houses changes but the people stay the same. 'Gentrification', on the other hand, involves a change in both the physical qualities of the neighbourhood *and* in the population's composition, with the arrival of new residents. It is the latter which is more responsible for the considerable extent of the revival, and, as might be anticipated, is held to be the greater agent of social dislocation.

The 'typical' model of gentrification envisages as a starting point an old, declining neighbourhood near the city's core inhabited by a low-income population, of perhaps diverse ethnic and racial backgrounds, mostly in rented units. A trickle of 'pioneers' enters, whose socioeconomic characteristics are often taken to be those of highly educated, upwardly mobile, young professional whites, allegedly attracted by the neighbourhood's social heterogeneity, convenient location, and promise of a (to them) novel way of city life. More pragmatically, they are also attracted by low rents and/or market values. Yet the newcomers' advent of itself is to destroy this very attraction. Further similar migrants are drawn in, as is the real estate industry, and the neighbourhood begins to take on an image of urbane chic. Prices rise, along with property taxes, and lower-income residents, be they renters or owners, are thereby dispossessed and must move elsewhere. An attempt to formalize such a transition has been made by Goetze, Kolton, and O'Donnell (1977), built around the notion of increasing confidence among potential investors in the surety of value escalation. And, interestingly enough, Levy (1980, p. 309) has observed that, as a final stage of this process 'the neighbourhood enters the "mainstream" of upper-income demand'. That is, the area becomes homogeneously wealthy, and the self-same variety-seeking people who maybe inadvertently set the change in motion find that they are no longer content with the new image.

Numerous case studies indicate that such transition may be catalysed by certain physical attributes. Most notable is that of historicity: an urban fabric that was once dismissed, or at least overlooked, now becomes celebrated for its architectural style and 'authentic' ambience. The relationship between neigh-bourhood change and rising middle-class interest in historic settings is amply expounded by Datel and Dingemans (1980). A second but related variable is location: *ceteris paribus*, the older the neighbourhood, the closer it is to the various attractions of the downtown.

The model outlined above offers no indication of the magnitude of displace-ment of low-income residents and there is, as yet, no adequate overall assessment. The debate which has arisen in measure reflects the not necessarily comparable findings of particular observers of particular locales. On the one hand, the National Urban Coalition (1978), along with considerable testimony at 1977 hearings before the US Senate Committee on Banking, Housing, and Urban Affairs (US Senate, 1978), claimed that such displacement was rampant. Yet Grier and Grier (1978) note that in both San Francisco and the nation's capital, cities frequently cited as locales of greatest gentrification, the number of displaced households was relatively small. Sumka (1979) does attempt to quantify, but having provided Cousar's (1978) figure of over 500 000 persons per year for 1974–76 for all of the United States, directly admits that 'the data are subject to serious potential biases of an indeterminable direction. For example, moves due to rent increases are excluded, although in some cases such increases may be the result of revitalization activity. On the other hand, evictions, which were categorized as displacement moves, may be the result of factors totally unrelated to revitalization' (1979, p. 484).

Further difficulties of measurement of displacement are set out by Goldfield (1980). He mentions that displacement 'cannot be extrapolated directly from rehabilitation statistics. Abandoned units, for example, are likely rehabilitation candidates and they involve no displacement. In addition, it is necessary to separate those who would have moved from the neighbourhood in any case . . . and those who are forced out by the mechanisms of private re-habilitation' (pp. 458–459). Even in a recent study of a particular city, Hodge

(1981) is unable to separate to his satisfaction involuntary moves caused by gentrification from other changes of residence.

Numbers are, naturally, of some importance, especially since gentrification-displacement has become a politically sensitive issue. Over and above the question of numbers *per se*, however, is the matter of the human cost borne by those displaced, be they few or many. It has been established in many diverse settings—in Boston (Fried, 1963), Lagos (Marris, 1961), Cape Town (Western, 1981), and Halifax, Nova Scotia (Clairmont and Magill, 1974)—that enforced departure from established communities has serious and multiple implications for those who are affected. Moreover, in those cases where substantial numbers of long-term residents remain within the gentrifying area, the ambience changes counter to their taste, and results, once again, in loss of community. This has been reported independently in two Philadelphia neighbourhoods by Levy (1978) and Cybriwsky (1978).

A NEGLECTED DIMENSION?

The literature of the urban renaissance also addresses reasons for the apparent reversal of trends in the cores of central cities. The most frequently cited factor is the long-term structural shift in the economic base of American cities. The manufacturing economy, which for so long sustained the United States' metropolises, has been eroding, while growth has been shifting to the tertiary sector, particularly white-collar occupations.

A large proportion of employment opportunities thus are, and are projected to be, in downtown commerce and business. Location of employment has ever been a determinant of location of residence, and therefore inner-city locales become more competitive as places to live (Ley, 1980). Partial confirmation for this may be seen in what appears to be a correlation between the degree of gentrification in a given city and the extent of its importance as a centre of white-collar employment (Lipton, 1977). Secondly, it has been mooted that the rising costs of energy—in for example, commuting, the heating and air-conditioning of large detached houses—are enhancing the competitiveness, once again, of inner-city neighbourhoods (Goldfield, 1976).

A third focus concerns demographic changes: the increase in the number of persons in the prime house-buying age-range of 25–34; the increasing preference for childless households; and the increasing number of households consisting of unrelated individuals and of single persons. To the extent that the sub-urbanization boom of the 1950s and 1960s went hand in hand with the baby boom of those years, the trend for smaller households points to a certain obsolescence of the lower-density residential environment. As a rather specu-lative final point, Fusch (1978) questions if many of the so-called suburban generation are unhappy with the supposition that 'everything has become the same in the suburbs', and therefore have in reaction looked to the inner-city, where their identities and individualism 'can receive full play' in a 'unique, old, restored house' in an historic neighbourhood (1978, p. 7).

What we feel to be underemphasized in the above is the role that the public sector has wittingly played in facilitating downtown-area transformation, as we shall show for Philadelphia. To view central city revitalization as the fortuitous outcome of a remote hidden hand in a *laissez-faire* economy, or of the vagaries of demographic changes, is to miss the agency of human intent. The direction of change in the present city is partly the result of deliberate planning, albeit planning which has had to mesh with broader economic and demographic currents. We assert this even in the light of a radical critique of the gentrification literature by Smith (1979), where he proposes that the back-to-the-city movement is founded upon the notion that it is not so much people, but rather capital that has returned. This, he states, is because profitability here has increased relative to other parts of the metropolis, such as the suburbs. This view has merit, but we would like to point out that such capital movements have of themselves been induced by prior planning intended to bring about this very flow.

Planning is not value-free. Planners can hardly avoid being more responsive to certain interests than to others, and furthermore cannot totally escape their own inbuilt cultural-professional predilections. As a result, what they create in the city not only will reflect that city's balance of power but also the planners' own cultural styles. This point—which has not gone unnoticed in the planning literature (Friedmann and Weaver, 1979; Marris, 1974; Pahl, 1970)— has not, it seems to us, been adequately integrated into discussions of gentrification. Our treatment of the 'new' Philadelphia will try to illuminate the relationships between the values of decision-makers and planners, and the attributes of the emergent urban landscape.

Gentrification has in a sense been planned for; it commends itself to the planners' own notion that an 'improved' city requires an 'improved' downtown. This being so, the attendant problems of gentrification, like displacement, are to be seen in a new light. Displacement is not merely an unfortunate or unavoidable byproduct of impersonal market forces, but an assumed social cost resultant from deliberate decisions concerning priorities in city renewal.

Displacement from gentrification is thereby but a modern-day manifestation of a long-term phenomenon. Urban renewal, expressway construction, and so many other large-scale public works projects conceived earlier for the commonweal, have entailed similar social costs. They too have been rooted in deliberate decisions by persons in the public service who have successfully promoted their particular vision of the to-be-desired city. A departure from gentrification's precursors, however, may be observed in that today's displacees are not provided with the same relocation assistance as was mandated for those displaced by programmes which were more explicitly public sector, for example, urban renewal. That is, given the conventional view that gentrification is a private sector process, those who lose by it, in an essentially free-market economy, are on their own. Should it not be suggested that, if gentrification has indeed been planned for, the public sector has a degree of responsibility towards those displaced?

THE IMPRINT OF PLANNING

The previous paragraph's assertions are the more demonstrable because of the central role that planning has had in the postwar evolution of Philadelphia. Jeanne Lowe (1967), in her appraisal of how America's metropolises were addressing their urban problems, *Cities in a Race with Time*, singled out Philadelphia as one of the two best examples of comprehensive planning strategy.[1] She praises Philadelphia's 'rational, experimental and coordinated approach . . . over the past two decades', indicating that the city 'substitut[ed] thought and studies for the national penchant to act first and think later, [and] then set goals, devised plans, established priorities and invented programs, strategies and combinations of leadership forces' (p. 313). So too, Kenneth Halpern (1978), in his survey *Downtown USA*, opined that 'Philadelphia is the only American city whose development has been guided by comprehensive planning for close to 30 years' (p. 103).

The central focus of Philadelphia's coordinated approach has been to strengthen the downtown, known in Philadelphia as 'Center City'. This is where the new image, the renascent Philadelphia, is to be most clearly seen. The emphasis on downtown is quite evident in the celebrated *Plan For Center City*, published in 1963 after many years of preparation (Philadelphia City Planning Commission, 1963). Credit for the plan's overall strategy and its creative aspects is attributed to Edmund Bacon, Executive Director of the City Planning Commission. However, this is not to suggest that planners single-mindedly pursued the aggrandisement of downtown alone against all other areas; they did try, also, to address various concerns at a citywide scale (see, for example, Philadelphia City Planning Commission, 1960). But it was in the downtown that enthusiasm for the plan's proposals drew together a broadly based and, in the event, remarkably powerful coalition of civic and business leaders, such that volition could be translated into achievement (Petshek, 1973).

Philadelphia, of course, has a three-century tradition of plans, going back to William Penn's original scheme for the city in 1682. Even then, the disposition of thoroughfares and open spaces was intended to give rise to a strong central focus. The grid plan, aligned to the cardinal points, called for a 'Publick Square' of 10 acres at the geometric centre, the intersection of the two broadest streets. It was not until well into the 19th century, however, that the city expanded sufficiently from its nucleus along the Delaware Riverfront to render this square the effective centre. With the construction on this site from 1871 of the monumental City Hall, the symbolic centre was forever fixed. For the building is, by custom, always to be the tallest in the city, and from the top of its tower a statue of Penn watches over his creation.

Penn's plan held—with the not-insignificant exception of new streets subdividing the original large blocks—until the first major revision was proposed in 1892, the Benjamin Franklin Parkway. This broad, treelined baroque boulevard, patterned after the Champs–Elysées, cuts diagonally across Penn's grid. Paradoxically, it enhances the centrality of City Hall by affording a fine vista from the north-west. Not unexpectedly, the city's major streetcar and passenger rail lines also converged on the node at City Hall, as did the subway system, prosecuted with great vigour over the first three decades of the 20th century (Warner, 1968).

We provide this brief retrospect to emphasize that not only has the downtown always been the favoured principal target of city improvement efforts, but also to point out some attendant social consequences. In the case of the Benjamin Franklin Parkway, for example, a working-class neighbourhood and industrial premises centered on Penn's Northwest Square were obliterated. This was justified by pointing to the benefits of such an attractive, landmark project accruing to the city as a whole. Yet, *particular* benefit went to those who lived in north-western suburban areas, such as wealthy Chestnut Hill, and who, possessing private means of transportation, now gained stylish access to their downtown offices with a minimum of traffic tie-up.

Observe the above distribution of benefits to which a given course of planning leads among those who inhabit the city. That is, there are benefits as between the city and its citizens as a whole; particular benefits to specific neighbourhoods and groups (and thereby implying a measure of distributive injustice to those who do not receive these particular extra-proportional benefits); and particular disbenefits to *other* specific neighbourhoods and groups. The distinction is germane to our discussion of Philadelphia's 1960 Comprehensive Plan and the 1963 Center City Plan, as well as to their later modifications; it is also germane to an evaluation of Center City gentrification.

SPATIAL STRATEGY IN CENTER CITY PLANNING

A representative depiction of recent intentions for Center City Philadelphia revitalization is provided in Figure 10.1, drawn in 1963 by the City Planning Commission. Although some specific elements have since been altered—thus Figure 10.1 was updated in 1976—the illustration taken as a whole represents an ambitious proposal that still applies. It addresses all major categories of urban land-use, and integrates them into a new landscape strikingly different from the chaotic mix of land uses of Center City 30 years ago. Yet its foundations are still in Penn's plan for streets and open spaces. Some of the illustrated proposal has been effected by now (and a little, such as Penn Center [see below], was already

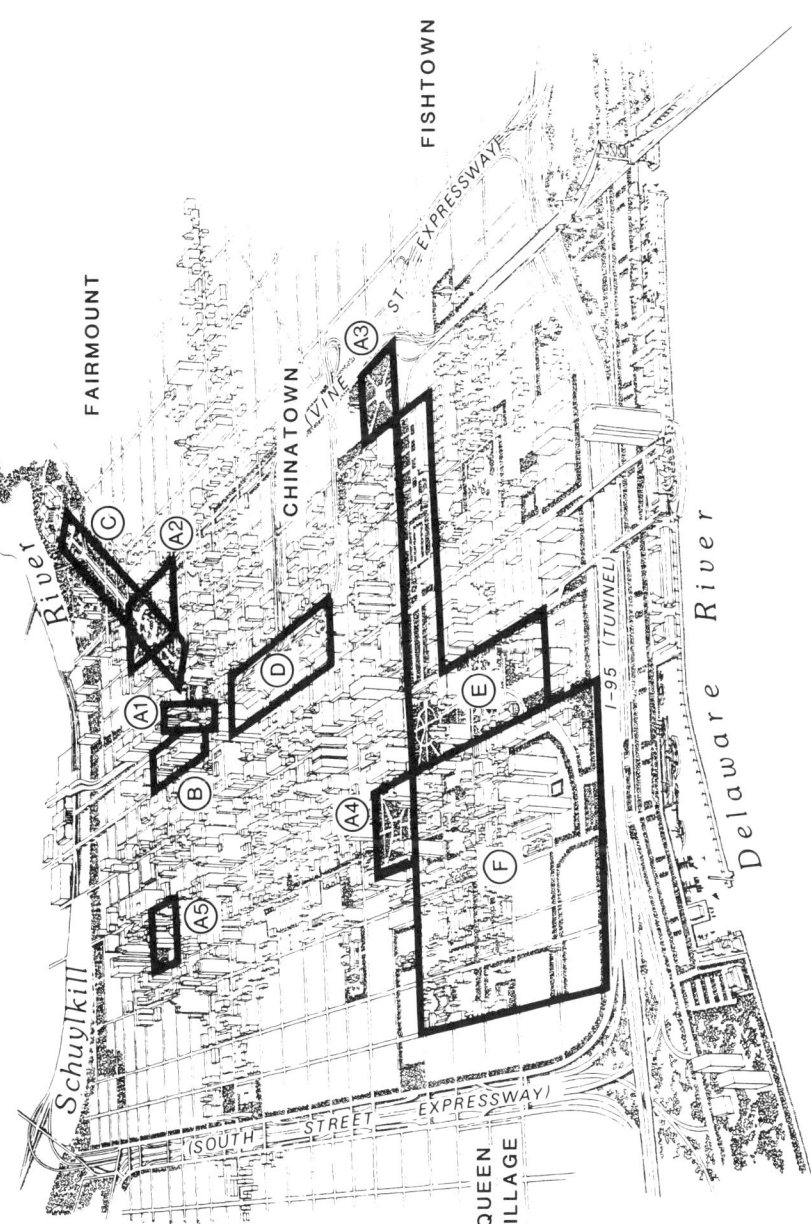

FIGURE 10.1. The image of a future Centre City Philadelphia as depicted by City Planning Commission in 1963. A–1 Centre Square (City Hall/Penn Square); A–2 Northwest Square (Logan Circle); A–3 Northeast Square (Franklin Square); A–4 Southeast Square (Washington Square); A–5 Southwest Square (Rittenhouse Square); B Penn Center; C Benjamin Franklin Parkway; D Market Street East; E Independence Park; F Society Hill

finished by the time the illustration was drawn) so the look of downtown is already significantly altered. Although much remains to be completed, the rapid pace of construction promises still more transformation of the city's core soon.

Edmund Bacon's Comprehensive Plan is highly regarded among urban planners. It demonstrated an enlightened appreciation of spatial strategy in altering an entire area. That is, specific renewal projects were purposely distributed in a manner that might simultaneously accomplish two desired goals: the elimination of unsightly and/or blighted zones; and the facilitation of 'spread effects' out from newly completed, publicly financed renewal projects, in a manner analogous to the growth-poles concept. One early example was the replacement of the so-called 'Chinese Wall', the 16-track-wide rail corridor running on brick arches into the very center of the city from the west. It was both ugly and obsolete, as well as forming a barrier to north–south automobile and pedestrian traffic. The Planning Commission, working with the Pennsylvania Railroad, which was the owner of the property and which had a prior interest in redeveloping the site, transformed the area from its foundations. Having put the rail tracks underground to an adjacent, newer station, a complex of modern office towers was built with a direct link for commuters. Furthermore, at rail and street level a pedestrian-oriented retailing complex, geared especially to the needs of commuters, was established. The entire development, known as Penn Center, attempts to make imaginative use of natural light, pleasing architectural form, and public open space.

Over the same period, towards the eastern end of Center City, Bacon's plan mandated extensive renewal of the oldest part of Philadelphia in order to enhance residential and recreational opportunities. Here, where many of the United States' most significant historical shrines (such as Independence Hall and the Liberty Bell) are located, renewal required the elimination of 'incompatible' declining commercial and industrial uses. These were replaced by a coordinated arrangement of landscaped malls, green squares and traffic-free pathways connecting various historical buildings, which collectively comprise Independence National Historic Park. The adjacent neighbourhood, Society Hill, was converted from an ageing and overcrowded, tattered district of low-rent residences and mixed commercial uses into an almost wholly residential showplace neighbourhood. Often cited in textbooks as America's most successful urban renewal project, it is now one of the metropolitan area's wealthiest neighbourhoods, as well as a significant tourist attraction. This accomplishment was possible in part because Center City Philadelphia has such historic character. The old city was recreated via 'authentic' renovation of colonial and federal-era townhouses, its ambience consciously accented by gas lanterns and cobblestones.

Lying between the historical district and the City Hall–Penn Center area is yet another more recent, largely publicly-funded project, Market Street East. It addresses the problem of long-declining retail sales in downtown Philadelphia, and therefore meshes well with other revitalization pillars geared to commerce, residence and recreation. (Since Figure 10.1 was first drawn in 1963, the actual *design* of the new buildings on Market Street East has been altered; the concept of the project has not.) The centerpiece of Market Street East is the Gallery, a four-level enclosed retailing mall with 125 shops and restaurants anchored by two large department stores. It was developed by the Rouse Corporation on land made available on advantageous terms by the Philadelphia Redevelopment Authority. Accessibility to the metropolitan-wide market is enhanced by ample parking, and the provision of a new commuter rail tunnel and station immediately adjacent, presently under construction. The latter is the largest (and most costly) public works project in the history of Philadelphia. The great commercial success of the Gallery since its opening in 1977 has led to the present construction of an even larger Gallery II on the next block.

The strategic spatial qualities of Bacon's plan are evident in these examples. The Penn Center project, for instance, just to the west of City Hall and thus toward the western edge of the central business district, was intended to stimulate private-sector investment in office and other commercial uses, thereby enlarging the business core. Indeed, since the completion of Penn Center, every bordering block has experienced new high-rise construction, mostly of offices. Such new construction has also comprised a significant component of hotels and apartments, attracted by the nearby Benjamin Franklin Parkway, in addition to the presence of these workplaces. Thus, with each spinoff from the largely publiclyfinanced original project, the proportionate contribution of the private sector has risen.

Similarly, the urban renewal projects in the historical area had a high degree of public-sector financing, whereas their subsequent spinoff developments have been more of a private-sector character, as is the pattern with gentrification. Thus, as prices escalated in Society Hill to render that development accessible only to the very wealthiest home-buyers, so did adjacent neighbourhoods come to be perceived as propitious loci for investment. Especially to the south of Society Hill, where there were tracts of equally historical housing, another fashionable neighbourhood, newly dubbed 'Queen Village', has evolved. It was previously Southwark, and had long been a principal receptor of poor immigrants to Philadelphia. By the mid-1960s it was a blue-collar, mixed ethnic neighbourhood (with a minority of blacks), oriented to employment in the Delaware River docks and to the industries of South Philadelphia. But the success of Society Hill contributed to the luring of higher-status migrants, first in a trickle, but then in ever-larger numbers, and now the neighbourhood is essentially gentrified. Philadelphia newspapers have reported this transformation under headlines such as 'Queen Village: Oldtimers Feel They Will be Forced Out'; 'The Newcomers Take Over'; '[The] Curse of "In" Neighborhoods'; and 'Housing, Prices Are Soaring in Queen Village'. Concomitant with the increase in purchasing power in such neighbourhoods is the evident commercial success of not only the Gallery project, but also several other small retail developments, both new and revivified, initiated wholly by private business.

Although not necessarily to the same comprehensive degree as in Society Hill and Queen Village, evidence of similar transformation is found in *every* neighbourhood in and near Center City. The degree of change varies with the idiosyncrasies of the given area, its advantages or conversely its obstacles. For example, tracts adjoining the stately Philadelphia Museum of Art, on a low hill overlooking the core of Center City down the length of the Benjamin Franklin Parkway, are also rapidly gentrifying, particularly where well-fashioned Victorian homes are concerned. Just across the Schuylkill River in Powelton Village we see the same process, stimulated by the proximity of two large universities. Other areas have predictably changed more slowly. That is, Fishtown, although seemingly well-located just to the north-east of Center City and possessing some homes of historical value, is yet dominated by warehousing and industrial land-uses. Similarly, certain predominantly poor black neighbourhoods adjoining Center City have seen less change, partly because their present residents are perceived by potential white investors as hostile and prone to criminality. The avoidance is most marked where large public housing projects are in place.

But even in these most unlikely locales there are signs of change, if only in the form of speculation in abandoned buildings, their shells affording renovation potential. Thus, within a radius of 2-3 km (1.5–2.0 miles) of Penn's statue, depending on the given sector, the expectations of Center City revival, via spread effects as envisaged in the master plan, are being in large measure fulfilled. Many view this as cause for civic celebration. A recent issue (June 1979) of *Philadelphia Magazine*—a glossy, consumption-oriented monthly catering to a supposed monied, urbane *bon vivant* market—focused on the topic of Philadelphia's renaissance. Its cover exclaimed 'The Hot New Neighborhoods—Come On Back!' The lead article, 'A New Philadelphia, Get It While Its Hot', announced that 'suddenly, Center City is bursting its boundaries'. A subsequent piece, entitled 'How To Get in on the Action', provided 'a guide to the busiest realtors and developers'. The general tone was apotheosized by the next article: 'Handicapping the Neighborhoods: A Panel of Experts Picks the Best Places to Live Today and to Buy for Tomorrow'.

VALUES AND HEGEMONY IN THE PLAN

In the particular case of the construction of the Benjamin Franklin Parkway, the question of the distribution of benefits was adumbrated. We have not yet explicitly addressed such matters as they are raised by the revitalization of Center City Philadelphia as a whole, nor have we spoken directly about the sociocultural values which underlie the official scheme for this part of the city. What we have just seen in *Philadelphia Magazine* reveals, of course, an exaggeratedly journalistic and gleeful bias, which does not reflect the aims nor the sole intent of the plan. The plan, however, does in its turn reveal its own predilections. In examining these now, we will find that our understanding of the social dimensions of downtown-area revitalization is improved.

Consider once more Figure 10.1, this time less as a depiction of tangible fabric, but rather as the expression of an idea. One is surely struck by the image of insularity conferred upon Center City. The downtown area is totally surrounded by barriers moating it from the rest of Philadelphia. Along the banks of the two rivers run multiple-lane expressways, connected at right angles by two other expressways which delineate the northern and southern boundaries of Center City, in fact precisely at the city's original limits as defined by Penn. At the very center, multistorey buildings circumscribe the apex that is City Hall but little detail is drawn beyond this 'walled city'. It must be said that the drawing was conceived for the particular purpose of highlighting potential Center City development. Despite this qualification, the *leitmotif* of downtown pre-eminence is palpable.

The expressway ring around downtown Philadelphia is hardly unique. Here, as well as in so many other large cities, such a scheme of transportation is intended to facilitate accessibility to the daytime workplace on the downtown island from distant, complementary commuter zones. To build such a system is also to gain an opportunity to expunge unwanted land-uses. It can also result in the interposition of barriers of limited permeability between downtown and inner-city 'blighted' areas. For the inner city, then, social distance is here being underwritten by the imposition of an extra complement of physical distance. Conversely, for the suburbs, social proximity is maintained by an investment to overcome physical distance.

This example from the expressway system brings into focus the question of *for whom* has the downtown been revitalized. It points out the unequal distribution of benefits from a given capital project, favouring in this case mainly white-collar suburban commuters. Further evidence of unequal distribution of benefits is offered, particularly, by the I-95 Expressway, along the Delaware River. To an even greater degree than in Figure 10.1—prepared several years before completion of this roadway—I-95 was depressed where it flanked Society Hill. It was covered over, the roof being landscaped with lawns, walkways and a fountain, affording uninterrupted access from Society Hill to a new riverfront park, Penn's Landing. The mile-long stretch of this roadway which included the tunnel proved to be the single most expensive mile of highway in the United States. By contrast, both to the north in Fishtown and to the south the expressway is elevated or, less frequently, at ground level, in conventional manner. Yet it is extremely interesting to observe that in one particular locale to the south, where it passes Queen Village, an eleventh-hour modification was inserted. Ingeniously designed barriers against noise from the highway were demanded by the community and obtained following litigation initiated by a coalition of Queen Village's new gentry. Still another modification to the network of expressways of Figure 10.1 was the eventual defeat of the proposed South Street Expressway (southern border) following protracted opposition by diverse community groups. One of the effects of the suppression of this road has been that gentrification has been able to diffuse more easily across what would otherwise have been a barrier.[2]

For a complete picture, it is necessary to point out, however, that this orientation of the expressway system to suburban commuters should also be seen in the light of the city's then-current problems. The loss of middle-class residents and industry to the suburbs, and the attendant erosion of the tax base, was in full swing at the time, with no grounds for assuming it would be soon moderating of its own accord. The future of the city appeared bleak if such loss were not staunched. Therefore, clearly, the city's aim had to be to hold and, if possible, to attract back middle-class residents. This strategy was complemented by the city's determination simultaneously to open for new middle-class settlement the extensive undeveloped tracts of land within municipal limits, as in the area known loosely as the Greater Northeast and in Roxborough (to the northwest). This is part of what the Comprehensive Plan set out to do, and, indeed, it can be said to have been quite successful in this attempt.

However, the conventional wisdom that 'success' is measurable in terms of the retention of the middle-classes is of itself culturally conditioned. Theoretically at least, the fiscal health of a city can be improved also by ameliorating the condition of its poorer residents. Certain programmes address this (such as job training , special education), but the general expectation in the United States context is that such efforts are prone to be palliative, rather than truly generative of city revival.

Thus, at a time when suburban growth was the dominant metropolitan process, the city felt that it could compete most effectively by incorporating into its plans a measure of the suburban world-view. For many of the suburban generation, the city was a place to be feared and avoided. Hence, it was no accident that one of the features of the Penn Center office complex, tailored to commuters, was the opportunity to work, shop, and board one's means of transport without having to set foot outdoors. Similarly, one of the outcomes of the current extension of a commuter rail link beneath the core of the central business district will be to reduce the distance for pedestrians between station and workplace. Furthermore, these considerations are not inapplicable to the commercial success of the Gallery, a wholly enclosed, well-policed pedestrian space to be directly linked to the new railroad.

There is also an element of the suburban motif in the design of Society Hill. A principal feature of the redevelopment plan was to replace the previous diversity of land-uses with an almost homogeneously residential landscape. This is in contrast to the modal pattern in row-house Philadelphia, where residential and non-residential (for example, the corner store, the industrial premises down the street) were interdigitated. So, in Society Hill redevelopment, the retail facilities are now neatly concentrated along a custom-zoned commercial block, while certain other uses—for example, the city's wholesale food distribution centre and some light industry—were removed from the area entirely. In their place were set green space, new townhouse developments architecturally compatible with the historical housing adjacent, and in one case three high-rise apartment towers of notable design.

Such reshuffling of urban land-uses has social meaning. The anthropologist and planner Constance Perin has explored with insight the manifestation of society's values in the built urban environment. She observed: 'Beneath producers' [of residential environments] maps . . . are assumptions about the kinds and quality of social relationships to result from land use relationships' (Perin, 1977, p. 83). Segregation of differing land-uses, or even of different categories within the same land use (such as housing), is seen as desirable by planners because homogeneity and safety are equated. Indeed, the mass appeal of neatly zoned suburbia is partially interpreted by Perin as resulting from the fact that, there, 'everything is in its place'. 'The city and the suburb contrast in the freedom to "avoid" people that each offers . . .'; or as an informant in the real estate profession confided to Perin: 'See, you have to understand [that] the fundamental feeling in suburbia is fear, let's face it' (1977, p. 87).

That the incorporation of suburban elements into the physical layout of Society Hill was purposive is seen in the tone of real estate advertisements of that time. For example, in the marketing of a specific property, the realtor inserted the following description into the 18 May 1958 *Philadelphia Inquirer*:

New parks, a marina, green pathways, Expressways & Nice People, all coming to enhance gracious living in SOCIETY HILL.

The realtor is not here selling the property but is selling the area, particularly what is new about it and stereotypically non-urban. Fear is to be assuaged by almost subliminal references to greenery, graciousness, and 'nice people'. Another revealing advertisement appeared in the same paper on 3 April 1966, by which time the Society Hill development was well under way:

Addison Court
in Society Hill at its finest

A new community of air-conditioned, contemporary style homes . . . with three bedrooms, two and a half baths, log-burning fireplaces, garden areas and sun decks, garages or private parking, spaciously designed interiors.

Addison Court has a charming and historic setting in an unsurpassed location where many distinguished civic and business leaders are now living.

Here, the prospective purchaser is reminded that the neighbourhood has already attained social cachet, and so it is more important that he or she be informed about the particular comforts available in the given development. The comforts and the privacy here offered for purchase might be seen as replicating suburban expectations rather explicitly. Even more explicitly, we read in Lowe's reporting of Mayor Dilworth (1956–62) 'candidly admitt[ing] that the new housing in center-city projects was deliberately being priced out of the average Negro's income range. "We've got to get the White [leadership] back," he asserted, and to do this "We have to give the whites confidence that they can live in town without being flooded"' (1967, p. 352).

Concomitant with the arrival of wealthier residents in Society Hill and other Center City areas is the emergence of new consumption-oriented styles of urban life, which in turn have caused visible modifications in the details of the city's built form. Perhaps the most evident example, as can be seen on Figure 10.1, is the provision of two riverfront parks in the place of obsolescent industrial and wharfage facilities. A case in point is Municipal Pier 30, now air-conditioned tennis courts where freighters until recently were unloaded. Or, in Queen Village, 22 new restaurants and bars catering to affluent tastes opened for business in the 1977 to mid-1979 period alone. One long-time local resident complained: 'Our neighborhood is being used as a playground for the rich!' (*Evening Bulletin*, 13 May, 1979). For Center City as a whole, the 1977 Census of Retailing for Philadelphia shows that bars and restaurants are the fastest growing sector. These and other examples of recreation and amenity-oriented additions to the urban landscape perhaps point to a 'new ideology of livability', guided by what Ley (1980), in the context of Vancouver, chose to call 'the canons of good taste'.

THOSE IN THE PATH OF PLANNING

The opening words of Bacon's *Plan for Center City* (Philadelphia City Planning Commission, 1963, p. 5) unequivocally and optimistically claimed:

> The well being of Center City Philadelphia is basic to the well being of the entire Delaware Valley region. Center City must always remain the principal place for doing business . . . For purchase of those special things which give richness to our lives and for those great cultural activities which set the tone for our contemporary civilization. In addition, Center City serves as a spring-board from which waves of revitalization spread outward as suburban families are attracted to urban living.

The 'new livability' to which Ley has referred, and which the above quotation encapsulates, applies only, however, to a select portion of Philadelphians. Yet one of the major justifications given for expending so much energy and public funds on the city's downtown has been that the improvement there would be an improvement from which *all* citizens might benefit. As ever, however, some have benefited more than others. The sociocultural values in the image of which downtown has been reshaped are those of the urbane upper middle class. It is they who are most comfortable with the new downtown. The protest is being increasingly heard from other Philadelphians that this monied class's style is coming to dominate what municipal publicists have tried to tout as 'everybody's neighborhood'. Furthermore, what to the middle-classes are beneficent 'waves of revitalization' may be viewed by many of the poor as malignant 'waves of displacement'.

It was Dilworth's predecessor as mayor, Joseph S. Clark (1952–56), under whom city revitalization plans first really began to roll, who once said: 'People take pride in the "spectaculars"—the center city rebuilding projects like Penn Center. But the hard guts of it is finding poor families a decent place to live.' 'Spectaculars' have certainly been realized, but much of the inner portions of the city remain as depressed as ever. Most of those areas which have been improved have new residents.

A case in point concerns displacement of poorer Puerto Ricans by middle-class whites in the Spring Garden neighbourhood, 1.6 km (1 mile) north-west of Center City, near the Art Museum (Cybriwsky, 1980). Pervasive resentment has occasionally flared into violence. For example, a well-publicized case in 1977 involved the fire-bombing of a white's newly renovated house by a Puerto Rican on the same block. It occurred on moving-in day, and damage ran to between $20 000 to $30 000 (*Evening Bulletin*, 3 June 1977). A friend of the accused, interviewed on the local television news, described the motive:

> There used to be friends of ours in that house. But this white guy comes in and kicks them out. And he thinks he's improving the neighborhood. All of us [Puerto Ricans] are going to get thrown out, one by one. The man will just come one day and say 'move'.

Beyond this frontier of change, the city numbers at least 25 000 abandoned houses (the exact number is not known) and great expanses of vacant lots. In 1979, official estimates were that more than 39 000 lived in private-sector substandard housing. In addition, in a city of approximately 1.6 million, 120 000 persons (90.9 per cent of them black) lived in public housing, much of which is described in a report by the Urban League of Philadelphia as 'generally atrocious, dangerous, and dehumanizing' (Lewis, 1981, p. 33). Philadelphia's poor are experiencing the full range of social ills which have come to be synonymous with inner-city slums: unemployment, inadequate services, discrimination, victimization by crime, poor health, lack of effective political voice, and stigmatization from their fellow citizens.

The persistence of such conditions while Center City revitalizes has bred a sometimes devastating cynicism regarding the true intentions of city improvement efforts. In the same Urban League report, Anthony Lewis (1981), a black community housing leader, correctly reports that the US Department of Housing and Urban Development criticized the City of Philadelphia for its continued racial bias in the distribution of federal housing funds. With some anger and hyperbole, Lewis draws his own conclusions: that there is a measure of anti-black conspiracy in Center City's renaissance. Lewis talks of the urban renewal efforts of the 1960s as 'Negro removal'. Proceeding to the 1970s, he asserts that:

> . . . more effective if subtle tactics were developed. These procedures came under various names including: 'triage', 'recycling', 'displacement', and 'gentrification'. Under this system, poor and black neighborhoods were allowed to decline. City services were cut and supportive programs were withdrawn. Private finance, particularly insurance and mortgages, was withdrawn through a process known as 'redlining'. When enough properties were abandoned and enough people forced or lured out of a neighborhood, services were not only renewed but increased. Rehabilitation money then poured in from many private and public sources. Inadequate housing was replaced with housing beyond the means of the poor. Soon whites and upper-income families replaced the blacks and poor in many neighborhoods known as 'Society Hill, Washington Square East and West, Franklintown and University City' (p. 31).

Lewis' depiction of the process lacks objectivity, but what is important here is the fact that, especially among minority-group citizens, widespread credence is given to such interpretations. Nor is it really correct to assert, as does Lewis, that 'the most severe housing dilemma facing Philadelphia's black community is neighborhood recycling and displacement' (p. 38). But, based on the broadly felt perception of injustice in the matter of shelter in a revitalizing Center City, Lewis' assertion speaks forcefully to the experience of many.

Similarly, the century-old *Philadelphia Tribune*, a newspaper which subtitles itself 'the voice of the black community', frequently editorializes against the unequally large apportionment of public funds to Center City, and has also bitterly attacked the recycling process. A particular case which illustrates the suspicions which have come to be so pervasive in much of the black community—but which is in itself of very localized importance—concerns an unanticipated impact of the new rail tunnel construction in Center City. It seems that much of the earth from the extensive excavations was heaped up on a vacant lot, about 3 km (2 miles) away, in a low-income black residential neighbourhood. An issue was made of this, as indeed it should have been. For, given the context of the awareness of those living in this particular area that the commuter tunnel certainly was not going to benefit them in the least, the selection of this site showed a certain insensitivity. 'They wouldn't do that in the suburbs', said one local resident to the *Tribune*, in its front-page lead story following damage to adjacent houses from erosion (19 May 1981).

This climate of mistrust has conditioned much black reaction to Center City revitalization. So, when the Gallery opened to great fanfare in 1977, certain voices urged a boycott. For several months, a sizeable group of Philadelphians, mostly from the poorest black neighbourhoods, marched chanting through the Gallery 'Boycott the Gallery', and 'Save our land—stop recycling'. The basic complaint was that $28 million in public funds, including hundreds of thousands of dollars in Community Development funds, had been spent in subsidizing the developer and two department stores, rather than improving the deplorable housing conditions in their neighbourhoods.

Another complaint lodged against the Gallery concerns jobs. A major justification for the vast public expenditures on this project was that it would create at least 1300 permanent new jobs, let alone those in construction. In the event, the *Tribune* complains that too small a percentage of these went to blacks, especially in the light of the large proportion that blacks represent in the city population as a whole and in the shopping center's clientèle (26 June 1981). Observing that the present construction of the second Gallery is being justified in the same terms (that is, 3500 construction jobs, 2000 permanent retail jobs, in addition to a large number of other opportunities in the office towers above), the *Tribune* editorializes: 'our community isn't buying this latest bait being dangled about . . . . The City has not heard the last word on Gallery II' (7 July 1981).

Clearly, then, a significant number of Philadelphians are disaffected by the changes in the Center City area. Specific references have been made to a Puerto Rican neighbourhood and to some black sources. The embitterment, however, is also felt in certain white neighbourhoods, and has been evident in Chinatown, in the path of the Vine Street Expressway. Income, along with the correlate of political influence, is the essential variable here, not race or ethnicity *per se*. That is, the protest seems to come more from the disadvantaged within a given ethnic/racial category, rather than being necessarily representative of that category as a unit.

With the rising socioeconomic status of the Center City area, the very textures of activity and style have altered there. Many long-term poorer residents have been obliged to go. Even those who yet remain, however, have lost a once-familiar milieu: 'this place isn't what it used to be'. Some of those portions of Center City which have not yet been redeveloped—for example, the largely black-oriented, rather honkytonk zone east of City Hall—are viewed by planners as redevelopment priorities. Here, the blue-collar unemployed pass the time in the pinball arcades and bars, while those with the new white-collar jobs in the offices above hurry past in three-piece suits.

CONCLUSION

What we note for a stretch of Philadelphia sidewalk appears to have been noted more generally by Rubin (1979) in her article entitled 'Aesthetic Ideology and Urban Design':

> The diversity of an urban population, or the cosmopolitan range of goods and services exchanged, is rarely taken as an index of urban success by students of urban culture. Instead, urban success is found in a catalogue of a City's noncommercial, nonindustrial institutions: a philharmonic orchestra, art museums, parks, religious and historical shrines, theaters, fine-arts architecture, and unified monumentalizing plans (p. 341).

The experience of Philadelphia over the last 30 years matches Rubin's observations to a remarkable degree. Certainly, the city makes great play over its 'cultural' and historical attributes. Certainly, the city's development has been fashioned by its Comprehensive Plan, perhaps more so than in any other city in America. In Center City, the nub of the planning effort, social diversity has been consciously diluted. To us, it seemed that this was an incorporation of essentially suburban characteristics, something the Center City felt compelled to do in order to be competitive in an apparently increasingly suburban time.

This paper has tried to demonstrate that the provisions of the Center City plan led to spatially focused private investment which brought about gentrification. That this was one of the plan's intents can hardly be gainsaid; it is spelled out in the plan's introductory paragraphs. Thus, in Philadelphia at least, it seems that it would be incorrect to consider gentrification wholly a private-sector phenomenon. Indeed, as a result of protests and lobbying, the City has come to accept a degree of responsibility in this matter. For example, the Office of Housing and Community Development, charged with the amelioration of living conditions in run-down areas, is trying in various ways to mitigate the social costs of displacement. But their efforts, critics claim, amount to 'too little, too late'. Gentrification now has its own momentum, and is perceived by many in power to be still delivering net benefit to the city.

Philadelphia is representative of numerous American cities in terms of both decline and a possible countervailing revitalization. The specific issues we have raised in this case study, although conditioned by the particular lineaments of Philadelphia's tradition of planning and the city's distinguished historical patrimony, also apply to other urban areas attempting to revivify their downtowns. From an even broader perspective, the social costs stemming from the city's most recent transformation are but latter-day manifestations of a theme which is ever-present in urban history: benefits and disbenefits of morphological change are dealt out unevenly, according to the ubiquitously uneven patterns of social power. Therefore, a central focus of social geography should always be upon the multiple social, political, economic, and moral forces which shape the city and whose interplay is implicit in the city's landscape.

NOTES

1. The other city is New Haven, Connecticut, known for its extensive use of federal urban renewal programmes.
2. To round out our overview of the expressway system, we note that eventual completion of the partially finished expressway along the northern boundary (Vine Street Expressway) is now scheduled for 1986.

REFERENCES

Allman, T. D. (1978). The urban crisis leaves town. *Harper's*, **December**, 41–56.

Barnekov, T. K. and Caron, J. E. (1980). *Quaker Hill: Reinvestment Displacement in an Historic District*, College of Urban Affairs, University of Delaware, Newark, Del.

Black, J. T. (1975). Private Market Housing Renovation in Central Cities. *Vohar lend*, **November.**

Clairmont, D. H. and Magill, D. W. (1974). *Africville: The Life and Death of a Canadian Black Community*, McClelland and Stewart, Toronto.

Clay, P. L. (1978). Neighborhood revitalization and community development: the experience and the promise. *Center for Community Economic Development Newsletter*, **August–October**, 1–9.

Clay, P. L. (1979). *Neighborhood Renewal*, D. C. Heath, Lexington, Mass.

Cousar, G. J. (1978). *Bulletin on HUD Estimates of National Displacement, and Pertinent Program Information*. Presentation at National Urban League Conference, 5 August.

Cybriwsky, R. A. (1978). Social aspects of neighborhood change. *Annals of the Association of American Geographers*, **68**, 17–33.

Cybriwsky, R. A. (1978). Revitalization trends in downtown-area neighborhoods. In S. D. Brunn and J. O. Wheeler (Eds.), *The American Metropolitan System: Present and Future*, Edward Arnold, London.

Datel, R. E. and Dingemans, D. J. (1980). Historic preservation and urban change. *Urban Geography*, **1**, 229–253.

Fried, M. (1963). Grieving for a lost home. In L. J. Duhl (Ed.), *The Urban Condition*, Basic Books, New York, pp. 151–171.

Friedmann, J. and Weaver, C. (1979). *Territory and Function: The Evolution of Regional Planning*, University of California Press, Berkeley.

Fusch, R. (1978). *Historic Preservation and Gentrification: A Search for Order in the Urban Core*. Presented at annual meeting of the Association of American Geographers, New Orleans.

Goetze, R., Kolton, K., and O'Donnell, V. (1977). *Stabilizing Neighborhoods*, Boston Redevelopment Authority, Boston.

Goldfield, D. R. (1976). The limits of suburban growth: The Washington, DC, SMSA. *Urban Affairs Quarterly*, **12**, 83–102.

Goldfield, D. R. (1980). Private neighborhood redevelopment and displacement: the Case of Washington, DC. *Urban Affairs Quarterly*, **15**, 453–468.

Grier, G. and Grier, E. (1978). *Urban Displacement: A Reconnaissance*, US Department of Housing and Urban Development, Washington, DC.

Halpern, K. (1978). *Downtown USA: Urban Design in Nine American Cities*, Whitney Library of Design, New York.

Hodge, D. C. (1981). Residential revitalization and displacement in a growth region. *Geographical Review*, **71**, 188–200.

James, F. J. (1978). *The Revitalization of Older Urban Neighborhoods: Trends, Forces, and the Future of Cities*, US Department of Housing and Urban Development, Washington, DC.

Laska, S. B. and Spain, D. (Eds.) (1980). *Back to the City: Issues in Neighborhood Renovation*, Pergamon Press, New York.

Levy, P. R. (1978). *Queen Village: The Eclipse of Community*, Institute for the Study of Civic Values, Philadelphia.

Levy, P. R. (1980). Neighborhoods in a race with time: local strategies for countering displacement. In S. B. Laska and D. Spain (Eds.), *Back to the City: Issues in Neighborhood Renovation*, Pergamon Press, New York, pp. 302–317.

Lewis, A. (1981). Housing for Philadelphia's Blacks. *The State of Black Philadelphia*, Urban League of Philadelphia, Philadelphia, pp. 30–34.

Ley, D. (1980). Liberal ideology and the postindustrial city. *Annals of the Association of American Geographers*, **70**, 238–258.

Lipton, S. G. (1977). Evidence of central city revival. *Journal of the American Institute of Planners*, **43**, 136–147.

Long, L. H. and Dahmann, D. C. (1980). *The City–Suburb Income Gap: Is it Being Narrowed by a Back-to-the-City Movement?* US Department of Commerce, Bureau of the Census, Washington, DC.

Lowe, J. R. (1967). *Cities in a Race with Time: Progress and Poverty in America's Renewing Cities*, Random House, New York.

Marris, P. (1961). *Family and Social Change in an African City: A Study of Rehousing in Lagos*, Routledge and Kegan Paul, London.

Marris, P. (1974). *Loss and Change*, Pantheon Books, New York.

Muller, P. O. (1981). *Contemporary Suburban America*, Prentice-Hall, Englewood Cliffs, NJ.

National Urban Coalition (1978). *Displacement: City Neighborhoods in Transition* National Urban Coalition, Washington, DC.

O'Loughlin, J. and Munski, D. C. (1979). Housing rehabilitation in the inner city: a comparison of two neighborhoods in New Orleans. *Economic Geography*, **55**, 52–70.

Pahl, R. E. (1970). *Whose City?* Longman, London.

Perin, C. (1977). *Everything in Its Place: Social Order and Land Use in America*, Princeton University Press, Princeton, NJ.

Petshek, K. R. (1973). *The Challenge of Urban Reform: Policies and Programs in Philadelphia*, Temple University Press, Philadelphia.

Philadelphia City Planning Commission (1960). *Comprehensive Plan: The Physical Development Plan for the City of Philadelphia.*

Philadelphia City Planning Commission (1963). *Plan for Centre City.*

Rouse, J. W. (1978). The lure of an urban life-style. *Conservation and new economic realities, Proceedings of a conference of The Conservation Foundation*, San Francisco, 18 November 1977, The Conservation Foundation, Washington, DC.

Rubin, B. (1979). Aesthetic ideology and urban design. *Annals of the Association of American Geographers*, **69**, 339–361.

Smith, N. (1979). Toward a theory of gentrification. *Journal of the American Planning Association*, **45**, 538–548.

Sternlieb, G. and Hughes, J. (1979). Back to the central city: myths and realities, *Traffic Quarterly*, **33**, 617–636.

Sternlieb, G. and Hughes, J. (1980). The changing demography of the central city. *Scientific American*, **243**, 48–53.

Sumka, H. J. (1979). Neighborhood revitalization and displacement: a review of the evidence. *Journal of the American Planning Association*, **45**, 480–487.

Sutton, H. (1978). America falls in love with its cities—again. *Saturday Review*, **August**, 16–21.

US Senate (1978). *Hearings of the Committee on Banking, Housing, and Urban Affairs: Neighborhood Diversity*, US Government Printing Office, Washington, DC.

Warner, S. B. (1968). *The Private City: Philadelphia in Three Periods of Its Growth*, University of Pennsylvania Press, Philadelphia.

Western, J. (1981). *Outcast Cape Town*, University of Minnesota Press, Minneapolis; George Allen and Unwin, London; Human and Rousseau, Cape Town, Pretoria, and Johannesburg.

Winters, C. (1979). The social identity of evolving neighborhoods. *Landscape*, **23**, 8–14.

Index

(Note: Page numbers in italics refer to maps and diagrams; government departments, legislation, etc. are listed under the country concerned.)